AF411958

INDIAN HISTORY CONGRESS MONOGRAPH SERIES

ESSAYS IN MODERN INDIAN ECONOMIC HISTORY

IN THIS SERIES

RECORDING THE PROGRESS OF INDIAN HISTORY:
SYMPOSIA PAPERS OF THE INDIAN HISTORY CONGRESS
1992–2010
Edited by S.Z.H. Jafri

ESSAYS IN ANCIENT INDIAN ECONOMIC HISTORY
(2nd edition)
Edited by Professor Brajadulal Chattopadhyaya

ESSAYS IN MEDIEVAL INDIAN ECONOMIC HISTORY
(2nd edition)
Edited by Professor Satish Chandra

HISTORY, IDEAS AND SOCIETY:
S.C. MISHRA MEMORIAL LECTURES IN HISTORY
Edited by S.Z.H. Jafri

ESSAYS IN MODERN INDIAN ECONOMIC HISTORY

Second Edition

Edited with an Introduction by

SABYASACHI BHATTACHARYA

INDIAN HISTORY CONGRESS
in association with

PRIMUS BOOKS
An imprint of Ratna Sagar P. Ltd.
Virat Bhavan
Mukherjee Nagar Commercial Complex
Delhi 110 009

Offices at
CHENNAI   LUCKNOW
AGRA AHMEDABAD BANGALORE COIMBATORE DEHRADUN GUWAHATI HYDERABAD
JAIPUR KANPUR KOCHI KOLKATA MADURAI MUMBAI PATNA RANCHI VARANASI

First published 1987
Second edition 2014

ISBN: 978-93-80607-98-6

Published by Primus Books

Laser typeset by Digigrafics
Gulmohar Park, New Delhi 110 049

Printed and bound in India by Replika Press Pvt. Ltd.

Contents

PART 4
INDIA AND THE WORLD SYSTEM OF INDUSTRIAL CAPITALISM

PART 5
TENSIONS AND STRUGGLES IN THE COLONIAL SOCIETY

Preface to the Second Edition

THE INDIAN History Congress has emerged as a representative organization for a large section of historians in India, providing its members with a forum to present their unpublished research work, using data from across the country. The annual sessions of the Indian History Congress are invariably attended by senior historians, who provide guidance to young researchers in their endeavours. In its multi-pronged activities, the Congress is perhaps one of the few organizations in India to provide a research and publication forum. To this end, it brings out an edited volume containing a selection of the research articles presented at various sessions. In fact, it is the meticulous selection of essays and rigorous editing of the volumes that has given cause for the University Grants Commission to recognize these proceedings to the level of a referred journal for the purposes of granting promotion to college and university teachers under the Career Advancement Scheme.

During its Golden Jubilee Celebrations in 1987, the Indian History Congress decided to publish three thematic volumes focusing on the Economic History of India. This three-volume set, entitled *Indian History Congress Golden Jubilee Year Publication Series* together contained over a hundred essays, with an introduction by eminent historians. The series met with much success, as it provided a panoramic view of 50 years of changing focuses and emphases of scholars on art, religion, and society and issues related to the historical roots of economic backwardness and the resultant economic under-development in India's colonial past.

These volumes on economic history were also important from another perspective. While inaugurating the first session of the Indian History Congress in 1935, Sir Shafa'at Ahmad Khan remarked that, 'economic history is almost a virgin field'. In the years following 1935, research in this area gathered depth and pace. In the subsequent decade and, in particular after Independence, considerable literature too was produced on the various aspects of the economic history of India. A nationalistic critique of colonialism during the process of decolonization was a major factor in developing interest in this topic. Meanwhile, since the mid-1950s the Marxist approach too gathered acceptance in the academic world of historians as an important factor in the explication of historical development. Together, the twin discourses of nationalist critique and Marxist approach became important contributory factors for a heightened interest in the economic aspects of India's historical past.

In challenging the imperialist historiography, Indian historians evolved considerable interest in studying society, religion, and art. They posited that Indian cultural past was essentially composite in nature and different communities lived side by side in a spirit of syncretism. In doing so, historians also examined the nature of religious identities and their role in shaping the contours of societal developments in our past.

Prints of the 1987 three-volume set were soon exhausted. Keeping in view their usefulness and steady demand among scholars as well as students, the Executive Committee of the 71st Session of the Indian History Congress, at University of Gour Banga, Malda, West Bengal, decided to reprint the three volumes, possibly with a new introduction by their respective editors.

To this end, I am grateful to Professor Satish Chandra, Professor Sabyasachi Bhattacharya, and Professor B.D. Chattopadhyaya for contributing substantial pieces for the new editions. And, it is indeed a pleasure to have these volumes released as a part of the preparations for the celebrations of the Platinum Jubilee Session of the Congress.

5 December 2013

SAIYID ZAHEER HUSAIN JAFRI
Secretary
Indian History Congress
Department of History
University of Delhi

Preface to the First Edition

THE EXECUTIVE Committee of the Indian History Congress at its meeting in Srinagar in 1986 had constituted the Golden Jubilee Celebrations Committee, which decided, amongst other things, to bring out a few thematic volumes containing articles published in the Proceedings of the Congress since its inception. Four volumes that are being brought out as part of the Golden Jubilee Celebrations deal with Indian art, religion, society and economy through the ages.

It may not be out of place to recall here the expectations of the founding fathers of Congress, Sir Shafa'at Ahmad Khan, the President of the first session in 1935, said: 'I have no doubt whatsoever that this body . . . is destined to play a momentous part in the building up of a vigorous school of Indian historians. . . . It knows no politics, it will not serve the interest either of our national life and thought propagandists who paint the glories of their country's past in a flamboyant language . . . nor will it support writers who are obsessed with prejudice and racial pride, have completely ignored those features which have maintained and preserved the continuity of our cultural life . . . I dread the prospect of long line of histories of India written by Muslims, Mahrattas, Sikhs, Bengalis and Pathans, each from their own point of view. . . . Should history be tied to the chariot wheels of perverted sectionalism which is now acting as a most serious obstacle to the growing nationalism of India on a whole?'

To what extent has the Congress, which has truly grown into an All-India body and is the largest organization of professional historians in the country, lived up to these expectations? The readers could perhaps look for an answer in the collections being presented here.

Each of these four volumes is preceded by short introduction from the editor, who has already provided the rationale of the concerned anthology. It is hoped that the series will reflect the commitment of the Indian History Congress to scientific and secular history and prove useful to all students of history.

I take this opportunity to thank Professor Satish Chandra of the Centre of Historical Studies, Jawaharlal Nehru University for taking up the responsibility of editing the present volume at a very short notice. On behalf of the editor as well as on my personal behalf, Dr. Muzaffar Alam, Associate Professor, Centre for Historical Studies, Jawaharlal Nehru University, is also to be thanked profusely for very significant help rendered by him. Dr. Bhairabi Prasad Sahu's unflinching help in proofreading is also gratefully acknowledged.

We are grateful to the Indian Council of Historical Research for making a handsome grant which has enabled us to meet partially the cost of publishing these volumes.

New Delhi
15 October 1987

D.N. Jha
Secretary
Indian History Congress

Introduction to the Second Edition

WHEN I was requested to write a Introduction to the second edition of the *Essays in Modern Indian Economic History* which I had edited twenty-five years ago, my first reaction was that it would be better to put together a new volume of selected papers submitted at the History Congress since 1985. However, as there is continuing demand for this volume, which covers the period 1935 to 1985, I have decided to say a few words about recent research by way of an Introduction to the present volume. I must add, however, that the Introduction I wrote for the earlier edition of this volume needs to be read along with the few pages I am now persuaded to add.

The question I want to address here is the following: Has there been a decline in scholarly interest in economic history? This complaint, or you may call it a lament, has often been heard over the last decade or two. In the decades preceding 1985, there was a huge spate of research in Indian economic history. It was then a new specialization. When, in 1935, Sir Shafa'at Ahmad, in his Presidential Address at the founding session of the Indian History Congress said that 'economic history is almost a virgin field', he was referring to an area of research that has begun to attract many young researchers. Several factors were responsible for promoting an interest in economic history. In late colonial India the Nationalist intellectuals, R.C. Dutt and Dadabhai Naoroji onwards, had focused upon the economic exploitation of India. That critique of colonialism was, by and large, limited to the nationalist public spokesmen, and it filtered down to the groves of academe only much later. One sees it in academic research in the post-independence years. An altogether new interest in economic history was generated when, after 1947, researchers began to address themselves to the issues raised by Naoroji or Dutt or M.G. Ranade. You may also recall a global trend that emerged in the process of decolonization in the 1950s and 1960s in Asia and Africa. There was heightened interest in the issue of economic under-development—which led to a search for the historical roots of economic backwardness. In post-independence India, specially during the Nehruvian regime, an additional factor was the intense public discourse on economic growth and national level planning and policy making. Further, the Marxist approach, with its emphasis on economic factors in the explication of historical development, began to be accepted in the academic world—quite contrary to the earlier trend when the Marxian approach was, more often than not, ignored as a 'politically inspired' and partisan approach. There was, thus, an unusually high level of engagement in research in economic history between the 1950s and the 1980s. Thereafter it was but natural that the high quantum of research in a specialization should level off; that is not necessarily evidence of decline.

Perhaps a more important reason is that in recent years the agenda of economic history has changed. The staple tools of the trade of economic historians used to be histories of public finance, domestic and foreign trade and balance of payments; principles of land revenue collection and tenurial relations; growth of railways and factories; banking and monetary history; sectoral distribution of the working population, and so forth. These are things which matter and justifiably continue to be subjects of study, but there are also other themes which have acquired a new importance. To mention just a few of: agro-ecology and environmental history affecting in the long-term primary sector activities in cultivation, forest and water resource exploitation; demographic factors bearing upon the 'carrying capacity' of land from the stage of hunting and gathering to sedentary agriculture; the expansion of the agrarian frontier with the enlargement of cultivated land area along with population; mortality, morbidity, life expectancy, family structure, etc. affecting the economically active population; the social traditions determining certain rights such as forest rights, or rights of pasturage, or use of the village commons; the influence of caste not only in obvious ways such as agrestic servitude or bondage, but in other ways as well, as in the transmission of artisanal skills or modes of operation of merchant communities; social and cultural aspects of the life of the urban working class, not only as labouring men but also as part of social networks in their habitation sites; the socio-political movements which formed a part of peasant resistance to economic exploitation and social exclusion. Thus, various non-economic factors bearing upon economic life in the broadest sense of the term have been focused upon in recent studies. That is not to say that these factors were not important in earlier literature but new research in recent years was much more focused on these aspects. It would have been useful to discuss the works of research which instantiates and illustrates these trends. In my Introduction to the expanded Indian edition (2005) of the *Cambridge Economic History of India*, vol. II, edited by Dharma Kumar and Meghnad Desai, I have reviewed this literature with bibliographic details. Readers who are interested may consult that review of literature. It is neither necessary nor possible to repeat that exercise here.

It was perhaps not fortuitous that while new aspects of economic life in the past began to be examined, many economists began to look beyond things 'purely' economic. This change was reflected in the new emphasis on the 'quality of life' which is now commonly used as an index of development, side by side with conventional growth indices like the GDP. This change in approach was also reflected in the discourse of 'development' as distinct from economic growth. As Amartya Sen and Jean Dreze have said in their recent work, *An Uncertain Glory: India and its Contradictions* (2013), 'the relationship between growth and development—their difference as well as their complementarity' has become a central theme with contemporary economists. Hence, Sen and Dreze recommend the inclusion, in the economists' agenda of research, social institutions, formation of knowledge and skills through education, level of nutrition, access to health care and its demographic consequences, and even political systems such as democracy or its antipodal alternatives. Parallel with this expansion in the ambit of economic thinking, one can see an expansion of the domain of economic history in recent times. Arguably, this new turn in economic history was implicitly anticipated by economic historians who made the study of the Political Economy their agenda. Or again, when Marc Bloch spoke of 'total history', he was beyond doubt pointing to the interconnectedness which the new agenda of research seeks to reveal in relation to economic life. Thus, the endeavours we have referred to are in part new, but also, in part a return to an old tradition of looking at the past.

To sum it up, the frontiers of the discipline of economic history have expanded in recent years. That is not a sign of the 'decline' of economic history, but a challenge to which the practitioners of that discipline must respond. Failure to do so might have been the signal of a decline; there is no evidence of such a failure in the publications since the late 1980s.

I am happy that the early explorations in economic history, of which some fragments are collected in this volume, are again being presented to a new generation of historians on the occasion of the seventy-fifth anniversary of the foundation of the Indian History Congress.

5 December 2013   SABYASACHI BHATTACHARYA

Introduction to the First Edition

THIS COLLECTION of essays has been put together in the hope that these selections from the Proceedings of the Indian History Congress would afford an impression of the research problems which have engaged economic historians in the past 50 years, the conceptual framework in which their research was conceived, and the methodology they employed.[1] I think it is no more than an impression that one may form, for the range and depth of historiography in this area of study did not get adequately reflected in the papers presented at the sessions of the Indian History Congress. That is so partly because in the early decades of its history the Congress was attended by small numbers; and partly because in recent times the limit on the length of papers allows authors to present only a fragment of their research output. Moreover, in a collection such as this the limits on space will not allow us to include a good number of papers which could have formed a part of this volume. The rubrics laid down by the Indian History Congress in terms of periodization (the traditional tripartite division ancient, medieval, modern) also proved to be a constraint. Despite these limitations—and the limitations possibly stemming from the editor's misjudgements—this selection of essays may have its uses.

It is useful in that it provides an overview of the continuities and changes in the professional historians' approach to the economic aspects of 'modern' Indian history. Second, this collection makes accessible to the reader a number of papers presented at the History Congress decades ago. I should mention here that it was decided to make room for such papers by excluding papers presented very recently. Sometimes a *locus classicus* like Sir Shafa'at Ahmad Khan's paper (1938) on British trade and imperial policy is not available even in some of the best libraries in India. (As far as I know only one library in Delhi possesses a copy of the proceedings of the Congress, 1938; see essay reprinted in Part 2 in this volume.) I will try to highlight some of these seminal contributions and the changing approach to Indian economic history reflected in the papers selected. It is neither possible nor necessary to provide here a fuller discussion of historiographic trends. It is not possible because we, the editors of the three projected volumes on economic history, decided to limit the editorial 'Introduction' to a few pages. It is not necessary because very recently the research trends in modern Indian social and economic history have been reviewed in the 'Survey of Research' series of the Indian Council of Social Science Research (Dharma Kumar and S. Bhattacharya in R.S. Sharma, ed., *Survey of Research in Economic and Social History of India,* 1986).

'Economic history is almost a virgin field and the material for the subject is voluminous.' It was a subject of study, Sir Shafa'at Ahmad said, which was 'insistingly claiming recognition and admission.'[2] That was in course of his Presidential Address at the founding session (8 June 1935) of what was then called the 'All India Modern History Congress.' What went into the making of this body, known to us since 1937 as the Indian History Congress? The first Presidential Address provides some important insights. Shafa'at Ahmad emphasised the need for 'a body that will serve as the focus of Indian historical research by which the unconnected and uncoordinated research, which are being prosecuted in different parts of India will be systematized.'[3] It was conceived as something like a clearing-house of research and 'an authoritative organ of historical scholarship.' Second, the first Presidential Address repeatedly makes another point: the exchange of ideas between individuals and institutions previously working in isolation would help develop a more generalized picture of 'Indian history as a whole'. 'There is a real danger in the microscopic examination of a small and insignificant bit of History. . . . History does not consist merely in the dissection of the tiny bits of facts without any principle or significance. History consists not merely in the organization, collection and examination of material but also in its interpretation. . . .'[4] Finally, Shafa'at Ahmad underlined the need for historians to respond to 'the new spirit of Indian nationalism'. He pointed out that, while archaeology and ancient history, had benefited from governmental initiative, the government had 'not encouraged researches in modern Indian history to the same extent'.[5] In isolation, mainly through private initiative, modern history research had developed in some institutions and regions. Hence an incipient danger: 'I dread the prospect of long lines of histories of India written by Muslims, Mahrattas, Sikhs, Bengalis and Pathans, each from their own point of view. . . . Should history be tied to the chariot wheels of perverted sectionalism which . . . is now acting as a most serious obstacle to the growing nationalism of India on a whole?'[6]

I have cited these extracts from the first Presidential Address delivered at the History Congress to capture the spirit that animated the efforts to form this body 50 years ago. In the historians' research output this spirit can be traced. It is true that to identify the dominant trend in Indian historiography, then or later, is not an easy task. The variety of research problems, and a kind of professional aversion to wider issues beyond the immediate empirical limits, make this task difficult. However, if one takes a long-term view and one looks beyond the general tendency of historians to treat their individual research problems in a discrete fashion, some integrating or organizing principles, some basic paradigms or interpretative frameworks may be identified. In the days of Shafa'at Ahmad the nationalist paradigm in historiography was beginning to develop.

In the area of Economic History this was in part a reaction against imperialist historiography, and in part it was an offshoot of the historical interests generated by the economic nationalists like M.G. Ranade and R.C. Dutt. If you bear in mind the colonial discourse in British historiography you can appreciate the significance of some of the early papers collected in this volume. Was the British empire acquired in 'a fit of absent-mindedness'? Dr. Bal Krishna's answer was loud and clear in his paper 'Was the British Conquest of India Accidental?' (1938, see Part 3 in this volume). 'The victories of Carnatic and Bengal were . . . the fruits of a long preparation on an extensive scale, and not of accidental circumstances. The intention and attempt to establish colonies were all along present from the establishment of the Company.'[7] Or again Shafa'at Ahmad's paper (1938, see Part 2): he establishes 'the importance of the East India trade in the determination of British foreign policy' leading to the 'commercial supremacy and political hegemony of the English' in the East.[8] Sometimes the nationalistic influence also led to the construction of heroic figures in India's past, almost as a response to the colonialist mythification of a Clive or a Dupleix (V.N. Pallai's paper, 1943, Part 1 in this volume).

In general, economic nationalism nurtured an interest in the question of growth and backwardness in the context of colonial-metropolitan relations, which raised basically historical questions contrary to the inclinations of the neoclassical school. M.G. Ranade is the best exemplar of this. 'The political domination of one country by another attracts far more attention than the more formidable, though unfelt domination which the capital, enterprise and skill of one country exercise over the trade and manufactures of another.'[9] Ranade suggested that along with this domination, there was an intellectual domination, that of the ideas of Political Economy evolved in England which pretended to offer 'one set of general principles (which) hold good everywhere for all times and places.'[10] Ranade, therefore, looked towards another intellectual tradition, that of the Historical Economists, especially those of Germany. It is interesting to note that some of Ranade's ideas are echoed by the historians represented here. For example. R.V. Oturkar of Bharat Itihasa Samshodhak Mandal: 'a temptation of using western terminology for using Eastern Society may be avoided,' he concludes in his paper (1945).[11] Shafa'at Ahmad expresses high regard for Ranade and 'the historical school of Maharashtra'. In this he was not untypical of his generation. That is not to say that the whole range of ideas of M.G. Ranade, R.C. Dutt, etc., was reflected in the professional writings of historians at that stage. The problems raised by the economic nationalists were addressed by professional historians somewhat later.

About the time India attained independence, a new wave of historical studies began. One of the Presidential Addresses (that of 1949) reflects a spirit of self-criticism that was probably widely shared: there was 'a tendency to "pottering", to go from one detail to another without trying to formulate conclusions . . . the tendency merely to reproduce materials has been perhaps carried rather too far . . . Indian contribution to modern Indian history has been very inconsiderable and the modern period of Indian history as we have it, is not of the Indian but of the Englishmen in India. . . . A nation's identity is rooted in the consciousness of its history. A new stage in the nation's growth is accompanied by a rewriting of its history. . . .'[12] This new impulse is reflected in a number of papers selected here. In the agenda of the economic historians; the problems uppermost were the policies of the colonial state, the impact of metropolitan capitalism on colonial trade and industry, and in particular the evolution of land revenue systems in various regions. The papers in part 2 and 3 in this volume are addressed to these questions (e.g. papers by K.K. Datta, Hari Ranjan Ghosal, Sarada Raju, Amales Tripathi, S.K. Barpujari, among others). At the same time, many of the continuities from the pre-colonial period to the so-called modern period in terms of social institutions, political structures, organization of production, etc., engaged historians (including medievalists like S. Nurul Hasan and S.C. Mishra). The reconstitution and incorporation of these institutions and structures into colonialism is a process that is yet to be adequately explored. It continues to be a fruitful area of research: the palimpsest character of the colonial social formation, the complexity of an economy and society where the detritus of the past settling layer upon layer form the text on which colonialism inscribes its signature. Some papers on this theme have been collected in Part 1 in this volume.

From the seventies one begins to notice a change. Incisive criticism was voiced in a Presidential Address (1970): 'the liberal nationalist approach' was found wanting because that approach was, while basically critical of colonialism, 'limited in its capacity to go to the heart of the matter for it does not fully explain the process of underdevelopment under British rule. . . . As historians we have to ask the question, what were the political, social, cultural and intellectual forces retarding economic development before 1947? . . . (What was) the historical process that inevitably led to the underdevelopment of India or "the development of underdevelopment" to put it in the apt and vivid manner of the pithy phrase of Andre Gunder Frank.'[13] While one does not find among the papers presented at the Congress many contributions framing the problem exactly in these terms, the incorporation of India in the world capitalist system certainly became a major theme. (As early as 1949 we have Amales Tripathi on the metropolitan transition to industrial capitalism and its consequences, and through the 'sixties and seventies' we have writings of which a few are collected in Part 4).

When we come to the 1980s one senses certain new trends. From the 1950s the opening up of the whole range of records of the British Indian empire for the first time, made accessible data on the making of industrial, agricultural and financial policies, on the decision-making process at the higher levels, the influence of interest groups and lobbies acting as pressure groups (which was conjectured but not proven until private papers of major political and official and business people became available), and so forth. This ground work was accomplished in the early decades after independence. In more recent years historical research began to push beyond the study of colonial economic policies per se, into the processes internal to the economy and society under the impact of these policies. In this process economic historians began to develop a culturally and socially sensitive economic history. Even the theoretically innocent study of empirical reality, e.g. the peasant household or the tribal economy, leads logically in the direction of integrating 'all relevant social sciences in history rather than to exemplify any one of them'.[14] It is not that the old concerns of Indian economic historians—the land revenue policy, the commercialization of agriculture, deindustrialization, the role of petty usury and trading capital, etc., are ignored, but they are overlaid with new ones and hence a possible enrichment of our understanding of the totality of history. The shift away from the older paradigms was also reflected in a shift of emphasis to class issues within the colonial context. Did the assertion of the unity of the people as a whole in the freedom struggle, cutting across class lines, involve the diminution of the significance of class exploitation and struggle in the nationalist historians' paradigm? Was the struggle of the whole people against colonialism struggle for the whole people? Did the received version of history render the oppressed and anonymous masses 'historyless' and is there a need to look at the possibilities of 'history from below'?[15]

Some historians began to address themselves to such questions in the last decade. Not many of them are to be found in this collection. However, one must remember that these are not problems which have never been studied before. Writings in the Marxist tradition explored some of these themes, e.g. works of D.D. Kosambi. In the professional writings presented in the History Congress these themes are touched upon, though at a different level of discourse. I put together in Part 5 a few papers which are concerned with tensions in rural society, conditions of the working class, the interface between peasant and working class movements and political parties, the response of tribal groups to external forces emanating from the colonial economy impinging on tribal economy and society, etc. More papers on similar themes are to be found among those presented at the Congress in the last few years, but we have not reprinted them here since these are readily available. In their more recent explorations of these and similar themes, in their reassessment of the paradigms of pre-independence vintage, in their attempt to put on the research agenda the 'history of the people' or the 'history of the oppressed' or 'history from below,' by whatever name you call it, historians of our days may be developing a new interpretative framework touching all aspects of history including the economic.

That seems likely. We must leave it at that, for proximity in time is not necessarily helpful in identifying the trend in a process of which we are a part.

Sabyasachi Bhattacharya

Notes

1. The readers may note that in my 'Introduction' the references are to the History Congress session year and the original pagination in the volumes of Proceedings. The details of the session of the Congress at which each paper was presented are indicated in the list on p. viii.
2. Sir Shafaat Ahmad Khan, Presidential Address, *All India Modem History Congress*, p. 15.
3. Ibid., p. 2 and pp. 59 et seq.
4. Ibid., p. 61.
5. Ibid., p. 49.
6. Ibid., pp. 9, 46.
7. Bal Krishna 'Was British Conquest of India Accidental?' *Indian History Congress Proceedings* (hereafter cited as *IHC*), 1938, p. 465.
8. Shafaat Ahmad Khan, 'Sir George Downing and the East India Company,' *IHC*, 1938, p. 483.
9. M.G. Ranade, 'Indian Political Economy (1892)' in *Essays on Indian Economics*, Madras, 1916, p. 92.
10. Ibid., p. 4.
11. R.V. Oturkar and S.N. Joshi, 'Institution of Watan,' *IHC*, 1945, p. 285; see Section I of this volume.
12. N.K. Sinha, Presidential Address, Modern History Section, *IHC*, 1949, pp. 208. et seq.
13. Bipan Chandra, Presidential Address, Modern History Section. *IHC*, 1970, pp. 31–2, 34.
14. E.J. Hobsbawm, 'From Social History to History of Society,' *Daedalus*, Winter 1971, p. 5.
15. I have discussed some of these issues in my Presidential Address, Modern History Section, *IHC*, 1982, and in an earlier paper, 'Paradigms Lost,' *Economic & Political Weekly*, Annual Number, Vol. XVII, pp. 690–7.

PART 1

Pre-Colonial Economy: Continuity and Change

1

Warren Hastings and Zamindari Rights

S. Nurul Hasan

B ETWEEN 1765 and 1793, i.e. between the acquisition of the *Dewani* of Bengal by the East India Company and the Permanent Settlement, the British administrators in India were greatly exercised about the question of land rights in India, particularly about the nature of zamindari rights.[1] There were some, like James Grant, who held that:

The Sovereign rulers in all parts, of Hindustan, if not through the whole of Asia . . . is declared to be the sole virtual proprietor of the Soil; not in the European feudal acceptation of the term . . . but in right and fact, the real acting landlord entitled to and receiving from the ryots or husbands-man a certain proportion of the gross yearly returns . . . fixed on a medium in Bengal, at one-fourth of the whole produce, according to a pecuniary estimation made about the year 1582, soon after establishment of the Mogul Government under Akbar.[2]

The opposite view was held by a large number of administrators, most notable among whom was Francis. He stated:

If the Nature of the Zamindary Tenure be attentively examined by the Test of Facts, I think it will appear to have no real Relation to the Feudal, Consequently that no Argument, in support of the Sovereign's proposed Property in the Soil, can be drawn from a Comparison of the two Systems. . . . The Mahomedan Conqueror did not divide the country among the followers, not did he make a new grant of the lands to the former Proprietors on condition of military Service. In general he left the possession of the lands where he found it, on the condition of a fixed pecuniary tribute, with which he maintained a standing army for the securing of the Acquisitions.[3]

Francis, in his well-known minute of 1776, categorically asserted that 'land is the hereditary property of the zamindar.' He holds it by the law of the country, on the tenure of paying a certain contribution to government.[4]

*32nd Session at Jabalpur, 1970.

A third view was that real proprietary right was vested in the ryots, a term used for peasants or 'village proprietors' or 'jeomanry' and the other 'real owners of the soil' who according to Holt Mackenzie's Minute of 2 June 1822, 'were transferred like a hold of inferior creation, into the hands of what we call the zamindars.'[5] This view was, of course, totally unacceptable to Law, who held that 'My opinion is that zamindar is indisputable proprietor of the soil, and the ryot but a vassal or peasant.'[6]

At the same time, some of the administrators realised that land rights in India were far more complex than the above-mentioned views implied. Sir John Shore, for example, in his Minute of 21 December 1789, held that:

The relation of a zamindar to government, and of a ryot to a zamindar, is neither that of a proprietor nor a vassal; but a compound of both. The former performs acts of authority unconnected with proprietary right; the latter has rights without real property; and the property of the one and the rights of the other are, in a great measure, held at discretion.[7]

Warren Hastings was among those who did not subscribe to any of the above-mentioned views. His views on the nature of the zamindar rights have been explained by him at length in two documents now included in the Warren Hastings Papers in the British Museum. Of course, at several other places also he has explained his views, but not at such length as in these two documents. The purpose of the present paper is to introduce these to scholars of history.

In the first of these documents,[8] Warren Hastings states:

I apprehend the term Zamindar or Landholder to have been originally applied by the first Mahummedan Conquerors to such Natives of Hindostan as they found in Possession of Lands whether extensive or otherwise. In the Persian Histories of India, the Raja of a Province, the chief of a Hamlet or Master of a few Acres are alike called Zamindar.

Warren Hastings then quotes from the *Ain-i-Akbari* to the reference to rights of a zamindar in Ain-i-Faujdar.[9] He then goes on to give examples of the action taken by the Mughal emperors against zamindars (Rajas or chieftains) and mentions the following cases: Jujhar Singh was obliged to pay a fine of Rs. 15 lakhs and surrender the whole of his country except a portion for his maintenance and 4,000 troops and sent to serve in the Deccan. He came back and overran the zamindari given to his relation, Pahar Singh. Jujhar Singh was attacked and slain. He then gives the example of Rao Hemun, zamindar of Bikaner, amir of 2,000 and governor of Daulatabad, who was removed by Aurangzeb and replaced by his son. Warren Hastings then gives the account of the action taken by Aurangzeb in the case of Jodhpur. He goes on to mention that Rao Buddh Singh, zamindar of Bonedeh, was given Mow and Jhatah on the decease of Ram Singh, even though the latter had left behind a son.

From the above instances, it appears to me that the Removal of Zamindar was frequently made by the Emperors of Hindostan according to their pleasure and sometimes even without a Fault on the part of a Zamindar, to serve a favoured courtier or enlarge the royal Revenues.

Authority similar to the emperor, proceeds Warren Hastings, was exercised by independent *Subadars*, such as Saadat Khan, Safdar Jang and Shujaud Daula who expelled several zamindars of Oudh. The Nabobs of Bengal also exercised similar authority. He then goes on to say:

I have already said that I never saw a written definition of the rights of Zamindars, nor did I ever hear that it existed, though I have taken some pains to enquire after such a writing.

From conversation with the Natives, I have always understood, that a Zamindar was liable to pay what Revenue the Sovereign thought proper to fix for the Zamindary, except certain Portions of Land allotted Rent-free for the Support of his Household. The Rent was generally easy, in order to enable him to assist the Sovereign with troops in his wars. He was not allowed to erect Forts or repair old one without Leave. He was not to keep more troops without Permission, than necessary for the Collection of the Revenue, or use the people oppressively, or harbour Robbers or Banditti in his Zemindary. For these offences, Rebellion or Non-payment of Rent he was liable to such punishment, as the Sovereign thought proper, generally fine, imprisonment or expulsion.

The second document, though prepared essentially in connection with the defence of his action in the Chet Singh case, is even more exhaustive, and is, therefore, reproduced in full.

A definition of the nature of the office of a zamindar, lent for the use of Mr Pitt, a day or two before the 13 June 1786; on which day he used it, and noted for the Benares Articles.[10]

'A zemindar by the constitution of the Mogul Government is the perpetual and hereditary servant of the Crown, entrusted with the cultivation, population and regulation of the lands which constitute his zemindary, and with the receipt and payment of the revenue, or Land tax. Their office is hereditary; yet they cannot enter upon their rights without a formal Act of Government, granting or confirming the same by an Instrument which is called a Sunnud Behaulee or patent of confirmation. The distinction which is made between the rights of property vested in the supreme Magistrate (who is called Hakime Wakt, or Magistrate of the Time, and means the actual Representative of the sovereign power) and the zemindar is very explicitly laid down in the Revenue Consultations of the close of 1773 or beginning of 1774, in opinions formally given by the Brahmins who compiled the Code of Laws, the Canongos (or Registers of the Revenue) Mahmud Rezza Cawn and Raja Shita Roy, in reply to questions which were put to them by the Board respecting the power of the Government to alienate or transfer zemindary property. These Rights were thus defined by the Canongos, Mahmud Rezza Cawn, and Shita Roy. The zemindar (they said) is the proprietor of the soil, the Magistrate of its produce; and from this distinction proceeded all the reciprocal rights and duties appertaining to each relation. In the same reference it was stated that the Magistrate might, if he pleased, alienate or assume any zemindary from its actual and lawful proprietor, but that if he did, unless for Rebellion, for notorious neglect of Duty or instances of disobedience, or other Enormity, or for Failure of Payment of his stipulated Revenue, he would be guilty of Injustice. This is conformable to the fundamental principle of Despotism, which is, that the sovereign shall not commit Injustice, nor offend against the Laws, but his Authority shall not be under any pretence resisted or disputed: the Check must be in his own Breast.

'The Obligations of the zamindar and the objects of his Trust will be found in the Sunnud which was granted by the Nabob Jaffar Ally Cawn, to the East India Company in 1757, which is drawn out in the same form with all zemindary Sunnuds, but I refer preferably to this, as it was written under the Authority of the Mogul government, and is therefore less liable to the suspicion of Informality than any made since the Companies accession to the Dewanny. This Instrument consists of a collection of all the different deeds which are officially necessary to the Grant of a zemindary. In this the preliminary Mandate, and that part which is styled the Muchilca (or obligation) answer to the Potter and Cabooleeat, or Deed of Lease and agreement interchanged with Cheyt Singh which are Counterparts of each other, the first conveying to the zemindar the property of Charge of the Lands on certain conditions, the last acknowledging his acceptance of it on the same conditions recited in the same words. These will be found in substance, if not in exact words, the same in the companies Sunnud, and in the Deeds bearing there names which were interchanged between the Company and Raja Cheyt Singh, who was to all Interests and purposes a zemindar, with equal rights and no other, as were held by the zemindars of Bengal and Behar, with this difference in the Authenticity of their tenures, that he derived his right from an original Grant made by the Nabob Shuja Dowala to him, his father having been a Collector in Trust, and he having succeeded to the same office, but neither zemindars by inheritance, and his Father not all.

'The destination which is marked above in the relative definitions of the rights of the sovereign, and the zamindar, strongly indicates the dependence of the latter, and the absolute right of the Magistrate to the produce of the soil, that is, to the revenue,, which was originally paid universally (as it now is in many places) and only in kind. . . . It is not to be supposed that the Magistrate was entitled to take whatever was above the surface of the ground, or contained in its entrails, and to leave the zemindar the bare earth for his subsistence. Such Cavils are unknown to the jurisprudence of India, as I presume it is equally repugnant to the spirit of our own.

'The zemindars were entitled to a share of the produce, or how could they live. But the Magistrate, whose authority was paternal, was the distributor of that share and determined its proportion. One of the duties of the Zemindar was to augment the population and revenue. Hence arose the practice of making occasional valuations of the land, which are called Hust-wa-bood, a compound word made up of the correspondent words, *is* and *was*. This may be assumed as an evidence of the right of the Magistrate to assess the lands at his option: For names prove the existence of things, and technical or official terms prove the existence and allowance of the practice implied by them; and the name Hustwa-bood, with its etymology, express that the actual valuation of the rent, or revenue differs from the former rate, and thereby proves the right of the Magistrate to augment the rent, as it would be an absurdity to suppose that the Magistrate would submit to the expense and trouble of making a new valuation for the sole purpose of reducing the rent, and establishing his own loss.

'Hence arises the distinction which is made, and constantly appears in the accounts of the revenue, between the Assel or Toomar, and the Aboaub. The first is the ancient or primitive rent fixed by Raja Toodulmul under the authority of King Acber throughout his dominions, and the last includes all the different assessments or additions which have been successively made and fixed since his reign. These distinctions are still preserved, and all the additional taxes enumerated, in the modern rent rolls, and accounts of the revenue. I believe they are not to be found in the Companies Sunnud, because (e.g. I mistake not) the Aboaub were by express condition excepted, and the Assel alone charged to the Company. This was afterwards given by the Nabob in Jagheer to coll. Clive, being about 2,22,000 rupees but the consolidated rent is, I believe more than four times that amount.

'Hence it follows, that the Magistrate possesses the right of raising the Zemindar's rents at his pleasure: that this right has been invariably exercised; and that it exists and has been exercised in all parts of the Mogul dominions equally, and in the same manner, the distinctions of Assel and Aboaub being universally the same.

'That the practice of the Company has been conformable to this right is proved by the improvements which have been made in their general revenue, which must necessarily and by the course of nature fail in some parts, and therefore could only have been improved by more than a proportionable augmentation in others; and by the practice of the government in Bengal, as well as the repeated order of the Company, in making annual settlements or agreements ascertaining the amount of each years revenue, which would be unnecessary if the quota was permanently fixed and the Magistrate had no right to vary, or increase it.

'That Raja Cheyt Singh held his zemindary on the same tenure as other Zemindar is demonstrable from the form of Mr. Burke's Charge, which states, and lest it should be mistaken or overlooked, has marked the words by Italic, that the zemindary of Benares was granted in continuation to Raja Cheyt Singh in "as full and ample a manner as he possessed it from former sovereigns"; but the manner in which he possessed it from former sovereigns must be that the universal tenure; which is far more limited and dependent than it has been ever made by the practice of the government of Bengal since the Company was in possession of it.

'In an argument upon this question the fairest and strongest evidence that can be adduced against a position of the charge, is the testimony given by one of the framers and supporters of the charge on an occasion which has no relation to it. This is equal to an admission by one of the parties in suit at Law. Mr. Francis has written a long and elaborate treatise upon the nature of zemindary tenures, and has described them exactly as I have done. This treatise is to be found in the records of the House of Commons, in some of their Committee Reports.

'I cannot dismiss the subject without taking notice of a very false and sophistical reasoning used in the charge, from a proposition made by me when Raja Cheyt Singh was not a zemindar of the Company, to prove the rights which he possessed when he became such. The fact is this. On the death of the Nabob Shuja Dowla, the majority of the council consisting of Genl. Clavering, Coll, Monson and Mr. Francis deeming themselves warranted to declare the treaty concluded with him void by that event, compelled his son Assaf Dowla to relinquish his sovereignty of the zemindary of Benares to the Company as one condition of the new treaty of alliance to be formed with him. I objected to this demand as an Act of Injustice and Breach of Faith; but I was not regarded. I now proposed as a qualifying measure that the zemindary of Cheyt Singh should be converted into an independency, and placed as Barrier between our provinces and the dominions of the Nabob of Oudh.

'The majority would not agree to this but chose to annex the zemindary a dependency to the other dependencies of the Company, and to receive the Raja in to the number of zemindars and Vassals of the Company. Yet Mr. Francis himself, who was one of that majority, and who if he was not concerned in framing the charge against me, is at least the most vehement of its supporters,, now maintains Cheyt Singh's right of independence on the grounds of the proposal, made by me for giving it, though he himself opposed the proposal, and prevented it from taking effect. Had my proposal been supported by Mr Francis, Cheyt Singh would have ceased to be a Zemindar, and I should have yielded him all the rights that were due to an independent prince in whatever intercourse I might have held with him. Mr. Francis with the other members who constituted the government of the time chose to receive him as a zemindar and in that character only could I regard him, nor could I without a breach of trust allow him to assume other privileges, or assert pretensions which were injurious to the rights and dangerous to the safety of the Company.'

From a perusal of these documents, it would appear that while Warren Hastings recognised that the word Zemindari denoted several types of rights, he was unable to distinguish between them, although in proposing independence for Cheyt Singh, he could see the difference between an autonomous chieftain and a zamindar.

He was also conscious of the fact that by the sanad of 1757, the original proprietors were deprived of their rights when zamindari was given to the Company. In 1772, he wrote:

From the best information I can get, on lands in every village have been time out of mind regularly divided, and marked out for Renging to the greater advantage, the good with the bad, and a reiat taking possession of any lands belonging to these division was immediately considered as proprietor and responsible for the whole.[11]

But later, defining *jama-i raiyat-i-khud kashta*, he writes that it was 'the rents of lands cultivated by tenants who reside upon them.'[12] Thus the *raiyat* here becomes a tenant and not a proprietor. Nevertheless, Hastings and Barvvell had proposed, 'to- secure the Ryots the perpetual and undisturbed possession of their lands.'[13]

Hastings, it seems, was unable to understand the full meaning of the term ryot, because of the definition which was given to him by a very knowledgeable person could not have made sense to him:

Anybody who lives in the territory of a *hakim* is his *raiyat*. The distinction and division is according to their ability and competence. The treatment meted out to them is according to their condition and status. Some of them are leaders of groups, others are its learned and the gentry, some are merchants, writers, scribes, professional people and artisans, others are in the services, or are labourers and load-bearers. Most of them are agriculturists. . . . [14]

Warren Hastings' concept of concurrent rights of the ruler and the zamindar is derived directly from an opinion that was given to him as follows:

The King is the proprietor of kharaj and of the country. Since the kharaj is from land, therefore he is also the proprietor of land. For the management of lands, he gives it to the zamindar. Therefore the Zamindar is the proprietor of the land of his zamindary.

The *raiyat* lives on the land, holding its title through the patta: It does not have the right to sell or gift away this land, consequently, the raiyat has proprietary right over land.[15]

In these documents, Warren Hastings has held that the Mughal rulers were arbitrary in removing the zamindars and also that their despotism was not arbitrary. He says that the Government had the right to raise the revenue and on another occasion asserts that 'the people were oppressed; they were discouraged, and disabled from improving the culture of their land.'[16] But at the same time he opines that 'rent was generally easy.'

In this connection, he wrote a strongly worded minute, criticising Grants' view that revenue could be enhanced. He wrote:

In his review of the land relations of the circars, Grant has argued that it was opposed to the ancient and modern theory and practice of oriental legislation. The doctrine of private individual landed property by inheritance, free of feudal tenure, extending beyond the period of a single life, but above all the law of the public expediency demanded taking from the peasant all except what was needed for his bare existence.

'From these premises it follows, that every land holder, of whatever denomination, ought to be dispossessed for the safety of the state, since the theory and practice are declared equally to be dangerous; that public expediency is the great law of society, and therefore every rupee should be exacted from the reiat which exceeds his natural wants; and that he ought to pay with thankfulness for the rare peculiar blessing of being under the dominion of a lenient, protecting sovereign state which when it hath squeezed from the people all that it can expediently take, will yet not have enough to supply its exigencies, and therefore in the vulgar judgment of mankind it ought to forfeit or resign its dominions altogether, as an invasion of every principle of society or the universal rights of mankind.'[17]

The present author has tried to show elsewhere that even Warren Hastings was unable to understand the complex land rights existing in India and why the confusion arose. But a study of Warren Hasting's views will always be of great interest to students of Indian economic history.

Notes

1. For an extremely interesting discussion of this problem, see R. Guha, *The Rule of Properly for Bengal*. The documents containing the detailed view of Warren Hastings, however, appear to have escaped the author's attention, neither have any of the numerous biographers of Warren Hastings, it seems, used these documents.
2. Firminger, *Fifth Committee Report*, pp. 11–170.
3. Francis to C. Boughton Rousff, 22, June 1776, India Office, Fr.incis Mss 53 (49) 26. Also quoted by R. Guha, op. cit., p. 102.
4. R. Guha, op. cit., p. 123.
5. Revenue Selections III-137. Similar views were expressed by Briggs, Lord Moira (1815) and Colebrooks (1820). For a powerful defence of the view that neither the

king nor the zamindars were proprietors of land, see the *Zamindary Settlement of Bengal*, Calcutta, 1879.

6. Thomas Law, *A Sketch of Some Late Arrangements and a View of the Rising Resources of Bengal*. Also quoted by R. Guha, op. cit., p. 177.

7. Firminger, op. cit., 11, p. 520.

8. Add. 29, 233f. 56a et seq.

9. *Ain-i-Akbari*, I, p. 283, Bib. Ind.

10. Add. 29, 234 Ff. 529–57 b; also 29, 202f. 329 et seq.

11. Add. 29,076, Procs. of the Committee of circuit for the settlement of the revenues of provinces, June-Sept. 1772. Proc. Kishunagur 10–20 June 1772.

12. Add. 29,076f. 26b.

13. R Gaha, op. cit., p. 122.

14. Add. 6,586 f. 127a.

15. Add. 19,503, Reply to 56 questions. F. 57b. The present author has examined the various Persian manuscripts and records of this period, but does, not propose to refer to those in this paper. This document is quoted because it is included in Warren Hastings Papers.

16. Warren Hastings Minute, 3 November 1772, quoted—Hunter, *Annals of Rural Bengal*, p. 385.

17. Add. 29, 233f. 68a and b.

2

Institution of Watan and its Influence on the Eighteenth-Century Maratha Society

R.V. Oturkar and *S.N. Joshi*

WATAN (HEREDITARY RIGHTS), Caste and Custom appear to be the corner stones of the eighteenth Century Maratha Society. We mean to discuss the features of Watan in this essay. Original material available in some sixty-eight papers, written in Modi script, as well as additional information already available will be utilised for the purpose.

Watan defined: Watan can be defined as a hereditary possession of a land or a privilege, recognised by the community on one side and the state on the other for enabling the possessor to perform the duties associated with its possession.

Before inquiring into the origin of Watan it is desirable to distinguish it from corresponding privileged positions. Watan should be distinguished from Inam which means a sort of present, may be hereditary, granted in recognition of some service already rendered. There is no duty necessarily attached to it, although local conditions may vary. The word Jahagir or Jagir has definite political, or to be accurate, administrative significance. A Jahagirdar owes the possession of his Jahagir exclusively to the state and he is expected to render a definite service to the state in return for it. A Jahagirdar is a petty prince or a chieftain exercising such political privileges and performing such administrative duties toward his people, as are assigned to him by the state. The Sanskrit word Vritti (वृत्ति) means a permanent means of livelihood assigned for a service of an ordinary nature. Historically Vritti and Watan differ from each other. In the Ādnyāpatra whose authorship is conventionally, attributed to Ramchandrapant of Shivaji II period there is a separate chapter describing the sature of their respective functions, from which it is clear that while the holders of Watan form a corporate part of the social structure, the holders of Vritti are only an additional emblishment that would enrich the Society and help to make life

* 8th Session at Annamalainagar, 1945.

beautiful and all sided. In actual practice the distinction between Watan and Vritti tends to blur, especially in the case of less important duties of life. Whatever else may be said about the Watan and the Vritti, they made life stable and the performance of a variety of services to the Community absolutely assured. The structure of the Hindu Society was rendered impregnable as it was founded on the bedrock of Watan and Vritti.

Let us now try to understand the nature and scope of Watan as evidenced by the original papers available. It is necessary to be specific. Treatment of Indian history has too often suffered from wide generalisations. The country is so vast and the period so extensive that Watan and Vritti might appear in different forms in different lands and in different periods. A living society cannot express itself through static institutions. That is why generalisations should be circumscribed with reference to a definite land and period with the help of evidence properly sifted and put forth. Importance of the publication of original papers cannot be exaggerated. Let us learn to sift and analyse before we venture to synthesise and generalise. The comparative evidence in different parts of the country at any difinite period would enable us to develop a sort of theory of the subject, on which the science of history and its philosophisation might later on be built up.

On a perusal of the 68 papers available, one is inclined to remark that in the eighteenth Century Maratha Society any conceivable profession under the sun could possibly be crystallised into a Watan, so deep was the idea rooted in the mentality of the people.

A paper of the year 1722 describes how three Sheikhs, Rustum, Imam and Dayal, acted as darweshis, tamed tigers and bears and obtained a watani right of showing them round in the six villages round about Haveli. The Patils were ordered that the darweshis should be allowed to collect two pice per house and to show tigers and bears to villagers. The Patils were further instructed that during their stay in the village they should be provide with a village coolie to carry their load and a night watchman to serve them as a guard. No other wandering darweshi would be allowed to move with his tigers through the villages where the said Sheikhs had obtained a watani right. From another paper, it seems that the darweshis collected one anna per house. In the absence of any clue to fix up its date it is impossible to establish any connection between the price level of the time and the Watan charge. All that can be said is that the Watan charge was capable of an occasional variation.

Other interesting cases of Watani rights may be briefly noted. A Gurav having obtained the right of supplying flowers in a small village, a Mali was prevented from doing the same and thus creating an additional Watani right there. On his deliberate attempt to do so a complaint was taken to his got-panchayat (community) which exacted from him a promise that he would refrain from doing so. The right of blowing Sambal, a musical instrument, had been obtained by the Gondhalis and they successfully complained against the Gosavis who attempted to use Sambal at a festival. The Gosavis were, however, allowed to celebrate Gondhal and the exclusive right of the Gondhalis to celebrate it was not recognised, as gondhal was looked upon only as a form of devotion to God. As late as in the year 1818, Captain Robertson issued orders allowing, the Patils and Kulkarnis to exact their conventional Watani rights from the villagers.

The object of granting a watan was to create a feeling of security in the mind of the watandar and secure his steady services for the village. An Abhaya patra (assurance letter) of the year 1782 issued to a Tamboli (betel leaf seller) of Garade contained an offer of a plot of ground where he could open his shop. He gave Rs. 15 to the village Hakim, as nazrana, and was bound to pay Rs. 2 per year as revenue to the State and 50 leaves per day possibly to the village authorities. The Abhaya patra bore witnesses of 18 different watandars of the village. The name of the assignee was Kasim bin Baji. Baji seems to be a Hindu name and Kasim was possibly a convert. Such was the spirit of tolerance that a change in religion did not deprive a person of a place in the corporate structure of the village. In another letter of the year 1769 we find that the Deshpandes of Saswad asked the Patil of Garade to prevent the grocer from dealing in betal leaves as the Tamboli had the exclusive right to do the same. Watandars were looked upon as the supports of the village organisation and were treated with courtesy and respect. In 1764 the following official letter was sent to a watandar Mhar of Hasuchi Wadi: 'You area watandar Chaugula of this, village and the Patil informs us that you have recently left your watan and your duties and gone away. You are hereby informed that you should not be afraid of anybody and you may safely resume your office and take possession of your lands.' Sometimes a watandar would find it difficult to pull on with the scanty watan income guaranteed to him. He could, on an appeal to the village, get additional land. In a letter to the Deshpandes of Saswad they were informed that as the Kumbhar of the village had been graced by God with a large family they (the village authorities) should see to it that he was properly provided for.

The different balutedars (artisans) of the village were not of the same rank, which probably depended upon the importance of the service rendered by the balutedars to the village. In one paper the balutedars are classified into three orders. The first order included the Sutar, Chamar, Mhar and Mang and claimed a share of Rs. 10 for each. The second included the Kumbhar, Nhavi, Parit, and Lohar and claimed only Rs. 5. The third consisted of the Joshi, Gurav, Sonar and a Mulana (Muslim) each of whom was entitled to Rs. 2½. This shows that seniority in the village organization was different from seniority in the caste organization. The untouchable Mhars and Mangs evidently enjoyed a grade and a share superior to that of the Joshis and Sonars who were touchables. It should be remembered, however, that the ranks of different balutedars often differed according to local custom. There is no reference to Patil and Kulkarni watandars in the paper mentioned above. Their case evidently differed from that of other watandars for they acted in the dual capacity of State officers and co-sharers in the village organisation.

It was but natural that occasional disputes should arise in connection with the exact contents of such watandari rights. Sometimes rival claimants in the family disputed for the possession of the right. Sometimes outsiders surreptitiously tried to establish their claim. Sometimes there was a rivalry as regards precedence in social ceremonies. For instance, there was a dispute between a Patil and a Joshi as regards precedence in the application of Ticca to the forehead on the occasion of (पचांग श्रवण) (listening to the religious significance of the day) ceremony. Such cases of dispute were settled in a variety of ways; but usually readiness was shown to refer the point to the village panchayat. In 1779 the Chamars and Mahars of Pargaon quarrelled over the right to take the five offerings (पंच महानिवेद्य) made to Holi. The whole Pandhar (village farmers) and bara balutyas (village artisans) gathered together in a meeting in which evidence of over ten persons was recorded, most of them supporting the claim of Chamars. In a dispute between the Patils of Walhe and Ingual regarding the right to take the thigh bone (फ़शा) of the goat killed for ceremonial purposes on the Dussera day, information was collected from 38 villages nearby and the point was settled in favour of the Ingulkar Patil (A.D. 1784). The claim to a thigh bone might appear to be very trival today, but the contending parties then were willing to lay a wager of Rs. 500 over the point of dispute. Sometimes villagers tentatively decided the quarrel and used to refer it to the authorities at Poona for an authoritative investigation and decision. Where the point of dispute had any religious significance the high priests of a holy place nearby such as Paithan were consulted. But they too collected information about the traditional practice prevailing in the locality, before giving their decision in the matter. In 1724, the smiths of Khalad quarrelled with the carpenters and claimed a separate watan for themselves. The quarrel came up for decision to the Deshmukh and Deshpande of Saswad. They referred the matter to the village authorities requesting them to call forth witnesses and note down their evidence. Thereupon a number of villagers gathered in a temple and gave evidence on oath. The letter contains a list of witnesses comprising a Carpenter, a Mali, a Nhavi, a Jyotisi, a Parit, a Chamar, a Gurav, a Mang, a Kumbhar, a Potdar, a Mahar and also a Moulana (a muslim) whose deposition could not possibly have been taken in the temple. It may be asked as to who had the legal right to decide such cases of dispute. The final legal right evidently vested with the State or whoever represented the State; but more often than not, the contending parties referred the matter to the local authorities, who used to take their consent in writing, Rajinama as it was called, thus binding them to abide by their decision. Should the contending parties approach the higher authorities directly, the latter would, as can be seen from instances cited above, send the papers to local authorities for further investigation. At times the State authorities sent their representative to ascertain such evidence. This practice evidently protected the complainant against local prejudices and one-sided reports.

There is one form of Watan which deserves a special mention. It is the Deshmukhi Watan. To enjoy a Deshmukhi Watan and to be a Deshmukh was an honour sought even by princes. Shahu on being released by Aurangzeb is found to be anxious to claim the Deshmukhi of Wai and even much later, when his position as a king was stabilised i.e. in 1718 and 1719 he appeared to be proud of styling himself as a Deshmukh. In a state document incorporating the decision of the Astta Pradhan i.e. the State Council over a case of conflict regarding the Deshmukhi claim, Shahu's name appears not as a king but as a Deshmukh. All this might appear to be very strange; but the reason is not far to seek. The respect that royalty can evoke is due to fear and possession of power; the respect for Deshmukhi on the other hand is functional and is due to the importance of the service that is rendered. The Deshmukh is responsible for seeing that land is brought under cultivation and revenue is collected. The change in political power rarely brought about a change in the Deshmukhs. In fact the new power had to coax the Deshmukhs into the recognition of their rule and more often than not, depended upon them for the collection of revenue. Poona was often the bone of contention between the Adilshahi and Nizamshahi in the seventeenth century and time and again it changed hands. Sometimes a few villages in the Poona paragana belonged to the Nizamshahi and the rest to the Adilshahi; but either powers collected their land revenue from Shitoles, the family which held the Deshmukh Watan of Poona irrespective of the political power that ruled over then. Most of the civil administration of the villages was looked after by the Deshmukhs, rendering the political power of the state over them all but nominal. Indeed to study the administrative system of the country under the Marathas one must learn to distinguish between administration of the state (राज्यकारभार) and the administration of the territory or the country (देशकारभार) and in the latter it was the (देशमुख) that counted most.

One more point and we shall have done. It is customary to describe the eighteenth century Society in India as feudal. Names are dangerous because they evoke wrong ideas about the state of affairs. Time has come when we should learn to find out the distinguishing features of the feudalism of the West and the watan bound society of the East. The points of similarity are superficial and differences appear to us to be fundamental. The Feudal lords owed their power and position to the state; not so the Deshmukhs. The Deshmukhs rarely disturbed the peace of the country by mutual aggrandizement; and were anxious to avoid becoming tools in the hands of conflicting powers. They sheltered the people within their jurisdiction by warding off the claims of contending powers.

It is not possible to deal exhaustively with this point. We venture to put forth a few ideas before this learned assembly with the object of stimulating discussion and a bit of cautious circumspection so that hasty generalisations and a temptation of using western terminology for describing Eastern society may be avoided.

3

The Ryotwari System and Agricultural Serfdom in Madras 1792–1827

Nilmani Mukherjee

THE STUDY of labour under the ryotwari system in Madras in the first quarter of the nineteenth century will not be complete without a reference to 'agricultural serfdom.' Cultivation in many of the districts was partly done by slaves. In 1819 the problem of agricultural serfdom came under special scrutiny of the government and some definite information was available regarding the condition of agricultural serfs in different districts.

In Salem by 1819 slavery had almost ceased to exist. The Collector could not discover that any *Puller* had sold himself as a slave of late years. Even some *Pullers* cultivated their own lands and had their own *Puttiams*. Those who cultivated the land of others, and who were not slaves, received a regular hire.[1] In Coimbatore, slavery was in existence in very few villages. The owner had the right to sell his slave without the land but it was a right very seldom, if ever, exercised. The highest price for a good slave was Rs. 50 though the price seldom was so high. The children of slaves were born slaves. On the birth of a child, the master presented the parent with clothes and one or two rupees. The master possessed power not only over the person but over the property of his slave, and he might make use of the cattle reared by the slave for agricultural purposes. The slaves were sold with the land, but, if they objected to serve another master, they were not forced to do so. This was probably a favour done to him by the master and not a right that he could claim.

The slaves had a share of the produce allotted for their subsistence,—about an eighth. In some instances land had been made over to the *Pullers* which they cultivated for their support. In many places, where actual slavery did not exist, a kind of bondage was introduced by the ryots undertaking to bear the expense of their *Pullers'* marriage upon condition of the latter binding themselves to the ryots exclusively for life.[2]

In Madura and Dindigul, slavery was founded, in the first instance, on voluntary contract. The slaves were never seized or sold for arrears of revenue.

*24th session at Delhi, 1961.

The origin of their bondage arose in a voluntary agreement on their part to become the slave of some man more powerful than themselves upon whom they thus imposed a more strict obligation to protect and maintain them and their families than merely serving them as labouring servants. The Brahmins, in consideration of their caste, did not receive those bonds of slavery directly in their own name, but had them generally drawn out in that of some of their *Sudra* dependents. These bonds were considered hereditary on the part of the bondsmen.

It was usual in the district of Tinnevelly for slaves to be sold or mortgaged either with the land or separately as the owner pleased. The master had all the command of his slaves' labour. They were apparently not bound to provide subsistence to their slaves except when employed in their business and then it was on the lowest scale of allowance, being generally no more than two measures of paddy a day. At other times their slaves were obliged to seek a livelihood at the hands of others, being bound only to return to their masters when the season of cultivation again commenced. The slaves were entitled, when the crops were reaped, to a small deduction from the gross produce called *carco*. It was usual when death occurred among them for their masters to assist them in the necessary funeral expenses, and on marriages, births and festival days to grant them presents according as their circumstances would admit. But the slaves could not claim these as a matter of right.

In an account of a person's property to know whether he was a fit security for another, it was usual, if he possessed slaves, to include them, a male slave being estimated in value from 3 to 15 C. *Chuckrums* and a female from 3 to 5 C. *Chuckrums*. But these were not accepted by the Government.[3]

The slaves in the district of South Arcot were mostly of the *Pully* and *Pariar* castes and the majority of them were chiefly devoted to the pursuit of agriculture. The number of both sexes including children was more than 17,000. The possessions and acquisitions of slaves were generally considered to be the property of their masters who, however, usually relinquished them to the family of the slaves.

Slaves could not marry without the consent of their owners who, as they defrayed the expenses of the marriage, virtually revived the contract of hereditary bondage for the offspring of slaves who were always regarded as the property of their fathers' owner.

The owners of slaves were required to provide them with food and clothing, to defray their wedding expenses and to assist them at child-birth and pay the cremation expenses. The food given differed according to the opulence of the owner, but it was always sufficient for subsistence. Otherwise, the owner permitted the slave to serve elsewhere during his poverty. The price of a male slave and family, when sold by their owner to another person, varied considerably and ranged from 10 to 50 *pagodas*. Formerly Muhammedans used to purchase

Hindus as domestic slaves whom they converted to Islam but such cases were becoming rare towards the close of the period under survey.

The Collector of South Arcot thought that slavery, as it prevailed in India, was free from many objections that existed in West Indian slavery. The slaves enjoyed the purchase-money and contiued on the land of their birth. In many ways they were better off than their African opposite numbers.[4]

Slavery in Trichinopoly existed on a fairly extensive scale. In the wet districts the number of *Pullers* was about ten thousand including those employed for the purpose of watching and feeding the cattle. In the dry parts there were about 600. But the *Pullers* were only to be found in those villages where there was paddy cultivation. Usually they were sold with the land but there were many cases in which they might be purchased independent of the land. The price of a *Puller* varied from five to ten *pagodas* according to his age and qualification. The slaves were more often than not kindly treated and it was the opinion of the Collector that the abolition of the *Puller* system would be followed by most serious and ruinous consequences to the revenue as well as to the *Pullers*. On emancipation, the slave would still have either to continue at the plough possibly under less favourable circumstances, or seek a livelihood that was not peaceable. He suggested that the lot of the slaves should be improved by increasing their emoluments. This they fully deserved for they were 'the creators of revenue' and the *mirasidars* merely 'payers of revenue, receiving a larger *warum*, than the creator of revenue, yet still they were an idle, useless race, born to consume the fruits of the earth.'[5]

Since there were agricultural serfs in different ryotwari districts each having its peculiar local factors, generalizations as to their condition are dangerous. But certain tendencies seem to stand out with some degree of clarity. The slaves were as a rule more kindly treated than one might imagine,— if for no other reason than that each of them represented an investment of capital and was a handy and valuable asset for cultivation while labourers were scarce. The same economic interest assured that the slave was provided with cloths and shelter and enough food.

Previously to the establishment of the British rule, the owners of slaves were in the habit of punishing them either by castigation or confinement for any misdemeanour or fault at their discretion but that power in British times was less and less exercised. Taken as a unit, a somewhat variegated unit, the slaves were on the whole better treated by their masters than the common class of free labourers.

During the period under survey, slavery, in general, appears as a slowly dying institution. The awareness on the part of the owners that the exercise of despotic authority over their slaves was not favoured by the British Government operated to prevent the buying of slaves. The slaves were considered to be less valuable when they could not be punished freely. In Coimbatore the virtual extinction of slavery was owing to an epidemic which caused the death of many of the slaves. Although no case of enfranchisement or manumission is on record, the slaves became virtually free in some peculiar circumstances. When the owners became poor and unable to maintain their hereditary slaves, the latter became practically free and worked for any person who might employ them. The extinction of the owner's family also resulted in the emancipation of the slaves.

But the emancipated slaves sometimes, out of sheer necessity, had to enter again into perpetual and hereditary bondage for about 20 to 30 *Pagodas* which a cultivator advanced, perhaps, for the celebration of a marriage ceremony. There was no instance of a slave ever discharging such a loan by his manual labour.

The policy of the Government was not in favour of slavery and orders were given that slaves should not be sold for arrears of revenue. This was, of course, with special reference to Malabar where alone it had occurred.[6] As the number of slaves in the Tamil Districts was fewer and their condition better, the Government thought any immediate emancipation of them would be inconvenient and cause distress to the slaves freed for want of any alternative employment. At the same time, however, the purchase of free persons as slaves was banned and all children born of slaves were declared free. But individuals could still contract, for a given sum, to labour for a term of years or for life. The Government laid down that such contracts should be in writing and binding only upon the individual who executed it and not upon his wife or children. Slaves were declared competent to possess and dispose of their own property without any interference on the part of their masters.[7]

Altogether it appears that the peculiar institution of slavery was disintegrating slowly during the period under review. The Government policy was not in favour of the institution, though it was not prepared to take any drastic action in this respect. But the attitude of the government was well known and this acted as a restraining factor. The operation of the old ryotwari system, and especially the destruction of *mirasi* rights, impoverished a number of big landowners who became unable to maintain slaves any longer as part of their establishments. The imposition of heavy ryotwari assessments also made the ryots cut down the expenditure of cultivation. They had to depend more and more on the labour of the members of their families. They could hardly afford to employ slaves for that purpose. The independent ryots possessing smaller holdings and cultivating smaller plots of land under the ryotwari system also did not so much require the labour of slaves. The general poverty existing in the ryotwari districts also acted as a deterrent. Only in the richer wet land districts of Tanjore and Trichinopoly agricultural serfdom lingered on to a considerable extent. The increasing use Of money as a circulating medium favoured by the ryotwari system also discouraged the institution of slavery which was linked on to an older system of economy. The ryots found it more convenient to employ labourers on money wages.

Notes

1. General Reports of the Proceedings of the Board, 3 January 1820, vols. 27 and 28, p. 362.
2. Ibid. Coimbatore District Records. 24 June 1819, vol. 612, pp. 50–2.
3. General Reports of the Proceedings of the Board, 3 January 1820, vol. 27 and 28, p. 372.
4. Ibid. South Arcot District Records, 12 September 1819, vol. 280, p. 131.
5. General Reports of the Board, 3 January 1820, vols. 27 and 28, p. 372.
6. Ibid.
7. Ibid.

4

Position of Patels and Karnums in the 'Ceded Districts' (i.e. the Present Districts of Cuddapah, Kurnool, Anantpur and Bellary) during the First Quarter of the Nineteenth Century

J.C. Dua

THE OFFICES of the *patel*[1] (the village headman) and the *karnum*[2] (the village accountant) have been very old and hereditary institutions indispensable for the local administration. They discharged multifarious duties and enjoyed considerable power and position. Every village had within itself, a complete establishment of hereditary revenue servants, a *patel* to direct the cultivation, realise the rent, maintain peace and order and manage its affairs in general; a *karnum* to keep the accounts and the land records of the village. He looked after the revenue administration of the village.[3]

The office of the *patel* was anciently bestowed on the founder of a village in return for the benefits which the state derived from his exertions and ever since became hereditary[4] and as such its being hereditary is distinctly an original feature. It seems that when the plan of taking the revenues by means of a share of the produce was introduced, and some kind of public administration was organised, the State felt the necessity of a literate person who could keep accounts.[5] This accounts for the existence of the office of the *karnum*. Of the two, as the *patel* continued to possess some 'magisterial powers and various duties of police and protection', he remained, at least nominally, superior to *karnum*.[6]

As such the main duty of the *patel* was to collect and remit the State's share of the produce. He also acted as the head of village police, the *munsif* and the magistrate of the village. Every village had one *patel*. But there were cases when some villages had more than one *patel*, while at times one or more villages shared one *patel*. Normally a *patel* was a landed person of wealth and his

*34th Session at Chandigarh, 1973.

position was more or less of an honour. Both the offices of *patel* and *karnum* were remunerated by lands on very favourable terms, other privileges and gratuitous services from the villages notwithstanding. The lands attached to their offices were, like their offices, hereditary.[7] The powers, functions and the economic position of the *patels* and *karnums* very often varied according to the political and economic condition of the district.

At the time when the districts under study were ceded to the East India Company (1800) Thomas Munro, the first Principle Collector of the Districts found most of the *patels* and *karnums* acting like Chiefs in their respective villages. The description as taking up the Government of his 'little Republic' may be justified because of the anarchy prevailing in the Districts due to the rapid change of the government during the past many years.[8] There was hardly any *patel* who could not muster a party of armed persons at a few hours notice. The *inam* land attached to the offices of *patel* which had given rise to the endless feuds,[9] had also rendered necessary for him to maintain armed persons. He was not only given the privilege and encouraged by the late government on the payment of a *nazranah* to plunder and extort money from the inhabitants but also to carry on predatory warfare against one another for political gains,[10] which had resulted into the impoverishment, if not almost depopulation of the villages.[11] This was a unique feature in the Ceded Districts that the persons like the *patels* and *karnums*, who were very peaceful in other provinces, should have acted like the captains of the banditri garrisoning independent castles.[12] Particularly in Gurramcondah, almost every head of a village favoured by political anarchy had become a *poligar*,[13] and inspite of his income being not more than two or three hundred *pagodas*, was regularly installed with all the form of a Chief of an extensive territory and his nominal officers of state subsisting on small portions of land. Many a time even a *karnum* was compelled to make over to him large tracts of the state land and to enter them in his accounts as waste.[14]

It was not only in the political field that the *table* and *karnums* had attained unduly unique position, but they had managed to improve considerably their economic status. The survey of the Ceded Districts conducted by Thomas Munro revealed that the amount of the *inams* of *patels* and *karnums* was seldom in any uniform proportion to the rent of their respective villages and that in some places it was as low as one per cent and in others as high as fifty—and that in many villages there was no *inam* at all.[15] But at the same time this was found that no native government had ever allowed more than 10% of the revenue as the total *inam* to both the *patel* and *karnum* in a village whose rent had exceeded five hundred *Pagodas*.[16]

It is not clear from the information available whether this variation was actually not seriously looked into by the previous rulers or there were some other factors conducive to this variation. It seems that it was mainly because of the frequent changes of the government, and the loss or rather concealment of accounts[17] which had brought about the variations. No doubt at the same time, we cannot completely rule out the previous proposition. Thomas Munro was of the opinion that probably the previous rulers paid little attention on the limiting of *inam* as whenever the *inam* was greater than usual, it was made answerable to complete the deficiencies in the village collections.[18] Even after 1800, Munro himself admitted that there were many villages, in which, the *patel* and even the *karnum*, were liable for deficiencies as far as the equivalent of their *inam* lands.[19] Moreover, even the assessment of those *warn* lands for deficiencies did not seem to have been regulated by any fixed principle. In some villages it was assessed only when accidental losses occurred, whereas in others it was a regular annual feature. In the latter villages the settlement was always fixed so high to make its realization impossible, without, of course, taking the *patels'* and *karnums' inams* at one-half or two-thirds of their produce.[20] A research in the Mughal age has also revealed such types of variations in the *inam* of the *patels* and *karnums*. The *inam* during that period depended on the customary practices and would vary from region to region and at times from village to village. . . . In any particular region, the rate during the Mughal age could not have exceeded the one prevalent (even) in the mid-nineteenth century. . . .'[21]

So, such a variation in the Ceded Districts was not a new phenomenon during the period preceding their cession nor in the region under review alone. But at the same time, it cannot be completely ignored that the political distrubances and frequent changes of government during the period prior to 1800 did play a significant role in creating variations in the *inams* of the *patels* and *karnums*. As already stated the *inam* land attached to their offices especially in the case of *patels* had given rise to endless feuds. It was not only an attraction for a *patel* to attack his counterpart in the neighbouring village and dispossess him from his *inam* land but would even attract him to drive his relations, if they possessed any *inam* land, from their land and seize their possessions.[22] At the same time even *poligars* used to give land to the *patels* on their helping them with the parties of armed persons. Normally the *patels* who had parties of ten, fifty and hundred were given a piece of land worth 9 to 24 *Pagodas*,[23] Those *patels* and *karnums* who refused to accede to the demand of the *poligar*, either of armed persons or of money, were treated very harshly and were even kidnapped, beaten and put into the confinement, till the required demand was met.[24] There are cases when a *karnum* was even compelled by threats to make over to the *patel* large tracts of the state land, and was to enter that in his accounts as waste.[25] The same land was later on declared as *inam* land attached to his office by the *patel*. At the same time, we cannot rule out the possibility of Thomas Munro being given the false accounts by the *patels* and the *karnums*. He himself felt that they were in habit of doing so in a general measure in the consequence of the change of government.[26] Thus all these factors account for the variations in the *inam* lands attached to their offices. It has been computed that in all there was an average of above 5 per cent of the total *inam* land which could be regarded as unauthorised *inam* attached to their office.[27]

Apart from this, for Thomas Munro, there were few other things which were quite peculiar in the character of the *patel* and the *karnums* in the Ceded Districts. He agreed that the *patels* and *karnums* would everywhere make small private collections by forwarding wrong accounts but it was an extraordinary feature in the Ceded Dictricts that many a time they would abscond with public revenue. They would not return unless they were granted permission to make up the deficiency by a new assessment upon the inhabitants.[28] In this way, a considerable amount of revenue was embezzled by the *patels* and the *karnums*. This affected the punctuality of the *tahsildars* to remit the revenues and at times resulted in loss to the government.

Another thing peculiar about the *patels* and *karnums* in the Ceded Districts was that they used great highhandedness in regard to the grant of *taqavi* to the *rayats*. It was the custom that the *patels* and *karnums* would appear as sureties at the *cutcherry* for a body of *rayats* to get them *taqavi*.[29] They often got the whole of the amount from the *rayats* the moment they would quit the presence of the *tahsildars*. Normally it used to be previously concerted and the *rayats* were brought before the *tahsildar* merely as a deception to obtain a sum of money for themselves. But the tragedy was that they would not stop there. Sometimes, the money thus obtained was called a loan which was to be paid whenever found convenient. But often the practice was that when the payment of *taqavi* back to the *cutcherry* became due, the *patels* and the *karnums* would exact the amount from the *rayats* in whose name it was originally disbursed.[30] Above all the accounts maintained by the *karnums*, the purpose for which they were holding that office, were always false and would amount to 30% to 40% of the actual revenues of the village concerned.[31]

Thomas Munro is of the view that the jurisdiction and power of the *patels* and *karnums* had been in no way inferior to that of any higher officer in the village. Though any one holding land, whether he was discharging the functions of a high civil office or was merely a village *taliari* was called a *Zamindar*, yet the actual position of the *patels* and *karnums* was far more superior to that of higher classes of *zamindar*, *deshmukhs* and *deshpandyas*, etc. The latter categories were all revenue officials, holding *inam* land or villages, and received a percentage on the collection as an allowance for performing the duties of their employment. But they held their office and land only during pleasure of the state, whereas in the case of the *patels* and *karnums* both the office and the *inam* were hereditary. As such the position of the *deshmukhs* and *deshpandyas* was inferior to that of the *patels* and *karnums*. And in actual practice, at the time of the cession of the districts, these were the persons who were all powerful and there were no *zamindars* excepting them.[32] But Munro is not correct in holding this view. He has exaggerated the position of the *patels* and *karnums* vis-a-vis the *deshmukhs* and *deshpandyas*. Actually the latter also held hereditary offices and worked in co-ordination rather their being infferior to the former. It is possible that because of the chaotic conditions immediately preceding the cession of the districts this development might have taken place temporarily. But in theory it is not correct.

Now the problem before Thomas Munro was that inspite of the flaws in the character and working of the office of the *patels* and *karnums,* it was not possible for him to do without them. It had been an ancient practice to entrust management of the village to the *patels* and *karnums* and the inhabitants were used to that. The Collector had merely to confirm what the *patels* and *karnums* had already done.[33] Moreover, they enjoyed considerable influence over the *rayats.* The *rayats* could be instigated by them to throw up their land for obtaining a reduction in the assessment.[34] They would be encouraged to do so for in case they obtained any reduction, the *patels* and *karnums* might also get the same concessions on the same pretext. Even those *rayats* who might be satisfied with original terms, in order to save themselves from the displeasure of the *patels* and *karnums,* would be induced to raise equal amount of objections.[35] At the same time they used to make better use also of their influence. It was only with their influence that the *rayats* could be persuaded to take up extra land, without which as much as ¼th of the total land would be a waste land.[36] They continued to enjoy the same amount of influence even in the later period,[37] and the Collector had to seek legal authority to punish the *patels* and *karnums* whenever the extra ordinary influence used by them was detected.[38] Munro did not want to entrust the *patels* and *karnums* with the power of fixing the revenue as there was a danger of their being partial to their relations and friends and biased towards their enemies. Above all they themselves too, were cultivators.[39] At the same time, he did not want any landowner holding the appointment of the *karnum,*[40] But inspite of these difficulties, Munro was confident that they were the persons most capable of making the settlement correctly,[41] only if certain checks were imposed upon them. As such their position and functions were kept precisely on the same footing as in theory they were meant for.[42] Those *patels* and *karnums* who had acquired political power and had attained the title of the *poligar* were reduced to the normal position. It was both administrative and agrarian necessity. It was an administrative necessity because unless the peace was restored, efficient running of administration would not be possible. These two officials exercised a considerable influence on the agrarian life of the villages. The *rayats* were under their command, the records of the villages were under their supervision and possession. The settlement of the districts was not possible if full co-operation was not forthcoming from them. Though it might be difficult to reduce them to the most honest village officials, it was at least certainly within the hands of administrators to finish completely the political power that they had attained because of political disturbances. That was done, even though at times military actions had to be taken against them.

In the beginning, since it was not possible to go into the details of revenue aspects, a *mauzawar* or village settlement was introduced. In this type of settlement the *patels* were made severally answerable for the rent of their own villages, and jointly for that of the whole of the district.[43] But this was not the final arrangement and the details had yet to be worked out. Later on, when the *Kulwar* settlement was introduced, the *patel* was to manage the whole village and was made answerable for the rent only of the lands which he occupied and every *rayat* was answerable for his own rent, and jointly they were made responsible for the rent of the whole village.[44] Apart from the other reasons for not introducing a permanent *mauzawar* or village settlement in the Ceded Districts, one important reason was that it would give much room for malversation to the *patels*. It would also have created many disputes between the *patels* and *rayats*, and would have become easier for *patels* to withhold the revenue.[45]

By the introduction of the village lease system in the Ceded Districts (roughly between 1808 and 1820) the settlement of village was made with the *patel* of that village. He was induced to undertake the rent of his respective village. One of the chief reasons of its failure seems to be the type of responsibility conferred on the *patels*.[46] No doubt the *karnums* were not considered to be fit for that purpose and it was though expedient to avoid forming the settlement with them. This was decided not because the Board of Revenue had any apprehension of the preponderance of the *karnums*, but because it was thought to be 'improper that the office of village Registrar should be united with the proprietary right in the village'. In case of emergency when there was no other person in the village able or willing to undertake the rent, the settlement could be concluded with the person holding the office of *karnum* but only after the office in question was taken away from him and conferred on some other person.[47]

Thus the *patels* and *karnums* kept on enjoying the respective position given to them in accordance with the practice of region. The *patels* were entrusted to manage the village. They had always held that office and were better qualified than any other person for that, and as such could not be removed without great inconvenience and probably loss of revenues.[48] The collector was only to confirm what the *patels* had already done,[49] and except in the case of misconduct and incapacity the collector could not remove them from the office, nor could interfere in their appointment.[50] As regards the *karnums*, according to the Regulation II of 1802 (Section I and II) the collectors were prohibited from dismissing them from their office without the authority of Board of Revenue.[51] Apart from regular duties assigned, *pattah* and *muchilkas* stating the amount of land with every *rayat* and the revenue to be paid by him, was to be countersigned by the collector incharge of the district, because it was felt that the inhabitants had more confidence in the collector than in that of the *patel*, and that they (the inhabitants) knew that it was intended to guard them against extra demands, and would be essentially guided by the *patels*.[52] Regarding the accounts maintained by the *karnums*, though it was known that they never gave perfectly true statement, yet they could give tolerably accurate accounts on account of fear of removal, or suspension.[53] At the same time the collectors were given authority to call the *karnums* for explanation about the accounts without assigning any reason because Munro felt that unless the *karnums'* accounts were constantly opened to the collector without any form of requisition it would be impossible to obtain within the year the necessary information for ascertaining the amount of revenue.[54]

Now the most important problem before the British administrators was to deal with the remunerations to the *patels* and *karnums* which traditionally were paid in the form of hereditary *inam* lands. As already stated that these officials had managed to get, apart from the legal *inam* land assigned to them, a considerable amount of illegally acquired land as well. Thomas Munro, the man on the spot, made up his mind not to settle anything unless the survey of the districts had been done, no matter how much time and money that might consume. He felt that the survey would bring to light the extent of unauthorised *inam* being retained by the *patels* and *karnums* in their own hands and as a result were enjoying the greatest part of the produce. There was no other means to detect the real value of those lands and their comparative value with the land held by the ordinary *rayats*.[55] Thus survey was essential to regulate a sort of semi-fœdual class, which at the cost of the common *rayats* and state revenues had emerged to be a fairly dominant class.

The survey revealed that all authorized and unauthorized *inam* land with the *patels* and the *karnums* amounted to acres 4,02,011-21-33.[56] Of this only 4/5th was cultivated. The whole of the State and *inam* land capable of cultivation amounted to acres, 1,20,66,923 of which the rent, as fixed by the survey, was *Star Pagoda* 39,54,417.[57] This means that about 5.36% of the total estimated rent was in the shape of *inani* with the *patels* and *karnums*..

The immediate action that Munro took as a result of survey was the fixation of the maximum, percentage of the *inam* land to be allotted to the *patels* and *karnums* in the Ceded Districts. He decided that in this respect the prevailing custom since the previous regimes should be adopted. Keeping in view the past practices Thomas Munro suggested the rate of *inam* to the *patels* and *karnums* as has been shown in the table below.[58] The table depicts that the percentage of *inam* was based upon the value of the land i.e., according to the survey rent fixed upon it. The range of the value of land taken into account is between C. Pagodas 50 to 6000. Accordingly the corresponding percentage of *inam* allowed to the *patel* ranges from 8% to .97 per cent and to the *karnums* from 12 per cent to 1.52 per cent. Thus if the survey rent was C. Pagodas 50, the *patel* got 8 per cent and *karnum* got 12 per cent worth of *inam* land in the village, in case it was C. Pagodas 100, they would get 6 per cent and 9 per cent; on C. Pagodas 300, 4 per cent and 6 per cent; on C. Pagodas 800, 3 per cent and 4 per cent; on C. Pagodas 1000, 2.8 per cent and 3.7 per cent; on C. Pagodas 2000, 1.9 per cent and 2. 55 per cent; on C. Pagodas 3000, 1.43 per cent and 1.9 per cent; on C. Pagodas 4000, 1.2 per cent and 1.57 per cent; on

C. Pagodas 5000, 1.06 per cent and 1.38 per cent; and on C. Pagodas 6000, 0.97 per cent and 1.25 per cent, respectively. The total percentage of *inam* allowed to the *patels* and *karnums* in a village worth of C. Pagodas 50 survey rent would be 20 per cent. In case the survey rent was C. Pagodas 100, the *inam* to the *patel* and *karnum* would come down to 15 per cent; on C. Pagodas 300, 10 per cent; on C. Pagodas 800, 7 per cent; on C. Pagodas 1000, 6.5 per cent; on 2000, 4.45 per cent; on C. Pagodas 3000, 3.33 per cent; on C. Pagodas 4000, 2.77 per cent; on C. Pagodas 5000, 2.44 per cent; and on C. Pagodas 6000, 2.22 per cent. The share of the *patel* in the total *inam* allowed in a village was always between 39% to 43.44%. This shows that the major portion of the *inam* went to the *karnum*. Munro has not given any explanation for this variation. It seems that this was because of the other legal and illegal means by which *patel* could manage to earn extra money. The excess of the above percentage of *inam* land if any, with the *patels* and *karnums* should be assessed according to the survey rent.[59] Thus, there was no fixed percentage of the *inam* attached to the office of the *patel* and *karnums*. At the same time the table also

TABLE 4.1

Survey rent in C. Pagodas	% of inam allowed to the patel	% of inam allowed to the karnum	Share of the patel in the maximum inam allowed in a village (in %)	Total % of inam allowed in a village to the patel and karnum
50	8	12	40	20
100	6	9	40	15
150	4.67	7.33	39	12
200	4.50	6.75	40	11.25
250	4	6.40	39.02	10.25
300	4	6	40	10
400	4	5.63	41.54	9.63
500	3.60	4.80	42.86	8.40
600	3.33	4.42	42.97	7.75
700	3.14	4.14	43.13	7.28
800	3	4	42.86	7
900	2.89	3.89	42.63	6.78
1000	2.80	3.70	43.08	6.50
1500	2.20	2.93	42.88	5.13
2000	1.90	2.55	42.70	4.45
2500	1.62	2.16	42.85	3.78
3000	1.42	1.90	42.94	3.33
3500	1.30	1.71	43.19	3.01
4000	1.20	1.57	43.32	2.77
4500	1.12	1.47	43.24	2.59
5000	1.06	1.38	43.44	2.44
5500	1.01	1.31	43.1	2.32
6000	0.97	1.25	43.24	2.22

depicts that as the survey rent increased the percentage of the *inam* attached to their office decreased.

Of course, in his report, immediately before his departure, Thomas Munro, while recommending the reduction of 25 per cent of the survey rent; suggested another formula for the fixation of the total *inam* to be allotted to the *patels* and *karnums* in a village. It was suggested that in the villages with not exceeding 250 pagodas rent, the total *inam* would be to the extent of 10% of the total village revenue; in the village with 250 to 500 pagodas rent, the *inam* would be to the extent of 7½ per cent; and that in the village with more than 500 pagodas rent, the *inam* would be to the maximum of 5 per cent.[60]

The percentage of the *inam* to the *patels* and *karnums* also comprised the *Marah Wurtana*,[61] i.e., the perquisites from the crops. Wherever the amount of *inam* together with the *Marah Wurtana* was less than the rate shown in the table, the difference was made up. In case the *inam* exceeded the approved percentage, both the *patels* and *karnums* were permitted to enjoy the whole as due to the unavailability of the official accounts of the previous government, there was hardly any means left of ascertaining the fact. But, as stated earlier, the excess was to be charged according to the survey rent.[62] This certainly did not prohibit them from taking any amount of state land on the usual survey rent. Taken on the face value of the *inam* recommended for the *patels* and *karnums*, their position was certainly given a great set back and it was considerably lowered.

A. Sarda Raju[63] has pointed that with the introduction of the new judicial system, all the offices connected with revenue collection were abolished except that of the *karnums*, and it was only in 1816 that the office of village headman was revived with very much curtailed power.[64] But is does not seem to be correct in regard to the Ceded Districts. Upto 1807 the office was very much in existence as it was only in 1807 that Munro had recommended the scale of *inam* to be granted to the *patels* and *karnums*. After his departure when the village lease system was introduced in the Ceded Districts, even Sarda Raju had accepted the reinstatement of the office of *patels*.[65] Thereafter it remained in existence.

As regards the office of the *karnum*, there are no two views that it remained as powerful as it was. His services remained indispensable under any mode of revenue collection. During the survey, both the *patels* and *karnums* had managed to get their land, *inam* as well as other, assessed very low.[66] Moreover, they could take any amount of waste land in their own names directly from the *amildar* on the fixed *cowle*, and were permitted to give that for their own advantage at a higher rate to the *rayats*, granting them *pattahs* specifying the quantity of the land and the rent. The government would not demand anything extra except the rates specified in the *kaulnamah* (agreement deed). So this was not only an extra source of income, but it proved to be a great boost to their position.[67]

With the introduction of the village lease system in the Ceded Districts, the position of especially the *patels* had become more important and they had become more indispensible. They were found to be the persons most qualified and best adapted to their village with respect to the interests of the government, and the *rayats*. As such the government wanted that they should rent their village. It was expressed that under the native governments, it was generally the *patels* who used to rent their villages. Even during the first year (1800–1) of the Company's government, it was found expedient to rent the village in the Ceded Districts to the *patels*. Of course, the Government accepted that since the introduction of the *rayatwari* system (1801–7) their duites had been to superintend the general administration of the village and to see that the cultivation was carried on to the full extent, whereas collection of the revenue was done directly by the state. With the introduction of the Village Lease System, they were expected to perform other duties as well.[68] But contrary to the expectations of the government it proved to be an uphill task to bring the *patels* round to accept the term and conditions of the government. Inspite of the several restrictions imposed upon them, they had been enjoying a considerable position and influence in the village.

They had thrown up the land and wanted the *bariz* (Jamma or Rent) to be considerably reduced. They could not only influence the *rayats* to restrain from accepting the land, but would create lot of problems for an outsider if he had accepted to rent the village. They could influence the *rayats* to restrain accepting the land, thereby making it impossible for the renter to fulfil his commitments to the Government.[69] The government was not in favour of renting the villages to the *karnums* due to reasons already explained.

In this way the government had to adopt a little harsh policy towards the *patels*. They were told that it was a part of their duty to direct and promote the cultivation of the State land, and to collect and pay the rent of the village to the government.[70] No doubt the *inam* was hereditary, but continued to be conditional and was a remuneration for their services. The only useful service that the *patels* could render under the existing circumstances was to rent the village. The Board of Revenue was of the opinion that in case they refused to accede to that or interfered in the operations of other renters, the collector was at liberty to dispense with their services and resume their *inam*.[71] In case the *patels* were allowed to refuse to rent the village and at the same time retain their service *maniyam*,[72] it was feared, that the refusal might become general, which would lead to a great loss to the government. At the same time, the persons who would undertake to rent the village, would certainly demand some abatement equivalent to the value of *maniyam* which would of course, involve a double expense to the Government.[73]

At the same time, the government did not want to be very harsh either and wanted to induce the *patels* only to undertake the rent of their respective villages. As such, the government had to moderate the rent to make it acceptable to the *patels*. This scheme certainly worked and it was not found necessary to deprive any *patel* of his office. Rather the Board recommended that they should not be removed unless there was a clear proof of embezzlement, tyranny, or contumacy on the part of the *patels*.[74]

Thus barring the political power that the *patels* and *karnums* had unlawfully attained because of the political distrubances immediately before the districts were ceded to the company they continued enjoying the influential position in the land revenue administration of the villages. Though with the introduction of the *rayatwari* system of land tenure (again after 1820) in the Districts, theoretically the position of especially the *patels* was once again given a set back, they continued to be as strong, influential and indispensable part of the village society as ever. Of course, the position of *karnums* remained unchecked. The British Government had acted rightly by not disturbing the local administration otherwise it would have certainly become very difficult for it to maintain the law and order to run revenue administration on smooth fooing.

Notes

1. Also khown as—*Reddi, Naidu, Naittamkair, Peddacapu, Maniakkaren, Monigar,* etc.
2. Also known as —*Kulkarni, Patwari, Shenabogue, Menon,* etc.
3. Madras Records Office, *Board's Consultations,* 5 January 1807; *Selections from the Records of the Bellary District, Political Revenue and Agricultural matters, 1800–1856,* ASO (D) 73, Letter from Thomas Munro to the President and Members of the Board of Revenue, 30 November 1806.
4. MRO, *Bellary Records,* 382/4, Letter from the Collector of Bellary District to the Board of Revenue, 22 August 1817.
5. Since a literate person was required and in the then South Indian society it were only the Brahmins who were educated, a Brahmin was chosen for that job. In South India and the Deccan Brahmins kept on holding this position, (see for reference MRO, *The Proceedings of the Board of Revenue on the interduction of the Village Lease in the Ceded Districts, 1811,* ASO (D) 31 and 32 Minute of the Board of Revenue, 9 May 1811). Whereas in Punjab and other parts of North India this does not seem to be the practice.
6. Baden-Powell, *The Indian Village Community,* pp. 13–14.
7. MRO. *Bellary Records,* 382/14, Letter from the Collector of Bellary to the Board of Revenue. 22 August 1817.
8. MRO, *William Thackeray's Report on Malabar, Canara and the Ceded Districts,* September 1807, ASO (D) 66; also see *Fifth Report,* 1812 (Madras, 1883), II, 709-45.
9. MRO, *Madras Board of Revenue Consultations, 31 Aug. 1801; Col. Munro's Report regarding Poligars in the Ceded Districts with a memorandun of Poligars, 1801–2,* RSO(D) 66 (21), Letter from Thomas Munro to the President and Members of the Board of Revenue, 12 August 1801.

10. MRO, *Selections from the old Records of the Bellary District, 1800–1807*, ASO(D) 72, Instructions issued by Thomas Munro, the Principal Collector to the Subordinate Collectors, 31 Dec. 1800; also *see—William Thackeray's Report . . .*, ASO (D) 66.

11. MRO, William Thackeray's Report. . ., ASO (D) 66.

12. Ibid.

13. For details about Poligars, J.C. Dua, 'Poligars: Their Rise in the Ceded Districts,' *IHC*, XXXIII, 1972 pp. 467–74.

14. MRO, *Col. Munro's Report Regarding the Poligars. . .*, RSO, (D) 62 (21), Letter from Thomas Munro to William Petrie, President and members of the Board of Revenue, 20 March 1802.

15. In case no *inam* was attached to the office of the *patel* and *karnum*, this does not imply that they served without any proper and adequate compensation, rather they continued to hold State land at a very low rent and the income thus derived by them was grater than the income derived by others from the *inan* lands.

16. MRO, *Bellary Records, 384/54*, Thomas Munro to the Collector Adorni Division, 14 April 1807; also—*Board's Consultations, 24 Aug. 1807, and Col. Munro's correspondence regarding the survey and rayatwari settlement of the Ceded Districts, 1802–1807*, ASO(D) 79, Thomas Munro to the Board of Revenue, 26 July 1807.

17. MRO, *Board's Consultations*, 24 Aug. 1807; and *Col. Munro's Correspondence regarding the survey. . .*, ASO (D) 79, Thomas Munro to the Board of Revenue, 26 July 1807.

18. MRO, *Bellary Records*, 384/54, Thomas Munro to the Collector Adoni Division, 13 April 1807.

19. *MRO, Selections from the Records. . .*, ASO (D) 72, Thomas Munro to Archibald Obins, Private Secretary to the Governor, F.S.G. 20 June 1805.

20. Op. cit., fn. 28

21. B.R. Grover,'Nature of Dehat-i-Talluqa (Zamindari Villages) and the Evolution of the Talluqdari System during the Mughal Age,' *IESHR*, II, 3 (July 1955), p. 259.

22. Op. cit., fn. 9.

23. Ibid.

24. MRO, *Col. Munro's Report regarding the Poligars. . .*, RSO (D) 62 (21), Munro to the Board of Revenue, 20 March 1802.

25. Ibid.

26. Op. cit., fn. 17.

27. MRO, *Selections from the Old Records. . .*, ASO (D) 72, Instructions issued by Munro to his suboradinate collectors, 31 Dec. 1800.

28. MRO, *Bellary Records* (1802) 396/346, Munro to the Board of Revenue, 26 June 1802; also *Selections from the Records of Bellary. . .*, ASO (D) 73, Circular issued by Thomas Munro, 10 Aug. 1801.

29. MRO, *Bellary Records* (1802) 396/346, Thomas Munro to the Board of Revenue, 26 June 1802.

30. MRO, *Selections from the Records of Bellary. . .*, ASO (D) 73, Circular issued by Thomas Munro, 16 June 1801.

31. MRO, *Public Sundries*, 123 A, *MBRC*, 19 May 1803; Col. Munro to his subordinate Collectors regarding the modes of conducting the Rayatwar settlement, 30 Sep. 1802; also—*Bellary Records*, (1805) 391/30, Munro to William Bentinck, governor of FSG, 8 May 1806; also. . . *MBRC*, 26 Sect. 1805; *Selection from the Records. . .*, ASO (D) 72, Munro to the Board of Revenue, 25 Aug. 1805.

32. MRO, *MBRC*, 26 Sep. 1805, and *Selections from the Records. . .*, ASO (D) 72, Munro to the Board of Revenue, 25 Aug. 1805.

33. Op. cit., fn. 3.

34. Op. cit., fn. 28.

35. MRO, *Public Sundries*, 123A, 31, *MBRC*, 19 May 1803, and *Col. Munro's Correspondence regarding the survey. . .*, ASO (D) 79, Thomas Munro to his subordinate Collectors, 30 Sept. 1802.

36. Op. cit., fn. 32.

37. APSA, *Cuddapah Records* (F. 1219), 419/348, Chaplin to the Board of Revenue, 2 Nov. 1809; also. . . MRO, *The Proceedings of the Board of Revenue on the Introduction of Village Lease in the Ceded Districts. . .1811*, ASO (D) 31 & 32, Minute of the Board of Revenue, 1 July 1811.

38. MRO, *Bellary Records*, F 1230, 388/42 Campbell to the Board of Revenue, 2 Nov. 1820.

39. Op. cit., fn. 3 & 35.

40. Op. cit., fn. 32.

41. Op. cit., fn. 3.

42. Op. cit., fn. 32.

43. Op. cit., fn. 27.

44. MRO, *Bellary Records*, 1806, 391/30, Thomas Munro to William Bentinck, Governor, FSG, 8 May 1806; also—*Selection from the Records of Bellary. . . .* ASO (D) 73 73 & 76, Circular issued by Thomas Munro, 10 Aug. 1801.

45. Op. cit., fn. 3.

46. MRO, *The Proceedings of the Board of Revenue on the Introduction of Village Lease. . .* ASO(D) 31 & 32, Minute of the Board of Revenue, 9 May 1811.

47. Op. cit., fn. 32.

48. Op. cit., fn. 3.

49. Op. cit., fn. 4.

50. MRO, *Bellary Records*, (1805) 408/154; 410/27, Circular—Collectors—Ceded Districts, 16 Aug. 1806; Also—*Bellary Records*, (1806), 408/215, Thomas Munro to Frederick Gahagan Collector of Adoni division, 16 Aug. 1806.

51. Op. cit., fn. 35.

52. MRG, *Public Sundries*, 123A, 31, Munro to his subordinate Collectors, 30 Sept. 1802.

53. Op. cit., fn. 3.

54. Op. cit., fn. 32.

55. MRO, *Bellary Records*, (1802), 397/73, Thomas Munro to the Board of Revenue, 29 Oct. 1802.

56. The total *inam* land in the Ceded Districts was acres 25,747 which was worth Star Pagodas 12,34,458. This shows that the *inam* land with the *patel* and *karnums* was

about 24.89% of the total *inam* acreage in the Ceded Districts and was worth 25.39% of the value of the total *inam* land.

57. Op. cit., fn. 17; also. . . APSA *Cundapah Records,* (1809), 626/245, W. Wayte, Secretary, Board of Revenue, to the Collector of Cuddapah, 14 Dec. 1809.

58. I am very much grateful to the Director and Mr. Jha of the Computer Centre, University of Delhi, for preparing this table for me.

59. MRO, *Bellary Records,* 384/54; and *Selections from the Records. . .*ASO(D) 72, Circular issued by Thomas Munro, 14 April 1807.

60. MRO, *Boards' Consultations,* 5 February 1808; *Col. Munro's Correspondence regarding the survey. . .* ASO(D) 79; *Selection of Papers from the Records at East India House relating to the Revenue, Police, and Civil and Criminal Justice under the Company's government in India, London,*1820–26, I, 94–98; *Fifth Report,* II,. 646–663, Report of Principal Collector of the Ceded Districts, 15 August 1807.

61. *Marah Wurtanah* were not collected in all villages. The rates also differed from place to place and item to item. For example on sugarcane and betel plantations, it was much higher than even the government rent.

62. Op. cit., fn. 59.

63. Raju, A. Sarda, *Economic Conditions in the Madras Presidency 1800–1850,* Madras, 1941.

64. Ibid., p. 20.

65. Ibid., p. 21.

66. Op. cit., fn. 17.

67. MRO, *Selections from the Records of Bellary,* ASO (D) 73, Circular issued by Thomas Munro (Undated) but issued sometime in 1801–02 (Fusly 1211).

68. APSA, *Cuddapah Records,* (1809) 636/245, letter from W. Wayte, Secretary, Board of Revenue to the Collector of Cuddapah, 14 December 1809; also MRO, *The Proceedings of the Board of Revenue,. . .* 1811, ASO (D) 31 and 32, Minute of the Board of Revenue, 9 May 1811.

69. MRO, *Bellary Records,* (F. 1219), 417/348, Letters from Chaplin, Collector to the Board of Revenue, 2 November 1809.

70. Ibid.

71. Op. cit., fn. 68.

72. A grant of land, or assignment of the government share of the produce therefrom, to the revenue officers, and the public servants of the villages.

73. Op. cit., fn. 68.

74. Ibid.

5

Land Settlement and Revenue Administration Under Maharaja Martanda Varma, AD 1729–1758

V. Narayana Pillai

MAHARAJA MARTANDA VARMA is known as the founder of the modern kingdom of Travancore, and is remembered as one of its greatest sovereigns. His greatness as a king depends as much on the administrative policies and the organization of departments as on his wars and conquests. It was his glory that he was able to establish a strong kingdom with safeguards for civil administration and military defence before the western type of Government machinery was introduced into India. Of all the measures initiated by Maharaja Martanda Varma, the settlement of the land is the most important, and a few facts which are bound to create a new interest in the subject are gleaned from original sources.

Not much is known about the condition of land revenue administration in Travancore before the time of Maharaja Martanda Varma, beyond a few facts gathered from epigraphical and other records. The earliest survey of the lands, of which records are available, belongs to the early part of the reign of Martanda Varma. The existing documents, however, point to the fact that there must have grown up a sound system of tenures and proprietary rights long before his time. From the very beginning of his reign Martanda Varma realised that as a preliminary to the organisation of a sound system of public administration the finances of the state must be placed on a firm footing, and for that the revenues should be carefully ascertained and properly collected. A complete survey of the State was necessary for the purpose, and as soon as he established peace in the kingdom he turned his attention to the settlement of the revenues from the land.

In 914 ME (AD 1739) some time after the suppression of the revolt headed by the Tampi-Pretenders, Martanda Varma appointed Mallan Sankaran, an officer with great experience, to carry out the land settlement. The old chronicle (granthavari) of the Sri Padmanabha Swami temple, Trivandrum, mentions

*6th Session at Aligarh, 1943.

that in 914 ME a settlement of the wet as well as garden lands in the State was conducted under the supervision of Kanakku Mallan Sankaran. Twenty-seven different tenures are mentioned including Kudijenmom, Pantara Otti, Pattam, and Virutti. It is stated that Ozhuku, Peru, Atavu and Ayacut records were prepared fixing the ownership of each plot of land as well as the responsibility for the payment of the dues to the Sarkar. This survey appears to have extended over a period of ten years, as records ranging from 913 to 922 ME are available in regard to the same. These records afford interesting details. A Kuri (writ) was granted to the ryots, and in some cases Karanams or Neettus were issued instead of the Kuri. Old records were examined in cases of doubt. Irrigation works were constructed and maintained by the Sirkar, and special cesses were imposed on the beneficiaries to recover the cost of the same.

As in wars and conquests the personal direction and control of the Maharaja was responsible for the brilliant results achieved in the governmental activities at the time. Numerous records exist which are eloquent in their testimony to the deep and abiding interest taken by Martanda Varma in the revenue survey and settlement. Communications after communications were addressed to officers in charge of the settlement work, directing them in their procedure or correcting them in cases of mistakes. The documents noticed in official or other publications may be passed over as they are already known. A few unpublished records may be summarised here, which I was able to read with the kind permission of the Government of Travancore.

Chattavarioyalas were addressed to Adhikaris (village officer) giving them detailed direction in regard to their duties and responsibilities. The records are interesting in a variety of ways and hence a summary of the same is given below. Prerecord dated 918 ME relates to the duties of the Adhikari of Vanehiyoor Pakuthi. Trivandrum taluk.

The Adhikari should see the collection of tax in money as well as in kind by Thantakaran, revenue peon, and should supervise the Chantirakkaran in charge of the palace. The Adhikari was given the power of appointing these and other subordinates. He should superintend the military training of Nayars by Asans, and should see to the disbursement of allowances due to them in proper time as well as the supply of bows and arrows, and gun power and shots. The Adhikari should enquire into complaints made to him and supervise the work of the Srikaryams of temples in the village. He should not attend to any thing other than his official duties. He may receive for his work an atukkuvatu, (perquisite) of one fanam for every 10 fanams due as atiyara, and an annual allowance of 300 paras of paddy and 360 fanams. The Adhikari had the privilege of taking with him ten peons when he went round the village on official duty.

The Maharaja paid the utmost attention to ensure justice and equity to all his subjects and to prevent corruption and malfeasance on the part of officers.

A record dated 11th Kartika 918 ME contains complaints to the Maharaja from aggrieved persons west of Karmana, regarding high-handed actions on the part of the revenue subordinates.

A document dated 24th Kartika 918 ME regarding instructions to Pillamars (accountants) in Vanchiyur Pakuthi, Trivandrum, affords interesting details about the method of settlement. The registration of wet lands should be effected in the presence of Kanakkan (accountant) of the Adhikari as well as of the Ahikaram. Direction is given to begin the preparation of the ozhukus of wet lands from a particular locality, and to register the lands according to lekkam numbers, giving the name of the owner and the amount due as tax. In regard to lands belonging to temples or Brahman Janmmis details regarding the tenant, etc., should be given in the ozhuku. Tax due to the Sircar must in every case be specified in the record. Tax from lands held in Pantara Otti (Sircar mortgage) should likewise be settled according to their yield. Detailed directions are given in regard to other tenures. For the settlement of dry lands the presence of four Naduvars was necessary. Specific rules were laid down in regard to taxes to be imposed on trees, such as coconut, jack tree, etc. The coconut trees were divided into four classes and tax thereon was fixed according to their yield. These directions even in matters of minute details removed the possibility of error as well as corruption on the part of officers and assured correctness and justice.

The foregoing details will show the thoroughness with which the settlement operations were directed and controlled. Although there existed from time immemorial rules fixing boundaries, arrears and proprietary rights over cultivable lands, the settlement of 914 ME (AD 1739) must be taken as the first organised attempt at an exhaustive survey of the whole kingdom with a view to the laying of the foundation for a sound revenue administration. The measure thus inaugurated was as wise as it was original that it was taken as the basis for all future land revenue settlements in the state.

This settlement covered only the ancestral kingdom of Martanda Varma, i.e., only the southern portion of what is now Travancore. The northern boundary of the original state (Venad) was pushed to the frontiers of Cochin by Martanda Varma by his conquests of Kayamkulam, Chempakasseri, Tekkumkur, and Vatakkumkur. A fresh survey was necessary in regard to the places newly acquired and in 926 ME the first settlement of Modern Travancore was undertaken. It was this measure more than anything else which served to consolidate the conquests of Martanda Varma, and to achieve the stability of State finances so essential for safety and progress of the kingdom. The settlements of 914 and of 926 assured the finances of the state and enabled it to organize a progressive administration on lines of permanent policies. The Maharaja paid equal attention to devise a governmental machinery for collecting the revenues thus ascertained and administering the affairs of the state. The state was divided into a number of mandapattumvatukkals (taluks) and each mandapattumvatukkal was sub-divided into properties, Pakuthies and Muris. The boundaries of these mandapattumvatukkals and properties were carefully surveyed and fixed (as evidenced by a record of the year 918 ME). Each mandapattumvatukkal was placed under the control of a Karyakkar who had under him Adhikaris in immediate charge of Adhikarams or Proverties.

The Karyakkas were under the control of Sarvadhikaryakkar who was responsible to the Dalava and the Maharaja. A record dated 3rd Chittirai 918 ME specifies the duties of the Karyakkar of Trivandrum mandapattumvatukkal. Roughly giving the boundary of the taluk and naming the 8 Adhikarams comprised in it the record preceeds to lay down the duties appertaining to the post of the Karyakkar. The Karyakkar should supervise the work of the Ahikaris, and deal out justice to complainants after making enquires through the Adhikaris. He may take as perquisite (atukkuvatu) one fanam for every ten fanams received by way of judicial fee, and any amount not exceeding one fanam presented by parties, who petition to the mantapattumvatukkal, remitting all excess amount into the royal treasury. He should supervise the work of the pillamar engaged in revenue collection and the affairs of temples within his jurisdiction. The Karyakkar had the power to appoint the Srikaryam (Manager of temple) and Pillamar in the temples under his charge. He should see to the proper performance of the pujas and the administration of the temple properties. It is interesting to note that in those days work commenced in the mantapattumvatukkal office at about 7 O'clock in the morning. Complaints received from the Adikarams were to be tried by the Karyakkar in the presence of four (respectable) men of the locality.

It may be seen from this how well-organized was the system and how well-defined were the powers and duties of the officers. In 929 ME, four years before the close of the reign, the settlement department was finally reconstituted extending its power over the whole of the new kingdom including Tekkamkur, Vatakkamkur and Champakasseri. A record mentions that in 929, Sarvadhikaryakkar and Pillamar were appointed and that revenues were properly collected and accounts maintained. Forts were constructed in various parts of the country and soldiers were garrisoned in them to keep the peace. In 930 Karappuram (Shertalai) was also added to the state, when it was constituted into a new mandapatumvatukkal.

These measures as well as the dedication of the kingdom to Sri Padmanabha Swami secured the consolidation of the State and laid the foundation for the greatness of modern Travancore. The future of the State was assured, and order and progress were established, for all time to come.

6

Slave Labour of Malabar
in the Colonial Context

Sebastian Joseph

THE LANDLESS agricultural labourers of Malabar were sunk fathoms deep in poverty and squalor. Their diminutive stature and sqaulid appearance demonstrated amply a tale of perennial undernourishment. Regarding this class Graeme makes a noteworthy observation:

In the interior, the wretched, half-starved diminutive creature stinted in his food and exposed to the inolemencies of the weather whose state demands that commiseration and amelioration which may confidently be expected from the humanity of the British government.[1]

These agricultural labourers were not the participants in a free labour market. To be more precise, they were the absolute property of their *Devarus* or lords. They could be forcibly employed in any work that their possessors pleased. This prodial or rustic class, known generally as *Cherumars* were engaged predominantly in the cultivation of rice lands and plantations.[2] They lived in the midst of fields in the small temporary huts which were 'little better than large baskets.[3] With an annual grant of sheer seven cubits of cloth[4] per head, a member of this class had to struggle to keep up his modesty.

There are any number of theories on the origin of agrestic slavery. The Brahmanical interpretation traces it back to the Parasurama legend.[5] The core of this argument lay in the Varna and Karma concepts that considered that individuals become outcastes or *chandalas* by sins against the laws of the respective castes. However, a disapproval of this view does not mean the non-acceptance of the antiquity of the system of agrestic slavery. That this class was indispensable to the process of agricultural production can be gathered from the fact that in Malabar alone there were 1,00,000[6] agrestic slaves according to a document of 1830. The term *Adimai* was generally used for the agricultural labourers of Malabar. This term *Adimai* was generally given to labourers of

*45th Session at Annamalainagar, 1984.

different castes such as Cherumars, Parriars, Vullams, Canacums, Erilays, etc.[7]

These cherumars who were literally serfs (Adimas) were the original inhabitants of the soil who were dispossessed of their lands by the succcssive invaders. Those serf castes who resided in the vicinity of the sea coast were better-off than their helpless co-brothers in the interior.[8] On the coastal areas, their labour was not indispensable althrough the year for the agricultural operations. And, hence they were allowed to work on their own account, to a considerable extent. However, in the interior taluks like Vettattunad, Sheranad and Vallbvanad in most cases, agrestic slaves were not allowed by their possessors to work for themselves.[9]

A cheruman or an agrestic slave was looked upon with disdain by all Hindu free born persons. This class was entirely considered impure and hence they were forced to erect their *chalas* (huts) at a far away place. They were supposed to keep themselves within the prescribed limits mentioned for each higher castes.[10] A Brahmin, when polluted by a cheruman, had to purify himself by prayer, ablution and by change of *Poonoos* or sacred thread.

These agrestic slaves were the victims of caste tyranny of an unprintable nature. A landlord could treat an *Adima* in the most inhuman manner and yet justify himself by stating that it was customary. The lash or coercive strokes were things too commonly used upon male as well as female slaves by the landlords.[11] These slaves were often seized and flogged and put in the stocks and their noses cut off in conformity with the crimes they committed.[12] Even after three decades of British rule, we come across cases of persons who caused the death of a cheruman by beating him, throwing him upon his back and thus amputating his nose.[13]

In the year 1835, several zillah assistant and native judges of the Western division were asked to report whether there were any final decrees whereby property in slaves has been recognised or rejected.[14]

On the revenue branch of the service the rights of the slave to possess and hold land and other property was not recognized during the first three decades of the British rule. It was found that there were about 377 slaves who held land on different tenures, paying revenue directly to the government.[15] The document further states that 'any complaint of the master taking forcible possession (of the property) would receive the same attention and would meet with the same redress as the complaint of a free man.[16]

Now the above one is an interesting piece of evidence. Inspite of the fact that these slaves were holding land on different tenures, they still belonged to some masters. Did it mean that it was not their economic position that determined their social situation as slaves? These 377 slaves had atleast partial control over their means of production. Yet the master had control over their person and he could make an attempt at controlling his property too, had the courts not interfered.

Even after decades of British rule, the condition of the slaves remained at an ignomable state. The cherumars remained precisely on the same state as they were half a century back. According to the Malabar district authorities, the cherumars were not one step raised in civilized life, or nearer emancipation.[17] If they remained beyond the periphery of civilized life, being exploited and tortured even in the early part of the nineteenth century, then their actual condition half a century earlier must have been certainly worse.

Infact, under the British rule, the price of the slave had risen. Every increase in their value was an additional obstacle to their freedom. An increase in their value was not due to the less availability of slaves on account of a fall in their population. On the other hand, according to a statement, the slave population of Malabar which stood below 1,00,000 before 1820, had risen to 1,44,000 in 1835 and to 1,59,000 in 1842.[18] This was an indication of the increase in the aggregate of slavery in Malabar. As stated by one official,[19] the longer period of British rule had proved some check on personal outrages and violence, such as mutilation. Beyond this, I believe the position of the cherumar to be stationary, and unless something more than negative efforts are made in his (slave's) behalf, he is likely to remain so.[20]

Slavery of Malabar was not a mutually beneficial social arrangement. In Malabar, it was only a myth that in times of famines and scarcity, the master would support the slave, because the maintenance of slaves even in ordinary times was scanty, and uncertain and in times of scarcity it was extremely doubtful.[21] It was not a 'perpetual labour given in exchange for perpetual maintenance'. It was true that a slave had opportunity for labour under his master. But he was not given a regular allowance for survival.[22] The allowance in the form of clothing and food scantily given to the slave was in the self-interest of the master himself. Because, starving them beyond a level, would have rendered them incapable of hard labour. This was not in any way different from his treatment of his pack oxen. For any thing beyond this, the slave had to look to his own extraordinary exertions at casual opportunities.

Price of Slaves

In Calicut taluk, a male able bodied slave was sold at 48 gold fanam (G.F).[23] The price of a female slave was 30 gold fanam and that of a boy and girl 10 gold fanam and 7½ gold fanam respectively. Cherumar were the only caste enumerated by Graeme in this taluk as slaves. Whereas in the Betatunad taluk we came across Yerupar, Karnakan, Pulayan and Parayan. While Yerular and Kannakan males were sold at 80 G.F. a male Pulaya used to fetch only 40 old gold fanam. Surprisingly a Pulaya woman used to fetch 64 old gold fanam. There is reason to believe that in this case atleast, the motivation was not primarily oriented towards considerations of productive labour. A male paraya used to be sold at 480 G.F. and a Paraya boy at 240 G.F. In the Changhat taluk the price of male Yerular and Kannakan was 120 G.F.[24] The price of Pulayan male was 60 gold fanam. The price of Pulaya boy ranged from 15 to 30 G.F.

The price of Yenular and Kanarakan stood higher than that of Pulaya in the Nedunganad taluk. The price of a Yerular was 120 gold fanam while that of a poleyan was only 40 G.F. However, a pulaya female fetched 75 G.F. in the taluk.[25] In the Walluvanad taluk also an Yerular and Kannakkan fetched 120 gold fanam. A pulaya male was sold at 75 gold fanam and a female was sold between 90 to 100 gold fanam.[26] The price of a Pulaya woman and the price of male Kannakans, Pannians, Kurumbers stood at 160 gold fanam in the Ernad taluk. At the same time a male Pulaya could be sold at a maximum price of 100 G.F.[27]

In the Shernad taluk also a Pulaya woman fetched between 100 and 110 G.F.[28] A male Pulaya was not paid more than 80 G.F. whereas a male Kunnakar could be sold at 110 G.F. even.'[29] In the Kurumbanad tatuk both Puiaya and Kulladee males were sold for 40 G.F. But surprisingly a Pulaya female fetched only 25 G.F.[30]

Lease of Slaves

Along with the sale of slaves publicly, one also come across evidence of large-scale leasing of slaves for a fixed period. The origin of this practice is shrouded in mystery. However, in a letter written from Nilgiris to J. Clarke, the Collector of Malabar, one finds a statement that the practice of leasing a slave was being continued by their proprietors in the Davala, Numbalcottah, Charrongcottah and Nelumbar division of the Wynad taluk.[31] Wynad was one area where, the Europeans had taken a keen interest in getting contracts, leases, etc., for a variety of purposes in a highly profitable way. Gold washing was one of the profitable areas the Europeans were interested in. The history of the gold mining and gold-washing started officially under the British from 1793 onwards.[32] A.M. Mascelles, a European was offered the lease of the 'gold-washing' of the district by the Tirumulpad of Nilamcur who also offered to guarantee in the lease the services of twelve families of slaves.[33] It had been always a normal practice in the area to include the slave families also in the lease for gold-washing.[34] This practice existed widely in the lower plains like Eddacherry and Carcoor also.[35] In the lower plains of Wynad, persons who had taken up farming of land on rents or gold washing used to have a specified number of slaves included in the lease.[36] These slaves were regarded during the period of lease as belonging to them.[37] The letter continues:

The slaves have themselves frequently told me that they belonged to such and such a Nair Chetty or Burgher and on enquiring I have found them to name a middle man or sub-tenant of one of the extensive free holders, who rented land and with it the slave from the landlord.[38]

Just as the land of Malabar was held under intermediary tenures, the slave too, as another form of property, could be held under lease by revenue farmers and gold-washers. The increasing economic activity by the Europeans and role the market forces have perhaps added to the frequency and severity of leasing of slaves in Malabar during the nineteenth century.

In the Wynad taluk, particularly, though the slaves did not remain always as the property of the same landholder, they always remained a part of the same property in the same property in the sense that they were attached to the same land that was sold, rented, mortgaged leased or hired out with it. When a large tract of land in Wynad passed from the possession of Namboolcottah Raja to the Nilambar Tirumulpad, all the slaves changed owners with the land.[39]

Transfer of the Slave: A Threefold Path

There existed generally three modes of transferring the usufrut of slaves. They were Jadmam, Kanam, and Pattom.[40] The transfer of a slave by Jenmam was nothing but a total sale of him. Just as a Janman holder of land claimed absolute ownership over his land, a purchaser of a Janmam right on the slave, too could claim almost an absolute right over the person of the slave.[41] When the full value of the slave was given, he was totally transferred to the new master. According to Buchanan, a young man with his wife used to be sold for 250 to 300 fanams.[42] Two or three young children will add 100 fanams, to the value of the family. Four or five children, with atleast, two of whom were beginning to work, would have made the slave family worth from 500 to 600 fanams.[43]

Under Kanum or mortgage, a proprietor received a loan of money, which was normally, two-thirds of the value of the slaves.[44] It is a pertinent point to mention that the original proprietor continued the practice of receiving annually a small quantity of rice, to show that his property in the slaves still existed.[45] In case the slave died while under Kanum, the original owner could demand the replacement of him by another able bodied slave.[46] As far as the person who advanced money was concerned, he could utilise the labour of the slave for the interest of his money for their own maintenance.[47]

Under the *Pattom* or rent system, for a certain annual sum, the master gave the slaves to another man; and the borrower commanded their labour. The annual charge of hire was 8 fanams (35.11½d), for a man and half as much for a woman. The *Pattomadar* had to meet the maintenance expense of the slave. Since profit was the ultimate motive, there was always a tendency on the part of the *Pattomadar* to diminish the expense on maintenance and to exact maximum possible labour from his slave during the tenure of hire. The slave on *pattoms* was much more a degraded individual.[48]

From the very practice of *Kanum* (mortgage), *Pattom* (rent), it is self-evident that the keeping of slaves was a profitable venture in the late eighteenth and early nineteenth century Malabar. The cost of his maintenance amounted to only a small percentage of the total income the slave produced by his own hard labour. A mortgagee would not have attempted the lending of money without interest to a mortgager, unless he was sure of making an amount of profit much more than that by way of interest would have fetched. It is further significant that this profit could be made even after meeting the maintenance cost of the slaves and a token annual payment of rice to the mortgager.

Hence, the question, was slavery profitable to an individual land holder is a crucial one. Then, one has also to find out the viability[49] of slavery as an economic system in order to ultimately tackle a greater issue, viz., the effects of slavery on the economy as a whole.

As has been mentioned already, the wage that a European planter paid to a coolie was 2 annas per day.[50] Whereas the wage that a slave received from his owner was two measures of paddy which amounted to 1 anna per day.[51]

Thus when his wage was paid through the owner, contractor, he not only pocketed fifty per cent of it but prevented the slave labourer from keeping even the other fifty per cent in cash. Two measures of paddy amounting to 1 anna, was a subsistance wage. Thus the slave was unable to save even one per cent of his wage even when he worked in the plantation as a hired slave. He could not spent any portion of his wage for the consumption of clothes, untensils or implements. Because the two measures of paddy was hardly sufficient for the consumption of his own family and hence there was no question of selling the paddy received as wage in the market to raise the money. If this was the case of the hired slaves of European plantations, the condition of the slaves directly under the masters, who were working in the paddy fields, was still worse as participants in a money economy. It is true that they were commodities in a market. But they themselves were rarely participating in the market as buyers andsellers of goods or services.

Notes

1. *Graeme's Report.* Tamil Nadu Archives (TNA), Madras, p. 37, para 30.
2. Buchanan, *A Journey from Madras through the Countries of Mysore, Canara and Malabar (1S07),* vol. II, p. 370.
3. Ibid.
4. Ibid.
5. Slaves are said to have been introduced by Parasurama for the tillage of the ground at the time that he gave the country to the Brahmins. Individuals became out-castes or *Chandalas* by sins against the laws of their castes and subjected them to servitude. It is extraordinary that the custom of making slaves of free born persons is not admitted, as having lasted to the close of the government of the Raja. . . (Graeme's p. 39, para 32).

Graeme's observation reflected the thinking of the dominant social elite which enjoyed the highest ritual status in his own contemporary Malabar. It is highly probable that Graeme's consulted this class exclusively to write his story or the origin of slavery in Malabar.

6. Babar, *Evidence before the Select Committee of the House of Lords 1830*, Quez. 3167, p. 284.

7. Buchanan, vol. II, p. 370.

8. Banaji, *Slavery in British India*, p. 83.

9. Ibid.

10. 'The rules of Malabar prescribed that a slave of the Pulayen, Woloorean and Brayer (Parayen?) castes should remain at a distance of 72 paces from a Brahmin and a Nair and 40 paces from Tean, and other castes generally 48 paces from a Brahmin and a Nair and 24 from a Tean...' (*Parliamentary Papers*, 1828, p. 920).

11. *Report from the Select Committee of the House of Commons, 1832* (Public), para 6, p. 339 Appendix.

12. *Parliamentary Papers (Judicial) 1828 Debosit on* No 8, Query 13, p 854.

13. Banaji, op. cit., p. 87.

14. Letter to the Provincial Court of Appeal and Circuit in Western Division, 26 November, 1835, 1833 to 1858, Slavery in Malabar (MSS) 1833 to 1858, Tamil Nadu Archives (TNA) herein after called *Slavery Papers* (MSS).

15. Letter to the Registrar of the Provincial Court of Appeal and Circuit, Northern Dvn., *Slavery Papers* (MSS), p. 19.

16. Ibid.

17. Letter to the Registrar to the Court of Sadr and Fouzdare Adalat, hereinafter called Slavery Papers, Fort St. George, *Slavery Papers* (MSS), Letters to Government, 1883 to 1858, p. 14.

18. Letter from R.W. Chattfield, Acting Senior Deputy Registrar, Calicut, 24 August 1842 to the Registrar to the Court of Sadar and Foujdaree Adalat, Ft St. George, Ibid., p. 100.

19. Ibid.

20. Ibid.

21. From R.W. Chattfield to the Registrar of the Court of the Sadar and Foujdare Adalat, Fort St. George. 24 August 1842, *Slavery Papers*, p. 102.

22. Ibid.

23. 3½ Gold fanam for Rs. 1,4 old Fanam for Rs. 1/-, 5 Silver fanam for Re. 1.

24. *Graeme's Report-Statistics*, pp. 41–3.

25. Ibid., p. 43.

26. Ibid.

27. Ibid.

28. Ibid.

29. *Graeme's Report*, p. 44.

30. Ibid.

31. A.M. Marcelles to I. Clarke, Collector of Malabar, Nilghirees, 4 March 1856 *Slavery Papers*, p. 469.

32. The question of gold mining and gold washing was taken up subsequently in 1828. In 1831 the collector reported that the privilege of collecting gold in the Wynad

and the Nilambar valley below it had been farmed out for the preceding 40 or 50 years. Lt. Woodty Nicholson of 49th Native Infantry and a Swiss Watchmaker of Devala and the Nilambur Valley, where they found a regular set of mines with shifts from 10 to 50 feet deep worked by 500 or 600 slaves belonging to the Nilambur Tiramulpad. See C.A. Innes, *Malabar District Gazetteers*, p. 15.

33. ARW Lascelles to J. Clarce, Collector of Malabar, 4 March 1856, *Slavery Papers*, p. 469.

34. Ibid.

35. Ibid.

36. Ibid.

37. Ibid.

38. ARW Lascelles, to Clarre, op. cit., p. 470.

39. Ibid.

40. Buchanan, *A Journey*, vol. II, p. 370.

41. Ibid., p. 371.

42. Ibid.

43. Ibid.

44. Ibid.

45. Ibid.

46. Ibid.

47. Ibid.

48. Ibid.

49. According to S.L. Engerman, viability is an ability of an industry to continue existing. In economic terms an industry would be considered viable if a market rate of return could be made on the replacement cost of capital. In the case of slavery the test for viability is the equating of the present value of the future stream of income from slaves with the costs of rearing them. If the present value computed on the basis of the market rate of interest, was less than the present value of rearing costs, slavery would have been economically unviable—there would have been no incentive for anyone to raise slaves. S.L. Engerman 'The effects of slavery upon the Southern Economy: A Review of the Recent Debate.' In *Explorations in Enterpreneurial History*, vol. 4, 1967, pp. 71–97.

50. W.J. Richmond to Clarke, *Slavery Papers* (MSS), p. 481.

51. C.R. Noister to Clarke, op. cit., *Slavery Papers* (MSS), p. 489.

7

A Note on Lakhiraj Lands

Saugata Mukherji

THE WORD lakhiraj is derived from an Arabic source, as indicated by authorities on revenue technicalities, being composed of two words, la which means 'no' and khirāj which stands for revenue or land-tax. Such grants were made in the Mughal period as rewards or payments for some services done. We may, however, reasonably infer that payment of this sort was quite prevalent in medieval India, as we come across so many instances of payment by land or assignments of land in lieu of cash salaries. Originally, the emperor or any other independent ruler made grants of lakhiraj land for services rendered to the community or to the state. These were known as badshahi grants. These were either cases of remission of revenue over a particular area of land already held by the grantee or new grants of land to a particular person or institution to be held free of tax.

Waste lands were also granted for reclamation and cultivation with the revenue wholly or partially remitted. Subsequently however, lesser authorities began granting lakhiraj and other charitable endowments which came to be known as hukumi or non-badshahi grants. In the days of declining authority and growing abuse of the office of the Kanungo, even petty officers with no authority indulged in making similar grants. Presumably, it was a convenient form of payment, (provided the village community sanctioned it) when the treasury was not over-full and where the ratio between the available supply of cultivable land and that of man-power was always traditionally in favour of the former.

It is curious to note that in many places, specially in Northern Bengal, lakhiraj tenures were loosely called jagirs. It was in fact this 'confusion' in terms that interested me originally because it could not be accidental. It is clear that grants of lakhiraj, large or small, were made on the same basic principle as assignments like jagirs with perhaps one important difference that jagirs were not hereditary possessions—indeed not possessions at all—but assignments of land held during the lifetime of an officer, while lakhiraj and other such grants—whatever they might have been originally—subsequently became

*21st Session at Trivandrum, 1958.

hereditary possessions.[1] Such proprietors, specially the larger ones, had a scope to expand into landholders on somewhat similar lines as the zamindars became proprietors. The real similarity of the grants of lakhiraj with the assignments of jagir becomes clear with the briefest examination of the nature of lakhiraj grants, starting from the possessions of the higher officials and descending to the base of the pyramidal structure formed by the ordinary mass of peasants and artisans and others of their class.

A point which should be cleared at the outset is: what does 'rent-free' land really mean? We find the British writers and revenue officials casually substituting the words 'rent-free' and 'revenue-free' for each other. It is, however, now agreed on all sides that very few tracts of land were indeed rent-free in Bengal or any other part of India in the medieval period. These lands were possessed in return for services rendered to the grantor, i.e., the overlord, who never failed to realise such services or 'presents' from the grantee—even though he might forego his share of the produce of that particular tract of land.[2] This becomes rent in a very real sense when we come to the lowest 'rung' of the ladder. This had long gone unnoticed but has been recently brought to light by several writers and mention should be made of a particular work in this field which clarifies the issue considerably.[3] Thus lakhiraj or revenue-free tracts of land were granted to zamindars who were then agents of collection of revenue, either as remuneration for their work or as reward for some special services to jagirdars for the maintenance of additional troops; to religious institutions and holy communities, and lastly to peasants, artisans and other menial servants and petty office-assistants. Thus, what can be loosely called 'feudal service' was expected in return for these grants. The nature of the service varied according to the position occupied by a person in the hierarchy, but the services which were imposed on peasants, workers, etc. were nothing else than the extraction of labour-rent.

The zamindars who were of old agents of collection of revenue were given, as part of their emoluments, nankar lands to be held revenue-free. The zamindar very naturally absorbed them gradually into this own property.[4] Apart from this, the zamindars and other local influential men were granted lakhiraj to induce them to take an interest in cultivation. In the days of declining authority, these men who had some sort of a real estate to begin with soon promoted themselves into the class of proprietors and it might be imagined that men of a lesser origin, the 'upstarts', were more energetic in this direction than the ancient nobles. The jagirdars also received over and above their personal jagirs other tracts of revenue-free land solely for the maintenance of troops. Several zamindars also held lakhiraj lands for the maintenance of troops and as cost of supplying boats to the Mughal rulers. The existence of 'nowara' and 'hissazut' lands attached to the Chandradwip Zamindari of Barisal in the days of the 'Mag' and 'Firinghee' incursions, the 'nawabad' lands of Chittagong and the Ghatwali lands in the western border districts of Bengal certifies to this. About Midnapur, O'Malley quoting J. Grant says: 'This district was held by a tenure different to any other known in the country . . . corresponded with the ancient military fiefs of Europe, inasmuch as certain lands were held lakhiraj . . . solely appropriated for the maintenance of troops;' and again, 'nearly two-thirds (of the Jagirs in the district) were assigned over for the maintenance of some thousands of barkandazes, match-lockmen or native Hindustani militia.'[5] Another community that benefited by lakhiraj grants to a great extent consisted of religious sects, temples and pious men who received grants either from the state such as aima, madad-i- maash, etc., which were placed under the supervision of the provincial sadar. Besides, the zamindars made similar grants like Brahmottar, Debattar, Mahatran, etc. to the Hindus and Piran, Chiraghi, Khairati, etc., to the Muslims. Grants were made to occupational groups like carpenters, ferrymen, milkmen, cobblers, weavers, agradanis and such others. Before the rise of the zamindari system, grants of waste land were made to communal services to men for helping administration and village defence and to artisans, local manufacturers, etc. In the Midnapur District Gazetteer we find that Chakran lands were granted to people of such diverse callings as simanadar, paik, gomashta, kumhar, napit, mali, dobi, astapahari (watchman), bearers and rasughirs (carriers of amin's chain of assessment). Thus, on a closer examination, it appears that lakhirajdars of this type rendered more services to the government than to the communtity and in such cases, labour-rent of this type coincides with the tax payable to the state.[6] With the transformation of zamindars into proprietors, communal lands became absorbed into private land, and as has been shown by a writer on the subject, rent-free lands were retained on condition of personal service to the zamindar. As the very name implies, these men, holding chakran lands, nucleated round the zamindar and rendered him personal service either in the form of labour or with their handiworks even though the zamindar was not entitled to produce rent in such cases. This clearly brings out to what extent 'non-economic compulsion' could be enforced by the nominal owner (or in this case overlord) of the soil in feudal India. It is clear from contemporary documents that some of the petty office-assistants and menials had to carry out in reality the most essential duties of the zamindar like looking after the law and order, village defence, etc.[7]

In the period between the grant of the Diwani and the Permanent Settlement, the Company became increasingly anxious about the so-called alienation of land and opposed all fresh grants of lakhiraj, even the perforce liberal grants of 'baze-zamine' in Burdwan district with a view to counteracting the effects of the famine of 1770 when the shortage of man-power in relation to land became most acute. Cornwallis, however, started the policy of outright resumption of alienated lands and this process continued, sometimes in full force, sometimes haltingly, till 1859. The attempt to raise the total amount of revenue receipts to the detriment of the broader agricultural and other interests of the country was, to say the least, unimaginative like so many other land-revenue policies of the Company. The Company mainly directed its attack against the petty holdings invalid lakhiraj holdings below one hundred bighas—rather than those bigger than it. The Baze-Zamin Regulations of 1788, the Regulation XIX and XXXVII of 1793 and the regulations about the resumption of invalid lakhiraj grants were the direct result of this attitude. The policy of invalidating the hukumi grants rather than the badshahi ones also hit the class of direct producers hard, those who had benefited by such grants as the 'baze-zamin' grants of the Raja of Burdwan. It is clear that the government leant in favour of the zamindars regarding the resumption of 'alienated' lands from the ryots. It is thus amusing to read the ravings of a representative of the zamindari interest, a self-styled 'love of justice', accusing the government in an article of having sided with the ryots in Sec. 28 of Act X of 1859.[8] The only thing that rings true in the whole article is that the existence of such numerous lakhiraj tenures was incompatible with the Company's modern revenue organisation, these being the relics of an old economy. This is evident from the fact that the decadent class of 'old' Zamindars and religious communities clung to these possessions with the despair of dying men. The appeals of an impoverished descendant of the great 'Chandradwip' Zamindars of Barisal and the laments and payers of a community of Brahmins in the same district might have been very pathetic, yet one cannot but sympathise with the Company's resumption of all these lands in 1800.[9] Such blows could not be avoided on the decaying 'old order' and on the remnants of a village economy.

In Assam, the question of lakhiraj tenures remained a vexed question till the 1880s. Here, it was aggravated by the existence of nisf-khiraj or half-free tenures which were originally revenue-free. But subsequently, some levies were made by local chiefs on parts of these lands. From contemporary records of administration, we gather that theoretically all such holdings were taken to have lapsed after the British conquest. Nevertheless, the actual existence of such lands caused the government to set up an *ad hoc* commission of enquiry with instructions to recommend the resumption of all 'alienated' lands (pending the lakhiraj enquiry) but to put into effect mild terms on these lands. The officials engaged, however, found it an impossible task and had to retain numerous lakhiraj grants as valid. After a protracted correspondence, continued with intervals till 1879, the government had to condone their unauthorised actions and to accept both lakhiraj and nisf-khiraj holdings. The nisf-kirajdars further held the waste lands as revenue-free. Such holdings, situated mostly in Kamrup, were in nature religious grants by the native Ahom rulers and dedicated to temples. Often, these were large tracts of lands, cultivated by sub-tenants who paid only the government rates as revenue but were bound to do service or pay in kind to their overlords (temples) in addition.[10] It is possible that this artificial continuation of labour-rent or some sort of rent in kind was a stumbling block in the process of 'monetising' rent and consequently the

Company's policy of modernising and maximising revenue. It also possibly affected the growth of a land market which had by then come into existence; but to what extent it is difficult to ascertain at the present state of information. Perhaps, an awareness of the peculiar situation led the government to make these lands compact and isolate them from the other revenue-paying territories where money-rent obtained, as Mr. Ward's note on this subject indicates.[11]

It is true that the introduction of money-rent by the British administrators did not signify any fundamental change in the nature of rent. But it was surely an indication of the coming social changes to which such relics of medieval economy could not be reconciled. Thus, Lakhiraj grants stood as symbol of 'feudal' service, military, civil or labour as the case might be. This survival of lakhiraj also signified the survival of an old set of relationships, little pockets of resistance against a general economic transformation. The Company's repeated attempts to resume all 'alienated' lands since the Diwani thus seem to acquire a special meaning. As has been very aptly remarked, these attempts 'stand for the efforts of the mercantile representatives of a comparatively superior economy to transform a backward community by converting a large fund of labour-rent into money-rent in a way suited to the requirements of its financial transactions. The failure of this effort merely proves how the natural economy of Bengal was to die hard.'[12] It was rather the unnatural continuation of a medieval feature that encouraged the reproduction of the old forces of production and for a long time thwarted the completion of a new economic process.

Notes

1. Baden Powell, *Land Systems of British India*, vol. I, p. 529.
2. T. Raychaudhury, *Bengal Under Akbar and Jehangir*, p. 33.
3. *Burdwan District Records* (New Series), vol. II, Introduction by R. Guha, sec. II.
4. Harington, *Analysis of the Bengal Regulations*, vol. Ill, p. 320. Quoted by Baden Powell.
5. *Midnapur District Gazetteer*, historical introduction by O'Mailey 'Land Revenue Administration.'
6. K. Marx, *Capital*, vol. III on 'Labour-Rent'.
7. Letter of the Collector of Birbhum, December 1787. Quoted in Burdwan Records (Introduction).
8. 'The Permanent Settlement Imperilled' by a 'Lover of Justice', 1859.
9. T. Raychaudhury, 'Some Old Documents of Barisal', *IHQ*, 1948.
10. *Assan Administrative Reports*, 1882–3.
11. Mr. Ward's note on the Kamrup Lakhiraj enquiry.
12. *Burdwan District Records*, n.s., vol. II, Introduction by R. Guha, sec. II.

8

The Role of the Banaras Bankers in the Economy of Eighteenth-Century Upper India

Kamala Prasad Mishra

FORM EARLY times there existed in India a system of indigenous banking, which though not organized on the modern pattern, but had certain of its essential elements.[1] The issuance of *hundis*, a credit instrument or bill of exchange, which enabled its drawee to transfer money from one place to another was a practice fully developed by the time of the Great Mughals.[2]

We will examine the system of banking with special reference to the Banaras bankers; noting their organization, relationship with the government and their role in the economy of the region during the period under review.

The city of Banaras, a great Hindu centre attracting large numbers of pilgrims and visitors from various parts of India, had developed into regional administrative headquarters and an important centre of trade and commerce during the eighteenth century. The opening of a mint at Banaras in about 1733 testified to the growing financial importance of the city a circumstance that must itself have added a few more bankers and merchants to the existing number.[3]

The main source on the Banaras bankers, is the record of their letters to their representatives and the Governor General at Calcutta and *vice versa* contained in the *Calendar of Persian Correspondence*.[4] A perusal of these letters, besides suggesting brisk activity in indigenous banking, throw light on many other important aspects; the high social status of the bankers, their relationship with the raja of Banaras, the nawab of Awadh and the British and the methods of their business organization. Though we lack precise data on their size and capital investment we are better served regarding their number. Fortunately, we have the recorded evidence of three eulogistic letters written and signed by the resident bankers of Banaras under three different dates.

The first is a paper in the *Nagari* script delivered to Lord Cornwallis at Banaras in September 1787, signed by sixty-six bankers who expressed their

*34th session at Chandigarh, 1973.

heartfelt satisfaction over the administration of justice in the city under Ali Ibrahim Khan, the chief judge and magistrate of Banaras under the British.[5] The second is a paper scroll signed by about two hundred and ninety *mahajans* and merchants of Banaras written in November 1787 as a testimony to Hastings' judicious and kind conduct towards the inhabitants of Banaras.[6] This, along with other similar testmonials signed or sealed by *amils*, zamindars, pandits, *ulema* and *muftis*, was sent to England to be used by Hastings in his defence during the impeachment proceedings against him. The third is again a complimentary letter to Lord Cornwallis presented in early 1792 on his return to Calcutta after achieving a grand victory over Sultan of Mysore. This is signed by six hundred and fifty-eight persons, 'the inhabitants of and sojourners in the city of Banaras' both Hindu and Muslims. Of the total number about two hundred appear to be *mahajans* and *sarrafs* that is resident bankers of Banaras.[7]

An analysis of their names reveals that the majority of them were Vaishyas, Agarwals and Khatris, traditional mercantile communities of the north Indian Hindu social system. These were followed by the Gosains and Brahmans in second and third position numerically. The absence of Muslims from the list of bankers may be largely explained by the general prohibition in Islam of the practice of charging interest on loans—one of the essentials of banking business. In reference to their original homes many of the Banaras bankers appear to have come from Gujarat, Rajasthan and the western region of the present state of Uttar Pradesh. This emigration of mercantile communities to Banaras from various regions was effected through a gradual process extending over centuries. For example, the ancestors of Sahu Gopal Das, a leading banker of Banaras in the 1970s, had come from Amroha, a town between Agra and Karnal at some time in the seventeenth century.[8]

The main concentration of the *kothis* or houses of the bankers was in New Patti within the city of Banaras. This *muhalla* was principally occupied by the respectable and important business magnates of Banaras, the Gujaratis, Gosains and Agarwals. Their influence and high social status may be judged form the exemption granted to them, along with the Raja of Banaras and members of his family, from furnishing security of appearance when defendants in civil suits. This privilege was allowed them by the British in consideration of the 'long established credit and responsibility of their houses.'[9] A further proof of their high standing in the social scale is provided by the conferment, by the Mughal emperor, of the title of 'raja' on two of the most influential members of their community Lala Bachhraj and Lala Kashmiri Mai.[10]

Bachhraj was the banker to the Nawab of Awadh as well as the Raja of Banaras. At various times he liquidated the nawab's arrears to the Company by granting bills in advance of payment by the nawab. For example, in 1784 he engaged to pay, and eventually did pay, a sum of Rs. 1,03,84,420 due from Nawab Asaf-ud-daula, being the balance of the year 1782–3 and subsidy for the use of the Company's troops for 1783–4.[11] He, along with Kashmiri Mai, was the principal receiver of the nawab's revenues from Raja Chet Singh, and after the transfer of the Banaras Zamindari to the Company became one of the chief remitters of the Company's revenues through the instrument of *hundis* payable by his correspondents at Calcutta.[12] He became treasurer to the Raja of Banaras in 1784 and received a *khilat* or robe of honour from the Governor General in 1785 for his services.[13] Similarly, Lala Kashmiri Mai began his career as banker and financier to the nawab, became the raja's and Company's treasurer at Banaras in the 1780s; and finally emerged as one of the biggest bankers of Banaras and north India with a number of agents at such towns as Bombay, Surat, Poona, Jainagar, Delhi, Lucknow and Calcutta.[14] It seems clear that the houses of Kashmiri Mai and Bachhraj acted in close co-ordination and sometimes operated as a joint concern.[15] For instance, in 1788 *hundis* for six hundred thousand rupees were drawn jointly by them on their representative at Calcutta and were paid into the Company's treasury as part of the nawab's tribute for the month of February 1788.[16]

Another leading banking house of Banaras was that of Bhaiyaram Gopal Das.[17] This house was first established by Kalyan Das and Chintamani Das[18] who, as stated before, had migrated from Amroha and settled at Banaras in the seventeenth century. Under Raja Chet Singh, Bhaiyaram became one of his principal advisers and acted for some time as his diwan. He, along with Kashmiri Mai and Bachhraj, had acquired such influence over the raja that the British resident, Graham, considered them as major obstacles in his scheme of obtaining a predominant influence in the Zamindari.[19] By about 1770, Bhaiyaram had some fifty-two branches of his house in various parts of India. He had two sons, Bhawani Das and Gopal Das. The latter being the elder looked after the business at Banaras. Besides Banaras, the house had its main branches at Calcutta, Murshidabad, Patna, Gaya, Allahabad, Lucknow, Jaipur, Nagpur, Poona, Surat, Bombay, Masalipattam, Madras, Ahmadabad, Baroda, Agra and Delhi. In the Banaras region itself it had two branch offices at Ghazipur and Mirzapur.[20]

The company had to depend a great deal in their financial transactions on the good offices of Indian bankers, two of which Kashmiri Mai and Gopal Das figure prominently in our records. The services rendered by the house of Gopal Das were so highly appreciated by the British that when Gopal Das died in February 1787, the Governor General asked the Resident at Banaras to pay a condolence visit to his brother Bhawani Das, and to assure Manohar Das, the eldest son of the deceased, of continued government patronage. Letters were also written in March 1787 to the Nawab and the Resident at Lucknow, the Governor of Bombay and the chief of the factory at Surat directing them to favour and patronize the firm as before.[21]

In 1789–90 when the Company's finances were under severe strain due to the long war in Mysore, the banking house of Gopal Das Manohar Das earned the gratitude of the Governor General by coming to the Company's aid. To facilitate the remittance of money they opened a new branch at Haidarabad in 1790 and paid out at Bombay no less than four and a half million rupees in cash within a period of twelve months.[22] The Governor General took a personal interest in the welfare of the family and directed Bhawani Das to settle internal differences among the sons of Gopal Das so that the unity of the family could be maintained.[23]

Notable among other banking firms of Banaras were those of Chaturbhuj Das,[24] Braj Raman Das Chaman Das, Ballabh Das Dwarka Das, Arjunji Nathiji, Jaitji Tralokji.[25] All held a position of respectability and through their agencies or correspondents transacted a considerable business, especially in *hundis*.[26]

Knowledge of and skill in business was handed down from father to son.[27] The bankers had their organized guilds[28] and worked in co-operation, settling their internal matters through arbitration within themselves. On occasions they also appear to have solicited the assistance of the official bureaucracy, from the Governor General to the Raja, the resident or other local chiefs.[29] They had their representatives or *gumashtas* posted at different branches of their respective houses. These agents were often members of their families, relations or persons of trust and responsibility associated with them through long service and business experience.

There might have been instances of indigenous bankers accepting deposits[30] but no conclusive evidence of their regular acceptance of deposits and of their paying interest there on—an essential element in modern banking is available for the eighteenth century. The Banaras bankers therefore appear to have carried on business mostly with their own capital. The unstable political situation of the century in which bankers were sometimes the easy victims of political disorders,[31] and the conservatism of the people which led them to keep their surplus wealth in small treasure chests in their own houses, may be taken as factors detrimental to the growth of deposit banking during the period of our study. The question then arises whence did the bankers draw their capital?

In origin all indigenous bankers appear to have been traders and merchants. The profit arising out of trade and the accumulation of wealth in their respective families, made easier by the Hindu social system, provided them with the necessary funds to start their banking business. Thereafter the profits of money-changing and banking could be ploughed back into the undivided family business.[32] The bankers' profits, in the main, arose first, from trade in coins and gold and silver bullion, which they sold or passed into circulation at a dearer rate than that at which they bought them; second, from the commission on *hundis*; third, from interest on loans; and lastly, from the insurance of goods and merchandise.[33]

We lack adequate data to make any reliable quantitative assessment of the capital investments of the Banaras bankers. No banker would then have wished to give a true account of his assets for he fear of exciting the jealousy of others, the demands of the state, or the attacks of night robbers or armed dacoits. He would also, at the same time, not wish to admit that his capital was small for had to establish his credit in the money-market.[34] All that can be safely observed is that the actual transactions of these men varied greatly in magnitude. In the case of big bankers, like Kashmiri Mai, Bachhraj and Gopal Das, their transactions might run into millions of rupees but there were many of inferior rank who dealt in smaller sums and served purely local markets. Furthermore, the amount of capital involved differed according to the nature of their functions and business networks. It would, therefore, be desirable to examine the various functions of the *sarrafs* and their role in the economy.

The primary function of the *sarrafs* appears to have been coin-testing and money-changing. The need for men specially skilled in the determination of the intrinsic value of the coins in circulation sprang from the variety of mints producing coins, differing from one another in both weight and fineness and from the treatment of all coins not as tokens whose purchasing power was fixed and guaranteed by the state, but as bullion, to be weighed and assayed.[35]

Under the Great Mughals the privilege of coining, in so far as gold and silver were concerned, was strictly guarded,[36] but minting was free, that is any one could take his bullion to the mint and get it converted into specie at a small charge. In practice, however, this was largely performed by the *sarrafs*.[37] Though there were a number of mints in the provinces to facilitate issuance of coins and bring them within the reach of the public yet the control of the imperial authority over them appears to have been nearly perfect so that the weight and fineness were pretty uniform, and there was little scope either for the mint officials to debase the coins or for the *sarrafs* to charge an arbitrary *batta* or discount. Since there was a standard Mughal rupee used throughout the empire, except at Surat, where a local silver coin called *mafvnudi* was also current, the *sarrafs* in northern India would mainly have been responsible for noting and allowing for the *batta* on coins not of the current, year.[38] And although they dealt mostly in the imperial currency[39] still their work could not have been light for Mughal coins were tri-metallic, that is of gold, silver and copper and need often arose <of changing one into another.

The silver coin called *rupya*, or in its Anglicised form the rupee, first introduced by Sher Shah and adopted by the Mughals, was the basic unit for all cash transactions, both commercial and administrative.[40] By the custom of the country all newly coined rupees were called *siccas* and passed at their full original value for one year, after which they were subject to a *batta* or discount varying from 2 to 3½ per cent, in the Banaras region,[41] according to their dates and passed under the denomination of *sanwats*.[42] The *sanwat* rupees were, however, the coins naturally most often used in day-to-day transactions, and even the government revenue was collected and paid into the treasury in *sanwat*.[43] The bankers had their agents who bought up these *sanwat* rupees in different parts of the country and sent them where they were current. Barlow summarised the situation in 1787 as follows:

The Ryot being obliged to pay his rents in the particular species of Rupees current in his Pergunnah, the Banker is enabled to rate it at what value he pleases. If the farmer has engaged to pay his Revenue to Government in Siccas the Banker charges him nearly the actual difference between Sunwats and Siccas, if in Sunwats the Banker takes the same Batta from the Collector for Bills on Calcutta in Siccas. In both cases the Rupees are sent back again to the Pergunnah from whence they came where the Banker's agent again disposes of them at an enhanced price to the Ryots.[44]

Thus in a situation like this when one kind of rupee formed the medium of revenue collection from the peasants and another that of revenue payment into the government treasury, the *amil's* banker who had the exchanging of them could always contrive to take a considerable gain for himself.

The second important function of the *sarrafs* was the issuing and discounting of *hundis*. In eighteenth century India the use of *hundis* or banker's drafts and bills of exchange was widespread. They were employed both for public and private purposes and were considered the most convenient and the safest means of transacting business where the money and distance involved were considerable. The system obviated the need to carry large amount of specie over long distances, which in view of contemporary transport and political conditions would have been both costly and risky[45]:

The *hundis* current in eighteenth century India were mainly of two kinds: *darshani*, i.e., bills payable on demand or sight and *muddati*, also called *miyadi*, i.e., bills payable after a stipulated period of time mentioned in the *hundi* and reckoned from the date of drawing. The evidence from eighteenth century English records suggests that the Banaras bankers made dealings in both these types.[46]

There was no fixed rule defining the amount of money that could be darwn by *hundis*. The amount varied according to the needs of the parties concerned and the availability of funds that a banker's correspondent was expected to furnish at a time. Sometimes a sum would be remitted by a number of bills and sometimes by only one. For example in February 1776 Raja Chet Singh's monthly revenue payment to the Company, amounting to Calcutta *sicca* Rs. 1,80,571, was remitted by a single *hunch* drawn by Kashmiri Mai on Kashinath, his son and correspondent at Calcutta,[47] two months later a nearly similar sum was sent by eleven bankers in twelve bills.[48]

Some idea of the commission charged by the *sarrafs* on *dakhilas* and *hundis* can be obtained from the scattered references in the English records of the period. The Company made use of the bankers in collecting the revenue from the *mufassal*. With the development of revenue farming in the eighteenth century in most of northern India, the bankers generally performed the job of sureties to the *amils* and paid the government revenue on their behalf in bills or *dakhilas* or notes as each *kist* fell due. For this they charged a commission called *bharai*, usually of from one to two and a half, per cent depending on the distance of the district from whence the revenue was payable and the comparative value of the different species of coins in which the revenue was paid.[49]

Once the revenue from the *mufassal* had been collected, the Banaras banker's *hundis* were then used to remit the payments of the raja to his overlord. Till 1775, while it was the nawab to whom such payments were made the technical problem was fairly easy. The Banaras rupees were current throughout the province of Awadh and the raja was allowed to pay in *Sanwat* rupees. It was therefore possible to make the payments in cash or by bill of exchange, and the two bankers to the nawab, Kashmiri Mai and Bachhraj usually despatched the money to Lucknow in coin, their expenses being paid by the nawab. After 1775, however, the whole arrangement had to be changed. The raja was required to pay the Company's revenue in Banaras *machhlidar* rupees, the name given to newly coined *siccas*. Since these rupees were not current in Bengal and would pass there only at a discount depending on their intrinsic value, the raja was asked to use bills of exchange, the exchange rate between Banaras and Calcutta *sicca* rupees being fixed by the Company, as was the bankers' *hundiyana* or discount.[50] A *Kistbandi* of the total annual revenue payable in equal monthly instalments was formed, and accordingly bills to the amount of 1,85,145 Calcutta *sicca* rupees drawn by the *sarrafs* in favour of the Company were sent every month. These were usance bills, or *miyadi hundis*, payable at 51 days after the date of their drawing.[51] In the remaining years of Chet Singh's rule the Company's annual revenues of twenty-two lakhs of rupees from Banaras continued to be remitted through the *sarrjfs' hundis*. In addition to this a sum of fifteen lakhs of rupees, paid by Raja Chet Singh as war subsidies in the years 1778–80, was also largely provided in this mode with the difference that while in the case of revenues bills had to be produced by the raja, in matters of war subsidies this was left to the resident.[52] After the expulsion of Chet Singh the Company entered into a new agreement with Raja Mahip Narayan Singh by which the revenue demand on the raja was increased to forty lakhs of Banaras rupees. The sum the raja was to pay in Banaras *siccas* to the resident, who was entrusted with the job of finding bills and sending them to Calcutta or elsewhere if need be, as directed by the Council.[53] So far as the raja was concerned the agreement relieved him of the responsibility of negotiating with the *sarrafs* for the timely supply of *hundis*. But this was a concession of very minor significance in view of the near doubling of the revenue demand upon him.

For the bankers of course the change made a great enlargement in their official business. In the collection of the land revenue from the *mufassal* the bankers' control over the *amils* and consequently upon the raja continued, moreover, unabated. In reviewing their situation in September 1788, Duncan reported:

From the system hitherto established in this country, the shroffs or Bankers can in fact, in a great measure, command the Raja and Government itself, with respect to the realisation of the Revenue; the custom being for each Kist to be realized not in cash, but by their Dakhilas or notes payable in a certain number of days from the dates thereof; and as the renters are generally in arrears to them, they of course exact their own terms from the latter for those Dakhilas, as well as sometimes from Government, before they will give in those of the ensuring Kists, after all which the realization of these Dakhilas becomes sometimes a second difficulty to the Raja, or rather to myself....[54]

Whether the charge for remitting money by bankers' *hundis* was moderate or not can best be judged by comparing it with the cost involved in transferring the same amount in specie over similar distances. That the resident at Banaras should find it less expensive to remit a sum of fifty thousand Banaras rupees to Calcutta by *hundis* than to escort cash to Calcutta is significant.[55] But we have an actual example to demonstrate the financial advantage in using *hundis*, even over so short a distance as from Banaras to Patna.[56] In June 1779, 1,98,431 Banaras *sicca* rupees were sent to Patna by boat, and after deducting the expenses of conveyance, insurance and so on, produced 1,84,541 Patna *sanwat* rupees. But a month earlier the same amount, when remitted through the instrument of *hundis,* had yielded 1,89,483 Patna sanwat rupees—or 4,942 rupees more than when the physical transfer of specie was made.[57]

The use of *hundis* was not confined to the collection and remittance of state revenues, for *hundis* were regularly employed by merchants and individuals for transacting business requiring the remittance of money to distant places. In the absence of data it is diffiult to form any reliable guess as to the volume of *hundis* used in mercantile transactions. However, some idea may be formed from the instance of the Banaras bankers' discounting of *hundis* to the value of twelve to fifteen lakhs of rupees a year drawn upon them by their counterparts from Nagpur alone.[58]

Being a prominent Hindu religious centre, Banaras attracted large numbers of pilgrims and visitors from all over India. These religious devotees and travellers, on account of the risk involved in carrying money, brought with them drafts drawn by their local brankers upon the Banaras *sarrafs* who would immediately discount and pay them the required cash to finance their stay and the other expenses related to the observance of the due rites and ceremonies in the holy city. This situation has been well summarised in a letter of the Banaras *sarrafs* to Duncan in March 1795:

. . . this is a country of Teeruth, or Religious Resort and visitation, in the course of which there arrive from other countries Hindoos, Pilgrims and Dukhin Traders . . . who bring with them large Drafts upon us, which we have to pay immediately and if they are not immediately supplied with cash, their disappointment will become very serious, and our good name and credit will be lost throughout all the provinces of India.[59]

Besides issuing and discounting *hundis* the *sarrafs* also generally provided insurance. There is no evidence of life or house insurance business of the modern type, but the *sarrafs* did conduct a considerable business in the insurance of goods carried by both land and water. The rates for goods and bullion were alike low, but it is striking to find that on occasion at least, the rate for bullion was the lower.

For example, in the 1770s we find the insurance rate on the despatch of bullion to Calcutta or Murshidabad at 2 per cent,[60] but in the 1780s the rate on the shipment of food grain to Calcutta or Dacca stood at between 2½ and 3 per cent.[61] The difference may be accounted for by the small size in relation to value of bullion consignments. It may more probably be explained, however, as the consequence of preferential treatment within the banking community when they were those who required insurance. We find a similar low rate of interest charged on loans given by one banker to another. This naturally brings us to a consideration of another function of the *sarrafs*, viz., that of providing loans to governments and individuals.

From scattered reference in the English records as well as in the Persian documents of the period, we see the great Banaras bankers assisting Mughal prince, the Nawab of Awadh, the Raja of Banaras and English Company with loans and advances. Thus, we find Prince Farrukhsiyar on his march from Bengal to Delhi in 1712, raising the sum of ten million rupees as a loan, on the security of the empire, from Nagar Seth and other leading bankers of Banaras.[62] Another Mughal prince Shigufta Bakht, eldest son of Jahandar Shah, was indebted to a Banaras banker to the extent of thirty thousand rupees, and so was Nawab Asaf-ud-daula of Awadh.[63] In 1788 Raja Mahip Narayan Singh took a loan of eighty-five thousand rupees from Shiv Lai Dube, a banker-cum-*amil* of Jaunpur, to pay off the arrears of his revenue to the Company.[64]

We have seen that some of the banking firms of Banaras, especially those of Kashmiri Mai and Gopal Das Manohar Das, came to the assistance of the Company by lending it several lakhs of rupees to relieve the severe strain caused by the Mysore war. In 1780, when the Company was engaged in war in Southern India, Kashmiri Mai at the order of Hastings paid to the resident at Banaras half a million rupees, although his financial position, so his letter to the Governor General suggests, was not very sound at that time.[65] In absence of any positive evidence it is difficult to state precisely the rate of interest charged by the bankers on such government loans. But it can be inferred that rate must have been less than what these bankers would charge from others, the zamindars, *amils*, traders, artisans and peasants.

From the information brought together in our survey we have seen that the Banaras bankers occupied a prominent position in the economic life of the country in the eighteenth century. They played a leading role in financing trade and agriculture; provided loans to government and individuals; and were instrumental in the collection and remittance of state revenues. With the growing trade of Banaras and also as a result of their financial transactions with the Company in the late eighteenth century the Banaras bankers appear to have consolidated their position and some of them, like Manohar Das, Dwarka Das, sons of Gopal Das, had been able to increase their business by the turn of the century.[66]

Whereas in Bengal the establishment of state controlled banks on European lines in the last quarter of the eighteenth century adversely affected the indigenous bankers and led to their progressive decline,[67] the Banaras bankers had been lucky in not having any such rival institution thrust into their midst in that period.[68] Thus they were able to hold their prime position as the financiers of trade and industries; and their *dakhilas* and *hundis* remained the chief instruments of revenue collections and remittance.

Abbreviations

Add. MSS.	Additional Manuscripts.
B.P.C.	Bengal Public Consultations.
B.P.P.	Bengal Past and Present.
B.R.C.	Bengal Revenue Consultations.
B.S.C.	Bengal Secret Consultations.
C.P.C.	Calendar of Persian Correspondence.
G.G. and C.	Governor General and Council.
G.G. in C.	Governor General in Council.
H. Misc. S.	Home Miscellaneous Series.
MSS. Eur.	Manuscript European.
P.R.O.	The Public Record Office.

Note: The manuscript sources used in this paper are from India Office Library, Foreign and Commonwealth Office London, the British Museum and the Public Record Office, Londn.

Notes

1. For the growth of banking in India see L.C. Jain, *Indigenous Banking in Inda*, pp. 1–26; C.N. Cooke, *The Rise, Progress and Present Condition of Banking in India*, pp. 11–19; *The Indian Central Banking Enquiry Committee Report*, 1931 vol. I, pp. 10–16.

2. Irfan Habib, 'Banking in Mughal India', in *Contributions to Indian Economic History*, Vol. I, T. Raychaudhuri, ed., pp. 1–20.

3. For example, Shiv Lal Dube, who came from Allahabad and opened a banking house at Banaras sometime in the mid-eighteenth century.

4. See *Calendar of Persian Correspondence*, 1759–93 in ten volumes.

5. *Add. MSS. 29202*, f. 129. For a similar testimony to the work done by Ali Ibrahim Khan followed by numerous seals and signatures of the residents of Banaras, in original and copies written in 1784, see *Add. MSS. 29217*, large paper roll 27'x 12½'.

6. See appendix 3 in Moti Chandra, *Kasi Ka Itihas*, pp. 442–5 and 321–2.

7. P.R O., 30/11/213, original in large paper folio and translation, ff. 26–37.

8. H.R. Nevill, *Banaras: A Gazetteer*, p. 119; Moti Chandra, p. 339.

9. Reg. VIII of 1775, see. X, in R. Clarke, *The Regulations of the Government of Bengal*, vol. I, p. 321.

10. C.P.C., vol. VII, p. iv of the index and no. 1775; ibid., vol. X, p. vi of the index.

11. C.P.C., vol. VI, no. 967.

12. See answer of Chet Singh's *Vakil* to the queries put to him at Fort William, 5 July 1775, B.S.C., 5 July 1775, Range A, vol. 29, pp. 420–1.

13. C.P.C., vol. VII, no. 370 and f.n. 4, p. 133.

14. Kashmiri Mai to G.G. in C., received 31 October 1786, C.P.C., vol. VII, no. 834.

15. A panel of arbitrators, presided over by Nagar Seth Chaturbhuj Das, to settle a dispute over the payment of *hundis* between Kashmiri Mai and Gopal Das, found convincing evidence of the joint working of the firms of Kashmiri Mai and Bachhraj. C.P.C., vol. VII, no. 1178.

16. C.P.C., vol. VIII, nos. 318 and 485.

17. Gopal Das was the eldest son of Bhaiyaram.

18. Brother of Kalyan Das.

19. Graham to Anderson, 5 December 1777, *Add. MSS. 45422*, f. 211.

20. Manohar Das to G.G. in C., received 9 March 1787, C.P.C., vol. VII, no. 1182.

21. C.P.C., vol. VII, nos. 1181 and 1211. Manohar Das and his widowed mother were honoured with robes sent from Calcutta, ibid., no. 1214.

22. C.P.C., vol. IX, p. xiv and no. 1588.

23. G.G. in C. to Bhawani Das, 2 October 1790, C.P.C., vol. IX, no. 626.

24. The title *ragar seth* (city banker) was applied to Chaturbhuj Das, but it was more in age or esteem that he was held to be the leading banker than of actually being so. The available evidence suggests that in relation to other big banking firms of Banaras, his business had considerably declined in the late eighteenth century.

25. The last two were Gujarati Brahmans, while the first three appear to have been Agarwals.

26. See their remittances through *hundis* to Bombay and Surat, in Duccan to G.G. in C., 26 September 1790, B.R.C., 8 October 1790, Range 52, vol. 19, pp. 681–8.

27. Cooke, op. cit., pp. 12–3.

28. A sort of informally chosen body representing all caste groups of bankers. Sec Jain, op. cit., pp. 39–42.

29. In the case of the *hundis* dispute between Gopal Das and Kashmiri Mal of Banaras in 1786–87, the intervention of the Governor General and the resident at Banaras was solicited though it was ultimately settled by arbitration,. C.P.C., vol. VII, nos.

729, 834 and 1178; G .G. in C. to Grant, 4 October 1786,.. P.R.O., 30/11/70, p. 201.

30. Jain has suggested that deposit banking in some form existed in India at the time of Manu. Habib, basing his argument on some scattered references in the Persian and English accounts of the period, has traced 'the rudiments of deposit banking' in Mughal India. See Jain, op. cit., p. 8; Habib, 'Banking ia Mughal India', pp. 17–8.

31. For example in 1742 when a Maratha horde entered Murshidabad, they invaded the house of Jagat Seth and carried away nearly thirty million rupees. See *Siyara-ul-mustakharin*, vol. 2, pp. 457–58.

32. *D.R. Gadgil, Origins of the Modern Indian Bus ness Class: An Interim Report*, pp. 34–35.

33. *R. Jenkins, Report on the Territories of the Raja of Nagpur, 1827*, p. 44.

34. Jain, op. cit., pp. 1–2.

35. Barlow to G.G. in C., 24 Aug. 1787, *B P.C.*, 26 December 1787, Rangs 3, vol. 30, pp. 962–3; Habib, 'Banking in Mughal India', pp. 3–7.

36. C.J. Brown, 'Some Remarks on the Mughal Currency', *The Journal of the UP. Historical Society*, vol. I, p. 152; Q. Ahmad, 'An Historical Account of the Banaras Mint in the later Mughal Period", *The Journal of the Numismatic Society of India*, vol. 23, p. 198.

37. Habib, 'The Currency System of the Mughal Empire', *Medieval Indict Quarterly*, vol. IV, p. 1.

38. Barlow to G.G. in C., 24 August 1787, *B.P.C.* 26 December 1787, Range 3. vol. 30, pp. 962–3; Habib, 'Banking in Mughal India', pp. 3–7.

39. It should be pointed out that the *sarrafs* had also to deal w ith the many non-Mughal coins which found their way into northern India, such as *rials, mahmudis, pagodas*, etc.

40. W.W. Hunter, *Annals of Rural Bengal*, p. 299; Habib. 'The Currency- System of the Mughal Empire', p. 2.

41. See Hastings' minute and observation relative to the Banaras mint, 12 June 1775, *B.S.C.*, 12 June 1775, Range A, vol. 29, p. 105.

42. The *sanwat* rupees, sometimes called *chalani* (current) or *peth*, were also known as *gauhar shahis* under Shah Alam's reign. Gauhar Shah was the name of Shah Alam prior to his accession. By *gauhar shahi* rupees, therefore, were meant those struck in Shah Alam's reign with the current year's issues called *siccas;* the latter became *sanwats* immediately after the coining of new *siccas*. In Bengal the system in the early 1770s was a little different. There all the rupees in the second year of their coinage passed at a discount of three per cent against those of the first year yet both were termed *siccas*. From the third year, and ever after, they were treated as *sanwats* and passed at a discount of five per cent. See Fowke to G.G. & C., 16 November 1775, *MSS. Bur. G.3.*, p. 9; J. Steuart, *The Principles of Money Applied to the Present State of the Coin in Bengal*, p. 16.

43. Habib, 'The Currency System of the Mughal Empire', pp. 4–6.

44. Ibid., pp. 965–6.

45. Gadgil, op. cit., p. 83; Cooke op. cit., p. 83.

46. For *darshani hundis* see Fowke to G.G. & C., 15 April 1776, *MSS. Eur. G. 4.* p. 25, and for *miyadis*, ibid., 25 January 1776, *B.S.C.*, 7 February 1776, Range A, vol. 34, n. p.; Duccan to G.G. in C., 17 October 1787, *B.P.C.*, 25 October 1787, Range 3, vol. 29, p. 350.

47. Fowke to G.G. & C., 3 February 1776, *B.S.C.* 12 February 1777, Range A, vol. 34, n. p.

48. Fowke to G.G. & C. 15 April 1776, *B.S.C.* 10 June 1776, Range A, vol. 36, n. p.

49. Grant to G.G. in C., 19 August 1787, *B.R.C.*, 29, August 1787, Range 51, vol,. 9, pp. 616–17.

50. The raja's annual revenue was set at 2,340,249 Banaras *machhalidar* rupees, which were treated as equivalent to 22,66,180 Calcutta *sicca* rupees, from which deducting 44,435 Calcutta rupees to cover the banker's discount, the total revenue to be paid by bills at Calcutta was eventually fixed at 22,21,745 Calcutta *sicca* rupees. This sum the raja was to remit in equal monthly instalments. Calculated on the above basis the exchange rate, including the bankers' discount, between Banaras and Calcutta would thus come to 105.3 Banaras rupees to 100 Calcutta rupees. See *sanad* granted to Chet Singh, 15 April 177, in C.U. Aitchison, *Treaties, Engagements & Sanads*, vol. 1, no. XXVII, C.C. Davies, op. cit., pp. 259–60.

51. Fowke to G.G. & C., 3 February 1776, *MSS. Eur. G. 3.*, p. 18; ibid., 30 March 1776; ibid., pp. 23–25; Bengal Council to Court, 20 March 1776, *H. Miso. S.* vol. 123, pp. 456–57.

52. Bengal Council to the Resident relative to the remittance of subsidies, 17 August 1778, *B.S.C.*, 17 Aug. 1778, Range A. vol. 49, pp. 134; Graham to G.G. & C., 29 Aug. 1778, *MSS. Eur. G. 3.*, p. 78.

53. See *sanad* granted to Raja Mahip Narayan, 14 September 1781, Aitchison, vol. I, No. XXIX, p. 69.

54. Duncan to G.G. in C., 12 September 1788, *B.R.C.*, 3 October 1788, Range 51. pp. 190–1.

55. Ibid.

56. The distance between Patna and Banaras via Baksar, according to J. Rennel, was 155 miles. (See *Memoir of a Map of Hindustan*, p. 319).

57. Graham to G.G. & C., 26 May 1779, *MSS. Eur. G. 3.*, p. 91; Graham to G.G. & C., 20 June 1779; ibid., pp. 94–95; Graham to G.G. & C., 16 July 1779; ibid., pp. 95–96.

58. Jenkins, op. cit., p. 44.

59. Enclosed in Duncan to G.G. in C., 23 March 1795, *B.R.C.*, 4 September 1795,. Range 53, vol. 34, p. 134.

60. See answers of Kashmiri Mai and Ram Chand Shah to the queries by Graham, enclosed in Graham to G.G. & C., 22 November 1777, *MSS. Eur. G. 3.* pp. 58 and 62.

61. See invoice of elevan boats of food grain despatched from Ghazipur to Calcutta, 23 July 1788, enclosed in Duncan to Hay, 30 July 1788, *B.R.C.*, 11 August 1788, Range 51, vol. 22, p. 711; invoice of grain despatched by Shanker Pandit to Dacca, 23 May 1788, in Duncan to G.G. in C., 29 May 1788, *B.R.C.*, 11 June 1788, Range 51, vol. 21, p. 1002; Duncaon to Hay, 2 July 1788, *B.R.C.*, 16 July 1788, Range 51, vol. 22, pp. 104–5.

62. *Rivaz-us-Salatin*, p. 269, as quoted in J.H. Little, 'The House of Jagat Seth', *B.P.P.*, XX, p. 130.

63. *C.P.C.*, vol. X, p. xxi.

64. V.A. Narain, *Jonathan Duncan and Varanasi*, p. 67.

65. Kashmiri Mai to G.G. & C., received August 1780, *C.P.C.*, vol. V, no. 1780. There are several other references of the prominent Banaras bankers providing the Company with loans. See *C.P.C.*, vols. 1 and 2, nos. 2801 and 329 respectively, and also vols. V to X.

66. See Duncan to G.G. in C., 23 March 1775, *B.R.C.*, 4 September 1775, Range 53, vol. 34, pp. 107–9; N.K. Sinha, 1, p. 143.

67. H. Sinha, *Early European Banking in India*, pp. 165–70.

68. Though a Company's treasury was established at Banaras in 1781 its main business was to receive the raja's revenues, in the remittance of which to Calcutta or to other Presidencies the services of the Banaras bankers were generally utilised. A Bank was established at Mirzapur in 1935–36 by a young Englishman but it failed within a year. About ten years later when the Banaras Bank was established by Col. Pew it met with a similar fate. See Cooke, or. cit., pp. 1203–4, 236–92.

PART 2

IMPACT OF MERCANTILE CAPITALISM

9

Sir George Downing and the East India Company

Shafaat Ahmad Khan

SIR WILLIAM FOSTER has remarked in one of his publications that no detailed account of Anglo-Dutch negotiations is to be found in published English works. The history of the foreign policy of Charles II has been traced with consummate skill by Macaulay, Ranke and others, but no attention has been paid to the luminous despatches of Sir George Downing from the Hague. I studied his published writings and despatches in 1916 when I was preparing material for the *East India Trade*. The lapse of time has tended to confirm the impression I had formed in those days, and my conviction of the supreme importance of the East India Trade in the determination of English foreign policy. Unfortunately, little material has been added to the information contained in Ait Zemas *Saken Van Staet en Orologh*, part IV, 1669; and, in Japikse's work published at Leiden, 1900. I indicated in 1922 the part played by Downing in the formulation of English demands, and his determined stand on behalf of the East India Company. Further details of Downing's career will be found in the *Dictionary of National Biography*, Lister's Life of Clarendon, and other works. Downing had taken a prominent part in the negotiations with the Dutch under Oliver Cromwell, and he went back to the Hague to resume the thread of negotiations under Charles II. A man of fertile energy, with the realistic outlook of a Restoration diplomat, Downing warmed both his hands on the fire of life, and accepted gratuities and donations from the East India Company. He was, however, steadfastly loyal to his king, and spared no efforts to advance his interest, and champion his country's cause. Downing was well versed in the intricacies of Dutch political life, and his bluff manners, strong commonsense, and manly beaming seem to have created an excellent impression in Holland.

It is unnecessary to detail the negotiations which were started by the East India Company immediately after the restoration of Charles II. Cromwell's victories over the Dutch had rankled in the minds of a proud and sensitive

*2nd Session at Allahabad, 1938.

people, and the re-enactment of the Navigation Act in the reign of Charles II had revived memories of a titanic struggle between the two great Protestant powers. I have dealt at length with the main causes of the Anglo-Datch conflict in the *East India Trade*, and reference may be made to this work for details of the chief causes of this hostility. The struggle between the two great Protestant powers tended to destroy the solidarity of the two great Protestant powers of Europe, and far-sighted statesmen clearly realised the danger of this conflict. The position was complicated by the warm advocacy of the cause of Charles' nephew, the young prince of Orange, against the pretensions of De Witte, who, though supreme head of the administration, was looked upon as usurper by the Orange party in England and Holland. It was clear to all sincere Protestants that a quarrel between the two Dutch parties would render Holland impotent and disorganised, and would contribute to the aggrandisement of Louis XIV. While the Orange party looked to Charles II for support; the De Witte faction was inclined to favour an alliance with France. Charles did not like the Dutch, and openly expressed his contempt for the plebeian merchants who had engrossed all power in their hands, and were inclined to look at every question from a commercial point of view. His instincts, his outlook on life, his tradition, and his interests were arrayed against a nation which was waging a fierce commercial war against the English whose interests in the East, in Africa and in America were diametrically opposed to the naval enterprise, commercial supremacy and political hegemony of the English.

The island of Polaroon had been restored to the English by the Treaty of Westminster; but the Company found it impossible to take possession, though attempts had been made in 1656, 1658 and in 1659 for that purpose. The Company resolved to send an expedition to seize the island, and Captain Dutton was sent as governor from St. Helena. The Dutch resorted to a technique with which the English Company had become perfectly familiar throughout their intercourse in the East. They insisted that surrender was to be made on the production of commissions not only from the Company, but also from the King. When the royal commission under the great seal was secured on 22 December 1660 (See Foster's *Court Minutes 1660–1663*), it appeared thoroughly unsatisfactory as it made no mention of the Treaty of 1654. The English merchants now launched a vigorous offensive on the entire Dutch system of monopoly. In a representation to the Council of Trade on 11 December 1660, they urged that in the treaty negotiations not only should reparation be insisted upon for damages already sustained, but for the future the English should have complete and unfettered right to trade freely in all parts of the East, without any molestation on the plea that the Dutch were at war with the natives of a particular place or had obtained an exclusive contract from a native customer (See Foster, op. cit., p. xv). The Council of Trade favourably reported upon the claims of the Company, and suggested the incorporation of this complaint in the proposed treaty with the Dutch. So far, the king had not been directly approached by the Company in its representations against Dutch competition in the East. On 28 January 1661, the Directors complained of the vexatious delays to which the Dutch had resorted with characteristic sluggishness, and referred to the persistent rumours of a strong fleet which the Dutch had equipped for the East. The Dutch had planned the capture of Bombay from the Portuguese, and there are many references to the Dutch desire in the minutes of the Company's books during the years 1650–59. They knew the strategic and commercial importance of Bombay, and it would have been easy for them to reduce Bombay, as the Portuguese power had shown alarming signs of decrepitude, and the Dutch had driven their commercial rivals—both Portuguese and English—from every South Sea island. Their mastery of the South Seas was unchallenged, while their conquest of Malaya and reduction of Ceylon made them the most formidable European power in Asia. They could not look with equanimity at the acquisition by their Protestant rivals of a port of great strategic importance to western India, and great concern was felt in London over the aggressive designs of the Dutch, who, it was reported on reliable authority, had fitted out a powerful fleet for the purpose. Negotiations had already been started in England for the marriage of Charless II with Catherine of Braganza, and the King made it clear to the Dutch ambassador that he could not allow any attack on Portuguese possessions in India. For further details of the occupation of Bombay by the King, and his transfer of the island to the Company, the reader is referred to my *Anglo-Portuguese Negotiations relating to Bombay*. Here, we are concerned mainly with the effects of their transfer on Dutch policy in India.

A treaty of peace had been signed between Portugal and Holland in August 1661, but it was not ratified by the Dutch until December 1662, and was not published at Batavia until March 1663. The interval was skilfully exploited by the adroit merchants in establishing their supremacy over the 'pepper ports' on the south-west coast of India. Quilon was captured in 1661, and Caranganur was stormed in the following year. Cochin capitulated on 28 December 1662. Cannanore was then attacked and yielded early in February 1663. The tide of the Dutch conquests flowed irresistibly, and the English merchants watched with feelings of jealousy and dismay the virtual disappearance of the Portuguese power from the South-West-Coast of India. They began to strengthen their position by establishing factories along the coast, and English settlements were established at Karwar, Porkhād (about fifty miles south of Cochin) and old Kayāl (near Tuticorin). The English President sent the *Hopewell*, in October 1662, to bring some from the Porkhād factory. The way was barred by Dutch ships, who informed the English captain a few miles from Cochin that the English would not be allowed to pass, as the whole coast was under blockade. The *Hopewell* was, therefore, compelled to return to Surat. The English President was furious with the treatment meted out to the Company's ship, and he decided to adopt a different method altogether. The Company's flag had been insulted by the Dutch shopkeepers, he wished to test whether the King's flag would preserve the ship from indignity. A royal squadron was sent under Lord Marlborough to take delivery of Bombay, and the vessels were to be laden home with the Company's goods. Oxenden now arranged with Lord Marlborough that one of the Company's ships, the *Leopard*, should complete her landing at Kārwār and Porkhād, from goods awaiting shipment and then proceed straight to England. When the ship arrived at Cochin, she found the harbour occupied by the Dutch. The latter prohibited the captain from proceeding to Porkhad, as it was a dependency of Cochin and the Dutch were determined to excercise their monopoly with the rigorous precision which had wrought havoc in Malaya, Ceylon and other places in South Seas. The *Hopewell* sailed for England without the loss of the cargo. The Dutch followed up their victory by compelling the Rajas of Cochin and Porkhad to sign treaties in March 1663, whereby they secured complete control of the pepper produced in those parts. The Company protested vigorously against the high-handed action of the Dutch, and Downing backed the claims of the East India merchants with his customary ability and vigour. His despatches from the Hague give a graphic account of his negotiations and show how fierce was the antagonism which embittered the relations between the two great Protestant powers. The despatch reproduced below shows the intensity of this conflict, and confirms the impression formed by me in 1916 that English foreign policy received a specific mould from the keen and sustained rivalry over the East India Trade.

Meanwhile, the negotiations with Holland dragged on, and Parliament was determined to preserve English commercial interests abroad. The King's championship of his nephew, the young prince of Orange, acted as a constant irritant to De Witte. The pretensions of the Company continued to mount the heights to which the timid and cautious ambitions of weaker nations could never aspire. They asserted the right of the English to reside in any part of the East Indies, and to trade freely with all the natives, except those who were 'immediate servants of the Dutch.' They were to be given permission to trade, notwithstanding any exclusive contract which natives might have signed with the Dutch. Moreover, an English passport was to be a sufficient protection from any interference from the Dutch, whether the vessels were English or native-owned, if the latter carried goods for an English factory. This was not all. All the rights and privileges secured for the English were to be enjoyed by every Indian or Asiatic nation that was in alliance with the King. De Witte criticised the Dutch ambassadors for entertaining these proposals, and a breakdown seemed imminent. The Dutch system in the East Indies regarded monopoly over the spices as the brick-pin of its political structure, and no Dutchman was prepared to part with a right which had been secured by them after nearly sixty years of continuous warfare. While the East India Company was intent upon driving a hard bargain with its rivals, the English Government was keen on the conclusion of a just treaty. It would be tedious to narrate the details of negotiations which consumed the energy of the parties, and involved constant reference to their respective Governments by representatives of the two powers. In the course of negotiations, the Dutch were amazed at the revival of an old claim by the English. The claim concerned two ships which were owned by the younger fourteen, the *Bona Spreanza* and the *Henry Bonaventura*. The former had been hired for a venture in Macao, and was captured by the Dutch in the Straits of Malacca. *The Bonaventura* had been, wrecked on the island of Mauritius and the Dutch settlers in that island had seized part of her cargo. These events occurred in 1643, and representations had been made to the Dutch Government for a number of years. The civil war dealt a servere blow to Courteen's prospects, and he took refuge from the importunities of his creditors in Italy and was made a bankrupt in 1650. He was alleged to have assigned his claims to Sir Edward Littleton and Sir Paul Pindar, and the creditors of the last two gentlemen took over these debts; but Courteen presented the claim himself and obtained 85,000 guilders in settlement. As it had been agreed that in the projected treaty all claims relating to the East Indies prior to 1659 would be barred, there was no reasonable ground for action by the parties. This seems to have roused the interested creditors to unwonted exertions, and as they had considerable influence at Court, the King's interest was enlisted on their side. Sir George Downing, the English Ambassador, pressed these claims with great vigour and ability. The State-General remained adamant, and declared that it was impossible to consider such an old claim. A breakdown of the negotiations seemed imminent, and Downing talked of quitting Holland. A compromise was, however, arrived at, and it was agreed that the claimants should have the right to prosecute their suit already begun, but all reference to the tribunal, which was to adjudicate on this issue was deliberately omitted. This elaborate vagueness was productive of considerable friction later on. Those who wish to study this matter further may refer to Volume VIII of the Duke of Portland's MSS Calendered by the Historical MSS Commission. The matter is discussed at inordinate length in that volume.

The treaty was signed on 4 September 1662, and ratified at Westminister on Christmas Eve. It was based mainly upon The Treaty of Westminster 1654, though it contained many important changes which were the result of increasing hostility and tension; between the two powers. Clause XV of the Treaty breaks fresh ground. The treaty is reproduced in Ait Zema's work, as well as in. Jean Du Mont's Corps Universal Diplomatique, volume VI, part II. Sir William Foster's *Court Minutes of the East India Company, 1660–1663*, reproduces clause XV of the Treaty, pages 351–3. The treaty provided for the surrender of Polaroon to any one- coming with a Commission from the King under the broad seal. It was agreed that the cession of Polaroon would cancel all claims for damages which had been sustained in the East Indies, and known in Europe, before 10/20 January 1659. The treaty specifically excepted the case of Courteen's two ships, and allowed the claimants to prosecute their case before a tribunal which was deliberately left vague. Claims made by individuals in particular cases after 1654 were to be decided by Commissioners to be appointed for the purpose. An interval of one year was allowed during which the English ambassador at the Hauge was to negotiate for settlement of claims on either side in consultation with the Dutch authorities. The treaty failed to establish peace between the two nations. Commercial supremacy in the East was the heart which sent the blood of life pulsating through the whole political system of the Dutch Empire, and the shrewd, calculating merchants of Amsterdam clung to these privilege with iron resolution. The English Company had formed expectations which were bound to be disappointed, and the wranglings between the two nations continued with ever-increasing bitterness. The Dutch monopoly in the East Indies remained undisturbed, while the compensation to the English for the severe losses sustained by them was ineffective, and the prospectsy of its payment were uncertain and remote. The Company had been assiduous in winning support in influential quarters, and the Committee resolved at a meeting on 13 March 1661, 'after some consideration how to obtain satisfaction, to give additional powers to the Committees formerly appointed to conduct this business and decrees that any two of them may use all just and possible means to obtain the required satisfaction; and, if they see occasion, they may, with the advice of the Governor and Deputy, dispose of a proportion, of what shall be recovered from the Dutch in such a way as they please, provided it does not exceed one-fifth of the sum recovered.' In other words, the Company offered a bribe of one-fifth of the sum that may be recovered from the Dutch to persons who helped the Company in its negotiations. The Dutch were unperturbed by these arrangements, and violated the basic provisions of the Treaty with a persistency which wore out the patience and exhausted energy of the English Company. Captain Dutton, who had been sent to Bantam returned to London, and related to his employers a tale of procrastination and malpractices by the Dutch. The Dutch Governor of Banas refused to hand over Polaroon, when Hunter, the Company's Agent tamely acquiesced in the repulse which the British had sustained. The Company made a strong representation to the King in the middle of July, 1663, and Charles II backed the claims of English merchants and requested Downing to exert himself in their behalf. Downing now appears on the scene, and the part he played in the negotiations was of particular importance. His policy may be summed up in his own vigorous words, 'I shall try to do all I can for the Royal Company but I am not optimistic. The only way to check the Dutch from doing such injuries or getting any remedy is to do them greater injuries, for your inaction they interpret as fear. They don't care for complaints.' (Downing to Bennett, 11 September 1663). The first Despatch dated 4 September 1663, O, S., refers to his arrival in Holland, and his visit to De Witte and other persons.

This is reproduced below. His second despatch expresses his general attitude towards the Dutch, and sums up the methods he adopted in his dealings with Holland. They were the methods, of a blustering, vigorous and able diplomat, who constantly indulged in bluff, to enhance his importance and the importance of his country, and received frequent largesses from a grateful Company for his brilliant advocacy and courageous opposition.

The third Despatch is dated 18 December 1663 and is of the utmost importance. Downing gives an extremely clear account of his conference with the deputies of the States-General end discusses the main points in the dispute with great clarity and force. The controversy centred round the four ships to which reference has been made above. Regarding the ships *Bena Esperanza* and *Henry Bonaventura*, the Dutch referred to the text of the treaty and asserted that the words *lis incepta* referred to legal proceedings; while Downing maintained that it meant diplomatic negotiations which had been going on between himself and the States-General. In the case of the *Hopewell*, the Dutch maintained that the ship was really bound for cochin, while the refusal of the Dutch to allow the *Leopard* to proceed to Porkhad was justified on the ground that the Dutch had conquered Cochin and Porkhad was a dependency of Cochin. Sir William Foster refers to Lister's Life of Clarendon for details of these conversations. The despatch is now published in extenso, and throws fresh light on the subject. The last despatch of Sir George Downing printed here is dated 18 March 1663, and describes a conference with the deputies of the States of Holland. 'It was,' says Downing, 'such a conference as I have never before heard of, for that it was in the place where the States of Holland doe assemble and the whole Estates or Corps were present with the nobles and all the Townes, and it continued from half ffive in the afternone till half nyne at night, they discussed the question of the *Leopard*.'

These despatches bring out the importance of the East India trade in the determination of British foreign policy and throw a powerful searchlight on the commercial rivalry of the two powers. The despatches have never been published in their entirety, though references to them are to be found in Lister's Life of Clarendon.

10

Danish Settlement of Balasore

Shahabuddin M. Gani

THE IMPORTANCE of Balasore as a great trading Centre is evidenced by the existence of five European settlements vying with one another for mastery in the trade of Bengal and Orissa. Balasore enjoyed the key position in Eastern Indian as all the ships to and from Bengal, Bihar and Orissa were loaded and unloaded here. Of the five foreign nations settled in Balasore the least known are the Danes. The English and Persian sources have noted their activities occasionally. However, the Danish sources are still lacking to construct their history in India.

The Danish East India Company was established in 1616 and a settlement was made at Tranquebar in 1620 on the south Eastern coast of India. From there they advanced to Masulipatam and then to Bengal. This Company failed due to want of patronage at home. A new Company was started in 1670 with more adventurous people.[1] The earliest reference of their presence in Balasore is found in the diary of Streynsham Master who visited this port in 1676. Foster informs that two Danish ships were spotted on Balasore Road in June 1673.[2] (Foster, *English Factories in India,* vol. II). Walter Clavel the English Agent at Balasore in his accounts of the trade of Balasore writes that 'the English and the Danes endeavoured to settle factories here (in 1633).'[3] Streynsham Master himself states that while he reached Balasore port on the ship Johanna on 24 August 1676, the Chief of the Danish factory sent his second in Command Sen: Quiman with his compliments to the ship on 27 August 1676.[4] Again after three days the Master visited the Danish factory in the town. On the second visit to Balasore he again met the Danish Chief Wilke Wygbert on 2 September 1676.[5] This Chief of the Danish factory was previously serving in the Dutch East India Company, where he lost one of his legs at Macosser.[6] Due to their illtreatment he left their services and joined the services of the King of Denmark to conquer a settlement in Bengal.[7] But afterwards some other persons of quality came to Bengal and peacefully concluded a treaty with the Bengal Government and obtained a settlement for the Danes, which Wygbert did not appreciate.[8] However, they got a handsome

*22nd Session at Gauhati, 1959.

piece of land in Balasore with house to establish a factory free of cost. A sum of Rs. 3,000/- was contributed by the local merchants. Perhaps Malik Quasim the Mughal Governor of Balasore also promised a help of Rs. 3,000/- to build a factory at Balasore.[9] Governor Quasim also introduced Wygbert to Nawab Shaista Khan, Subahdar of Bengal (1663–1678 and 1679–1688) and helped him to procure a Parwana from the Nawab to trade free of custom duties in Bengal and Orissa. The Danes had to spend about four to five thousand rupees to obtain this concession.[10]

Fitch Nedham the English Agent of Dacca informed on 30 November 1676 that the Danes were trying to obtain a new firman like that of the English.[11] And, on December 3rd he informed that the widow of Jaco (Juan) Gomes, the mother of De-Soita had arrived at Dacca and was vehemently throwing out her upbraiding speeches against the English.[12] Nedham further told that the Danes had been granted a Firman as desired by them. Which was then with the Rai, who would deliver it to them after receiving some presents.[13]

As regards their activities in Balasore the sources are scanty and very little is known to history. But there are evidences in the later period to indentify the existence of Danish factory in Balasore. The Danish settlement had an area of seven acres.[14] This area is still known as Dinamandarga. It was fortified by a natural moat which connected it with the river and defended it from land attacks. On the north side the industrious merchants had excavated a dock. A skeleton of a ship was also lying there up to the end of the nineteenth century.[15]

John Beams calls Dinamardanga was worst situated than the other foreign settlements, since it was far away from the town.[16] The Danish settlement of Serampore was also known as Dinamarnagar.[17] This settlement was granted by Alivardi Khan.[18] Mahabut Jang, Subahdar of Bengal to Mr. Soetman, Chief of the Danish establishment through the influence of M. Law, the French Agent of Cassimbazar.[19] They were granted sixty bighas of land of which they occupied only three bighas in Serampore and the rest 57 bighas in Ackna.[20] During the American war the English ships were not safe on the seas so the Danes enjoyed a boom period in Indian Trade. John Palmer, known as the prince of merchants in Calcutta was then working as Danish agent at Serampore who himself realized not less than one lakh of rupees a year.[21]

The prosperity of the Danish factory came to an end in 1801 when England and Denmark became hostile countries. The English immediately occupied the Danish settlements of Serampore and Tranquebar which were, however, restored to them after the Peace of Amiens.[22] Balasore could not be occupied, as Orissa was then under the Marathas which was conquered by the English in 1803. Denmark was a neutral country then, and other vessels took the advantage of employing Danish pilots and passed safely on seas under the Danish colours protecting them from Freeh privateers.[23] The war was renewed again between Denmark and England. Captain George Elliot, son of Governor-General Minto, seized three rich vessels of the Danes on the Hughli,[24] and the British soldiers took possession of the Danish factory of Serampur and Tranquebar. Mr. N.B. Edmonstone, secretary to government, in the Political government. Department., Fort William also sent orders on 27 January 1808, to the Magistrate of Cuttack, 'to issue orders to the officer commanding at Balasore to take possession in the name of His Britania Majesty of all factories and buildings, all property and also all papers, accounts and records belonging to His Danish Majesty or the Danish East India Company situated in or near Balasore.'[25] The then acting Magistrate of Cuttack George Hartbwell likewise asked Lt. Col. Marley to make prisoners of war of all civil, military and marine officers and all Europeans in the Service of the Danish Majesty or of the Danish East India Company. Concluding the letter Hartwell wrote that 'it is the desire of the government, that care be taken in the execution of those order that the utmost degree of humanity, liberality and attention be manifested towards the persons, whom they arrest.[26] Captain C. Fagan, Commanding Officer of 2nd Bn. 19th Regiment of Native Indian stationed at Balasore town immediately took possession of the Danish establishment of Balasore.[27] However, the private property in the Danish factory was returned to their owners except the factory and buildings of the Danes.[28] When the peace was concluded between these two countries all the properties of the Danes were restored to them. But the records in the judicial papers of Cuttack show that the Danish factory comprising a big building was renovated and was utilized by the English Company.[29] After some months G. Webb, Magistrate of Cuttack, informs Dowdswell that the building of the Danish factory did not belong to the Danish Company but to a gentleman Mr. Pruscolin, the late Danish resident, who was at that time residing at Serampore.[30] Perhaps the officers of the Danish Company abandoned the Balasore factory and migrated to Serampore. James Peggs, the late missionary at Cuttack, writes that the Danes had an acre of ground and a few trifling buildings just enough to give them authority to hoist the Danish ensign or Sunday morning.[31] They must be some private traders who had settled here permanently like that of Charles Dacosta the Dutch.[32] However, the brankrupt Danish Company could not be maintained by draining the home treasury. Finally the king of Denmark according to the wishes of his people disposed of their possessions of India in Tranquebar, Serampore and Balasore to the English East India Company for the sum of twelve and a half lakhs of rupees on 11 October 1845.[33]

Notes

1. *Cambridge History of India (CHI), vol. V*, p. 114.
2. 'Early English Trade in Orissa,' *OHRJ*, vol. VII, no. 3 and 4, pp. 213, er. seq.

3. *The Diaries of Streynsham Master: Indian Records Series, 1675–1688*, II, ed: PC. Temple, 1911, p. 84. See also Wilson, *Early Annals of English in Bengal*, vol. I, pp. 17–19.

4. *The Diaries of Streynsham Master*, vol. I, p. 300.

5. Ibid., p. 319.
   Bowray says that Captain Wilkins was the head of the Danish factory and he was an able Commander, who was previously a tailor by profession, *Countries around Bay of Bengal*, pp. 182–190, Master himself again calls him. Witbert, *Diaries*, vol. I, p. 303.

6. *Diaries of Streynsham Master*, vol. I, p. 319.

7. Ibid.

8. Ibid.

9. Ibid.

10. Ibid., pp. 319–20.

11. Ibid., vol. II, p. 77 et seq.

12. Ibid., vol. II, p. 91.

13. Ibid.

14. O Mallay, *Bengal Dist. Gazetteers, Balasore*, pp. 189–90.

15. W.W. Hunter, *History of Orissa*, ed. N.K. Sahu, p. 184.

16. John Beams, op. cit., p. 311.

17. Ghulam, Husain Salim, *Riyazas-s-Salating*, Persian Text, Asiatic Society of Bengal, 1895.

18. Charles Stewart, *History of Bengal*, p. 341 and Jadunath Sarkar, *History of Bengal*, vol. II, p. 452.

19. W.H. Carey, *The Good Old Days of Honorable John Company*, vol. II, p. 277.

20. Ibid., p. 278.

21. Ibid., pp 279–80

22. Ibid., and *CHI*, vol. V, pp. 114–15.

23. Carey, p. 280.

24. Ibid.

25. From G. Hartwell, Magistrate, Cuttack to Lt. Col. Marley, Commanding in Cuttack, 1 February 1808. *Judicial Papers, Orissa State Archives*, vol. XII, pp. 12–13.

26. Ibid.

27. G. Hartwell to N B. Edmonstone, 9 February 1808.

28. G. Hartwell to Lt. Col. Marley, 7 March 1808.

29. G. Hartwell to George Dowdswell, Secretary to Govt. in the Judicial Department, Fort William, 15 June 1808.

30. G. Webb to George Dowdswell, 9 August 1808.

31. James Peggs, *History of General Baptist Mission w'th Orissa* by Andrew Sterling, 1856, p. 271.

32. M.L. Melville, Acting Jt. Magistrate, Cuttack to C. Lusington, Secretary to Govt., Foreign Deptt., 15 May 1818, *OSA*, vol. XIV, pp. 5–8.

33. *CHI*, vol. V, p. 115; Carey, op. cit., vol. II. p. 280.

11

British Salt Monopoly in Orissa

K.M. Patra

THE MANUFACTURE of salt was a flourishing industry along the eastern coast of India. As a common day-to-day necessity of all people, trade in the article fetched good profits. The monopoly of salt trade even prevailed in Mughal times when it was assigned to a favourite or to the highest bidder. But it is believed that the monopolist in the Mughal times 'had neither the ability nor the organization to make his monopoly exacting'. The situation became different after the British victory at Plassey. In course of a few years, a new system of strict monopoly both over the manufacture and sale of salt was introduced in Bengal.

Soon after the introduction of salt monopoly in Bengal, the East India Company explored the possibilities of extending it to Orissa. Salt was much cheaper in Oiissa and naturally a considerable quantity of it was smuggled from Balasore to Bengal. In 1786 an argreement was made with Rajaram Pandit, the Maratha Governor of Orissa, by which the salt dealers became subject to the orders of the British Commercial Resident at Balasore without whose 'parwana' no salt could be imported to Bengal.[1]

But the agreement did not work satisfactorily and smuggling was not checked. So in 1790 George Forster, an envoy of Lord Cornwallis, brought the matter to the notice of Maharaja Raghuji Bhonsle at Nagpur. He suggested that the Company might be allowed to purchase all salt produced in Orissa. Raghuji did not agree with him on the ground that the British monopoly of trade would ruin native merchants completely.[2]

The British conquest of Orissa in 1803 was closely followed by the extension of salt monopoly, in the first instance, to the northern division of the province from river Subarnrekha to river Mahanadi, On May 4, 1804, a temporary regulation was enacted by the Governor-General in Council for management of the salt department in the above noted region.[3] Robert Ker, the Collector-cum-Magistrate of the northern division of the province, supervised the manufacture and sale of salt in Orissa until the arrival of James King in

*29th Session at Patiala, 1967.

1806. The latter took over the charge as the first Salt Agent of the province with his headquarters at Balasore.

The Salt Agent controlled the manufacture of salt along the coastal region for a distance of about 100 miles. In 1807 there were 11 'aurangs' as the salt enclosure were called, in this region.[4] Each 'auranga' was divided into several sub divisions termed as 'bhowris'. Each 'bhowri' in turn contained a convenient number of 'chattis' and each 'chatti' a certain number of 'chulhas' or fire places. The salt manufactured in the 'aurangas' was of two kinds, 'panga' or boiled salt and 'kurkutch' or solar evaporation salt. The first variety was superior to the second one, and therefore it was sold at higher rates. The northern coastal region mainly produced 'panga' salt. The quantity of salt manufactured in the 'auranga' rapidly increased under the supervision of James King. In 1807, he informed the Board of Trade that he would be able to send 90,000 maunds of salt from his agency.[5] Only four years after, he wrote to the Board that there was every prospec of realizing 4 lakh maunds of salt in his Agency.[6]

The British authorities had to face certain difficulties in the initial period of their salt monopoly in Orissa. The crux of the problem was the question of setting terms with zamindars in whose estates salt 'aurangs' were situated. Before the British conquest of Orissa, the zamindars in the sea coast made large profits from the salt trade. When it ended with the introduction of British monopoly, they made oppressive demands on the 'malangis' who were only poor raiyats of their estates.[7] James King negotiated with the zamindars and finally an agreement was reached with them by which they made over their salt and fuel lands to the government for payment of 1½ annas per maund on all salt manufactured within their estates. They also agreed not to interfere with the 'malangis'. In 1811 James King recommended that in addition to the grant of 1½ annas per mound, the zamindars should receive certain quantity of salt as 'khorakes' or diet allowance for the use of their families. This was also sanctioned by the Government.[8]

Another difficuly which James King had to face was the problem of fixing the wages of the 'malangis' By the temporary regulation of 1804, they were paid at the rate of 25 rupees per 100 maunds of salt. But as this rate was not profitable, they were unwilling to come forward for taking advances which hampered production.[9] The government was willing to enhance the rate in order to encourage the production. But it was felt that the extra amount paid to them would only be extorted by the zamindars if they were left to realize their land revenue from the 'malangis'. So the Government wanted that the terms should be settled first with the zamindars. When that was decided in 1811, the price paid to the 'malangis' was raised to Rs. 35 per 100 maund.[10]

Thus the intial difficulties were solved, and the salt monopoly was firmly established in the northern part of Orissa by 1811. Two years after, by the regulation 22 of 1814, the monopoly was extended to the southern part of the province. All salt regulations of Bengal were also enfored in Orissa by the said regulations.

The immediate effect of the government monopoly was a sudden rise in the price of salt. The enhanced price of salt was found to be one of the main cause of popular dissatisfaction which led to Rebellion of 1817, only two years the extension of salt monopoly to the whole of Orissa. Walter Ewer, the Special Commissioner, brought to the notice of government that the price of salt during the Maratha rule was 3½ to 4 annas per maund or less than one 'kahan' of 'kauris' at the place of manufacture. It might have been sold by the merchants at best at the rate of three 'kahans' per maund in the interior of the province. The price of salt in 1817 was upwards of 24 'kahans' of 'kauris' per maund which was more than 6 times the average rate under the Maratha Government. The people also faced much difficulty in procuring salt, an article of daily consumption, even at high rates. Even remarked: 'I certainly believe the salt monopoly to be a real and unexaggerated grievance to the inhabitants of a large part of the district, and that the introduction of it with its consequences has materially curtailed the already scanty comfort and circumscribed enjoyments of the Coriah rout'.[11] Thus the early management of salt monopoly like that of the land revenue, was disastrous to the people as it was conducted by 'the fatal policy of a too sudden leap from one extreme to other.'[12]

In order to remove the grievances of the people, a Commissioner was appointed in 1818 with the powers of general control over all departments of the province. Robert Ker, the first Commissioner, took much interest in redressing the popular discontent against salt monopoly. To reduce its price, more salt on easier terms than before was supplied by the government. Previously salt was sold to the merchants only at the 'aurangs' along the sea coast of the province. They were allowed to purchase not less than 20 maunds and so the retail dealers charged high price for it in the interior of the province.[13] During the administration of Ker in 1818–19, 9 'gaols' or store-houses were constructed at different parts in the interior of the province for the convenience of retail sale. The article was disposed of in quantities as small as one maund. It was also sold at most of the preventive 'chowkeys' in the province which were thirty in number. The Salt Agent was directed to exercise a very strict control over the conduct of his 'gola' and 'chowkey' officers for preventing their fraudulent charges of higher price than the authorized rate.[14] Ker's vigilance improved the administration of department and brought great relief to the people.

In May 1819, the Government of Bengal established a new Board for the administration of salt monopoly in the Presidency. It was known as the Board of Customs, Salt and Opium. The new Board of course, brought no change in the administrative set-up of the salt department in Orissa. Besides the creation of a new Board, a new regulation (regulation 10 of 1819) was also passed in

1819 which rescinded the regulation 22 of 1814 and consolidated all rules for the administration of salt monopoly in the Presidency. It laid much emphasis on the prevention of smuggling of salt. All native officers of the government including the village policemen were required to be vigilant on this matter, and any wilful neglect of the duty was to be punishable by fine and even dimissal from office.[15] This regulation was strictly enforced in Orissa, and it continued to be the basis of administration of salt monopoly in the province for a long time.

Till 1823 the administration of salt monopoly in Orissa was under the jurisdiction of a single Salt Agent. He shouldered all responsibilities of manufacture of salt in the entire sea coast of Orissa from river Subarnasekha to lake Chilika. He also supervised the sale of salt and prevention of smuggling in the province and export of salt to Sulkia in Bengal. To lessen such huge burden of a single Salt Agent and for better administration and supervision of the Agency, the Governor-General in Council decided in 1823 to divide the Agency into two distinct divisions, the northern division and the southern division, with river Dharma as the dividing line.[16] After five years the province was divided into three seperate divisions which in course of time came to be known as districts. Each division or district remained in charge of a Collector who was also entrusted with the duties of a Salt Agent.[17] Thus, Orissa was divided into three salt agencies which were administered by the Collectors of Balasore, Cuttack and Puri. The administrative activities of those officers were co-ordinated by the Commissioner at Cuttack and supervised by the Salt Board at Calcutta. The said Board controlled all salt agencies in the Bengal Presidency.*

The three agencies of Orissa were capable of producing huge quantities of salt. Of course, the amount of production varied according to demand, both in view of local consumption and public sale at the Calcutta market, leaving apart the seasonal calamities. The salt producing capacity of three Orissa agencies were best expressed in the out-turn of 1853–54. The estimate of salt to be produced was for 19,63,000 maunds of both 'panga' and 'kurkutch'. The actual amount of production came up to 16,88,564 maunds of which 6,72,999 maunds were produced in the Balasore agency, 3,00,508 maunds in the Cuttack agency, and 7,15,057 maunds in the Puri agency.[18]

The manufacture of salt was conducted by close supervision of the Salt Agents. However, the immediate control and responsibility for production rested on the shoulders of the 'aurang' darogahs. Under the darogahs, there were a number of contractors or 'chooleas' with whom the government entered into an annual contract for the supply of certain quality of salt known as 'taidad'.

*There were 7 Agencies in the Presidency such as, Puri, Cuttack, Balasore, Hijli, Tamluk, 24-Parganas and Chittagonj.

These 'taidads' varied from 30 to 700 maunds and the contractors employed the required number of 'malangis' for its manufacture.

These 'malangis' were the real community who manufactured salt for the government. Two advances were given to them during one season. Before the beginning of the manufacturing season they were paid the first advance through their 'chooleas'. In the middle of the season, they were paid the second advance according to the quantity of salt produced by them, and in the end of the season, their accounts were finally settled. The wages paid to the malangis varied at different periods.

In 1826 the payment was fixed at Rs. 50 per 100 maunds of salt. In fact, they had to deliver 115 maunds, the extra 15 maunds were charged for wastage in transportation and also for payment of *Zamindar's* land revenues. Besides the cash payment, each 'malangi' was allowed to take two pots of salt monthly for his own use. This amounted to about 2 maunds for each 'malangi' in one season.[19] In 1836 this privilege was withdrawn, and the 'malangis' were required to buy salt for their own use.[20] This measure must have caused much hardship to them. It was further aggravated by the reduction of their wages. In 1838 the government decided to reduce the rate of payment to 5 annas per maund in order to bring down the cost of production and raise the net profit.[21]

The result of such a reduction of wages was utter destitution of the 'malangis'. Their petition to the Salt Board clearly stated how it had deprived many of them of their mere subsistence, in consequence of which some lost their lives and others were compelled to leave the 'aurangs'. They hoped that the government would enhance the rate of payment at least by one anna on the ground that they produced a variety of salt superior to that of Bengal manufacturers.[22]

The government was, however, mainly concerned with the net profit from the salt monopoly for which it was necessary to reduce the cost of production to the minimum. So the rate of payment to the 'malangis' fluctuated on this prime consideration. It was raised occasionally when the demands of salt in the market increased. The extreme poverty of the 'malangis' was never mitigated, and they had to work with mere subsistence wages as most of them had no other means of livelihood.[23]

The salt monopoly in Orissa yielded much profit to the Company's Government. In 1822 Andrew Stirling observed that 'the finest salt of all India' was manufactured in the coastal region of Orissa, and it gave annually to the Company 'a net revenue falling little short of 18 lacs of rupees'.[24]

In course of time the net profit from the salt monopoly soared very high. In 1853–54 the net profit from the retail sales in three agencies of Orissa amounted to Rs. 8,96,173. In that year the export of salt from Orissa was about 12 lakhs of maunds and as the government duty was Rs. 2–8 annas per maunds, the net profit would have been about 30 lakhs of rupees. Thus, the net revenue derived from the salt monopoly in Orissa both from local sale in the province and public sale at Sulkia was about 39 lakhs of rupees towards the end of the Company's rule. It was more than the double of the land revenue of the province which was about 17 lakhs of rupees after the long-term settlement of 1837. The salt monopoly, therefore, was the principal source of revenue to the British Government in Orissa. In fact, it 'formed the second principal source of revenue to the Company's Government in Bengal the net annual receipt from it often exceeding a crore of rupees and sometimes even amounting to one crore and a half.'[25]

It is certain that the huge profit from the public sale of salt at Sulkia did not find its way to Orissa and was never utilized for benefit of the people. The amount received from the local sales in the province was invested in the production of salt and management of the department. No doubt the revenue derived from the salt monopoly was 'entirely the creation of the British Government', but perhaps no other source of revenue was so entirely based on narrow commercial outlook of the Company.

Consequently, it evoked much adverse criticism from the contemporary writers. Lt. Col. James Caulfield in his *Observations on our Indian Administration* remarked that salt being an indispensable article and one that must be procured at any hazard by all classes should be 'left unshackled to the public.' He advocated that the government should allow 'a free and unrestrained use of this simple necessary of life.'[26] J.W. Kaye, in his well-known work on *The Administration of the East India Company*, remarked: 'Of all the great sources of Indian Revenue on one has been so much assailed as monopoly of "salt". It is here that the philanthrophists will find his most palpable object of censure, the partisan of free-trade his most vulnerable point of attack, advocate of the Company his least defensible position.'[27]

Even George Plowden, who was appointed as the Commissioner in 1853 by the Government of India 'to enquire into and report upon the manufacture and sale of and tax upon Salt in British India', had to report against monopoly. He found that the tax was 'very productive' and it was raised at 'a small proportionate cost'. He calculated that only 8 annas reduction in duty would involve a loss of 36 lakhs of rupees in the Bengal Presidency including Benaras. Of course, the people were accustomed to pay it without complaint. But it had pressed hard upon labourers and other poor people of India. He stated, 'I am very strongly of opinion that the tax is positively too high, even at its present reduced rate. A tax of 500 per cent appears to me a very high tax to impose upon any one article of consumption, when naturally the article in question is comparatively very dear in the territory to which the Tax applies.' However, Plowden could not advocate for the abolition of the tax as it was 'impossible to point out any equally productive source of revenue' in India.[28]

The only redeeming feature of the British salt monopoly in Orissa was that to some extent it encouraged the trade and commerce of the province while they were in a process of decay. The certainty of profit in the export of salt from

Orissa to Sulkia 'golas' led to the construction of large number of boats at Balasore and other smaller ports of the province. When the export of salt was over for a season vessels were engaged in transporting surplus agricultural products of the province and some other articles to different parts of the country. The port of Balasore flourished due to the export of huge quantities of salt from the place.

The British salt monopoly continued only four years more after the end of the East India Company's rule. In course of time the strong prejudice of Indians against the Liverpool salt had vanished on account of its low prices. On the other hand, the government manufactured salt showed a constant tendency of becoming more expensive, as a result of which the Liverpool salt gradually took possession of the market.[29] In 1863 the government abandoned salt manufacture and the salt agencies were closed. The operations were brought to an end in Balasore on 28 February 1863, in Cuttack on 23 April 1863, and in Puri on 30 July 1863.[30]

Notes

1. *Calendar of Persian Correspondence*, vol. VII, no. 435.
2. Ibid., vol. IX, no. 605.
3. Bengal Judicial (Civil) Proceedings, no. 26 of 5 Sept. 1805, Government to Commissioner of Cuttack, 4 May 1804.
4. Cuttack Salt Records, Acc. no. 9, Salt Agent of Cuttack to Board of Trade, 20 July 1807.
5. Ibid., vol. 24, Board of Trade to Salt Agent of Cuttack, 27 August 1807.
6. Ibid., Acc. no. 531, Salt Agent of Cuttack to Board of Trade, 11 January 1811.
7. Cuttack Salt Records, Acc. no. 9, James King to Board of Trade, April 1806.
8. Parliamentary Paper, HC, 1856, vol. 26, Report of the Commissioner on Salt in British India, part III, Bengal, appendix C, no. 3.
9. Cuttack Salt Records, Acc. no. 531, Salt Agent of Cuttack to Board of Trade, 25 July 1808.
10. Bengal Revenue Proceedings, no. 15 of 17 July 1818, Walter Ewer to Government, 13 May 1818.
11. Bengal Revenue Proceedings, no. 15 of 17 July 1818, Walter Ewer to Government, 13 May 1818.
12. G. Toynbee, *A Sketch of History of Orissa 1803–1828*, p. 70.
13. Guide to Orissan Records, vol. II, Salt Agent to Board of Trade, 18 May, 1817, p. 53.
14. Bengal Revenue Proceedings, no. 25 of 19 May, 1820, Stirling to Blunt, 29 February 1820.
15. H. Shakespear (Compiler), an Abstract of the Regulations of Government, vol. IV, p. 84.
16. Cuttack Salt Records, Acc. no. 575, Government of Bengal to Commissioner of Cuttack, 24 July 1823.

17. Bengal Judicial (Civil) Proceedings, no. 1 of 27 November 1828, Extract from Proceedings of Governor-General in Council, 23 October 1828, no. 164.

18. Parliamentary Paper, HC, 1856, vol. 26, Report on Salt in British India, part III, Bengal, appendix C, no. 3.

19. Balasore Salt Records, Acc. no. 753, Salt Agent of Balasore to Commissioner of Cuttack, 22 September 1854.

20. Cuttack Salt Records, Acc. no. 124, Salt Agent of Cuttack to Commissioner of Cuttack, 4 November 1836.

21. Ibid, Acc. no. 164, Commissioner of Cuttack to Salt Agent of Cuttack, 4 March 1840.

22. Ibid., Acc. no. 170, Petition of Malangis to Salt Board, 25 October 1842.

23. Ibid., Acc. no. 328, Salt Agent of Cuttack to Commissioner of Cuttack, 29 October 1857.

24. A. Stirling, *An Account of Orissa Proper or Cuttack*, p. 5.

25. H.R. Ghosal, *Economic Transition in the Bengal Presidency 1793–1833*, p. 102.

26. James Caulfield, *Observations on our Indian Administration*, p. 63.

27. J.W. Kaye, *The Administration of the East India Company*, p. 670.

28. Parliamentary Papers, HC, 1856, vol. 26, Report on Salt in British India, part III, Bengal, pp. 175–84.

29. C.E. Buckland, *Bengal under the Lieutenant-Governors*, vol. I, pp. 286–87.

30. *Annals of India Administration*, vol. VIII, p. 302.

12

The Deplorable Condition of Saltpetre Manufacturers of Bihar, 1773–1833

N.P. Singh

THE SALTPETRE manufacture was done throughout the province of Bihar by a class of persons known as *Nuneas* and *Beldars*.[1] They were a class of persons who used the hoe, but all *Nuneas* and *Beldars* did not make saltpetre, many were employed to dig tank and to make roads.[2] In Bihar the number of those who could make saltpetre was about 500 houses.[3] Their chief employment in the fair season was to make saltpetre.[4] In the rainy season they weeded and ploughed the paddy and maize fields and performed other operations of agriculture and horticulture for daily hire. When the English East India Company's monopoly in saltpetre rendered its business illegal, the *Nuneas* and *Beldars* made privately as much of this article as they could sell. As this meagre quantity of saltpetre did not offer them opportunity for sufficient employment, they be took themselves to prepare culinary salt (muriate of soda) from a saline earth that was found in large parts of the province of Bihar.[5]

The *Beldars* of Purnea and the *Nuneas* of Saran, Champaran, Tirhut, Patna and Gaya ordinarily received advances from the Company officials for the smooth running of their business.[6] Sometimes these officials with connivance of the *Mahtos* stopped payment of these advance to the *Beldars* and *Nuneas* and this deprived them of their means of subsistence.[7] These poor and helpless manufacturers of saltpetre were not only employed by the Company, but were prohibited from working for any other person.[8] By the illicit business of the article, that of necessity followed, the Company was a considerable loser.[9] When the investment of saltpetre was to be diminished, a certain amount of deduction was made from each factory and in each factory a few men would be thrown idle and they would not readily find other employment.[10] We find that in 1802 *Nuneas* were forced to supply saltpetre on a very reduced price by the officials of Singhia, Muzaffarpur, Kurhani, Darbhanga, Mau, Chapra, Dighwara and Dumri factories which were the largest saltpetre depots in North Bihar.[11] In the same year in the district of Tirhut Gudadhar Sen had been appointed

*35th Session at Jadavpur, 1974.

Tehsildar of *Nemuck Sayer Mahal* on a monthly salary of Rs. 50. Further, the collector recommended that each *Nunea* should be granted a *Putta* specificaily specifying as to what quantity and at what weight each *Nunea* was to deliver his saltpetre.[12] It was recommended with a view to stopping embezzlement and to protect the interest of the *Nuneas*. The collector also strongly recommended the appointment of Gomastahas with their *Amlas* for each Kuthi in order to ensure faithful discharge of duty by *Tehsildars*.[13] The collector, while speaking about the mode of collection mentioned in the same letter dated 28 October 1802, to Acting president of the Board of Revenue, that the manufactured saltpetre used to be divided half by half between the Government and the *Nuneas* and the Government was required to pay 2 annas from their own share to the proprietor of the soil, the payment being called *Huck zamindary*.[14] This was true in respect of pergunnah Beesarah of Tirhut only.[15] In other pergunnahs of Tirhut the proprietors of the land were paid out of the *Nunea's Share*, the mode of collection of which the collector was not in a position of ascertaining in spite of his best endeavours.[16] The government used to take all the saltpetre and pay money to other sharers.[17] It is further mentioned that the saltpetre delivered by the *Nuneas* used to undergo another process of refining before it was delivered to the commercial resident and in so doing every 1½ maunds of the commodity used to go down to only one maund in weight.[18] But this was in no way detrimental to the interests of the *Nuneas* as they used to be paid before the second process.[19] The weight also differed at different stations of delivery.[20]

From the beginning the *Nuneas* were subject to numerous undue exactions. They paid to the government half of their produce as *Sayer* or tax for the manufacture of saltpetre, out of which one- fourth was paid to *Zamindars* on whose estates the *Kuthis* were situated. Besides this, they had to pay *salamy* and *russom* to the *Moostajeers* and others which amounted to Rupees 6-8-0 on each Kuthi under the following denominations: *Moostajeers* Re. 1-0-0 *Russom Canongoe* Rs. 1-8-0, *Zilladar* Re. 1-0-0, *Barmottar* Re. 1-0-0, *Malernaa* Re. 1-0-0 and *Pauslans* Re. 1-0-0.[21]

The mode of weighment was also very much objectionable. In pargumnah Beesarah of Tirhut saltpetre was received from the *Nuneas* at the rate of 17 seers to the *Pusseree* and 48 seers to the maund which made 2 maunds 4½ seers and four chattaks when delivered to the saltpetre factory of the Company by the farmer. In Tirhut proper the rate was 17 seers to the *Pusseree* and 40 seers to the maund which made one maund and twenty-four seers when delivered to the Company at 5 seers to the *Pusseree* and 40 seers to the maund.[22] Due to this over-weighment the poor manufacturers were put to a great loss. In 1811 they presented a petition to the Court setting forth, in detail, the hardship they were exposed to due to this excessive rate of the *Pusseree* and unfair weighment. The Court after having considered their petition fixed the *Pusseree* at five seers on July 5 of the same year.[23]

Mr. H. Parry did not like this order and asked the Company's Vakil to make a motion before the Court of Appeal at Patna for the revision of the order of the Zillah Court concerning the fixation of the weight at 5 seers to the *Pusseree*.[24] The Court of Appeal at Patna refused to rescind or modify the order passed by the zillah Court although the Collector of Tirhut and the Commercial Resident were interested in modification of this order. This shows a glimpse of the independence of the judiciary even in the beginning years of the nineteenth century. This judgement proved to be boon to the indigenous manufacturers but it meant a heavy loss to the saltpetre farmers. H. Parry, the Collector of Tirhut, went to the extent of advising the Revenue Board that the attention of the Vice-President in Council should be drawn towards this subject and under his authority an order might be issued to fix the old established *pergunnattee* rate of 17 seers to the *Pusseree*. But no such order was passed by the government and the order of the zillah Court fixing the weight of five seers to the *Pusseree* and forty seers to the maund remained in force since then.

The *Nuneas* paid to the government and the *Zamindars* a large part of their produce as sayer for the manufacture of saltpetre. So the advantage which the government derived from the Namuck Sayer Mahals cannot be denominated as land revenue. It may properly be defined as a tax payable by the manufacturers of saltpetre for the liberty they enjoyed in respect of gathering saltpetre from the villages, ruined buildings and other places where earth could be found impregnated with this article.[25] The collection thus made from the *Nuneas* was known as the Namuck Sayer and was an important branch of public revenue in Bihar. Although the Sayer Collection on Hat, Bazar, Gunjete had been abolished in the year 1790 by the Company's government, but Sayer Collection on saltpetre continued unabated. In a letter dated 20 March, 1795, G. Arbuthnoth, Collector of Tirhut, described the Namuck Sayer as a tax collected from the manufacturers of saltpetre as *Haokmy Share*.[26]

After 1800 due to the increased demand of saltpetre in the English market the saltpetre manufacturers of Bihar had to be forced to accept advances on account of the Company. Even after the enactment of Regulation VIII of 1812, which re-established the saltpetre monopoly, the practice of forcing advances on the *Nuneas* continued.[27] Besides, the price given to the *Nuneas* for their hard earned saltpetre was extremely low which was not sufficient for their subsistence.[28] The records of the period disclose that for one maund of saltpetre, the pykars received one rupee and fourteen annas from Company, out of which the *Nuneas* were given only one rupee and six annas.[29] But sometimes in 1813 and 1814 the price payable to the pykars was reduced to one rupee and seven annas per maund out of which only fourteen annas remained as the manufacturer's share. Due to this unremunerative price the *Nuneas* sold a portion of their produce to private merchants.[30] In 1814 the *Nuneas* of Bihar submitted a petition to the Board of Trade praying for an increase in the price of the article.[31] Another petition was submitted by the *Nuneas* of Bihar which stated that the remuneration given to the manufacturers was extremely poor.[32] The petition also stated that the pykars or middleman exploited the manufacturers in many ways.

The Company's indigenous servants oppressed the *Nuneas* regularly. On 28 May 1812, a petition was presented to the Board of Trade by the *Nuneas* of Bihar accusing the *Diwan* and *Gomastahs* of the Company's factory of Patna of having committed 'various acts of Injury and Oppression' against them for a long time.[33] The inferior servants of the Patna factory unfairly weighed their saltpetre and charged *salamy* from them on every occasion of weighment.[34] The petition also stated that on drawing the attention of the Commercial Resident towards these excesses of the *Amlas,* they were confined, beaten and disgraced by the peons of the Residents office.[35] In the end the petition stated: 'such Acts of oppression and Tyranny have never been committed towards any class of people but the Looneeas of Zilla Behar within the dominions of the Company.'[36] On 1 September 1813, another petition was presented by the *Nuneas* which alleged that the *Diwan* had misappropriated government property to the value of six lacs of rupees and that he might be immediately suspended along with his *Amlas.* The *Diwan* was suspended by Government and an extrajudicial Enquiry Commission was set up against him.[37] The Enquiry Commission's examination of the charges against the *Diwan* was continuing for the last one year and a half and in the meanwhile a third petition was submitted by the *Nuneas* to the Registrar of the Diwany Adalat at Patna praying that they might be permitted to withdraw from further prosecution of the charges.[38] Two more petitions were received by the Registrar for the withdrawal of the charges against the *Diwan* of Patna factory.

On a critical examination of the charges against the servants of the Patna factory it seems that they were true. But the petitioners' attempt to move the higher authorities against the arbitrary actions of the *Diwan* of Patna factory and his *Amlas* was foiled by the desertion of some of their own men who were heavily bribed by the *Diwan* and induced to submit counter petitions in his favour. Possibly the complainants' patience had been exhausted by the annoyance and delay involved in the carrying on of the prosecution. But it may be safely concluded that the allegations, against the *Diwan* and his *Amlas* were sustantially true.

Notes

1. Francis Buchanan, *An Account of the District of Purnea in 1809–10,* pt. V, p. 549.
2. Vide Prinsep, *A History of Political and Military Transaction,* vol. II, p. 426.
3. Rickards, *India or Facts Submitted to Illustrate the Character of the Native Inhabitants,* vol. I, p. 126.

4. Harington, *An Elementary Analysis of the Laws and Regulations*, vol. I, p. 663.

5. Buchanan, op. cit., p. 549.

6. Bengal Separate Department Proceedings, 7 June 1837.

7. *Calcutta Review*, January, 1930, pp. 41–2.

8. H. Wilson, *A Review of the External Commerce of Bengal*, pp. 27–8.

9. Home Department Public Consultations, 24 August 1816.

10. Bengal Board of Trade (Salt) Consultations 21 December 1807; Letters from; Monsieur D. Dayot to Governor-General, 31 January 1817 and 7 July 1817 (Foreign Department Miscellaneous).

11. Letter dated 28 October 1802, from J. Rattray, Collector of Tirhut to Thomas Graham, Acting President and Members of the Board of Revenue.

12. Ibid.

13. Ibid.

14. Ibid.

15. Ibid.

16. Ibid.

17. Ibid.

18. Ibid.

19. Ibid.

20. Ibid.

21. Ibid.

22. Letter dated 11 March 1816, from H. Parry, Collector of Tirhut, to J. Dean, Commissioner in Bihar and Benares.

23. Letter dated 9 August 1815, from H. Parry to the Rev. Board.

24. Letter dated, 18 August 1815 from H. Parry to Francis Legros, Commercial Resident, Patna.

25. Letter dated 21 July 1801, from the Board of Revenue to the Governor-General in Council.

26. Letter dated 20 March 1795, from G. Arbuthnoth, Collector of Tirhut to the Revenue Board.

27. Harington, op. cit., vol. III, pp. 722–3.

28. Bengal Board of Trade (Commercial) Consultations, 22 April 1814.

29. Ibid.

30. Commercial General Letter (from Court) to Bengal, 9 February 1814.

31. Bengal Board of Trade (Commercial) Consultations, 22 April 1814.

32. Ibid., 6 May 1814.

33. Two copies of the English version of the petition are preserved in the Patna Judge Court Records.

34. Ibid.

35. Ibid.

36. Vide Petition of Mukur Singh (English translation) annexed to A.J. Colvins' Letter to H. Douglas, 28 October 1813 (Patna Judge Court Records).

37. Letter from Robertson, Registrar, Patna Diwani Adalat to H. Douglas 27 May 1815 (Patna Judge Court Records).

38. Ibid.

13

Some Trading Activities of Indians in Russia in the Eighteenth Century

Surendra Gopal

A T THE turn of the eighteenth century a flourishing Indian trading community already existed at Astrakhan, the city at the mouth of the Volga where the river falls into the Caspian Sea. The Indian traders specialised in importing not only Indian goods but Eastern goods in general from Persia and Central Asia into Russia. To Persia they exported not only Russian goods but also Western European goods purchased from Russian or European merchants. But the Russians protested against the excessive profits earned by the Indians. The Russian government thereupon asked all the eastern traders (excluding the Armenians) not to indulge in retail business and confine their operations to the city of Astrakhan only. Thus when the eighteenth century dawned the Indian trading community in Russia was concentrated in the city of Astrakhan.[1]

In the eighteenth century, although this policy was not formally repudiated, we find loosening of restrictions on the Indians. The contemporary Russian documents describe them as going to different Russian cities. They carried Eastern goods, mainly of Persian origin from Astrakhan to Moscow[2] and purchased European goods in Moscow to be sent to Astrakhan.[3] The Indian merchants living in Moscow stood guarantee for incoming Indian traders and undertook to pay any dues and debts contracted during their stay in Moscow.[4] The Indian merchants from Astrakhan went to the cities of Derbent,[5] Kracnoyar,[6] Kizilyar,[7] Tsatrsini[8] and other cities for purchasing and selling goods. In the cities of Derbent and Kizilyar some of them lived more or less on a permanent basis and acquired landed property.[9] They sometimes had their relations among the Indian merchants living in Astrakhan[10] or sometimes they were merely agents or servants of Indian merchants of Astrakhan. Similarly the documents refer to Indian merchants visiting the important Makarevsky fair to make purchases.[11]

*29th session at Patiala, 1967.

The Indian share in export to internal cities of Russia was considerable as is evident from the following figures. In 1724 the Indians exported goods worth 97.7 thousand Rubles while the Russian merchants sent goods worth 43.3 thousand Rubles. Next year the Russians surpassed the Indians. The share of the Indians slumped to 33.6 thousand Rubles while that of the Russians went up to 63.3 thousand Rubles. Other merchants of Astrakhan shared with Indians this decline. They could send goods worth only 17.6 thousand Rubles.[12] The participation of Indian traders in the internal trade of Russia appears to have been the result of Peter the Great's policy of encouraging commerce and crafts within this empire. However, as the Russians gathered experience the Indians along with other eastern merchants lost this trade. This is evident from the fact that in 1750 the Indian merchants applied to the Czar for permission to trade in the cities of Russia.[13] The demand was occasioned by the loss of Persian trade of the Indians of Astrakhan which had been so far the mainstay of their profits.[14]

Apparently the request of the Indian merchants was not considered favourably, for we find them adopting expedients to circumvent the restrictions and keep the trade going. They started employing Russian citizens, Tatars[15] and Kalmuks,[16] Agrizhanets[17] and Armenians[18] who were not forbidden like other eastern merchants, by the Czar from selling goods in Russian cities to carry merchandise on their behalf to Russian cities. Sometimes the above mentioned persons carried the articles merely as servants of the Indian merchants. On other occasions the profit was to be shared in certain proportion. In some cases it was stipulated that in case of loss, the carrier of the goods would not be held responsible. The Indian merchants also advanced monetary loans and the carriers purchased goods out of this sum from Indian merchants for sale in the cities of Russian Empire. After the goods had been sold, either interest or a share in profits was to be paid to the Indian traders. The money advanced by the Indian merchants was also used by the agents to purchase goods in Russian cities. When such persons returned, the Indian merchants reserved the option to purchase from them outright at prevailing market prices, or to purchase a part of the goods and direct how the rest was to be disposed of in the Astrakhan market.[19]

Thus despite the ban imposed by the Russian authorities on the activities of the Indian merchants, the Indians were able to bypass them in practice by hiring agents. This shows the flexibility of the Indian mercantile community and their capacity to adjust to new situations.

As in the previous century, the trade with Persia was an essential ingredient of the activities of the Indian trading community in Astrakhan but in this century the nature of this trade underwent certain modifications as a result of the growth of new factors.

The Russians stimulated by the policies of Peter the Great wanted to control as much as possible the import and export trade of Persia. On the one hand they tried to encourage the indigenous commerce by concluding various alliances with the Persians on different occasions and utilised their success in some wars with Persia to extort trading concessions.[20] They started employing extra- mercantile methods to eliminate their trade-rivals. In 1745 the Indians in Astrakhan were forbidden to write to Persia uncensored letters, a step which drew instant protests from the Indians.[21] The Russian authorities asked their Consul in Resht to be careful about the nationalities of traders coming from Persia to Astrakhan. Indians should not be allowed to come in the garb of Tatars or Persians.[22] Moreover, other objective conditions in Persia also hampered the trade of the Indians.

After the fall of the Safavid dynasty anarchy overtook Persia. She faced a series of foreign invasions, mounted by her two neighbours Russia and Turkey.[23] From the north-east, Uzbegs and from the east Afghan tribes began to hammer at Persian frontiers.[24] The Persian capital Isfahan fell into the hands of the invaders in 1722 and the rule of the Safavids came to an end.[25] Even when Nadir Shah succeeded in establishing his authority over the whole of the country, it was so devastated that some invaders appeared to have run over the territory.[26] Due to political instability economic activities in the country had been dislocated. The land route from India had become completely unsafe.[27] The sea route was seething with pirates. The Imam of Muscat had declared war against Persia. His navy kept on attacking the Persian ports. As a result the sea-trade from India had considerably declined.[28] Naturally the Indian traders in Astrakhan, who drew supplies of Indian goods from their Persian based country-men were starved of the same. Hence the Indian traders in Astrakhan concentrated their attention on Russian and Persian goods.

The Indian traders were again successful in adapting themselves to the new conditions. The table given below shows that after the Armenians (who had always enjoyed a privileged position both in Russia and Persia) the Indians commanded the second place and they closely competed with the Russians, whose trade with Persia surpassed that of the Astrakhan Indians only in certain years. The Indians also fared better than the Persians.*

| | Exports to Persia in Rubles | | | | Imports from Persia in Rubles | | |
Year	Indians	Armenians	Russians	Persians	Indians	Armenians	Russians	Persians
1737	25324	24807	22202	—	90948	92387	76670	—
1738	21312	332700	14707	23912	57034	54892	42597	49257
1739	24834	241220	52686	42198	186878	179190	94007	131291
1740	84704	254379	55100	40854	109201	221212	53864	136411
1741	53800	362655	45108	19359	72823	201194	43489	30054
1742	20935	261044	47685	11165	15726	18632	69889	7574
1743	53384	433564	25331	13024	64297	356281	17095	40118
1744	24739	644315	61856	22002	64173	467192	175004	65689

*The table has been compiled on the basis of R-1.0., Doc. no. 114.

To keep up their trade with Persia the Indians in Astrakhan had recourse to several expedients. They employed agents of Bukharan,[29] Persian, Armenian[30] and Tatar[31] extractions. These carried goods to Persia on behalf of Indian merchants sometimes on the basis of a share in the expected profit or sometimes as mere servants.[32] The Armenians were the most important agents employed by the Indians of Astrakhan to prosecute their Persian trade.

The trade of the Indians with and in Persia was suffering because of local chaotic conditions. In 1740 the Russian Consul at Gilan reported that a Tatar agent of Indian traders in Astrakhan was arrested and his goods seized by the local Persian authorities. He was not beaten only because of the timely intervention by the Russian Consul, who now advised the governor of Astrakhan that in future Indians should not be sent to Persia for there was no trade.[33]

It is in the above context that we find Indian traders migrating from Persia to Russia. In 1741 eighteen Indian merchants from Persia arrived in Baku[34] and the same year seventeen Indians from Gilan arrived in Astrakhan.[35] These Indians were of Multani, Lahori and Marwari origin.[36] This loss of trade in Persia impelled the Indians to seek imperial permission to trade freely in the internal cities of Russia.[37] The Indians contended that after the death of Nadir Shah the Indians were being killed in Persia and all sorts of restrictions were imposed on them which made it difficult for them to carry on their trading activities.[38] Indeed we have to marvel at the ingenuity of the Indian traders who despite tremendous odds continued to carry on their business without any political support from any quarter.

The Russians authorities became deeply concerned at the disruption of the Persian trade because it cut off the supplies of Indian goods. They started making determined efforts to find an alternative route to India from Russia via Central Asia, i.e. Khiva and Bukhara. The Russian rulers and the Russian authorities repeatedly sent embassies and missions to establish the new route, which would be safer and dependable.[39] This task was facilitated and this urge was strengthened because they had by 1735 captured the Kazakh steppe, which bordered on the Central Asian khanates.[40] To give concrete shape to Russian ambitions Orenburg was established in 1735 to act as a forward post on the road to India via Central Asia.[41] The Russian authorities adopted measures to lure Indian and other eastern traders of Astrakhan and Central Asia to Astrakhan in the hope that this would help in the establishment of direct trade between Russia and India.

An Indian trader of Astrakhan who is named as Marwari Baraev in Russian documents was initially consulted in this connection by the Russian Empress.[42] He testified to the fact that disturbed conditions in Persia had adversely affected the coming of Indian merchants to Astrakhan from Persia. In Bukhara the Indians had numbered about 300 persons but they had left for Kabul and other places owing to attacks by the Khan of Kokand. Marwari

Baraev promised to bring back the Indians if the security of their persons, and property was guaranteed.[43] Marwari Baraev was granted 1,000 Rubles by the Russian authorities for establishing a Company in Orenburg to trade with India.[44] The Russians were serious about this project. The tax returns show that the value of goods coming from or going to Orenburg was mentioned both in Rupees and Rubles.[45] Presumably on this basis Kemp states that Orenburg replaced Astrakhan as a focal point for the activities of Indian merchants in Russia.[46]

But Mrs. Kemp's contention seems to be doubtful.[47] Conditions in North and North-Western India were not favourable for expansion of land trade and the long route through Khiva and Bukhara was also not safe because of internal strife between the khanates and the constant incursion of the nomad tribesmen. Astrakhan continued to be the chief centre of the activities of Indian merchants in Russia although henceforward not trade but usury became the prime occupation of the Indians.[48] But the establishment of Orenburg marks a definite progress in Russian attempts towards finding a direct trade route to the Central Asian markets and India and is the culmination of a century of sustained efforts in this diection.

Notes

1. For details regarding the activities of Indian traders in Russia in the eighteenth Century see my paper, 'Indian Traders in Russia in the eighteenth Century,' submitted to the Indian History Congress, Mysore, 1966.
2. Russko-Indiiskiye Otnosheniya v XVIII v., (R-I.O), Moskva, 1965. Doc. nos. 1, 2, 29, 35, 87, 102.
3. Ibid., nos. 27, 87.
4. Ibid., nos. 6, 32, 43.
5. Ibid., nos. 41, 49.
6. Ibid., no. 73.
7. Ibid., nos. 84, 103, 133, 140.
8. Ibid., no. 144.
9. Ibid., nos. 55, 84, 96, 140, 195–93. This again contradicts Kemp's contention that Indians did not invest in land. Quoted in Baikova's Rol sredney Azii v Russko-indiiskikh torgovykh svyazakh, Tashkent, 1964, p. 167.
10. Ibid., no. 133.
11. Ibid., no. 56.
12. Ibid., no. 194.
13. Ibid., no. 134.
14. Ibid.
15. Ibid., nos. 133, 191.
16. Ibid., no. 191.
17. Ibid., no. 44 [Agrizhants were those persons who were born out of wedlock between an Indian father and a Tatar mother].

18. Ibid., no. 82.

19. Ibid., no. 41.

20. Ibid. nos. 54, 60.

21. Ibid., no. 126.

22. Ibid., no. 77.

23. Percy, Sykes, *A History of Persia*, vol. II, pp. 233, 237–39, 251–53.

24. In 1696 an Englishman from Meshed reported that there had been no caravans either to or from India due to disturbed conditions. Lockhart, Lawrence, *The Fall of the Safavi Dynasty and the Afghan Occupation of Persia*, p. 289; In 1751 reports said that between Balkh, Afghanistan and eastern Persia there was a terrible anarchy. R-l.0., doc. no., 180; In 1739 Tabriz reported complete absence of any business. R-l.0, doc. no. 80; In 1792 Indian merchants in Astrakhan could not obtain any supply of Indian goods from Indian merchants in Persia as the trade of Bandar Abbas and Basra with India had been completely dislocated. R-1.0, doc. no., 199; In 1800 again Orenburg reported that it had no goods from India as Bukhara which supplied it with Indian goods did not have any. R-1.0, doc. no. 213.

25. Sykes, op. cit., vol. II, p. 229.

26. R-1.0, doc. no. 134.

27. Ibid., 180.

28. Lockhart, op. cit., pp. 391, 392, 398, 403, 446.

29. R-1.0, doc. no. 191.

30. Ibid., nos. 42, 53.

31. Ibid., nos. 44, 49, 94.

32. Ibid., no. 44.

33. Ibid., no. 94.

34. Ibid., no. 95.

35. Ibid., no. 98.

36. Ibid.

37. Ibid., no. 134.

38. Ibid.

39. Ibid., nos. 137, 165–169, 179–183, 200.

40. G. Wheeler, *The Modern History of Soviet Central Asia*, p. 29.

41. Baikova, op. cit., p. 177.

42. R-1.0, doc. nos. 72, 74.

43. Ibid., no. 74.

44. Ibid., no. 75.

45. E. Ya., Lyusternik, Russko-Indiiskiye Ekonomicheskiye Svyazi v XIX veke, p. 12.

46. P.M., Kemp, *Bharat-Rus*, pp. 104, 106.

47. Baikova supports Kemp. Baikova, pp. 180, 181. However, Baikova, like Kemp, fails to adduce sufficient proof in favour of her statement.

48. The extensive money-lending activities of Indians in Russia needs to be described in a separate paper.

14

The Britain–China–India
Trade Triangle, 1771–1840

Tan Chung

BRITISH INTEREST in China began with the woolen textiles. It was believed that once British 'home spun' gained access to such a market, the key to British prosperity would be found. According to Sir William Foster, it was not spice-hunting, as generally held but actually the quest for the Chinese market for woolen cloth which led Britain into the 'Brave New World.'[1]

Two centuries later, British merchants in the East had a different perspective. The East India Company which had inspired King Charles II (1160–85) to make tea a British national drink,[2] went on a tea-buying spree as soon as it had settled down in the China market. The Court of Directors instructed their Canton supercargoes in 1730 to make their European rivals 'sick of their voyages for tea' at any cost.[3] This set both the pattern and the pace of Britain's 'China trade'. The East India Company's tea 'investment' (i.e. purchase) increased from 6 million lbs. per year in the decade 1771–80 to 35 million lbs. per annum during the period 1831–37. While in the 1770s Britain took 33% of the total tea exports from Canto (the only Chinese port open to maritime Western nations), this share increased to 54% in 1781–90, to 74 per cent in 1791–1800, and reached the highest point of 80% in 1801–10. Although British buying continued to increase in the next decades, their monopoly of the Canton tea market slackened because of keen competition from the USA merchants.[4]

Britain's China trade acquired a tea-orientation. In the statistics given on next page more than 90% was payment for Chinese tea.

It was good strategy for the East India Company to show profuse enthusiasm in a Chinese commodity in the initial stage. By their wise manoeuvre, the EICs Canton supercargoes not only established themselves as the favourite customers of the semi-official Chinese hong merchants, but also succeeded in using the good offices of the latter to grease the palms of the Manchu customs authorities for the smuggling of Indian opium into the forbidden Chinese

*34th Session at Chandigarh, 1973.

kingdom. The expansion of Indian exports to China would not have been so smooth and rapid without the apparent tea-obsession of the East India Company in the eighteenth century.

TABLE 14.1: EICs Investment in China Goods 1761–1833

1761–1770	£ 4,365,847
1771–1780	4,576,975
1781–1790	10,997,770
1791–1800	14,055,250
1801–1810	16,900,000*
1811–1820	18,700,000*
1821–1830	19,098,326
1831–1833	5,314,081

Sources: For 1761–99 from E.H. Pritchard, *The Crucial Years of Early Anglo Chinese Relations*, New York, reprint, 1970, p. 396; for 1800–33 from Morse, op. cit., II, III, IV passim.

Note: Whenever there is conversion from Canton currencies into British currency in this essay, the rates are: 1 Spanish $ = 0.72 tael, 3 taels £ = 1.

*An estimate based on incomplete records.

Even when tea was utilized as a catspaw, the Chinese herb served the British national interest well. It acted as a moderate and harmless stimulant, and when accompanied by milk and sugar, provided a good refreshment, 'without which the poor diet of the factory workers would not have kept them going' during the hectic days of the Industrial Revolution.[5]

Second, despite the myth about the Company's 'losses', there was good lucre in the tea trade. There was no advertisement about it, but we can easily see this when we examine the Company's accounts. The prime cost FOB of the Company's tea investment at Canton was s 2/9 per lb. (£ 26,49,589 for 7,79,37,000 lbs.) in 1771–80, s 1/3 (£ 89,74,822 for 1,424,57,000 lbs.) in 1781–90, s 1/3 (£ 110,37,948 for 2,009,70,000 lbs.) in 1791–99, and s 1/4 (£ 1,52,51,000 for 2,444,44,000 lbs.) in 1801–10, all of which included the Chinese government 'exactions' and the wasteful expenses of the Company's establishments at Canton-Macao. Afterbeing shipped to London, the tea was sold at s 3/5 per lb. {£ 1,02,77,592 for 6,03,24,000 lbs.) in 1771–1780, s 3/2 (£ 1,86,92,387 for 11,92,50,000 lbs.) in 1781–1790, s 2/11 (£ 2,83,21,901 for 19,01,85,000 lbs.) in 1791–1800, and s 3 (£ 3,60,93,069 for 24,04,38,000 lbs.) in 1801–1810.[6] In other words, the Company's gross profit in importing Chinese tea always stood much higher than 100% and never fell below s 1/8 per lb. during the three decades from 1781 to 1810. It was this bright prospect which had made the British traders so enthusiastic in importing Chinese tea.

Third, the British Exchequer received as much as one-tenth of Britain's total revenue from the tea consumers, collecting in 24 years between 1814 and 1837, a total of £ 8,26,40,531—an average of £ 34,43,355 per annum.[7]

Fourth, tea played a pivotal role in British economic development. It made round trips all over the world via London on British bottoms, making England the entrepot of tea in the world on the one hand, and developing British shipping on the other. Tea also brought a boom for another important British colonial enterprise, as every handful of it invariably went down the pot with several spoonfuls of West Indian sugar. Both tea and sugar were the two most highly taxed articles in Britain, the per capita consumption of which doubled during 1843–57, 'four times as fast as the growth in population in Great Britian.'[8]

Fifth, it was tea which enabled the Indian interests to transmit private British fortunes as from India homewards. The East India Company had annexed India for the purpose of among other things, appropriating the Indian revenue as openly admitted by Sir John Shore in 1789.[9] Personal friends and relatives of the decision makers of the EIC were given contracts for servicing the British Raj. In the process the Indian revenues were dropped into private British purses. They were, then, shipped to China in the shape of Indian goods. When tea was purchased at Canton, the Company paid to the hong merchants what it had received from private British traders who had the proceeds of their Indian goods. Before leaving India, they had signed bonds with the India government which obliged them to remit their proceeds to the Company's Canton treasury. The latter, after receiving the proceeds, issued them bills of exchange with which they could draw cash from the Company's London office. The exchange rates (between the tael and the Spanish dollar in which the Company's Canton receipts were registered, and with the pound sterling, in which the bearer of the bills was to be paid in London) were generally generous. In the late 1820s, a tael of silver was offered from s 7/3 to 6/7, while in 1787, when the Company's Canton treasury needed replenishment urgently it absorbed £ 13,00,000 from private Englishmen at as. high as 7s. 7½ d. per tael.[10]

II

What was of prime significance to the Indian interest was Indian opium. The British-Indian opium enterprise had two components: the Bengal opium and the Malwa opium. The former was a real child of the British Raj, and the latter, of illegitimate origin, an adopted child. The Company's Bengal opium monoply took shape as soon as Englishmen arrived at Patna after the Battle of Plassey. In 1773, the Company officially took over it. From then on, East India was developed into the leading opium-producing country, surpassing Turkey, the land of Afyon. The table below outlines this development.

TABLE 14: Development of Bengal Opium Enterprise 1771–1840

Period	Poppy-Growing Area (Bighas)	Average Annual Production* (chests)
1771		1,400
1775		3,000
1797–1800		4,186
1801–1810	45,736 (in 1808)	4,042
1811–1820	45,492 (in 1818)	4,039
1821–1830	1,27,181 (in 1828)	6,000 approx.**
1831–1840	2,82,792 (in 1838)	15,081

Sources: H.R.C. Wright: *East Indian Economic Problems of the Age of Cornwall and Raffles*, London, 1961, pp.109, 113, Morse, op. cit., III, p. 339; *Bengal Commercial Report*, vols. 30–52; B. Chowdhury, *Growth of Commercial Agriculture in Bengal*, Calcutta, 1964, pp. 18, 46.

*   Figures indicate the Company's sales at Calcutta.

**   record of 1823 missing.

Malwa opium, the produce of a wide area from Rajasthan down to the Deccan, rose as a non-Company enterprise, emulating the example of the Bengal opium and competing with the latter in the China market. The Board of Customs, Salt and Opium of the Bengal government inquired into the matter and discovered in 1820 three advantages of the Malwa over the Bengal in the China market:

(1) The Chinese could get 75 per cent of pure extract from the Malwa and only 57 per cent from the Bengal moister;

(2) The Malwa cakes were small and flat, thus easier to smuggle into China than the large and globular Bengal cakes;

(3) The Malwa chest adopted the Chinese picul system (a picul weighing 133⅓ lbs. which was the weight of opium in a Malwa chest), thus was more convenient for Chinese counting than the two-factory-maunds (weighing 149 lbs.) Bengal chest.[11]

This discovery coincided with a change in the Company's attitude to the Malwa opium. It gave up its earlier dog-in-the-manger policy and flung open the gates of Bombay to facilitate the export of Malwa opium to China. Subsequently, the Malwa opium enterprise was brought under the Company's monopoly. In 1820, Malwa opium valued at Rs. 32,15,317 passed through Bombay on its way to China. In the next two decades, Bombay's average annual export of Malwa opium to China was Rs. 41 lakhs in 1821–30, and Rs. 1 crore plus in 1831–1840.[12]

The combination of the two opium enterprises formed a formidable trade offensive against China as shown in Table 3 below. We may note that the Company followed its much advertised policy of 'restricted production' of Bengal opium until 1820 (see Table 14.2).

TABLE 14.3: Shipment of Indian Opium to China 1795–1840 (in chests)

Period	Bengal	Malwa	Total	Annual Average
1795–1800	12,261	Nil	12,261	2,043.5
801–1810	25,648	13,219	38,867	3,887
811–1820	29,649	14,396	44,045	4,404.5
1821–1830	52,867	62,067	114,234	11.423
1831–1840	77,608	165,940	243,548	24,355

Sources: *Bengal Commercial Reports*, vols. 13–52; H.B. Morse, *The International Relations of the Chinese Empire*, Shanghai, 1910,1, p. 209; Hsin-pao Chang, *Commissioner Lin and the Opium War*, Harvard, 1964, p. 223.

Under the self-imposed restriction, the Company selected the most fertile land for poppy cultivation and improved the packing to make the Company's stamp on the Bengal opium chests a symbol of quality. The Company then exacted a high price from every chest it had sold. In the Canton customs Register (the 'Hoppo Book')[13] of 1753, a picul (of 133 1/3 lbs.) of opium was listed at a price of taels 50 (equivalent to £ 17)[14] making it s 2/7 per lb. But between 1810 and 1823, a Bengal opium chest (of 149 lbs.) was seldom sold to the Chinese dealer at less than 1,000 Spanish dollars (equivalent to £ 240), with the highest prices of 2,600 and 2,500 dollars offered to a Patna chest and Banaras chest respectively, in 1822, making he Bengal opium price in China as high as £ 40 to 41.7 lb. The Company was quick in grasping this prospect and sold its Patna chests at Rs. 4,400 and its Banaras chests at 4,420 in its January sale at Calcutta in 1822.[15] The exchange rate at that time was 204 Bengal rupees for 100 Spanish dollars. The Company was selling almost at 2,200 dollars, leaving very little profit margin to the opium exporters.

If this intense profit hunting on the part of the Company gave a lie to the humanitarian claims of its 'restrictive policy' the developments after 1820 all the more proved that the Company's lofty sentiments were no more than hollow effusions. The year 1820 was significant not only for the Company's new patronage for Malwa opium, but also for its decision to expand poppy cultivation in the Bangal presidency, leading to a spectacular increase in the production of Bengal opium. The effect of all this on the China trade was evident. The export of Indian opium to China in 1821–30 nearly tripled the previous record. And in 1831–40 the export of Indian opium in ten years could compare to what had been exported earlier in a whole century. In 1821, opium overtook tea to become the first commodity of the triangular trade (the import of which to China was worth 9 Spanish dollars against 8.4 million of Chinese tea for Britain).[16] It remained the number one staple in China's foreign trade until the late nineteenth century.

When the British imposed themselves as the rulers of India, they were eager to explain to the whole world that they had brought civilization and enlightenment to the sub-continent. There could not but be moral constraint against this close association between an 'enlightened' government and an infamous commerce. The explanation went round that the Company's interest in opium rose from the expediency of balancing Britain's China trade. Henry Dundas even told the British Parliament in 1796 that Bengal would be impoverished of silver if opium was not sent to China.[17] Either Dundas deliberately lied, or he had not consulted the trade figures of the previous four years which we reproduce below.

TABLE 14.4: British–China Trade Balance 1792–95 (in £)

Year	British investment in China goods	British–Indian imports to China excluding opium	Trade balance in favour of Britain
1792	15,22,100	14,61,221	−60,879
1793	12,79,623	20,13,570	+7,33,947
1794	15,66,196	14,64,427	-1,03,669
1795	11,56,280	14,04,761	+ 2,38,481
		Overall balance	+ 8,07,780

Sources: Morse, *Chronicles*, II, pp. 201, 203, 305, 256, 265, 266; Pritchard, op. cit., p. 402.

Indian cotton occupied a substantial share in the second column of the above table. In the period 1817–33, Indian cotton realized £ 2,25,13,767 in China. The Company's total China investment being £ 3,11,68,933, it needed to absorb only £ 1,14,04,615 from private proceeds of Indian goods, as the import of British goods had fetched £ 1,97,64,318. Even a half of the cotton proceeds could make up the deficiency, let alone the availability of proceeds from Indian imports other than opium and cotton valued at £ 45,65,864.[18] So there was no need to import opium to China to balance the British trade during this period. Earlier, in the seven years between 1802 and 1809 (excluding 1806), the total Indian cotton exported from Calcutta and Bombay to China was valued at Rs. 5,20,28,904, showing an average of Rs. 74,32,701 (equivalent to more than 0.9 million pound sterling, if we calculate at the rate of Re. 1 = sh. 2.6).[19] We have already seen (from Tables 14.1 and 14.2) that the average annual British deficiency in her trade exchanges with China in the decade 1801–10 stood at about 0.6 million pounds, which could have been easily made up by the proceeds of Indian cotton which would exceed a million pounds a year on an average. In short, if opium were to play such a limited role of balancing Britain's China trade, not many chests of it would have been traded in the eighteenth century and it would have been totally given up in the nineteenth century.

The dichotomy between the moral constraints on one hand and the calculations of political and economic advantages on the other in British commercial interests' association with opium was reflected in the Company's opium policies. On one hand, rhetoric was continuously broadcast, like the statement by the Court of Directors in 1817 that 'were it possible to prevent the use of the drug altogether except for the purpose of medicine, we would gladly do it in compassion to mankind'.[20] Not only were the Company's ships forbidden to carry opium to China, but even the licenses issued by the Indian authorities to the opium clippers were camouflaged. In the licenses issued in 1828 to the *Hercules* of Mackintosh and Co., the *Louisa* of William Clifton, and the *Jane Eliza* of Crattenden Mackillop and Co., it was specified that these ships were to sail to China to export a few thousand rupees of saltpetre and nothing else.[21] Actually, each of these ships left Calcutta with lakhs of rupees of goods, mainly opium. The *Jane Eliza* carried no saltpetre on board at all.[22] On the other hand, as Dr. D. Butter, examiner of the Banaras Opium Agency, candidly admitted in 1835, 'The great object of the Bengal Opium Agencies is to furnish an article suitable to the peculiar tastes of the population of China'.[23] And the China-bound opium was called 'provision opium' in the Company's factories.[24]

The first advantage of the opium trade was the profit. No other commodity could be as profitable as opium, which needed little investment, and a single pound of it in weight could fetch many tonnes of pound sterling in value. Second, the source of this profit was not India, but another country about which British public opinion was totally unconcerned. As the trade in opium not only did not impoverish India but, on the contrary, helped to strengthen the Indian economy in no small measure, there was approval from London.

Earning profit was both economically and politically important for the Company because it had to find the means to maintain its Indian regime. Opium was a most convenient instrument to enlist the riches of China in support of the British Raj. This support can be quantified from Table 14.5. This table records five great leaps. In the 1780s there was a sharp increase of about 200%; then there was nearly another 200% increase in the next decade.

TABLE 14.5: Bengal Government's Opium Revenue 1773–1840

Period	Recorded in Rs.	Recorded in Sterling £
1773–1780		269,979
1781–1790		987,021
1791	27,50,906	
1792	29,09,157	292,751
1793–1796		10,39,103
1797–1800	80,27,756	13,54,595
1801–1810	5,19,18,505	
1811–1820	7,37,64,078	
1821–1830	9,70,61,926	
1831–1840	14,34,17,299	

Sources: Data for 1773–84 from D.E. Owen, *British Opium Policy in China and India* (reprint, New York, 1968), p. 37; for 1785–90 from P.J. Marshall, *The Impeachment of Warren Hastings*, Oxford, 1965, p. 166; for 1791–92 from Holden Furber, *The Private Records of An Indian Governor-Generalship*, Harvard, 1933, p. 30; for 1792–1809 from Miburn, op. cit., II, 220; for 1797–1817 from Morse, *Chronicler*, III, 339: for 1818–40 from *Bengal Commercial Reports*, vols. 30–52.

In the first decade of the nineteenth century there was another 100% increase. Then, the revenue in the third decade doubled that of the first, and that in the fourth decade doubled that of the second. There is another angle to look at the increase of Bengal government's opium revenue. In 1792, it accounted for 5.2 per cent of the Bengal revenue (Rs. 29,09,157 out of Rs. 5,54,80,267); its weightage rose to 7 per cent in 1812 (£ 7,28,940 out of £ 10,425,052), to 10 per cent in 1822 (£ 14,93,554 out of £ 1,41,63,277) and further to 20 per cent in 1842 (Rs. 1,82,79,956 out of Rs. 9,08,35,565).[25]

The importance of this revenue can be further illustrated. In 1815, when the Chinese government was taking steps to check illegal traffic, the Select Committee of the Company at Canton was worried that there might be a serious defalcation in the part of the Honourable Company's Revenue of Bengal.[26] In 1817, the Indian government had a costly war with the Pindaris, expending Rs. 3,87,35,875. The only presidency whose finances were not in the red was Bengal, where Rs. 55,68,188 of opium proceeds made up 7.5 per cent of its revenue.[27] And thanks to the prosperity of the opium trade, the Company's Canton committee could rush two million Spanish dollars to India to ease the financial crisis.[28]

Opium accrued revenue for British Raj, and simultaneously remitted back to England a part of this revenue which had become private fortunes. There was no better vehicle like opium which could transmit British fortunes homeward from India and simultaneously replenish the sources of these fortunes. In this regard, Indian opium had a greater strategic importance in the trade triangle than Chinese tea and British textiles. The British manufacturing interests should have strongly resented the westward commodity movement of the triangular trade. But the double utility of opium as both the generator and transmitter of the Indian revenue harmonized the internal contradiction of Britain's China trade between its import-orientation and its urge of expanding British exports. For what might have been the loss of Britain's China market was compensated by the gain of her Indian market. The vital link between opium trade and the export of British manufactures is best illustrated by the panic among Manchester industrialists in 1839 that the stoppage of opium trade in China might seriously affect the Indian purchasing power for British cotton goods.[29] This was why the British manufacturing interests firmly supported British military action against the Chinese government's persecution of the native and foreign opium traders.

III

The classical view that commerce achieves an equilibrium between demand and supply is not valid in our discussion of the trade triangle which was a peculiar phenomenon of imbalances. If we use Calcutta and Bombay to represent India,[30] the trade balances in 1821–30 between the three countries were: £

1,23,39,499 from Britain to China (Chinese goods to Britain £ 1,95,78,552, British goods to China £ 72,39,053), £ 1,77,73,655 from China to India (Indian goods to China £ 2,11,62,645, Chinese goods to India £ 1,03,38,990), and £ 93,32,415 from Britain to India (India goods to Britain £ 3,31,99,318, British goods to India £ 2,38,76,903).[31] The trade balances between London, Canton and Calcutta in 1801–33 were: £ 3,00,20,666 from London to Canton (£ 6,11,25,681 of goods from Canton to London, £ 3,11,05,015 of goods from London to Canton), £ 1,24,08,444 from Canton to Calcutta (£ 3,23,69,453 of goods from Calcutta to Canton, £ 1,99,61,009 of goods from Canton to Calcutta), and £ 2,28,43,136 from London to Calcutta (£ 6,24,17,860 of goods from Calcutta to London, £ 3,95,74,724 of goods from London to Calcutta).[32] In both the triangles there was no overall balance.

This external rhythm of the trade triangle, *viz.* India being the starting point, Britain the receiving end, while China a mid-way station in the India-to-Britain wealth movement, enable us to discover that the imbalance was caused by the difference in political, status between Britain and India. We also see that international commodity movement has a tendency to flow from the politically lowly placed nations to the highly placed.

Two major developments of the first dimension of the triangle, i.e. trade between Britain and China may be noted: (1) whereas British silver used to be imported to China in the eighteenth century (Table 2), from 1829 onwards, Chinese silver began to flow to Britain. (2) British cotton textiles made their debut in Chinese market in 1830. The Company may be blamed for obstructing the expansion of Chinese market for British manufactures in general,, and the late introduction of British cotton textiles to China in particular. In the seventy years of vigorous trade with China (1760–1833), it imported British cotton textiles to Canton only during the last four years of its China trade monopoly (1830–33), and imported only £ 1,16,000 of British cotton textiles to China annually.[33] After the 'free trade' era began in 1834 with the closure of the Company's Canton establishments, the import of British cotton cloth suddenly leaped to a new record of £ 16,40,781 in 1837 more than 14 times of the EIC's sale.[34]

The detailed distribution of commodities in the Sirto-British commercial exchange in 1817–33 was as follows: out of a total of £ 1,28,47,494 of British imports to China, 85.2 per cent (£ 1,09,26,379) being woollens, 8.1 per cent (£ 10,31,343) being metals, and 3.6 per cent (£ 4,65,388), cotton textiles; out of a total of £ 3,39,34,106 of Chinese exports to Britian 92.5 per cent (£ 3,13,63,087) being tea, 5 per cent (£ 17,00,636) being silver, and 1.5 per cent (£ 5,08,546), silks.[35]

The second dimension, trade between India and China, was originally meant to be a one-way India-to-China wealth movement, using China as a relay station and finally transmitting the wealth to Britain. That an opposite China-to-India movement also emerged was due to two factors. First, since the introduction of opium to the triangular trade was meant to play a double function of transmission of wealth and simultaneously replenishing the Indian treasury, the private opium exporters had to remit a part of their gains back to India to sustain their opium adventure (as there was quite an exaction on their gains by the Company's Calcutta opium sales). Second, as the China-bound Indian ships always sailed back without specific assignments and with plenty of accommodation, a return cargo from China was inevitable for additional profit and also for taking ballast to stand the storms of the Pacific. Third, the British-Indian Opium traders often bartered their opium with Chinese smugglers for goods without paying customs duty, and shipped them back to Calcutta for re-export. Many Americans and Portuguese found it convenient and cheap to buy Chinese tea and nankeens at Calcutta.[36]

The details of commodity exchange between India and China may be separately illustrated according to the statistics of Calcutta and Bombay. During 1795–1840, the Rs. 32,49,73,000 of Calcutta exports to China was dominated by two commodities: Rs. 20,93,02,000 of opium accounting for 64.4 per cent of the total, Rs. 9,08,00,000 of cotton making up 27.6 per cent; the third important commodity, viz. grain, amounting to less than 1 per cent (Rs. 25,61,000). The returns from China during the same period were dominated by silver, which occupied the lion's share of 67.1 per cent (Rs. 15,26,89,000) of the total Calcutta import from China (Rs. 22,59,03,000). This means that 72.7 per cent of the value of opium exported from Calcutta to China came back in the form of silver. Other Chinese imports were: tutenag (Rs. 1,52,81,000) 6.7 per cent, tea (Rs. 89,55,000) 4 per cent, vermilion (Rs. 31,94,000) 1.4 per cent, nankeens (Rs. 29,80,000) 1.3 per cent, camphor (Rs. 26,89,000) 1.2 per cent, alum (Rs. 29,93,000) 1.3 per cent, cassia (Rs. 14,83,000) 0.6 per cent, etc.[37]

According to 27 years of records of Bombay during 1801–39,[38] there was a total of Rs. 29,62,14,000 of export to China, shared by 49.7 per cent of cotton (Rs. 14,70,66,000), 40 per cent of opium (Rs. 11,80,29,000), in addition to 2.7 per cent of shark's fin(Rs. 80,69,000) and 1.2 per cent of sandalwood (Rs. 37,23,000), etc. We should remember that opium became an export of Bombay only from 1820 onwards. In the first seven years, it trailed behind cotton as the second largest export to China. From 1827 onwards, it began to take lead. During the 1830s, the opium-cotton ratio was 7:5.

Like Calcutta, the Chinese returns to Bombay were dominated by silver. During the same 27 year period, 54.4 per cent of the total import from China (Rs. 24,47,08,000) was silver (Rs. 13,25,81,000). The next important import was sugar (Rs. 3,04,46,000), 12.4 per cent of the total. Interestingly enough, the Chinese first learnt how to make brown sugar from the Indians in ancient times. The former probably first perfected making white sugar in the sixteenth century and subsequently exported it. Chinese white sugar must have earned its reputation in India, as in Indian vernaculars white sugar is called *chini*.

Bombay was a successor port to Surat in international trade. Surat, in turn, succeeded Cambay one of the greatest ports of the world half a millennium ago, which Chinese merchants used to frequent. In its import of sugar from and its export of sandal-wood (and olibanum, etc.) to China, Bombay still maintained some of the traditional economic ties of the two ancient Asian neighbours even under the British Raj. Other Bombay imports from China were: raw silk (Rs. 2,83,80,000) 11.6 per cent; cotton textiles including the nankeens (Rs. 1,27,54,000) 5.2 per cent; tea (Rs. 38,53,000) 1.6 per cent; (Rs. 32,28,000) 1.3 per cent; porcelain (Rs. 20,67,000) 0.8 per cent, etc.[39]

The third dimension, trade between Britain and India, is generally regarded as a topic outside the scope of the Britain-China-India trade triangle. This may be briefly dealt with by way of concluding this essay.

First, trade between Britain and Calcutta: the total of Rs. 49,72,59,837 of the latter's export to the former in 29 years, 1801–30 (excluding 1823) consisted of 43.5 per cent of indigo (Rs. 21,28,65,919), 29.2 per cent of raw silk (Rs. 9,82,98,973), 8.5 per cent of cotton and silk textiles (Rs. 4,13,58,579), 6.4 per cent of sugar (Rs. 3,08,43,061), 4.6 per cent of raw cotton (Rs. 2,24,22,688), 3.2 per cent of saltpetre (Rs. 1,55,34,215), etc. The British returns of Rs. 30,40,06,683 included Rs. 5,69,53,726 of cotton textiles (18.7 per cent of the total), Rs. 5,29,23,887 of metals (17.4 per cent), Rs. 3,92,73,502 of liquors and confectionary (12.9 per cent), Rs. 1,86,50,578 of woollens (6.1 per cent), Rs. 1,16,10,509 of cotton yarn and twist (3.5 per cent), Rs. 99,29,345 of glasswares (3.3 per cent), Rs. 88,86,352 of boots and stationery (2.9 per cent), Rs. 80,64,319 of western clothing including hats and books (2.7 per cent), Rs. 57,01,072 of oilman's store (1.9 per cent), Rs. 57,75,886 of carriages and saddlery (1.9 per cent), Rs. 18,18,654 of musical instruments (0.6 per cent) Rs. 15,54,358 of empty bottles (0.5 per cent), etc.[40] The Bombay records are quite fragmentary. A glance at 16 years records, 1819–35 (excluding 1834) shows similar patterns to the Britain–Calcutta exchanges. The 16 years of Bombay's exports to Britain, valued at Rs. 10,51,45,038, were dominated by raw cotton (Rs. 5,71,82,001) comprising 54.4 per cent. Next was silver and gold (Rs. 1,14,42,979) making up 10.9 per cent. Other items worth mention were: 4 per cent of raw silk (Rs. 42,37,313), 3.6 per cent of pepper (Rs. 37,79,550), 3.5 per cent of coffee (Rs. 37,23,577), and 3.5 per cent of elephant teeth (Rs. 36,52,100). The British returns of Rs. 11,68,92,355 consisted of 46.7 per cent of cotton textiles (Rs. 5,46,37,848), 21.7 per cent of metals (Rs. 1,49,14,469), 7 per cent of liquors and eatables (Rs. 82,39,460), 3.4 per cent of cotton yarn and twist (Rs. 39,21,872), 3 per cent of woollens (Rs. 34,24,584), 2.3 per cent of articles for wearing apparel (Rs. 27,34,418), 1.8 per cent of cochineal (Rs. 20,90,177), 1.7 per cent of glass-wares (Rs. 19,37,509), 1.2 per cent of books and stationery (Rs. 13,97,845), etc.[41]

The salient features of the trade between Britain and India were: (1) it followed the classical pattern of trade between the colony and the metropolis;

(2) a substantial part of the exchange concerned cotton and its products; (3) a good portion of the British imports catered to the needs of Europeans rather than Indians.

The Indian exports were essentially raw materials, while her imports were generaly finished products, the majority of which could be manufactured in India. The exchanges of cotton and its goods show a process of transforming India (which had been a renowned cotton textile producer of the world) into a massive consumer of British cotton textiles some of which from the Indian-grown cotton.

Many items among the British imports to the two Indian ports, can be treated as non-essentials. Even some of the apparently beneficial items which we have included in the category of 'metals' were originally classified as 'military stores' and 'naval stores', both of which amounted to Rs. 78,00,000, and accounted for 2.5 per cent of Calcutta's total import from Britain during 1831–40.[42] Similarly, things like books and stationery were useful things. But their import to India was more aimed at strengthening the alien rule than developing the native economy.

As alluded to earlier, in ten years (1821–30) Calcutta and Bombay exported in excess £ 9,322,415 of wealth to Britain, and £ 10,773,655 to China (which, too, was ultimately transmitted to Britain). In other words, two million pound sterling were the annual Indian tribute to Britain. But even the articles from Britain which formed a part of the British payment for Indian exports, those military and naval stores, books and stationery, liquors, carriages, hats and boots, were all for the consumption of those who were devoting their time and energy in India to the cause of transforming Indian revenue into private fortunes, then into Indian exports to China, and then into Chinese exports to Britain. This was the strange manner in which the trade triangle was complete. At last we see the equilibrium in the trade triangle under-review, namely: Indian opium for the Chinese, Chinese tea for the Britons, and British Raj for the Indians

Notes

1. William Foster, *England's Quest of Eastern Trade*, pp. 5–6.

2. M.E. Wilbur, *The East India Company and the British Empire in the-Far East*, pp. 302–14.

3. H.B. Morse, *The Chronicles of the East India Company Trading to China*, vol. I, p. 162.

4. William Milburn, *Oriental Commerce*, London, 1813, II, 486; Morse, op. cit., vol.IV, pp. 253, 325, 343; *Irish University Parliamentary Papers*, XXXI, p. 182.

5. J.A. Williamson, *A Short History of British Expansion*, p. 38.

6. Data from Pritchard, op. cit., p. 395; Morse, op. cit., passim; Milburn, op. cit., II, p. 534.

7. *First Report from the Select Committee House of Commons*, 1830, Appendix, p. 84; *Ya-p'ien chan-cheng*, II, p. 655.

8. A.H. Imlah, *Economic Elements in the Pax Britannia*, p. 160.

9. Amales Tripathi, *Trade and Finance in the Bengal Presidency*, p. 17.

10. *First Report*, Commons, 1830, T.G. Lloyd's witness, Q. 4181.

11. *Bengal Commercial Reports*, vol. 31.

12. *Bombay Commercial Proceedings*, vols. 57–76.

13. 'Hoppo', the Pidgin English name of the Canton Customs Superintendent, was the corruption of the Chinese wood *hu-pu*, meaning the Revenue Ministry to which he belonged.

14. H.B. Morse, *The Trade and Administration of China*, pp. 328–9.

15. John Phipps, *A Guide to the Commerce of Bengal*, pp. 259, 266.

16. Morse, *Chronicles*, vol. IV, pp. 20, 22.

17. F.S. Turner, *British Opium Policy and its Results to India and China*, p.135.

18. Morse, *Chronicles*, vols. II, IV, passim.

19. *Bengal Commercial Reports*, vols. 14–21; *Bombay Commercial Proceedings*, vols. 40–46.

20. Turner, op. cit., p. 44.

21. *Home Miscellaneous*, 1828–40 (National Archives of India), S. no. 440.

22. *Bengal Commercial Reports*, vol. 40.

23. D. Butter, 'On the Preparation of Opium for the China Market', *Journal of Asiatic Society of Bengal*, vol. V, 1136, p. 165.

24. George Watt, *A Guide to the Economic and Commercial Court*, p. 131.

25. Data for 1792 from Furber, *Governor-Generalship*, p. 30; J. MacGregor, *History of Oriental Commerce* (House of Commons, 1847–48, c. 974), p. 235; for 1842 from Yen Chung-p'ing ed., *Chung-Kuo chin-tai ching-chi-shih fung-ihi tsu-liao hsuan-chi*, Shanghai, 1955, p. 25.

26. *Foreign Secret Proceedings*, National Archives of India, 8 December 1815, no. 1.

27. Tripathi, op. cit., p. 162, Morse, *Chronicles*, III, p. 339.

28. Morse, op. cit., p. 308.

29. Chang, op. cit., p. 193.

30. This leaves out the third port, Madras, statistics of which are not available.

31. Calculated on statistics of Morse, *Chronicles*, II–IV; *Bengal Commercial Proceedings*, vols. 58–68; converted at Re. 1 = s 2.

32. Morse, *Chronicles*, II–IV; *Bengal Commercial Reports*, vols. 13–52; conversion Re. = 1 = s 2/6 before 1814.

33. Morse, *Chronicles*, vol. IV, pp. 248, 271, 339, 369.

34. *Irish University Papers*, vol. XXXI, p. 178.

35. Morse, *Chronicles*, vols. III, IV, passim.

36. *Bengal Commercial Reports*, vol. 19.

37. Ibid., vols. 13–52.

38. The missing years were 1806, 1810–18, 1834, 1836.

39. *Bombay Commercial Proceedings*, vols. 39–79.

40. *Bengal Commercial Reports*, vols. 13–42.

41. *Bombay Commercial Proceedings*, vols. 56–75.

42. *Bengal Commercial Reports*, vols. 43–53.

COLONIAL STATE: POLICIES AND CONSEQUENCES

15

Was British Conquest of India Accidental?

Bal Krishna

The Indian Empire a Blind Acquisition

The idea of the accidental acquisition of the Indian Empire by the British has crystallized into a universal belief. It is being reiterated from to time in books and speeches as a self-evident maxim of the political histories of England and India. It claims many staunch adherents in both countries, but the study of the records of the British East India Company will shake the reader's faith in this popular doctrine. The presentation of these facts is not only of academic interest, but is fraught with political significance of the first magnitude. The theory of the fortuitous acquisition brings in fatalism and divine imposition. Then it implies the sudden and fortuitous loss of the doctrine will wash away the very foundations of human effort, enterprise, intelligence, British heroism and political genius. Although national vanity is tacked by explaining the Indian conquest on the principle of Caesar's inimitable message of 'Vini, Vidi, Vici', history and truth are often murdered by such catchwords. Research too receives a crude setback. History repudiates the idea that empires can be gained like prizes in a lottery. I am writing these pages in the hope that my onslaught on the popular belief should bring to light the true causes of the British conquest of India.

The idea of blind acquisition of an empire more extensive, more populous and more prosperous than that of ancient Rome, was probably given currency by Professor Seeley. 'Nothing greater that has ever been done by Englishmen,' said he, 'was done so un-intentionally, so accidently as the conquest of India.' Further on, the learned professor explains himself thus: 'But in India we meant one thing and did quite another. All along we have been looking one way and moving another'. Seeley's school of thought has thus propounded the theory that the object of the English in coming over to the East was trade alone and not conquest of territory. But I maintain on the basis of documentary evidence

*2nd session at Allahabad, 1938.

that commerce and conquest were the main objects soon after the advent of the English in the East. Conquest was never lost sight of, although it was subservient to commerce for the first sixty years.

It is purely fallacious to believe that the East India Company was a mercantile body which in its corporate capacity of merchants was, through the stress of circumstances, and much against its own will, forced to become sovereign of Bengal. A judicious reading of the charters, letters patent, and records of the Company can lead us to the one conclusion that its nature, scope and aims were, soon after its establishment, enlarged, and that the mercantile body of the time of Elizabeth, in course of time, but long before the acquisition of the Bengal sovereignty, had been transformed into a body politic. Throughout its long career, we find it working as a department of the state for the commercial and political conquests of the heathen nations of Africa and Asia. We ought not to be misled by its commercial concerns. It was engaged in commerce, as the state is universally engaged now in producing, distributing and exchanging millions of pounds worth of goods, by being the biggest capitalist entrepreneur and merchant rolled into one. The East India Company likewise was not a purely commercial corporation, but also a political organization to extend the conquest of England and ruin the power of her European rivals in the East.

'It was in charter as in deed a new state, erected within the state itself, which enriched it and increased its strength abroad.'

This aspect is fundamentally essential for the right understanding of the events immediately preceding and following the memorable battle of Plassey, and if we lose this key, we shall be launched into an inextricable labyrinth of historic confusion. We are sure that this focal truth alone can afford us the right perspective in viewing the history of the progress and development of the Company. With the loss of this guiding light, we are bound to wander in a wilderness of loose and incoherent facts.

Territorial Conquests of
The Portuguese and The Dutch

The Portuguese, from the first appearance of the Dutch and English in the Indies, were determined to keep them out of the Oriental trade by force. Thereupon the Dutch invested their East India Company, with the avowed object of conquest and colonies, with authority to make peace or war with the Eastern princes, to erect forts, to choose its own governors, maintain garrisons and to nominate officers for the conduct of the police and the administration of justice. Armed with such vast powers and fortified with a burning ambition to build up an extensive commerce, the Dutch had a meteoric success in routing the Portuguese forces in many places of importance and were soon in possession of large islands, a well-exercised navy, strongly fortified places and good harbours. They were accordingly well secured against the Portuguese and their new rivals of the English nation.

The Dutch had soon learnt the lesson that they could not trade in the East unless they could capture the countries under the control of the Portuguese. *The English following in the wake of the Dutch had only one alternative, either to cease trading and sink into obscurity or to oust the Portuguese and the Dutch from their possessions and settlements.* It is true that the English could not successfully cope with the Dutch in the East Indies for more than a century but it does follow that the idea of making conquests for the preservation of trade and the honour of the country was not present all along, or that they did not make attempts to secure territories.

Commerce, conquests and colonies were welded together in the careers of the Portuguese and their Dutch successors. The experience and practice of these nations had made it clear to the English that commerce could not be carried on without fortified factories, naval and military supremacy and state aid. The English could not proceed on purely commercial lines in the teeth of armed opposition from their firmly established rivals.

English Attempts for Territorial Acquisition

I will now take a very rapid survey of the attempts made by the East India Company to gain colonies in the East and to secure fortified places in India for founding an empire here.

1. The English took possession of *St. Helena* in their very first voyage.
2. *Struggle for the Spice Islands:* The Dutch made treaties with the rulers of Amboyana, Banda and Pulo Ai in 1600 and 1602 for assisting the natives in the expulsion of the Portuguese and for exclusive purchase of spices. The English were trying to enter into similar treaties with other rulers. In 1620 they even succeeded in procuring the surrender of three places in the Island of Banda, namely, Pulo Ai, Poolaroon and Lantor. This success was short-lived, as the English were soon defeated and almost expelled from the places by the Dutch. Thereafter the former made supreme efforts to establish themselves in India.
3. *Colony at Saldanah:* Edward Dodsworth pointed out to the Company in November 1615 the advantages of having a colony at Saldanah. Five years after Capt. Schilling took possession of the Bay of Saldanah and the adjoining continent of Africa as far as no Christian prince had any fort or garrison within the limits. Thus he opened the way to colonization in South Africa.

4. *Capture of Ormus:* In 1622 the English captured Ormus, the greatest emporium of Euro-Asiatic commerce of those days in the mouth of the Persian gulf. Its custom-house alone is said to have earned £ 31,875 per annum to the Portuguese. If the views of the English Captain as reported by P.D. Yalle can be relied upon as representing those of this nation or the Company, then no more proofs are required to show the existence of political ambitions during the first thirty years. The Captain observed that in case the Persians would deliver to the English the fortress of Ormus, *as they had desired it from the beginning,* the English would people the Island, restore its trade as formerly, and would keep four ships there for the protection of its trade and for guarding the sea against the Portuguese as well as other enemies. They would, moreover, transport a good number of people from England, and whole families with wives and children to dwell in Ormus, as the Portuguese did before, and then they would prosecute the war against the latter at Muscat and everywhere else.[1]

5. *Early attempts for forts in India:* So far as the efforts to secure fortified places in the Indian soil are concerned, we find that the possession and fortification of Muzafarabad are discussed by the English at Surat as early as 1615.[2] Sir Thomas Roe favoured a vigorous offensive as 'the nobler and safer part' and the most likely to impress the Indians.

   A most significant attempt was made by Capt. Keeling for securing territories and expelling the Portuguese from their Eastern possessions.[3]
   Roger Haves gives the terms of a treaty entered into with the Zamorin on 4 March 1615. The latter promised the cession of the castle and island of Cranganor together with the town and the fort of Cochin to the English, if they should be successful with him in capturing those places from the Portuguese.

6. *Plans for the Conquest of Bombay:* After having fortified Lugundy in Java and Armagaon on the Coromandel Coast, the Company suggested the advisability of establishing a settlement at Bombay, the 'London's Hope' in Arabia, or at some other suitable spot in the Indies. In pursuance of this object, the English entered into an alliance with the Dutch. Six English ships laid seige to Bombay in October 1626, pillaged the town; set all the houses on fire, and returned.[4] It formed the first attempt of the English to capture Bombay from the Portuguese.
   In 1628 again, ships were twice sent on voyages of discovering the situation of Danda Rajapuri, Rajapur and Bombay on the Konkan coast, but no fortifications were undertaken at 'Bombayee',[5] as it was too much exposed to Portuguese depredations.

7. *Policy underlying fortification of Armagaon:* The various reasons, commercial and political, for having fortifications, have been outlined in a letter of 27 May 1626, which relating particularly to the necessity of a fort at Armagaon, gives the underlying motives of the whole policy.' Were we once fortified, we

should draw infinite of all sorts of people and, more special, such as are fitting our Negotiations; and, in time, *we should get the whole Government of the place into our own hands*, and doubt but, if we continue thus, we shall be subject to all casualties and the Dutch will never leave us in quite, 'till they have, by one means or other, rooted us out.'[6]

8. *Schemes to Capture Portuguese Possessions:* One more evidence is furnished by Wylde, the President of the English Factory at Surat, in his Remonstrance to Cromwell. He entered into a treaty with the Great Mogul to aid him by sea, in the taking of the Portuguese cities of Diu, and Daman. He entertained the Lord Protector with interesting details of the power and riches of the Portuguese and then suggested the capture of their dominions by sending a naval expedition from England. 'So may the work be done in one year, for Jacatra being surrendered, all the rest must follow, as wanting provisions or starve. And this done, there will be little to be with the Portugull as being inconsiderable by sea, whereof we must endeavour to make ourselves masters before we can enjoy all those rich trades to ourselves alone.'[7]

Charles I condemned the Company for not having fortifications like the Portuguese and Dutch, and therefore granted charters to Courteen Company and the Assada Merchants 'to take possession of all such lands as they shall discover.'

9. *Colonies in Africa and India:* Interesting accounts of the proposals for establishing colonies in the islands of Madagascar, St. Helena, Re-union (called England's Forest) and Mauritius; of the occupation of Madagascar, the despatch of several ships with colonists on board and of the efforts to make it a successful colony since 1636 onward, are now available in Foster's Court Minutes. Then the war with the Dutch after the fifties forcibly brought to the mind of the English statesmen the paramount necessity of having fortified places in the East. President Blackman from Surat and Spiller from Isphahan in Persia wrote strong minutes on the necessity of founding colonies. The former pointed out in 1653 that Bombay and Bassein could be captured from the Portuguese without any difficulty.

In 1653, Spiller commended the strong, policy of the Portuguese and the Dutch in having fortified places in the East and particularly a castle 'about Surat or on the coast of India' for enjoying a commanding trade and increasing English 'strength, force and honour in these Oriental parts.'[8]

The petition of the E.I. Company in 1654 to the Lord Protector for 'a national interest in India,'[9] proposed the acquisition of Bassein and Bone Bay (Bombay) in India, and the town and castle of Mozambique in Africa with the several fortifications, privileges, trade and other benefits belonging to these places.

Similarly, the decision to re-occupy, fortify and colonize Poolaroon and St. Helena, furnishes additional evidence of the colonizing spirit of the East India Company.

10. *Cession of Bombay:* When it is remembered that vigorous efforts were made by the English since 1626 to take possession of Bombay, it is only then that the full significance of the cession of that island to the King of England in 1662 can be realized by the reader. What could not be obtained by force of arms, was diplomatically secured through gift. Why Bombay and not any other place should have been obtained in dowry, becomes intelligible from the preceding and subsequent events. This donation cemented the friendship of the English and Portuguese, so that the allies should be able to successfully oppose the growing power of the Dutch.

The ambitious and aggressive policy of Charles II will be revealed from the words used in the Commission given to Sir Abraham Shipman:

'Our maine designe . . . being to gain to our subjects more free and better trade in the East Indies, and *to enlarge our Dominions in those parts,* and advance thereby the honour of our Crown , and the General Commerce, and Weale of our subjects. . . ."

11. *Militant Policy of the Company:* A few years later Gerald Aungier, Governor of Bombay, sounded a trumpet call by postulating to the Company that 'the times now require you to manage your general commerce with your swords in your hands.' When the Mogul Emperor was engaged in a war with Bijapur, Golcondah and the Marathas, the Company adopted their new policy of aggressive militarism. They resolved to enter into a war with the Mogul, because in their own words 'we have no remedy left. But either to desert our trade or we must draw that sword His Majesty hath intrusted us with, to vindicate the rights and honour of the English Nation in India.'[10]

The following extract is interesting in revealing the imperialistic ambition. 'If it should be asked, How the Dutch can maintain 170 forts and fortified places in India, while 2 or 3 can hardly be supported by the English Company? The answer is the same: All the Dutch stock would not maintain their 170 forts one year but for the ingrossment of spice, and their skill of making their natives pay the charge of their fortified places: And this last we say is all the foundacon of their greatness and power: For how have they engrossed Spice trade but by fortifications? And how have they maintained their fortifications, but singly by that skill which we now recommend to your invitacon.'[11]

In another letter they write:

"It is our ambition for the honour of our King and Country, and the good of posterity, as well as of this Company, *to make the English Nation as formidable, as the Dutch, or any other Europe nation, are, or ever were in India; but that cannot be done, only by the form and with the method of Trading Merchants,* without the political skill of making all fortified places repay their full charge and expences."[12]

Finally, we may produce another memorable despatch wherein it is laid down '*that which we promise ourselves in a most especial manner* from our new President and Council is that they will establish such a politie of civil and military power, and create and secure such a large revenue to maintain both at that place, as *may be the foundation of a large, well-grounded, sure English Dominion in India for all time to come*.'[13]

Imperialism Continued: Though the Company sustained an ignominious defeat and suffered heavy loss in trade and prestige in trying sword with Aurangzeb, the Directors did not give up their political ambitions. They issued the following instructions to their 'General of India' in Aug. 1688.

'Though our war be over, you must continue to train and exercise in arms all our Factors, Writers and English Servants of all degrees from the highest to the lowest according to our former orders, because we must for ever hereafter keep ourselves a martial Nation in India.'

Dr. C.R. Wilson has justly remarked that "nothing can be further from the facts than the generally accepted picture of the mid-day halt of Charnock at Su anatee growing to be a city, 'chance-directed, chance-erected,' 'spreading chaotic like the fungus.' Had the English confined themselves to 'mere trade,' had the merchant remained 'meek and tame where the timid foot first halted,' there would have been no Calcutta and no British India."[14]

The English after 1700 resorted more to force than presents for opposing the demands of the native officers and even of the governors of Bengal. Instead of 'to be always giving to every little rascal,' the Governor of Fort William showed boldness in clearing his goods by the use of the military.[15] At the death of Aurangzeb in 1707, Fort William was considerably strengthened by building two new bastions and by employing sixty new Indian soldiers. On account of the enhanced security, the English were able to oppose the demands of the Nabob for a levy of one lac of rupees from them. A threatening message was sent to Patna to the effect that 'If any of our people there are plundered, we will take satisfaction at *Hugli*, or anywhere we find it convenient to do.'[16]

12. *A Secret Scheme to Conquer Bengal:* The English continued to gather strength in Bengal and minutely studied the political situation of the whole country through their agents. By the middle of the eighteenth century they felt themselves strong enough to conquer Bengal from the Muslim forces. A confidential scheme for the conquest of Bengal was sent to the Company by Colonel Scott. Herein he brushes aside all objections and fears as groundless and argues that the English could not have any dread of invasion from Delhi. '500 disciplined troops might defend the pass,' says he, 'against the whole power of Indostan and secure us from that quarter.' No European nation could contest the conquest with the English, as the latter would have the absolute command of the Hugly river. The Marathas could not disturb

the peace of Bengal if the passes would be fully defended by forts and troops. In short, in his opinion an annual supply from Europe of 2,000 men for three years, would be necessary and quite sufficient to make the English conquest secure and lasting.

An experienced officer like the Colonel was convinced of the inherent weakness of the rulers and the ruled in Bengal, and consequently he developed the project of suddenly capturing the government of the three provinces. The subsequent events leading up to the battle of Plassey are the natural developments of such projects.

13. *The Conclusion:* We have now finished our survey of the repeated attempts of the English East India Company to found colonies in Africa, the Indian Archipelago, in Persia and India from their very first voyage in 1601 to the Bloodless Revolution of 1757 in Bengal. There is scarcely any long period wherein an abatement of this ambitious programme is visible. On the contrary, every succeeding decade reveals more vigorous efforts being made for the establishment of an English Empire in the East.

The victories in the Carnatic and Bengal were consequently the fruits of a long preparation on an extensive scale, and not of accidental circumstances. The intention and attempt to establish colonies were all along present from the establishment of the Company; the only thing hidden from human ken was the wonderful magnitude and the extraordinary stability of the empire founded by the English in India. This study pre-eminently emphasizes the pregnant truth that the conquest of India by the British was not achieved by a stroke of fortune, but through sturdy struggles and steady sacrifices extending over more than two centuries.

Notes

1. P.D. Valle, vol. I, p. 8.
2. Letter Rd., vol. III, p. 208.
3. Purchas his Pilgrimes, E.S., vol. VI, p. 496.
4. Marine Records, vol. 43.
5. This name is still used by the Indians.
6. Factory Records, Miscellaneous, vol. IX, p. 135.
7. B.M. Sloane Ms, 3271. cf. Dr. Khan, *Anglo-Portuguese Negotiations Relating to Bombay 1660–1677*, p. 435.
8. Ibid. 10 April 1655, p. 272.
9. Ibid., p. 374. C.O. 77, vol, VII, no. 92, Decision to obtain Danda Rajapura, Bassein and Bombay or any other places in 1658. Court Minutes, vol. 1655–59, pp. 250, 252. cf. Court Minus, 1650–54, Introduction, p, iii.
10. Letter Book, vol. 8, pp. 79, 225–27=Bruce's Annals, vol. 3, p. 568.
11. Letter Book., vol. 8, pp. 37, 264–5. Fort Gen. Letter dated 14 January 1686.
12. Letter Book., vol. 7, p. 500.

13. Letter Book., vol. 8, pp. 242–3. Letter on 7 January 1686, pp, 467–8.
14. *Bengal Past and Present*, vol. I, p. 30.
15. Hedges, *Diary*, vols. II, LVII.
16. C.R. Wilson, E. Annals, vol. I, p. 178.

16

Genesis of the Diwani Grant of 1765

Kali Kinkar Datta

THE YEAR 1765 marked a turning-point in the history of the Bengal *subah* and also of India as a whole. In the month of August of this year Shah Alam II, the unfortunate and shadowy Emperor of Delhi, made a grant of the *Diwani* of Bengal, Bihar and Orissa to the English East India Company. Shah Alam's *firman* of the 12 August 1765, granting the *Diwani* stated: 'that whereas, in consideration of the attachment and services of the high and mighty, the noblest of exalted nobles, the chief of illustrious warriors, our faithful servants and sincere well-wishers, worthy of our royal favours, the English Company, we have granted them the *Diwani* of the provinces of Bengal, Bihar and Orissa, ... as a free gift and *altamgau*, without the association of any other person . . . it is requisite that the said Company engage to be security for the twenty-six lakhs of Rupees a year, for our royal revenue, which sum has been appointed from the Nawab Najm-uddaula Bahadur, and regularly remit the same to the royal *sarkar*; and in this case, as the said Company are obliged to keep up a large army, for the protection of the provinces of Bengal, etc., we have granted to them whatsoever may remain out of the revenues of the said Provinces, after remitting the sum of twenty-six lakhs of Rupees to the royal *sarkar*, and providing for the expenses of the *Nizamat*. It is requisite that our royal descendants, the Viziers, the bestowers of dignity, the Omras, high in rank, the great Officers, etc., have the said office in possession of the said Company from generation to generation, for ever and ever.'

The language of the *firman* was more or less conventional. It need not lead one to think that the *Diwani* was a voluntary gift of the Mughal Emperor. In the first place, transaction was a logical sequel to the growing helplessness of Shah Alam II in the face of various hostile forces. Driven from pillar to post and post to pillar by the adverse influences of cruel destiny and also his personal failings, he found even Delhi too hot for him, chiefly due to the malignant hostility of the Wazir Imadulmulk. His three attempts in 1759, 1760 and 1761 to bring Bengal and Bihar under his influence by undoing the verdict of Plassey ended in smoke. The battle of Buxar (23 October 1764)

*15th Session at Gwalior, 1952.

confirmed the verdict of Plassey. It resulted in the defeat of three of the important rulers of northern India, Shah Alam II, Shujauddaulah and Mir Qasim. Immediately after it, Shah Alam II, not quite happy on his virtual dependence on Shujauddaulah and with his usual vacillation, threw himself almost at the mercy of the English and entered into negotiations with them which after Clive's return to India in May, 1765, drove him to make the *Diwani* grant. As for the new Nawab of Bengal, Najmuddaulah, he had already been reduced to a figurehead according to the terms of the treaty of twentieth February 1765, between himself and the Calcutta Council. The *Diwani* was a logical step after it and supplied a legal cloak to the *de facto* authority of the English in Bengal.

It must also be noted that the *Diwani* was a natural concomitant of the eclipse of Mughal rule throughout India, in a sense the culmination of an idea, which had originated a few years back in consequence of it. Already, before 1759 an officer was made by the Delhi Emperor to invest in the English East India Company with the duty of collecting the revenues of Bengal. Clive wrote in his letter to Pitt, dated the 7 January 1759:'. . . application has been made to me, from the Court of Delhi, to take charge of collecting this payment, the person entrusted with which is styled the King's Diwan. . . . But this high office I have been obliged to decline for the present, as I am unwilling to occasion any jealousy on the part of the Suba (Nawab of Bengal), especially as I see no likelihood of the Company's providing us with a sufficient force to support properly so considerable an employ, and which would open a way for securing the Subaship for ourselves.'[1]

Again in 1761, Emperor Shah Alam II made an offer of the *Diwani* to the English, 'on condition of their being answerable for the royal revenues' from Bengal. But the Council in Calcutta did not accept it. They thought as follows: 'It would be a source of perpetual contest and ill-will with the Nabob but lest such an appointment might at any time hereafter be thought advantageous we will for the present defer coming to any resolution thereon and only write the King that we shall soon send our Requests in form.'[2]

The Council in Calcutta informed Major Carnac on the 6 July 1761, that 'with regard to the Dewannee of these provinces, . . . it would be a source of continual jealousies between the Nabob and the Company, we do not think it advisable to sue for it at this time.'[3] Mir Qasim, in fact, was opposed to the acceptance of *Diwani* by the Company and he was assured by the Governor in Calcutta that he will 'never deviate from the treaty (with him) and will always be ready to assist him.'[4]

The Court of Directors approved of the Calcutta Council's view, with regard to Shah Alam's *Diwani* offer of 1761, and wrote to them: 'Your refusal of the *Dewani* of Bengal offered by the King, was certainly right, and we are well satisfied with the just and prudent reasons you give for declining that offer.'

But the situation had completely changed after the battle of Buxar and the Calcutta Council's treaty of the 20 February 1765, with Nawab Najmuddaulah. The Company, in fact, now wanted the *Diwani*. The Select Committee in Calcutta wrote to Lord Clive, its President and Governor, on the 21 June 1765: 'And this My Lord would appear to us the most favourable occasion that may ever occur for obtaining Sunnuds from the King for the Dewanny of Bengal a point of great consequence to the Company much desired and strongly solicited by General Carnac, but without effect, a price being expected and demanded that was thought by the Governor and Council more than equivalent to the advantage. Times are since altered, the King is now dependent on our Bounty, his whole hopes of protection and even subsistence rest upon us. It cannot therefore be supposed he will prove obstinate in denying request of little consequence to him in his present circumstances, but advantageous to us, his greatest benefactors, we may say his only friends. We therefore beg leave to recommend this as one of the most important Points to be negotiated.' The negotiations were carried on by Shitab Ray and Muniruddaulah,[5] then the two good friends of the English in Bengal and Bihar and resulted ultimately in securing for them the coveted *Diwani* with its enormous advantages. The Select Committee in Bengal wrote to the Court of Directors on the 8 September 1766: 'It was in the prosecution of our plan, of giving permanency to your influence, that we obtained from the King a grant of the Dewanny; and with the same view we entered into an agreement with the Nabob, the consequences of which are that the revenues of the three provinces being now entirely under our direction, we no longer depend, for the support of our military establishment, on the bounty of the Subah.'

Notes

1. Malcom, *Life of Clive*, vol. II, pp. 126–8.
2. *Public Consultations*, 4 July 1761.
3. *Vansittart's Narrative*, vol. I, p. 263.
4. *Calendar of Persian Correspondence*, vol. 1, p. 118.
5. Letters from Shah Alam II to the Company's Governor, dated 2 August and 11 August 1765. *Calendar of Persian Correspondence*, vol. I, pp. 423–4.

17

The Revolt of Zamindars in Akkalkot, 1830

A.R. Kulkarni

AKKALKOT[1] WAS a small Jagir created by Shahu, in the eighteenth century. When Shahu was released in 1707 from the Mughal captivity, he was opposed by the supporters of Tarabai at various places. The Patil of Parad, a place 25 miles south of Daulatabad made a vain attempt to resist Shahu, and died in a pitched battle. The widow of the Patil surrendered and sought protection from Shahu. Shahu pardoned her and promised to treat her only son as his, and later on granted him the Jagir of Akkalkot, (Sholapur district, Maharashtra) and was named as Fattesingh. The Jagir was granted to him in perpetuity, and was thus brought within the royal fold. He was treated as prince, and perhaps he would have succeeded to the throne of Satara had he not preferred a small jagir to a state.[2]

The fifth Raja of this Jagir, Shahaji II (1828–56) faced a small rising of the people in his state. When the British wrested power from the Marathas in 1818, a period of unrest ensued throughout the Maratha country. Chatur Singh of Satara, the Ramoshis, the Koils, the Shibandis (fort garrisons) of Kolhapur, the Bhils of Khandesh, etc., revolted against the British authorities. The Maratha soldiers who were deprived of their former positions became rebels.[3]

The State of Satara was created by an agreement between the East India Company and the last Chatrapati of the Maratha State. It was a diplomatic move of Mountstuart Elphinstone, who wanted to please the people of the Maratha country and also to enlist their support for the British Raj. The Jagirdars of Satara nominally remained under the supremacy of the Raja of Satara but actually they had entered into separate treaties with the Company.[4] Thus the seeds of distrust and dissensions were sown by the company from the very beginning.

The Raja of Satara (no longer the Chatrapati of the Maratha State) by the Treaty of 1819 had not only accepted the British paramountcy, but had also

*33rd Session at Muzaffarpur, 1972.

agreed to circumscribe his freedom and authority. He could not have any relations with the people outside his state, including the Jagirdars, without the previous sanction of the British Resident stationed in his court.

The Maratha Jagirdars were broadly grouped under three heads: (1) The old Sardar families like the Nimbalkars of Phaltan, the Dalles of Jata and the Ghorpades of Mudhol; (2) The ministers of Shivaji and his successors, Pratinidhi, Angre and the Raja of Akkalkot, and lastly (3) the jagirdars created by the Peshwa like Raste, Patwardhans, etc.[5]

Raja Fatte Singh II (1789–1822) of Akkalkot had entered into an agreement with Captain James Grant, the Political Agent of Satara, on 3 July 1820, by which he agreed to be under the protectorate of the Raja of Satara.[6] Article 11 of this Treaty assured the Raja that so long as he remained loyal to the Treaty, the Company would protect him from the Raja of Satara.[7] In view of this Treaty an agreement between Satara and Akkalkot was signed on 11 July 1820.

These agreements were faithfully observed during the period of Grant (1818–20) but the disputes between the Raja and his Jagirdars on several issues began to develop after his departure. It seems that this problem of relationship between the Raja and the Jagirdars was discussed at length by the Raja with James Grant when the question of transfer of power to Raja was under consideration of the company's government. From the Diaries of the Raja, it seems that the Raja's demand for a complete control over the Jagirdars was not conceded by the company. The ambiguity regarding the relationship caused much friction between the Raja and his jagirdars in the subsequent period.

Maloji (1823–28) was succeeded by his infant son Sahaji II (1828–56). Tulajabai, the widow of Maloji acted as protector of the infant Raja and his brother Fatte Singh, but the Regency rights were exercised by the Raja of Satara as per the Treaty of 1820. It was against this rule of the Raja of Satara that the people of Akkalkot revolted in 1830 and the British had to intervene to suppress the revolt.

The local watandars and inamdars resented the administration of Pratap Singh, and under the leadership of Shankarrao Sardeshmukh, a watandar of Borgaon, they challenged the new administration. The infant king was arrested, the fort of Akkalkot was captured, and thus the capital was brought under sway by the rebels.

As it was incumbent upon the Satara Govt, to restore order and peace in the Jagir, the joint forces of Satara and the company congregated on the frontiers of Akkalkot. The rebels held the fort for some time, though they had to surrender it later to the superior forces of the company. But in the course of this pitched battle of 10 July 1830, between the two forces, Captain Edmund Sparrow of the company was wounded and died immediately. This perhaps irritated the British, who ruthlessly subdued the rebels. To commemorate this event Colonel Robertson, the Resident of Satara constructed the tomb of Captain Sparrow which is situated by the side of the road to the new palace.[8] The force of the company restored peace in few days and Captain Jameson was appointed to administer the State on behalf of the Company.

The original documents, available in the Parasnis Museum and the Bharat Itihas Samshodhaka Mandal, Poona, throw some light on this Akkalkot affair of 1830. It is possible to explain with the help of these sources the strained relations between the Raja and his jagirdars, the role of the company, the causes of the revolt, how the people of Akkalkot resisted the combined forces of Satara and the company, what happened on the day of revolt, and how was it finally crushed, etc.[9]

When James Grant left Satara by the end of 1829, all the suppressed bickerings came to the surface. For instance, the Raja of Satara was insisting since long that his jagirdars should attend the court at Satara held on the Dasara day. But this compulsion was resented by the Jagirdar as too expensive. Besides it was felt as humiliating. The Raja of Akkalkot earlier on the advice of James Grant, transferred one of his villages to Satara in lieu of this attendance.

The relations between Satara and Akkalkot did not improve and the Raja of Satara had lodged a complaint with Captain Briggs, the Resident to investigate into this problem. Chaplin, Commissioner of Poona, and Elphinstone, the Governor of Bombay, had sought explanations from Akkalkot, but as the Raja had assured loyalty to the Treaty, and that he would always seek the favours of the company[10] in case of dispute with the Raja of Satara, this enquiry was dropped as unnecessary.

The native rulers always found the frequent transfer of the European officers as inconvenient to them, as they had to cultivate friendship with every new officer afresh. The Jagirdar therefore requested Malcolm, the Governor of Bombay, to send efficient Residents to Satara and that the reports of all the earlier officers like Elphinstone, Grant, Briggs, etc., be preserved for the benefit of the new officers.[11] It is needless to say here that every new officer of the company was well posted with information about the region in which he had to work.

The outbreak of the revolt took place on 10 July 1830. Earlier, the Rajmata Tulajabai on 30 June 1830 had conveyed the explosive situation in Akkalkot to Malcolm.[12] Her complaint was against the officers appointed by the Raja of Satara to manage the state affairs during the period of regency. These officers, according to her misbehaved, violated the traditions of the Jagir, destroyed the canon, auctioned many things including the valuables of the royal household, etc. Thus the prestige of the Royal family was at stake at the hands of these officials. The new garrison employed by the Raja had imprisoned, beaten and put to disgrace the old nobles of Akkalkot. She therefore requested the Governor that these officers of Satara be immediately removed.

Raja of Satara who was waiting for some excuse to interfere with Akkalkot sent fresh forces under the pretext of subduing the zamindars. Tulajabai categorically stated that the zamindars were not at fault. She maintained that as the privileges and purses of the zamindars were stopped, some of them out of sheer disgust were deserting Akkalkot. It may be hazarded here that the Rajamata might have instigated the disgruntled zamindars to rise against the Satara administration. Malcolm, however, received this letter on 13 July i.e., three days after the outbreak of the revolt.[13]

Both Robertson and Dinkarrao Mohite, the commander of the Raja wrote to him giving a full account of the situation in Akkalkot on the day of the outbreak of the revolt on 10 July 1830. Both mentioned how Edmund Sparrow died of wounds on the battlefield itself. From the Raja's side the casualties were few: three persons died and eight to ten persons were severely wounded. Dinkarrao Mohite, the commander of the Satara Raja reported in detail the happenings of the 10 July. It seems that the people of Akkalkot gave a heroic resistance on that day. Skirmishes took place between the forces of Satara and the Deshmukhs and Sardeshmukhs who were deserting Akkalkot with their familes. Part of the town was set to fire. The officers of the Raja of Satara who were expelled from Akkalkot joined the commander. The Commander who had arrived from Sholapur made efforts to get canon to harass the rebels. It was raining throughout the previous night which obstructed the movements of the army.[14]

As the situation was getting worse, Robertson requested the Raja on 11 July to send two new big guns with ammunition and gunners, two hundred troops of the company including the gunners, and two elephants from the royal stables. The Ahmednagar centre of the company was earlier instructed to send canon to Akkalkot, and the Raja was informed that in case those canons reached in time, no additional canon be required from Satara. He should await a letter from Poona on this behalf, and send only two hundred troops, if canon from Ahmednagar were on its way to Akkalkot.[15] From these elaborate preparations one could guess the gravity of the situation. However, it seems that by 12 July normalcy was restored as Malcolm refers to a proclamation of the 13 July in his letter to Rajmata of the same date. This was in fact his reply to her earlier letter of 30 June 1830. She was asked to obey the orders of Col. Robertson, to avoid any further deterioration of the situation in Akkalkot. He also promised her that protection would be given to her son, if she desired to send him to the company, and attempts would be made to redress her grievances. It was also pointed out that if she failed to report to Robertson immediately, the royal family and the people of Akkalkot would suffer for this and no appeal would be entertained from her.[16]

This episode was concluded on 17 July 1830. Malcolm congratulated Pratap Singh for his prompt help and timely action. He assured him that if the people of Akkalkot disregard the proclamation, they would be punished. This would cause immense loss both to the rulers and rebels of Akkalkot.[17]

Tulajabai agreed to report to the company in Poona within a period of ten days. It appears from her letter that she was not satisfied with the decision, but she was helpless and had to accept the decision without any reservations. She writes to the Resident that the company had made her to accept the proclamation without paying any attention to the problems she had raised in her letter of 30 June 1830.[18]

The Raja of Akkalkot was unwilling to go to Satara from Poona where he was enjoying the protection of the Company. He resented the Satara administration and expressed his fears that he would be locked up in the houses specially constructed for the people of Akkalkot. These houses would be as good as prisons. However, the Raja had no other go but to meet Pratapsingh at Satara.[19]

The company suspected Tulajabai as the brain behind this revolt. The Diary of Raja Pratap Singh makes an interesting note in this respect, 'Jameson reported that Shahaji is a good boy, but Tuljabai has spoiled him. He, therefore, writes to me that she should be sent to her parents' place for some time and be paid minimum maintenance. She would be observed for two months and if she did not show any improvement in her behaviour, she would be separated from her son.'[20]

Thus this attempt of Akkalkot to cede from Satara failed in 1830, but this did not put an end to the friction. The Raja of Satara was deposed by the company in 1839, and the Satara State lapsed to the Company in 1848. All these territories went under the direct control of the Company.

Notes

1. This paper is based on original papers preserved in the Parasinis Museum, Deccan College and Bharat Itihas Samshodhak Mandal, Poona. The author is indebted to Shri Y.N. Kelkar who gave a few letters from his personal collection.
2. *Ithihas Sangraha*, year 2, vol. 3, pp. 6–7.
3. 'Maharashtra Under the Company, 1818–57', Dr. P.V. Ranade, Thesis, University of Poona, chapter 4 discusses at length the unrest in Maharashtra.
4. Memoir on the Satara Territory Selections from the Records of the Bombay Govt. no. XLI, n.s., Bombay, 1857, pp. 52–7.
5. *Grant Duff, History of the Marathas*, vol. II, pp. 326–8.
6. *Memoir on the Satara Territory*, pp. 52–5.
7. Ibid., pp. 52–5.
8. *Rojnishi of Pratap Sinha*, Ms. vol. 5, pp. 146–61, dt. 19 to 27 March, 1822, Alienation Office, Poona.
9. A.N. Pradhan, *A Monograph on Akkalkot*, pp. 59–60.
10. *Parasnis Museum Ruman*, no. I, File 8: 11, dt. 23 July 1826 *RIF*.

11. Raja to Malcolm dt. 5.12.1828 *RIF*, 8 : 19
12. Tulajabai to Malcolm dt. 30-6-1828 *RIF*, 8 : 7.
13. RIF, 5 : 2
14. Satara Daftar preserved in *BISM*, Poona letter no. 9, dated 10 July 1830.
15. *Parasnis Museum RIF*, 8 : 13.
16. *RIF*, 5 : 2.
17. *RIF*, 8 : 4.
18. *RIF*, 8 : 9.
19. *BISM*, dt. 23-9-1930.
20. Selections from Peshwa Daftar, vol. 42: 62, dt. 5 January 1831.

18

Land Revenue and the Economy of Broach in the First Half of the Nineteenth Century

S.C. Mishra

AN ATTEMPT has been made in this paper to bring out two major aspects of the economy of Gujarat, immediately after the establishment of British rule. The major fact which draws attention is the crushing burden of the *land revenue,* 'rent' as it termed in the then official parlance, which is uniformly above 60% of the gross produce, leaving the cultivator with barely the subsistence and in bad years, not even that. The second appears to be the continuous revenue tradition which was carefully maintained by the English rules; they exercised great caution in disturbing any facet of the usages to which the agrarian population had become used. An additional feature which may be noticed is the virtual absence of *zabti* or measurement as the basis of revenue assessment, collection in kind also appears to have been the universal practice in the whole of Gujarat—including the areas which produced the cash crop of high quality cotton and was the centre of textile manufacture in the seventeenth century.

The pargana of Broach (Bharuch) was seized by the English in 1774 after ousting its Nawab of a flimsy pretext. It was, however, handed over to the Sindhia in 1786 and ceded back in 1803. The other five parganas were ceded by the Peshwa: Ankleshwar and Hansot in 1802, Jambusar, Dahej and Amod in 1817.

Land in this region was traditionally divided in two categories: the first was government land, paying full revenue; the other was alienated which was held on the payment of either a nominal quit rent or was entirely rent free. This classification was the price reason for the first survey of the area by Lieut-Colonel Monier Williams begun in 1811 but completed in 1820. It is with the government lands that the early in English officials were primarily concerned.

The principles and practices are laid down in an early revenue letter from the Court of Directors to the Governor in Bombay, dated 10 January 1810

*39th Session at Hyderabad, 1978.

which in turn is based on a report dated 31 May 1807 despatched from Bombay. 'The principle on which the jumma or rental is annually settled in the Guzerat (sic), seems to be an equal division of the produce of the tulput land in cultivation between the Government and the farmer.'

As a rule, this theoretical division was commuted into money to the cultivator's disadvantage. There was a broad computation of the revenue payable in consonance with the quality of land and the crop harvested. However, the principle of bhag batai was operative in as much as 'as a security for the payment of the Government rent, the crop can neither be reaped, housed, threshed out nor sold without the permission of the collector or one of his authorised agents.'[1]

Division of crops and collection in kind remained the operative system in Broach till 1837–38 when the *begotee* rates were introduced.[2] With this introduction, i.e., cash revenue based on bigha-wise measurement, extended over the district in about six years, the position of the cultivators was no better. The revenue fixed was on the higher side; the average revenue for ten years preceding the fixation of the *bighoti* rates was Rs. 15,95,476; for the next ten years, it was Rs. 18,500,00, 'showing an increase of 15% (which was) out of all proportion to that of either population or cultivation.'[3]

That the jamabandi amounted to half the produce has been noticed; this was the system when the district passed under the English in 1803. This was also the practice in the twenty years, 1784 to 1802, when the pargana was under the Sindhia. The revenue letter from Bombay to London dated 20 February 1808 notes with a certain satisfaction the *rise* in the revenue during the four years of English rule. The average of yield during Sindhia's rule had been Rs. 8,35,105; under the English, the collections were: in 1803–04, Rs. 10,54,539; in 1804–05, Rs. 11,30,647; in 1805–06, Rs. 11,26,997; and in 1806–07, 12,24,583. This had been achieved by a general improvement in economy, as the Bombay Government put it, while adhering to the accepted principles, namely, 'that the established customs of the natives should be adhered to, affected only by such well-weighed improvements as have for object, the guarding more effectually, their own established systems, from such vicissitudes and abuses as experience has shown them to be liable; in short, to ameliorate their condition, without subverting the foundations of their hereditary rights; the preservation of which, as interwoven into all their manners and impressions, must tend, it is conceived most efficaciously, to their permanent happiness.'[4]

The Directors concurred in this policy. They noticed in their letter of 10 January 1810, 'Much has been effected since the cession of Broach to the Company, in the way of purging the ancient Moghul system of the abuses which had crept into it under the Marhatta administration: the great, the intolerable evil of which was, not the excess of its imposts, but the mode of levying them.'[5]

These were admirable sentiments and there is little doubt that the rationalisation effected by the English contributed towards the improvement of the Broach economy. The Governor's revenue letter of 14 April 1810 mentions this improvement: 'The general improvement in the state of the inhabitants of this district is further very observable in the number of substantial houses to be seen in the village where huts of mud and straw stood about four years ago.'[6]

This optimistic picture is, however, belied by some of the information which comes not from this period but from the late forties of the century. In his report dated 28 January 1847, J.M. Davies collector of Broach, was conscious of the 'stringent mode of taxation' his apology for the same being that 'it had the advantage of squaring the damands of the Government with the circumstances of the season.'[7]

Cotton was at this time focusing the attention of the Manchester textile interests; its lobby was active both in London and Bombay, exploring and advocating the possibility of growing cotton in India—provided the Company's administration would provide the necessary facilities and infrastructure. Alexander Mackay deputed by the Manchester and Liverpool Chamber of Commerce surveyed Gujarat and Maharashtra for this purpose; the Bombay Committee also investigated this potentiality in depth. As such, figures for cotton serve as an index for the problem at hand; namely the incidence of land revenue and the peasant economy in this context.

Thus the collector of Broach, J.M. Davies, reported that in 1837–38, in one particular village, Nudhara, 'the whole value of cotton raised on Government lands was estimated at 3,352 rupees, of which 2,603 ruppees were set aside for Government.' The number of bighas producing cotton was 392; thus the yield per bigha was Rs. 855 of which the revenue charged was Rs. 6.64 leaving the cultivator Rs. 1.91 only.

The following figures given by Davies, as he writes, 'speak for themselves.'[8]

Year	Average Assessment per bigha	Average Return per bigha	Nett return to cultivator	Remissions
1837–38	462	47 lbs. 6.3.2	1.13.00	
1838–39	1.8.11	15 lbs. 2.5.6	0.12.7	
1839–40	3.5.6	41-2/3 lbs. 4.6.7	1.1.1	

These figures are based on the price level of cotton as under: For a bhar of kapas, seed cotton of 960 seers equal to 312½ lbs. of cleaned cotton:

1837–38:	36.00
1838–39:	48.00
1839–40:	33.00

In terms of village wise statistics, the same pattern may be indicated as follows: for three villages, the land revenue charged and the amount left to village alone are indicated:[9]

Year	Gross value of gross produce: cotton grain	Taken as assessment	Left to growers	Village
1837–38	3352 + 4206	2603 + 3267	749 + 939	Undara
1838–39	2711 + 3810	1624 + 2282	1087 + 1528	Undara
1839–40	2475 + 7065	1574 + 4495	901 + 2570	Undara
1837–38	358 + 2541	296 + 2106	62 + 432	Soorwaree
1838–39	1079 + 2520	476 + 1116	603 + 1413	Soorwaree
1839–40	630 + 3446	395 + 2163	235 + 1283	Soorwaree
1837–38	1137 + 912	635 + 511	502 + 401	Awadur
1838–39	280 + 223	123 + 99	157 + 124	Awadar
1839–40	1085 + 777	614 + 641	471 + 336	Awadur

In another statement, the collector furnished the crop wise estimate of the 'amount of produce and the value thereof at the present market price of one beega of land together with the Government assessment thereon': (dated 1 February 1847).[10]

Produce	Average in Broach maunds	Value thereof	Average assessment	Ryot's share
Kharif				
Dhangar or rice	9–3.4	5.2.3	4.0.0	1.2.3
Bajiee	8	5.11.11	2.6.11	3.5.0
Jowaree	7½	4.2.5	2.6.11	1.11.6
Moogh	2½	1.12.5	2.6.11	—
Muth	5	2.13.8	2.6.11	0.6.9
Chowla	2½	1.11.5	2.6.11	—
Tull	4½	5.12.3	2.6.11	3.5.4
Gowar	7¼	4.5.3	2.6.11	1.4.6
Rabi				
Kuppas	3	3.14.9	2.6.11	1.7.10
Toor	5¼	3.14.2	2.6.11	1.7.3
Wheat	5¾	7.2.6	2.6.11	4.11.7
Sugarcane	40 (gur)	40	2.6.11	37.9.1

The collector noted that 'better crops like sugarcane, dhana, safflower and mustard are raised to a very limited extent the great expense attendant on the first and the want of any extensive demand for the other restricting their general cultivation.' Secondly, the 'value of wheat was considerably above the common average this year.' He also noted that generally two or more crops were combined together, such as pulses with jowar and tull (oil plant), but the estimates were given for each separately.[11]

These statistics reveal the burden placed on the cultivator, especially if he raised cotton. The structure of price system, involving as it did the middleman both at Broach and at Bombay, with its with fluctuations added to the uncertainty under which he suffered. For the collector the government too was a party in this loss for it 'is but too frequently made to bear a portion of the ryot's loss in either a large remission, or a heavy outstanding balance at the close of the year.'[12]

These figures which indicate the share taken over by the government refer *only* to this component of the produce taken away from cultivator. They do not refer to the additional imposts, certainly minor by comparison to the land revenue but still a charge on the cultivator. They do not also refer to the cost of production to the continuing annual investment in terms of seeds, manure, bullocks and labour—not to speak of the 'capital' base denoted by land.

The first is given by Major Williams in his Survey, citing the instance of one village, Umlesar, in the Broach pargana. The total payments to the Government amounted to Rs. 15,642.3.43. Of this, Rs. 12,402.0.0 was the Jamabandi and Rs. 3,100.2.0, the *vera* an additional impost 25% of the Jamabandi which formed 'an acknowledged part of the revenue as jumabundy.' An additional Rs. 140.1.43 was collected as Baubtee, a composition of miscellaneous charges formerly levied 'for individuals,' possibly as expenses but continued 'on account of Government.'

In addition to the above, local village charges pertaining to functionaries and other, called *parchooran* or miscellaneous, amounted to Rs. 1,307.1.0. The total disbursement thus was Rs. 16,950.0.43.[13]

These figures are one-sided in as much as they do not give the income or the return of cultivation in that year; they do not also indicate if the veyra formed a part of the total rental or was supplementary to it. In any case, if the Jamabandi plus veyra are taken as land revenue, and computed as half of the total produce, the cultivator still had to pay nearly 9% to 10% in addition. The portion left to him thus was no more than 40% of the produce.

A clearer picture is furnished by Alexander Mackay in his analysis of the economy of this district. Mackay was deputed by the Manchester Chamber of Commerce to investigate the potentialty of Indian cotton lands for intensive cultivation. In his report he argued that India could be a viable source of high grade cotton, an efficient alternative for the southern American states— provided adequate incentives were given, the oppressive 'rental' structure was overhauled efficient infrastructural services were provided and the Manchester textile interests were inclined to favour Indian against American cotton.

Mackay calculated that the *cost of cultivating* four bighas of land worked out to Rs. 6.8.4 which gave Re. 1.10 as the cost per bigha. The collector, J.M. Davies too had estimated the same at Re. 1 as. 12. At this rate, the average for 16 bighas, necessary for producing a candy of clean cotton, is as under:[14]

Government assessment at Rs. 2 as. 2 per bigha:	34.00.00
Other exaction at 20% of the above	6.12.00
Expenditure on land at Re. 1 as. 10 per bigha:	26.00.00
Interest on money borrowed:	3.00.00

Average total cost of production for one candy of clean cotton of 784 lbs. 69.12.00

Thus when the price of cotton per bhar is Rs. 30.0.0, which it was in 1842–43, 1844–45, 1845–46, the return to the cultivator on 16 bighas is Rs. 8.12.0. If it is Rs. 28.0.0, the return falls to as. 4; this year, it was necessary to give remissions of Rs. 1,28,656.0.3. Similar remissions were necessary in 1841–42 (Rs. 2,446,1) 1843–44 (6465.10.11) in 1844–45 (51,617.2.7) and in 1845-46 (4,40,328.11.5). Likewise, balances had to be written off.[15]

The following table makes this clear:

Years	Price per bhar: 2½ bhar make one candy of 784 lbs. of clean cotton	Remission	Balance written off
1837–38	36	n.a.	n.a.
1838–39	48	n.a.	n.a.
1839–40	33	n.a.	n.a.
1840–41	43	1,28,656	1,96,640.83
1842–43	30	—	2,01.942.1.6
1843–44	33	6,465.10.11	1,06,508.10.0
1844–45	30	51,617.2.7	1,29,543.2.7
1845–46	30	4,40,328.11.5	13,956.10.7
1846–47	30		

It may be noted that these figures indicate the total remissions given. However, as Mackay noted, a fall in the price of cotton had an immediate effect on the price of other crops, especially grains; for it meant a transfer of land to those crops which in turn produced a glut leading to a fall in price.

Another revealing insight is furnishad by Mackay. The average yield of a bigha in Broach was about Rs. 5/-. Deducting the government assessment, Rs. 2 as. 2, and the cost of production Rs. 1 as. 13, the cultivator, in an average year, was left with Re. 1 a. 1 per bigha, about 25% of the total produce.[16]

In his Survey, Williams estimated the living expenses for a family of husband and wife with three children as under:

Food:	grain 18 maunds for adults and 13½ maunds for childern: 4 kulsees 12½ maunds Rs. 13.00 per kulsee	Maunds: 36+40½ Rs. 62.00
Clothing:	cloth of the coarsest kind for all:	Rs. 20
	Total	Rs. 82

Other needs like milk could be met, Williams estimated, without financial expense; the family would hold some cattle feeding on the village green. Given this estimate, and given the above income of Re. 1 a. 1 per bigha, per season minimum holding of 40 bighas could be considered a viable one at which the cultivator would maintain himself in an average year.[17]

And 40 bighas, as Monier Williams noted, was not a normal but a large holding; the bulk of the holding were much below this level.[18]

The guidelines which were used for the fixation of the annual 'rental' by the district officials appear to have been primarily twofold. First, they had no wish to kill the goose, to disrupt the traditions which had been accepted by the agrarian populace. As such, they rationalised the prevailing system, legitimised the existing hierarchy and did no more than correct the abuses. Certainly, in 1803 and after, they felt more secure; in 1774, when Broach was first occupied, their plea had been for farming; this was no longer the case in 1803.

Second, the Bombay Government, chronically in deficit owing to its Maratha involvement, was in search of stable revenues, as high as they could go. The price level thus played a crucial role in determining the actual amount. In 1835–36, Kirkland, the collector, raised the revenues because the price of cotton had touched an all- time high of Rs. 56.00 per bhar. This injudicious enhancement caused distress and had to be subsequently revised.

It is not possible in the scope of this brief paper to go into the details of the social constitution and the economic condition of the agrarian classes and into the variations in the revenue demands *visa-vis* the different qualities of land and different products. The main purpose has been to indicate the crushing burden of land revenue and ancillary charges which took off nearly 60% of the total produce of the land—and used at least 50% of the same in non-productive activities.

The administrative charges for collection do not appear to have been much. Reporting in 1810, the Governor of Bombay in the revenue letter of 14 April 1810 provided the following figures:

Estimated Jama for the year 1808–09	14,31,076.2.86.
Actual collections	14,21,846.0.37.
Customs yield	1,18,410.2.65.
Total Receipts	15,49,436,0.0.
Disbursements	
Allowances to Covenanted servants	23,199.3.96.
'Native' establishment	21,522.0.0.
Judicial establishment: For the Northern division as a whole	1,70,876.1.43.
Total Disbursement	2,20,985.0.0.
Allowance of the Covenanted Servants	1.621% on the jama
Native Establishment	1.503% on the jama
Revenue, Customs, Judicial Total	14.262% on the jama
For 1849–50, Mackey gave the following figures:	
Gross Realisable Revenue	16,07,256.0.0.
Allowance to Covenanted European Officers	55,150.13.8.
Huzoor Cutcherry charges	32.579.14.31.
District charges	63.115.15.1.
District hereditary officers	27,738.0.8.
Village officers, hereditary and stipendiary	80,723.10.3.
Village Expenses	48,579.2.0.
Total	2,97,887.8.9.

The district expenses had, during the intervening half century, gone up by Rs. 76,902 while the revenue had increased by Rs. 57,820.[19]

Since this paper deals with the government lands and not with the alienated ones, it is not possible to go into the yield from the privileged land holding designated by these categories. A preliminary scrutiny was made into this area by Monier Williams and certain resumptions were made. Broadly speaking, the beneficiaries in these categories were not the cultivators but the handful of renter, non-cultivating elements.

The agricultural product price structure remained the yardstick for revenue assessment for much or the nineteenth century in Broach. This trend is reflected in the several settlement, revenue revisions, reductions and enhancements. Yet, so long as revenue remained the base of the official economy, so long as budget remained a gamble in monsoons, the revenue was close to the maximum surplus which could be extracted from the peasant. Broach was obviously no exception in this regard. Nor were the English the first to initiate this trend. Nevertheless, the pattern of agrarian economy which came to be generated—or which was already an established fact—did not allow the poorer peasantry to gain even when Broach was supplying one of the most demanded agrarian commodity—cotton.

Notes

*For clarification of the currency figures cited in this paper: two currency systems are used. The first used in the Bombay Presidency up to 1835 used the units, rupee, quarter and reas, the last being an account unit, 400 to a rupees and as such 100 to a quarter. After 1835, in which later figures are given uses the usual rupee, anna and pie, current upto decimalisation.

1. 'House of Commons: Papers related to the East India Affairs' 22 June 1813, cited as Item 2, 2, in *Annotated Bibiliography of the Economic History of India*, vol. II, part V, no. 9, p.121–2. (Parliamentary Paper).

2. Alexander Mackay, *Western India: Reports Addressed to the Chambers of Commerce of Manchester, Liverpool Blockburn and Glasgow*, p. 124.

3. Mackay, op. cit., 124–5.

4. PP: EIA, os. 6 and 7, pp. 119–21.

5. Ibid., no. 8, para 129, p. 123.

6. Ibid., no. 7, para 54, p. 121.

7. House of Commons: Report of the Committee appointed by the Government of Bombay, on the Decline of the Cotton Trade; etc., 21 July 1847: cited as Item 16-112-5 in vol. II, part VI of the *Bibliography*: 28 July 1847: Appendix P: J.M. Davies Collector of Broach: 28 January 1847

8. The table given below is based on two tables given to the above: 'Statement showing the Extent of Cotton Cultivation in the Broach Collectorate...' p. 41 and 'Statement showing the Value of One Pound of Cotton...' p. 43.

9. Accompaniment no. 1 to the above, p. 42.

10. J.M. Davies, 10 Feb. 1847, p. 44.

11. Idem: marginal notes on Statements nos. 1 and 2.

12. J.M. Davies, 28 Jan. 1847, p. 40.

13. Lieutenant-Colonel Monier Williams, *Memoir of the Zilla of Baroche*: Being the Result of a Revenue Statistical and Topographical Survey of that Collectorate, Executed by Order of Bombay Government: Selections from the Records of the Bombay Government, no. 3: Bombay: Reprinted for Government at the Bombay Educational Society's Press, 1855: Cited as Item 2.42–38 in vol. I, part I of the Bibliography, pp. 64–7.

14. Mackay, op. cit., pp.130–2.

15. Accompaniment no. 2 in J.M. Davies: 28 Jan. 1847, p. 42. For Remissions in these, see Statement showing the Extent of Cotton Cultivation . . . p. 41.

16. Macay, op. cit., pp. 120–22,158–60. See also pp. 128–32. For the estimate of the cost of production at Re. 1 as 10 per bigha, see p. 158.

17. Monier Williams, op. cit., p. 53.

18. Ibid., p. 54.

19. *PP: EIA*, no. 7, p. 120; Mackay, op. cit., p.139.

19

The Agrarian Structure of the Madras Presidency: Impact of British Administration

Sarada Raju

THE MAIN elements of the agrarian structure were the village community, the system of land holding and land tenures, and the ubiquitous caste system. The entire institutional framework was based on the village community with its integrated economic and social organisation. The system of land tenures comprised a complex set of relations including those between the state on the one hand and the agriculturists on the other, and the interrelations between the different categories of the agricultural population in several tenurial forms. The back drop was provided by the caste system, based on distinct rights and privileges as well as duties and obligations.

Before analysing the agrarian structure we may briefly delineate the general condition of South India in the Pre-British period. After the decline and disintegration of the Vijayanagar Empire in the latter part of eighteenth century, the political configuration of the country was a changing mosaic, with the Muslim states, the Maharattas, the scions of ancient local rulers, the erstwhile Viceroys of the Vijayanagar Empire and other chieftains contending for regional power. The advent of the European traders, first the Portuguese and the Dutch, later the English and the French, intent on securing commercial privileges by intrigue and armed might, aggravated the situation. In the later period the influence of the Portuguese, and the Dutch waned, while the British East India Company began to transform itself from a commercial to a political entity, with the French on the side wings as strong rivals. The middle of the eighteenth century saw significant realignments of politcal forces and the emergence of new political equations which culminated in the establishment of British rule by the end of the century.

The early reports of British Collectors and other officially inspired observers team with accounts of the desolate state of the country, the reduction

*35th Session at Jadavpur, 1974.

in population the neglect of cultivation and the general distress. This picture of political disturbance, bordering on anarchy, and of economic deterioration set the norm for all subsequent descriptions of the state of the country in the centuries preceding British rule. The Official pattern is fully reflected in Srinivasa Raghava Iyengar's monumental work. It is true that there were some officials who bore testimony to the flourishing condition of agriculture, industry and commerce, not only in earlier periods, but even during the greater part of the eighteenth Century. But most of the official reports of the early period belong to the former category.

However, many pre-British observers present a different picture. It is not only the European and other travellers who visited the country in the balmy days of the Vijayanagar Empire, such as Barbosa, Paes, Vartheama and Ceasar Fredrick who are full of encomiums on the fertility, abundance of goods and general prosperity of the people. Even those who came a century or so later, including Tavernier, Robert-de Nobili, Father Martin and others, expressed similar opinions. Finally, we have also the evidence of the early collectors and other officials of the East India Company who contrasted the desolation and destruction of the recent past with the flourishing condition of the country in the period before the Mysore wars. Munro in a letter dated 11 January 1805 declared, 'There are few districts in India which do not in the ordinary year yield more grain then is required for consumption.' Total famine or failure of crops was unknown, though local famines did occur. On the whole, it does appear from the vignettes of life and conditions available for the pre-British period, including the greater part of the eighteenth century, that the tenor of social and economic life was not unduly disturbed for any length of time, whatever the political climate. The continuity and vitality of the village community through the centuries also indicates that misrule, plunder and oppression were interludes and not the norm, of rural life.

The village community represented a well-ordered set of agrarian relations. The first British collectors, Place, Munro, Hepburn and others were unanimous in their praise of village organisation and village solidarity. Descriptions of the structure and working of village polity abound in the Records of the Board of Revenue, The Fifth Report of the House of Commons, Wilk's Historical sketches, etc. The distinctive feature of the village was the spirit of community feeling, mutual cooperation and self-reliance. And this set the tone of agrarian relations. The question of equity is certainly relevant, but the thesis of exploitation could no doubt be applied with equal facility to most societies of the period. To some extent, all ancient societies (as well as some not so ancient) took for granted the subordinate status of the working classes, and their exploitation was the accepted norm.

The evolution of agrarian relation is closely connected with land tenures and the revenue system, and the whole fabric of relations is interwoven with the life of the village community. There was a multiplicity of tenurial forms which confronted the new rulers. The differences in tenure may be traced to the origins of the village, i.e. the formation of villages—an interesting topic well worth investigating. The three main systems of tenure were the zamindari, the Ryotwari and mauzawar. Of these the system of joint villages prevailed with various modifications over a great part of the Presidency. Under each of these main systems and sub-systems, there were different forms of tenancy as well as labour as a fruit and the whole naturally presented a bewildering variety to the alien rulers. Their ignorance of the customs and practices as well as the language of the people certainly impeded their understanding of the situation. And it is hardly surprising that they not only confused themselves, but transmitted a part of this confusion to subsequent generations of inquirers. As far as the different components of the agrarian society were concerned, they were well aware of the nature of the interrelations, of their rights and duties, and the configuration of the tenurial substurcture to which they individually belonged, because, the whole was clearly defined by custom and tradition.

Tenancy was of different kinds ranging all the way from the Kanamdars of Malabar and the Uicudies of the Tamil country, who were owners for all practical purposes, since they paid the land revenue, found all the agricultural inputs and rendered only a nominal rent to the landlord, to certain categories of Poracudis whose status was similar to that of the landless labourer. Similarly in regard to agricultural labour, also, there were differences. The majority were serfs attached to the soil, such as the Pannaiyal, Muladal, Adamai, etc. Serfdom was in fact, a form of land tenure, with rights of occupancy which were well recognised. It was said that they even claimed 'mirasi' or heredity right in the 'incidents of their villeinage'. There were also the labourers who come from outside the village on agreement for term and who were free to leave at the end of the term.

The caste system was firmly integrated with this structure of agrarian relations. The landlords as well as the majority of tenants belonged to the Brahman, or other 'upper' castes, while most of the labourers, and in particular, the serfs, belonged to the lowest castes. But while this was the overall pattern, it does not indicate the entire picture of tenurial or agrarain relations. In practically all the villages, the village functionaries, including the taliari, the totti, the leather worker, etc., all of whom belonged to the lowest caste, held a plot of land as their vritti, i.e. as the perquisite of their profession. Similarly, while most of the bigger agriculturists belonged to the Brahmin, Vellala, Reddy and Kapu families, every one who contributed to the village economy was entitled to some land, i.e. even weavers, potters, barbers and other artisans, as well as traders.

The above different elements of agrarian society whether based on land tenure, profession or service worked in fairly close harmony and cooperation.

The system of village administration with the Headman at the apex, supported by the punchayat, the council or Sabha and the caste panchayats, ensured the smooth functioning of the socio-economic organisation. The inscriptions of earlier centuries, the accounts of foreign travellers and early official reports do not highlight discord among the different elements, or glaring violations of humane conduct in owner-labour relations. Undoubtedly there were individual cases of cruelty and ill-treatment. There was frequent oppression by rulers or their officials of the people as a whole but not of the body of workers by landlords. The available accounts indicate harmonious rather then discordant relations.

We need not seek for an explanation of the smooth relations, apart from the inherent character of the system. In pre-British times, and also during the first few decades of British rule, the natural growth of population was constantly checked by epidemics, famines, war and the absence of health and medical facilities. The early reports make frequent references to the low level of population and the scarcity of labour. His report on the Jaghire speaks of the great difficulty of procuring labour due to the paucity of inhabitants throughout the Carnatic. Employment was very easy to obtain. Only higher reward would induce people to enter new service and not always then.[1] We hear that extensive areas were left uncultivated because population was low. In such circumstances it was in the interest of the landlord to treat the workers well. There are occasional references to landlords owning a large number of serfs unable to maintain them because of reduced circumstances, and hiring them out to others, or allowing them to seek employment else where. But the serfs, it is said, would prefer to go back to their old master if he could afford to employ them. An enquiry into the conditions of serfdom in the Madras Presidency in 1940 revealed that the treatment was generally lenient and that landlords showed concern for the welfare of serfs. In fact it was stated that the position of serfs was better than that of free labourers. They were better fed and clothed, and many of them were of 'a stout, athletic appearance.' Hence they were no doubt reluctant to leave their masters and exchange their economic security for a precarious livelihood as free labourers. Thus apart from the evil of segregation, it appears that even the lowest class of labourers was not badly treated in general,[2] and landlord labour relations were fairly smooth.

The above account perhaps presents a rather roseate picture of general conditions and agrarian relations in the earlier period. It may be said that wisdom precludes generalisation about India, past or present. However, the favourable aspects have been stressed partly as a corrective to the over emphasis on distress, disorder and devastation in earlier Britsh Reports as well as the leather Manuals, Srinivasa Raghava Iyengar, etc.

One of the earliest measures undertaken by the new rulers was the scrapping of the village system of administration in spite of all the encomiums showered on it by their own spokesmen. The entire Revenue and Judical administration was re-organised on a centralized basis. The Ryotwari system of assessment of Land Revenue was introduced since, as Bentinck observed, it offered the best opportunity for a continuous increase in revenue. Concerted action on the part of the entire cultivating body could have defeated this purpose. Of the various village functionaries only the Karnam and Taliari were retained and others, including the Headman, were divested of authority and duties. It is true that local British official opinion was not unanimous in advocating the change.[3] The Board of Revenue was strongly in favour of continuing the village organisation, and fixing the assessment of the village as a whole. The Board declared that the dissolution of the village community would be like dissolving a joint stock British Company and asking each shareholder to trade separately so that he could be taxed separately. A committee appointed in 1815 to review the Revenue system expressed the opinion that the British system was unknown and unsuited to the country. Even the Court of Directors was at one time prepared to endorse the views of the Board of Revenue. But some of the district collectors supported the centralized system, and they received the blessing of influential elements in England.

The foundation of the new policy was that in India—unlike in England— all land belonged to the ruler, and the cultivator was only a tenant with no parmanent right to the land. As usual the Board of Revenue raised its voice in protest, and refuted the assumption of state proprietorship. Munro who was later the chief architect of the Ryotwari system of Madras, at one time bore testimony to the existence of private property in land. He also declared that earlier rulers usually favoured moderate assessments. Writing to the Board he stated that from accounts and enquiry he found 'no instance in which the Governments share was more than 1/3. In many it was not 1/5 or 1/6 and in some not 1/10 of the gross produce.' In spite of these views and in spite of the existence of innumerable inscriptions and records testifying to the sale and purchase of lands, the British authorities reiterated the opinion that there were no cases of sale and purchase of land because that the ruler owned all land. Policy makers in England, as well as many officials in India endorsed this view. The Indian Famine Commission Report of 1880 asserted that 'In India the immemorial and unquestioned custom of the country is that the land holders do not own the land.'

What was the reason for this *volte face* in regerd to landed rights on the part of the Court of Directors as well as of Munro and other officials with local experience? True, there was the desire to optimise the revenue, which was almost a point of honour for many of the collectors of the early decades. In fact quite a few collectors, took pride in declaring that they were able to maintain full revenue collections, and even obtain bumper collections, although the previous season had been one of severe famine with consequent reduction in population and cultivation. The abolition of private trade and private transactions deprived the company's servants of opportunities for acquiring quick fortunes. This rendered the payment of increased salaries obligatory. The needs of the bureaucracy, the maintenance of large armies, mounting Home charges and other direct and indirect remittances of England, necessitated a continuous expansion of revenue. Since land was the main source of revenue, the optimisation of revenue rates and its rigorous collection became an imperative measure of policy.

The authorities found in economic theory a convenient instrument for rationalising the above policy. Malthusian-Ricardian theory of rent declared that rent was an unearned income, having no effect on profit or prices. This rendered the landlord's rent a particularly suitable source of tax revenue. As Stokes[4] observes these ideas could not be applied to England, but India was an altogether different proposition. Having decided to appropriate the entire landlord's share of rent, the policy makers set out to prove that in India the state was the landlord. The theory of rent was combined with Benthamite Utilitarianism to the support the arrogation of property rights by the state. Apparently the greatest happiness of the greatest number of English man justified it. It was the Benthamite James Mill who was responsible for drafting many of the despatches from England relating to the Ryotwari settlement. A Revenue Despatch to Madras dated 12 December 1821 declared that the 'surplus produce (i.e. the whole rent of land) should in all be taken as Revenue.' These authoritative views influenced the thinking of the Company's officials in general, and long after utilitarianism, ceased to have any influence in England, it emerged, thanks to Mill as 'the corner stone of the Indian administration.'[5] Even Munro who had earlier advocated a moderate assessment on a permanent basis changed his views when he returned from England. Overriding the protests of the Board of Revenue who pleaded for the retention, of the village leases, the government introduced the Ryotwari system on the principle of high assessments and periodical upward revision. The Ryotwari system was soon extended over the greater part of the presidency.

The first effect of the new revenue and administration system was the disintegration of the ancient village community. The process was accelerated by the factors which were operative later, such as the opening up of the country through Railways, commercial contacts with the outside world, etc. The exhorbitant assessments and rigidity of collections resulted in heavy dependence on professional money-lenders. There was a great increase in land transfers and sales both on account of sequestration for non-payment of revenue and foreclosure by the creditors.

At the same time, the decline of industries and the destruction of handicrafts forced the artisans to fall back on land. This coupled with the slow, but perceptible increase in population during the course of the century radically altered the land–man ratio. Land began to acquire value and prices and rents rose in the second half of nineteenth century. The period witnessed the growth of large groups of landless labour, comprising those who lost their lands through sequestration or to the money-lender, and those thrown out of employment in industry. There was increase in litigation due to the substitution of contractual relations in place of customary ones. The influx or money-lenders from outside also led to some tensions though not so severe as those culminating in the Deccan Riots. However, the caste system which the rulers left untouched provided some continuity, while the headman still exercised some unofficial authority.

There was a general deterioration in agrarian conditions during the course of the first half of the nineteenth century. We find numerous reports of the growth of pauperism during this period. There was some measure of improvement in the second half, and a few districts such as Tanjore, Krishna and Godawari experienced greater prosperity. But even in this period, on the whole, the position of the peasant and the agricultural labourer does not indicate appreciable progress. Certainly compared to the potential of the country and the remarkable development of other countries in the same period, the improvement was negligible. Serfdom was abolished in 1840 but since the system was based on custom rather than contract the agrarian relations were not conspicuously altered.

The disintegration and dissolution of the village community as a consequence of the British Revenue and Administration system has been well-documented and adundantly lamented. But the question may be asked whether the village community was such a perfect institution and whether it was worth preserving. No doubt it contributed to the survival of the economy and of society and thus served both the people and the rulers, who should be assured of Revenue. Hence the fact that warring armies left the agriculturists alone. The individual cells of the politico-socio-economic structure survived. But did the village play a positive role in strengthening the total structure of the nation.

Each village was no doubt a closely knit unit, largely self-sufficient, with decisions by concensus and the village headman, hierarchy of officials and village councils ensuring a more or less even tenor of life. The internal cohesion which represented withdrawal and isolation from external influences was the antithesis of regional and territorial cohesion. It aggravated the fissiparious tendencies inherent in a society which was a conglomerate of diverse castes, languages, religious belief and cultural practices. It resulted in the lack of national even regional unity. Only a powerful ruler equipped with a strong army and an efficient administrative organisation could keep the region united. The ego-centricism of villages combining with the mutual jealousies of local rulers paved the way for conquest by successive predatory elements from outside. If the villagers had not been insulated against the worst repercussion of political changes and armed conflicts, they would have become aware of the great difference between Rama and Ravana. They could have roused themselves out of their complacency and organised themselves on a regional basis to resist an invader or support a good ruler.

Notes

1. Place's Report on the Jaghire 1799, Report form Geenway Collector of Jaghire in Proceedings of the Board of Revenue 26 August 1800.
2. Elijah Hoole, *Personal Narrative of a Misson to the South of India*, p. 174.
3. Hodgeson, *Report on Dindigul 180S, p. 25. Proceedings of the Board of Revenue,* 5 January 1818.
4. Eric Stokes, *The English Utilitarians and India*, p. 80.
5. Ibid.

20

The Revolution Behind the Revolt

H.R. Ghoshal

THE DISCONTENT in 1857 due to social innovations was certainly more widespread, though less deep-seated perhaps, than that caused by the absorption of great principalities and extinction of ancient sovereignties. The combined effect of both was sufficient to precipitate a serious crisis. It may be doubted, however, if the economic causes of the conflagration were not more powerful than the social and political. Truly speaking, the economic transformation which took place in India during the last sixty years of the Company's administration brought more misery on the country and its people than the political. And it affected nearly all sections of the population to a greater or less degree.

First of all, with regard to the land settlements. Although commercial consideration was the uppermost in the minds of the Company's directors and most of their administrators in India, and British merchants and adventures regarded India as a fat milch cow, it must be admitted that some of the British officers were sincerely solicitous of the well-being of the Indian people. Mountstuart Elphinstone, Thomas Munro, Tucker, Bird and Thomason, among others, were genuinely inspired by a desire for the good of the governed. Yet much of the settlement proceedings and many of the land revenue tended to the severe oppression and annoyance of considerable sections of the people. Lord Cornwallis's Permanent Settlement itself failed to commend itself to the class for whose benefit it was introduced. The sunset law, which accompanied the institution of the Permanent Settlement, by substituting the system of auctioning away zamindaris and mahals in place of the time honoured practice of distraining the zamindars for non-payment or heavy arrears of revenue, at once led to the ruin of a large number of zamindars and their estates in Bengal. The fact was pointed out by Rickards in one of his speeches before the commons in 1813.[1] Indeed the bulk of the issues of the *Calcutta Gazette* and its supplements from the year 1794 are full of advertisement for the sale of mahals belonging to ancient families of zemindars in Bengal.[2] As an instance we may cite the case of the Pathan raj of Birbhum, one of the biggest zemindaris,

*20th Session at Anand, 1957.

which went into liquidation within a short time of the introduction of the Permanent Settlement. Another great defect of the Permanent Settlement was that some estates were assessed too heavily and others too lightly. Besides, the Permanent Settlement was not at all welcome to many of the landholders and farmers of revenue. As late as 1833, and even atfterwards, the zemindar of Tirhut proved extremely recusant in coming to terms with the settlement officers, resisting their operations 'in a litigious spirit'.[3] In such cases, Government temporarily took up the management of unsettled mahals and held them khas.[4] But khas management itself was a source of oppression. The Commissioner of Saran wrote to the Collector of Tirhut on 18 December, 1833, about 'the continued injustice sustained by the landholders by the present extensive system of khas management or temporary engagements with malik or farmers.[5]

Bengal and Bihar were not the only victims of a revenue law. In the provinces where ryotwari settlements were carried out, in the greater out, in the Madras Presidency, Bombay and the ceded and conquered provinces (later called the North-Western Provinces), equal and greater hardship was suffered by the landholding middle classes, who were not exactly in the position of zemindars but nevertheless acted as intermediary agents between the rent-payers and government. Settlement operations in the south in the opening years of the nineteenth century deprived 'many of the chief people of their official rank and official emoluments, and cast them adrift upon the world.'[6] The discontent caused by this predicament was one of the contributory factors leading to the Vellore mutiny of 1806.[7] When the Company obtained from the Nawab-Vizier the ceded territories (1801) and from Sindhia the conquered provinces (1803), all sorts of properietor presented themselves. Striving after justice, the settlement officers completely did away with the claims of the revenue farmers, mostly talukdars, and brought the village occupants into direct relations with Government. The talukdar was for the most part regarded as 'a fraudulent upstart and an unscrupulous oppressor'; and to oust him was held to be 'as great an achievement as to shoot a tiger'.[8] Mr. Robertson, the Lieutenant Governor of the North-Western Provinces remarked in his despatch to the Court of Directors of 13 August, 1851, that in Farrukhabad 'the obligations of a treaty and the direct orders of Gorvenment were but lightly dealt with; and in all a total disregard was evinced for act of even such men as Warren Hastings and Lord Lake.[9] The settlement instituted in the newly annexed dominion of Oudh in 1856 struck down the privileged classes in the same wreckless way.

More iniquitous than all this was the Company's resumption procedure begun from 1819 for examining into the validity of rent-free tenures, such as jagirs, *madad-mashes, brahmottars,*[10] *devottars,*[11] etc. Numerous such teneurs existed in almost each district of the Bengal Presidency, most of them dating from Mughal times. To swell the Government revenue the resumption officers called upon the holders of all such grants to present them for inspection. Those who failed on account of their farmers having been lost or destroyed were forthwith deprived of the privilege they had been enjoying. And a great many of the documents submitted were declared forged. At the same time jagirs were resumed and assessed on the death of the jagirdars. In many cases there were injustices owing to the resumption officers' ignorance or misapplication of the regulations.[12] It is not possible to estimate how many thousand respectable persons had actually to submit to the inevitability of confiscation in this way, how many old families were reduced to indigence by the harsh doings of the over-zealous revenue officers. The oppression attendant upon the proceedings did not always escape the notice of government. In a letter to the Sadar Board of Revenue, Calcutta, dated 2 May 1837, the Secretary to Government in the Revenue Department wrote:' His Lordship is very anxious that no unnecessary alarm should be given to landholders, by the institution of suits on insufficient grounds to establish the liability to assessment of lands attached to permanently settled mahals . . . ,'[13] The resumption proceedings were however carried out in the most drastic manner, and in spite of government's notes of warning, and the warnings of some of their officers, in the North-Western provinces as well as in Bengal, Bihar and Banaras. In a like manner the Inam Commission, established in the Bombay Presidency in 1852, went, according to Seton Karr, into the titles of no fewer than thirty-five thousand estates, great and small, during the first five years of its operations, three-fifths of which were confiscated.[14] That resumption was a great deal responsible for the 1857 flare-up is clear enough. As early as 1829 a big crowd made a demonstration before the Court of the Resumption Officer of Patna under Mir Abdullah and Rahat Ali as a protest against the severity of the resumption laws.[15] Then, during the anti-British plot of 1845–46, the Magistrate of Patna, discovered a bundle of papers in one of the wells which contained a petition 'praying for the removal of all the functionaries at Patna and stating that the country would never recover from the effects of Resumption Laws.[16]

Ever since the acquisition of the Diwani of Bengal, a systematic oppression had been practised by the Company's dalals and servants connected with the supply of their investment. The oppression continued, in spite of occasional attempts to check it, until the winding out of the Company's cloth factories after 1817. Often it was of a severe kind and drove many weavers to voluntary exile or compelled them to give up their profession altogether.[17] Beating and flogging the weavers in the factories were by no means uncommon.[18] The oppression as such was not confined to the Bengal Presidency. A graphic account has been given by Richards of similar maltreatment of weavers under the Surat factory in the Bombay Presidency. The oppression and exploitation of the opium- growers in the Company's opium factories in Bihar also became notorious. But nothing like the treatment meted out to the ryots by the

European indigo planters. Buchanan, writing about 1810, has noted that the zamindars as a class were dead against indigo.[19] And a collector in East Bengal remarked later that there was not a single instance of an Indian zamindar starting indigo manufacture who had not in the end been ruined by his selfish European neighbours.[20] Indeed the whole system of indigo cultivation was vicious in theory, and such a system, as the Indigo Commission observed in 1860, could be worked 'only by oppression and ill-usage.' As the Company's Government countenanced such oppression, people had reasons to feel great resentment against them on this score.

If not within the purview of this paper to discuss the causes of the collapse of the cotton industry which came about in the early decades of the last century. But it may be noted that the root cause of the calamity was the Industrial Revolution in England. The Charter Act of 1813, which abolished the Company's trading monopoly, and the cessation of the Napoleonic War (1814–15), as well as the drastic reduction of import duties on British cloth, enabled England to flood the Indian market with her machine-made fabrics, while in foreign markets she was able to oust Indian piece-goods almost completely during the next one decade and a half.[21] The tragedy produced by this catastrophe begs description. About fifty lacs of women lost their employment as spinners, and vast numbers of weaver and other classes of persons connected with the industry were entirely thrown overboard. In 1832 Lord Bentinck painfully observed: 'Cotton piece-goods, for so many ages the staple manufacture of India, seem thus for ever lost. The sympathy of the Court is deeply excited by the report of the Board of Trade exhibiting the gloomy picture of the effects of a commercial revolution productive of so much present suffering to numerous classes in India and hardly to be parallelled in the history of commerce.'[22] Within the next quarter century some of the other indigenous industries, such as the manufacture of mixed fabrics of cotton and silk, indigenous jute manufacture, the ship-building industry and indigenous mining suffered much the same fate. At the same time the large influx of British private traders created a competition in many other branches of trade as a result of which Indians were gradually ousted from their position. The dissatisfaction produced by all this was vented in contemporary newspapers. Thus in 1836 a Bengali newspaper remarked that owing to the advent of European architects, cabinet-makers, jewellers, and tailors, indigenous workmen were reduced to such a state of misery that they became 'as thin as needle.'[23]

Such was the position when Lord Dalhousie's Government issued peremptory orders stopping the pensions of some descendants of ruling families. Among them was Nana-Sahib, the adopted son of the ex-Peshwa. It may be doubted if he would have jumped into the movement, if he had not faced this economic crisis. He suddenly found himself stranded by the Company's orders in 1853, and had no otherway than to take up arms against the Raj that had deprived him of his legitimate due. Four years he waited sullenly; and when the chance came, he was quick to embrace it. A similar economic predicament drove Kunwar Singh of Jagdishpur to side with the rebels. He had a long-standing grievance against the Company's economic policy. Dr. K.K. Datta points out that once when his father's estate was going to be resumed, Kunwar appeared at the head of a band of armed men before the court.[24] And when he was finally left in the lurch by government's withdrawal of protection, he was desperately driven to join the insurgents.[25] Nor would the movement have received the support of the talukdars and zemindars, had not the Company's harsh economic measures almost bled them white. Mainly for the same reason, the common folk, the Santals, Kols, and other aboriginals of Chotanagpur and the Santal Parganas sided with the rebels, though not quite actively.[26] Then, the sepoys themselves had a host of economic grievances against the government which have been discussed by Dr. Sen.[27] That the economic factor was more important than the social or political may also appear clear from the text of the proclamation issued in the name of the Hindus and Muslims of Delhi to the people of India in 1857 which throughout stresses the economic misery brought about by the Government's Policy, and in the end mentions about the attempt 'to subvert every one's religion.'[28] It may well be concluded that the rising would have remained localized, if there had not been so deep-seated an economic discontent, such wide-spread impoverishment brought about directly or indirectly by British policy, such iniquities in the emoluments and privileges of the soldiery, as we have noticedabove.

Notes

1. H.R. Ghoshal, *Economic Transition in the Bengal Presidency*, p. 34.
2. Ibid.
3. From Secretary, Sadar Board to Commissioner of Bhagalpur, 21 November 1834, Muzaffarpur Collectorate Records.
4. From Commissioner of Patna to Collector of Chapra, 10 April 1834, Muzaffarpur Collectorate Records.
5. Muzaffarpur Collectorate Records.
6. Kaye, op. cit., p. 112.
7. Ibid.
8. Ibid., p. 116.
9. Ibid., p. 126.
10. Grants for the maintenance of Brahmans.
11. Grants for the maintenance of deities.
12. From Secretary, Sadar Board, to Commissioner of Bhagalpur, 30 May 1837; from same to same, 4 December 1838—Muzaffarpur Collectorate Records.
13. Muzaffarpur Collectorate Records.
14. Kaye, op. cit., pp. 128–29.
15. K.K. Datta, *Biography of Kumvar Singh and Amar Singh*, p. 63.

16. Ibid., p. 65.
17. Ghoshal, op. cit., pp. 19–25, 29–30.
18. Ibid., p. 25.
19. *Purnea Report*, p. 393.
20. *Minutes of Evidence before Select Committee on Affairs of E.I.C., 1832*, vol. I, p. 210.
21. Ghoshal, op. cit., pp. 41–5.
22. *Gen. App. to Report from Select Committee, 1832*, p. 275.
23. B.N. Banerji, *Sambad Patre Sekalker Katha*, vol. III, pp. 74–5.
24. K.K. Datta, op. cit., p. 91.
25. K.K. Datta's *Biography of Kunwar Singh* coatains an admirable account of his activities in connection with the movement of 1857–8.
26. See in this connection P.C. Roy Choudhury, *1857 in Bihar (Chotanagpur and Santal Parganas). See also Report of Bihar Regional Jljecords Survey Committee, 1956–7*.
27. Sen, op. cit., pp. 21–3.
28. Ibid., p. 1.

PART 4

India and the World System of Industrial Capitalism

21

Some Reflections on the East India Company's Charter of 1813

Amales Tripathi

The year 1813 was a turning point in the history of the East India Company as well as of India. So far as the Company was concerned it lost its monopoly of Eastern trade, which was being assailed for more than a century and had already been shorn of some of its rich plumage. Principles of free trade were adopted with a few obvious limitations in the charter granted to the Company that year. So far as India was concerned, for the first time her economy felt the full impact of the Industrial Revolution, the implications of which were henceforth rapidly worked out in thousand and one ways to the detriment of native trade and industry. Its inherent logic of expansion set on foot an inexorable scheme of exploitation—more comprehensive and broad based than the Company ever dreamt of or was capable of putting through because that scheme now embraced not only India's consuming classes but her raw materials and her proletariat. India's external trade had been throttled by a series of prohibitive tariffs, her shipping either destroyed or discouraged by a ruthless and unequal competition, private trade, her industrial capital either rendered idle or diverted to the internal commerce crippled by a shameless plunder, euphemistically called land by the lure of Permanent Settlement, her credit system suppressed or absorbed by European banks that exclusively favoured the alien interests[1] her revenue freely spent to procure investments, a disguised drainage to England for which no return was made[2] her rural population ruined by the rigours of the advance system and the New Dispensation of Land[3] so that she fell an easy prey to the vast potentialities of the Industrial Revolution, let loose after 1813.

The years between 1813 and 1833, when the Company's trade was abolished altogether, gave the *coup de grace* to a long process of India's economic decline. Yet the Parliamentary debates on the Charter of 1813 and the evidence adduced by the witnesses on behalf of the Company show no adequate comprehension of the approaching denouement. Warren Hastings, Sir John

*12th Session at Cuttack, 1949.

Shore, Robert Thornton, John Tierney, Thomas Graham, Colonel Thomas Munro, Thomas Sydenham, Joseph Ranking—to name a few of them, were all of opinion that opening of trade would fail to achieve the end sought—namely, the extension of British commerce in India.

The Indian goods were better and cheaper than English goods but did not have a good sale in England because of tariffs which made them dearer than latter by an average of 20 to 25% (Joseph Ranking), Indian calicoes paid £ 3 16s 8d% on importation and a further £78 6s 8d on home consumption; muslins paid a 10% duty on importation and £ 31 6s 8d% on home consumption, wrought silks and coloured goods were entirely prohibited and so on. Said Ranking: 'If the duty was 20% or 40% less it would still be very high and I think many of these classes of goods would be consumed in this country.' If the trade was thrown open, even if the Indian goods were largely smuggled, they would surely drive the British goods out of the home market. This was also the conviction of many witnesses including Lord Wellesley. 'Had this (i.e., imposition of 70 or 80% advalorem duty) not been the case,' wrote H.H. Wilson later, 'had not such prohibitory duties and decrees existed, the mills of Paisley and Manchester would have been stopped in their outset and would scarcely have been again set in motion, even by the power of steam.' According to Parkinson the Indian goods were so dearly prized that, in spite of the duties, muslin was sold to the tune of £ 14½ millions during 1793 and 1810 and the heroines of Jane Austen and Henry Tilney of Northanger Abbey boasted of buying the real India stuff for 5s a yard. Thomas Garland said the same thing about Indian sugar: 'If it be brought here as cheaply in point of freight and the duties are equalised, I have no doubt that it could have a very serious effect upon West Indian Produce.' As for British exports to India the superior skill and industry of Indian manufacturers, the unchangeable habits and customs of the Indian consumers and finally their grinding poverty would for ever stand in the way of any extension.[4] The European goods increasingly exported by private traders to India had caused a glut (Sir John Malcolm), were selling at a loss (Thomas Graham, Thomas Sydenham, William Davies, Martin Lindsay, etc.), were consumed by Europeans mostly (Major General Alexander Kyd), could sell better if offered at a much cheaper rate (Thomas Sydenham), provided of course, the habits of the people could be changed—which, if at all possible, would be a slow and long-term affair (Munro), the printed cotton goods, though showing doubled exports, were bought by the Portuguese mostly (Martin Lindsay), and so no. The picture drawn by these witnessess was really gloomy and free trade, on this information, would be ill-advised and unprofitable, probably suicidal for, it would mean capture of English and the continental markets by the Indian piece goods, on the one hand, and colonisation of India by Europeans on the other. Lord Wellesley solemnly warned that 'the trade of India was vital to the Company in their political character' and as such should be left unmolested in the interests of good governance of that country.

Behind all arguments we discern the East India Company grimly fighting for its exclusive privileges. These pessimistic witnesses were either the ex-servants or the proteges of the Company, the Nabobs who had themselves shaken the pagoda tree and were now trying to preserve the fruits thereof within a closed circle. First, though the Company repeatedly declared its trade to be a losing concern, it was a mistake to assume so and its own arguments were often misleading, self-contradictory and unconvincing, (Charles Grant Senior's evidence). Political power since 1757 had only strengthened its mercantile status in the country. The consequent control over finances procured an inexhaustible enlargement of its commercial capital, surplus revenues could be sunk in investments, debts could be incurred for that purpose to an unlimited extent,[5] internal trade could be entirely monopolised and raw materials as well as skilled labour (weavers, for example) could be commandeered by virtue of sovereign authority newly obtained. Greater revenue facilitated further conquests and conquests gave virgin fields for exploitation (cf. Malwa opium). The Company could at last manipulate the economic life-lines of India—saltpetre, salt (Beveridge), cotton, silk[6]; and opium.[7] The tariff-walls raised before England did not quail it in the continental, coastal and Asiatic trade lay ample compensation. The old shipping interest, the role of which in combating free trade has been laid bare by the able researches of C.H. Philips[8] actively encouraged this pretension. The first decade of the nineteenth century saw its dogged determination to resist all attempts of Dundas and others (Wellesley included) to allow India-built or home-built ships of smaller tonnage to carry goods from and to England at a less rate of freight. The new shipping interest which tried to force the monopoly of the old hereditary bottoms was really the counterpart of private traders who tried to break the monopoly of the East India Company.

The third ally of the company was the London merchants who were averse to lay the out-ports open to Indian trade. At first in favour of free trade like other unprivileged merchants, they took alarm at the vehement pamphlets from Edinburgh and Glasgow and turned completely round to support the Company's cause. They were monopolists at heart and their idea of free trade was confined within the limits of the port of London.

Counter arguments put forth by the Company's enemies read like so many dissertations on practical application of Adam Smith's theories of trade. It was really the author of the *Wealth of Nations* and the Manchester economists who fought their intellectual battle for them. But they were the true prophets in the circumstances radically altered by the Industrial Revolution. The monopolists were vainly struggling against the forces of adolescent capitalism whose inherent logic of growth inevitably necessitated a complete removal of all medieval restrictions—social, economic, political and psychological.

The challenge of the Company's monopoly, irresistible in 1813, had been sounded even from its date of inception. The hostile forces in the first period may be divided under two major heads (1) the commercial capitalists who had been left out of this exclusive privilege, entailing enormous profits, (2) the mechant manufacturers who suffered from the trade policy of the Company, i.e. growing imports of cheaper and finer Indian manufactures that threatened to deprive them of the home as well as the continental markets.

The former registered their defiance by interloping, by formation of rival trade associations like that of Courten during the Civil War or that of Papillon after the Glorious Revolution. The free trade it sought was, however, a conditional and limited free trade conceived not as a general principle as was to be the case is the nineteenth century, but as *ad hoc* proposals to remove certain specific restrictions that bore down upon the complainants. In practice, it meant no more than the removal of the other man's privileges in order to supplant them with one's own. It was the expression of a particular class interest.

The second party of opposition consisted of the staplers, the bullionists and mercantilists who attacked through pamphlets and Parliament and forced the latter to promulgate the tariff legislations of 1700, 1701 and 1702, to induce the Company to push the sale of British manufactures even at a loss and to prevent the Company from freely exporting bullion which should better remain at home and augment industrial capital. They were frankly protectionists in the best Colbertian sense.

It was true that monopoly was the only basis on which merchant capital could be attracted to foreign adventures in the sixteenth and seventeenth century. When productivity of labour was low and the number of workers engaged seldom numerous, it was difficult to imagine a substantial profit being naturally made by investment in production. Unrestrained competition would then be more detrimental than helpful for growth of trade, the profit of which lay in taking advantage of price differences. As Dobb has said: 'until the progress of technique substantially enhanced the productivity of labour, the notion could hardly arise of specifically industrial surplus-value derived from the investment of capital in the employment of wage-labour, as a natural economic category, needing no political regulation or monopoly either to create it or to preserve it.'[9]

This progress of technique and productivity of labour were in the womb of time and monopoly, still advantageous in the early decades of the eighteenth century, stood its ground against the above-mentioned opposition after making a few judicious concessions, reflected in the union of old and new companies in 1708, or the tariff settlement or agreement to export English staples of a specified value.

Then the Industrial Revolution took place, not all at once as the term 'Revolution' may lead us to suppose, but gradually spread through a long period. But great increase in the power of production was registered from the beginning and the industrial capitalists, a class rapidly becoming conscious of its power and interests, so long satisfied with protection against Indian imports, wanted now the total abolition of monopoly which acted as fetters- on the full development of the new economic system.

With the change of circumstances the economic policy, advocated by them, had been undergoing important changes. In the period of Marx's 'Primary accumulation' or what Dobb has called 'the period of acquisition' their creed was crude bullionism. In the second phase, 'the period of realization' they wanted capital in a liquid form and markets for the products of that capital. In this phase emphasis falls more on a favourable balance of trade than on import of specie. Further development of capitalism was marked by shifting of emphasis to yet another economic concept, *viz.* favourable terms of trade, whereby (1) nascent industries would get protection from foreign manufacturers, (2) raw materials would be secured at a cheaper rate which would further encourage home industry, and (3) colonial markets would be forced to maintain an inelastic demand for home manufactures. The political and economic pressure envisaged in the assumption of such inelastic demand made the trade of this phase a 'scarcely veiled plunder,' while the growth of home industry was postulated on nothing but ruin and destruction of colonial economy.

The Sumptuary laws of 1700, 1701 and 1720, mentioned above, fulfilled the first demand of the capitalists. Those were still more strengthened by decrees of 1765, 1779, 1782, 1783, 1787, 1797, 1798 and 1799. Over and above heavy protection the home industry was given bounties in 1779 and 1781; excise duties on exports, imposed in 1794, were repealed in 1785[10] and a mere 2½% was fixed as duty on their importation into India. So far as the other two demands were concerned, however, though the Company ruined India's internal trade, partially destroyed India's industry and drained much of her Industrial capital—it was unwilling to put them through as completely as the industrialists would desire.

The industrialists could never be satisfied with the Company's efforts to push the sale of British goods in the East. They considered, and rightly so, the Company to be a rival manufacturing corporation (for proofs of rivalry see letter of Court, 1 March 1783 expressing alarm at the import of Manchester muslin) which had factories in India where they could exploit the Indian skilled labour and absorb her cheap raw materials[11] to the utter exclusion of other merchants. They were more bent on selling products of these factories profitably in Europe than on selling English goods in India or China mostly at a loss. They lately obtained political power, by affording vast financial resources and administrative authority to the Company, had only added to its strength as rivals.

Then again the question of raw materials. It was not the interest of the Company to send cotton or silk to England cheaply so that British factories could turn out finished goods at a cheaper rate and overwhelm the Indian and Continental textile markets. But the Company in both the respects, had to climb down before the mounting opposition of industrialists. The exports of British manufacturers were ever on the increase since the first decade of the eighteenth century and from 1857 we find a trickle of raw materials flowing to England. The trickle would be a torrent after 1813. As early as 1769 (letter 17 March, 1769) the Directors wished the manufacture of raw silk to be encouraged in Bengal and that of silk fabrics discouraged. Raw silk imports averaged in the first decades of the nineteenth century between 351, 825 lbs. to 624, 878 lbs. or 400,000 lbs. according to Macgregors account (p. 134). Imports of this stuff, a losing concern since 1776,[12] were bolstered up by reduction of import duty to 1s. 3d. per lb. of 24 oz. in 1765 and tariff perference of over 20% in the first quarter of the nineteenth century. Various attempts were made, by importing silk worms from China (1771) or by introducing Italian methods of winding (1770–75), to improve the Bengal produce.

Though the cotton of the E. I. Co's dominions was the worst that came to the British market, its exports were encouraged in response to the industrialists' demand. The first export took place in 1791 and during the American embargo it amounted to 46,185,476 lbs., 25,822,216 lbs. of which were consumed by British manufacturers.[13] The following figures for exports speak for themselves.

Year	Export of cotton wool (in lbs.)
1800	6,629,822
1810	27,783,700
1812	915,950
1813	497,350

The sudden rise in 1810 is explained by the American embargo of 1808.[14]

Export of indigo recommenced about 1790 and after the destruction of San Domingo plantations during the French Revolution it increased to a great extent. The annual value of this export realised in England about £ 3,600,000. Plantations began to be set up for the first time—in Bengal and Tirhoot, financed by the Company and the European banks.

The result of this policy had been foreseen by Edmund Burke—'Its effect must be to change the whole face of that industrious country in order to render it a field for the produce of crude materials subservient to the manufacturers of Great Britain.'[15]

But the industrialists were not satisfied with so small results. Nothing short of free trade, they thought, could open the abundant material resources of India to the full exploitation by British industries. They truely surmised this export to be merely a way of sending remittances home particularly when remittances could no longer be made in handwoven cloths in view of duties and machine competition.

The unprecedented growth of industry in the latter half of the eighteenth century put emphasis on volume of export-demand for the products of home manufacturers. In an age when industrial investment was little developed and the dominant interest consisted of the privileged insiders of the chartered trading companies, the monopoly gain on a given turnover was the natural focus of interest. But with development of industry it was gradually perceived that greater export meant greater opportunity for the employment of labour in home manufacture and increased employment represented a widened scope for investment of capital in industry, since each additional labourer was a potential creator of additional surplus and more employment meant more creators of surplus value. Whereas a change in the terms of trade (and hence presumably in the prices/cost ratio) tended to increase the rate of profit to be earned on a given capital and so was retained as an object of policy, an expansion in the volume of trade, provided that it could be purchased without any unfavourable reaction on the terms of trade, would enable a larger volume of capital to be employed at a given rate of profit. This proved to be the main ground of assault of Adam Smith and the free-traders of the late eighteenth century on the monopoly of colonial trade which served to throttle any expansion of the market in the interests of establishing a set of monopoly prices. 'The government of an exclusive company of merchants is perhaps the worst of all governments for any country whatever', declared Adam Smith and 'to expect that the freedom of trade should ever be entirely restored in Great Britain is as absurd as to expect that an oceana or Utopia should ever be established in it. Not only the prejudices of the people but what is more unconquerable, the private interest of many individuals irresistibly oppose it.' These vested interests had to be overcome, however, for 'the East Indies offered a market for the manufacturers of Europe greater and more extensive than Europe and America put together.'

Thus spoke the master, apologist and philosopher of industrial capitalism. When the War of American Independence shut off the vast markets of a continent and the wars of French Revolution and Napoleon's continental system threatened to shut off another, the demands of British capitalists for freedom in Eastern trade rapidly gathered momentum. America not only bought goods but supplied cotton, West India supplied sugar and England felt the immediate need of turning to the Old world to redress the balance of the New. The growth of privileged trade after 1793, a result of that demand, was remarkable. The 3,000 tons of shipping, provided in the Dundas agreement, were soon insufficient for trade with Bengal alone. In a letter from Hon'ble G. Udney, Member of Council to the Marquess of Wellesley[16] we get the tonnage occupied by private trade with Bengal in the following years:

Years	Tonnage
1794	2,473
1795	5,346
1796	4,657
1797	3,787
1798	6,223
1799	7,748

In 1802, after a prolonged discussion between Dandas and the Court of Directors—the E.I. Co. agreed to empoly extra ships for carriage of private trade. During 1803–10, 20,277 tonnes were used by private traders alone. The results were astounding, some said, a 200% increase of trade with India. The Company's agents, though admitting this figure, spoke of its unprofitability during the Parliamentary debates (Martin Lindasy, William Davies). But they did not give the true picture of things. The spring which the trade received from the operation of this agreement was such that upon a comparison of the exports and imports by the Company and by private traders during the years 1802–11 it is evident that the latter have had nearly an equal proportion of that trade; a circumstance the more deserving of notice at this time, because the amount of the exports appears to have been doubled within the period of the charter. In the article of the manufactured cottons there has been an increase so great as almost to surpass belief, the average of the annual export in that article between 1792–96 having been only £ 730 while the average between 1807–11 was £ 96,980. In 18 years from 1793 to 1811 they imported indigo to the amount of £ 15 million sterling.'[17]

This evidence was corroborated by Thomas Courtenay, Forbes,, the Chancellor of Exchequer (Castbreagh), the Earl of Clancarty and the Report on the External Commerce of India (28 December 1804).

Hamilton has given us a calculation of returns obtained by private and privileged traders during 1793–1809. The former's (the officers and crew of the Company's ships) amounted to £ 75,43,076 while the latter's rose to £ 2,12,17,283. In 1810–11 privileged trade showed a return of £ 21,99,322, next year, of £ 11,69,023 and in 1812–13, of £ 2,553,627, In the last year the Company's trade ruturns showed only £ 808,975.[18]

This actual expansion of commerce under the aegis of privileged traders, even unsupported by the arguments of the Manchester school, was sufficient to refute the Company's contention that there was no scope for extension of trade with India.

Let us, then, summarise their grievances on the eve of the renewal of charter.

They fell in the following categories.

1. High freight rates had been charged (£ 15 per tonne for homebound and £ 5 per ton for outgoing voyages).
2. Certain commodities had been barred.
3. Ships could be chartered at lower rates but the old shipping interest had prevented it.
4. Privileges, the foreigners, for example, the Americans, enjoyed in India, were denied to the Britishers. The growth of American trade was alarming. In 1806–07 they as well as other European nationals exported goods worth £ 19,58,000 and imported goods worth £

1,600,000 while the Company's imports were only £ 12,00,000. In 1808–10 the Americans exported to the tune of £ 17,05,814 and imported goods worth £ 16,27,612.

5. The system of pre-emption exercised by the Company over the native producers virtually shut out the private traders.

6. British capital, most needed for development of India's- material resources, had been debarred by various laws from purchasing of lands by Europeans, settlement of Englishmen in India, etc. The question of investment of British capital is very important, for untapped agricultural and mineral resources of India not only promised rich dividends for surplus capital but fulfilled an essential condition of capitalist development at home by procuring cheap raw materials.

Remedy sought, as mentioned above, was complete freedom of trade and in the parliamentary debates Lord Grenville opened the charge against the Company in the approved manner of Adam Smith. 'No sovereign, I confidently believe, has ever yet traded to profit, no trading company, I greatly fear, has even yet administered government for the happiness of its subjects—so strange is the necessity of this unprecedented case, that we must carry on our commerce at a loss in order to govern our empire to advantage.'

In easily the most able and scathing criticism of the Company's method of investment he asked, 'What is the real condition of an empire whose industry is supported only by advances made from its revenues?' Deploring the laws that excluded British Capital from India—which consequent growth of commerce would have rendered into wealth for Indians—he said, 'Where capital which sets to work the industry of a people and is furnished only from the taxes which they pay, where the sovereign, himself the exporting merchant, sends out their manufacture without return, himself the internal trader, purchases it only from their own resources, himself the master manufacturer, maintains the artisan at the cost of the labourer, and claiming to be himself also the paramount proprietor of the soil, actually collects in kind the raw material in payment of this territorial revenue, by what part of such a trade can the country profit? What freedom what security what competition can exist in commerce so conducted? What health or vigour in the community which thus draws from its own veins the only nourishment by which the vital cirulation is maintained? . . . .'

'What I object to is that peculiar policy which not only exacts the tribute but monopolises the commerce, compels the payment and forestalls the resources which should provide it. . . .'

In contrast, the private Britisher's trade would be a trade of barter—not a trade of remittance to be supplied by the surplus revenue or public debt.

As for the arguments adduced by the Company's agents regarding the impossibility of extension of commerce, Grenville indignantly pointed out that such would have been the reaction of Cicero about Britain or of some counsellor of Henry VIII or Elizabeth about the wilderness of North America. 'Who tell us that the trade we now carry on with India must in all future time be limited to its actual amount? . . . . By commerce, commerce will increase and industry by industry. So it has ever happened, and the greater creator of the world has not exempted India from this common law of our nature. The supply first following the demand, will soon extend it. By new facilities new wants and new desires will be produced. And neither climate, nor religion, nor long established habits, no, nor even poverty itself, the greatest of all present obstacles, will ultimately refuse the benefits of such an intercourse to the native population of that empire.'

Let us hear Tierney and we will get the other side of the medal, for this eloquent appeal for free trade was not entirely 'for the benefits of the native population of that empire.' Rank self-interest took the guise of righteous indignation and masqueraded for lofty humanitarianism. 'He had not heard', said Tirney, 'that any of the advocates of the happiness of India had ever proposed to allow any one manufacture of India to be freely imported into this country. The general principle was the Great Britain would force all her manufactures upon India, and not a single manufacture of India in return. It was true that they would allow cotton twist, but then having found out that they could weave, by means of machinery, cheaper than the Indian, they would say to them, 'leave off weaving, supply us with the raw materials and we will weave for you'. Now although this was a natural principle enough for merchants and manufacturers to go on, it was rather too much to talk of the philosophy of it, or to rank the supporters of it as in a particular degree the friends of India. They might argue very well as merchants, but very badly as philosophers; and indeed he could see no over-abundance of the milk of human kindness in this new Birmingham philosophy. In England, where the woollen manufacture was our staple, we prohibited in exportation of wool in the raw state, but in India (for which we professed such friendship) we were to take care that the cotton wool should only be imported in the state of the raw material. Although we pretended such anxiety for the good of India, we wished that it should only be a nursery for the raw material, but that all advantages of the manufacture should remain with us. They were to supply us with the material, that we might rival their manufacturers in every market of the world.'

But monopoly, turned to bay, was fighting a lost battle. In the new economic milieu, the impersonal forces of capitalism would bear down upon and overwhelm this instinctive opposition of vested but basis-less interests. In Tierney we hear the swan song of a fast vanishing age and an out-worn economic system. A new era had dawned, consequent on the mechanical and organisational revolution, which had transferred the means of production from the hands of the commercial capitalists and feudal overlords to those of the industrial bourgeoisie and the inexorable logic of their expansive ethos demanded a reorientation of economic policy from the state that would serve the cause of unfettered capitalist development. This the State could not deny as it was itself the reflection of the prevalent economic system and the instrument of the owing classes.

The conflict again is nothing but the symptom of the inherent contradiction of capitalism.

'In order to expand, in order to find a room for every new accumulation of capital, industry requires a continuous expansion of the market (and in the last analysis of consumption.) Yet in order to preserve or to enhance the profitability of capital that is already invested, resort is had from time to time to measures of monopolistic restriction, the effect of which is to put the market in fetters and to cramp the possibilities of fresh expansion. In the period of the system's adolescence the contradiction has generally displayed in the form of a conflict between the interests of an older generation of capitalists, already entrenched in certain spheres of trade and usury where capital had earliest penetrated and the interest of a new generation who had become investors in newer trades or industries or the newer methods of production. In the seventeenth century the contradiction found expression in the conflict between rising industrial capital and the merchant princes with their chartered monopolies; in the early nineteenth century in the challenge that the new class of factory capitalist threw down to the whig aristocracy and the whole Mercantile system. In each case the complaint of rising industrial capital was not only that the existing regime of monopoly caused an undue share of the profits of trade and of manufacture to accrue to a privileged circle, but that it limited growth and expansion—set narrow frontiers to the industrial investment field."[19] The nature of the conflict determined from the beginning who should be the ultimate victor. The free-traders won, the charter was passed. Within less than a quarter of a century the misgivings of the monopolists were belied. Between the charter of 1813 and the charter of 1833 we find British goods, specially cotton textiles, flooding the country from end to end[20] the native manufacturers being submerged and wiped out, helpless before cheap mass production. Indian textiles now exported to England were 'very low cloth, checks for sailors or lower calicoes or velvets,'[21] 'calculated for the lower classes' (Toone—do), and as they could not pay for the adverse balance, now becoming a permanent feature of the Indo-British trade, bullion began to be exported to England. The predictions of Burke add Tierney proved only too true. India was henceforth to be chiefly the exporter of raw materials. The seed of colonisation was being sown in India, mines were sunk.[22] Coffee and indigo plantations and silk filatures set up, which exploited the abundant humanity of India so that rich returns could be obtained from the British capital invested therein at an increasing degree.[23] What was left of the native spinning industry was destroyed by the large import of cotton twist, machine made and therefore cheaper than hand-spun.[24] The Third Committee showed its indignation at the salt monopoly of the Company which made a profit of 800 to 1000%. But behind this solicitude for the people of India was the desire to introduce Liverpool salt (Ramsay and Sir Charles Forbes). In 1826 the heavy protective duties were lowered in favour of India. Silk manufacturers of all kinds, prohibited until that year, were to be allowed into England on payment of a flat rate of 30% advalorem import duty, cotton manufacturers were to pay 10% advalorem and the reduction was comprehensive. But as Digby says in *Prosperous British India*, 'These burdensome charges were subsequently removed but only after the export trade had, temporarily or permanently been destroyed.' Duties on Indian raw material like cotton were entirely taken off (Sullivan—in reply to the Board of Control query). The result was an unbelievable cheapening of these articles. In 1793 one lb. of cotton fetched shilling ¾d., in 1815 11½d, and in 1831 5d. only. In 1793 one lb. of raw silk was priced 21s., in 1815 18s. Id., in 1831 13s. 7½d. only. So that these goods could be brought more cheaply, a cry arose in England to abolish the insidious inland transit and customs duties.[25] The charter of 1813 did not grant all Europeans full power to reside and own lands and invest capital in India. Hence the outcry against license system in the replies of the important Chambers of Commerce to the queries of the Board of Control, viz. the Manchester Chamber of Commerce, the Glasgow Chamber of Commerce, the Liverpool East India Committee, the Hull Committee all asked for absolute freedom of investment. This was a pointer of the shape of the things to come. The development of capitalism had reached a stage in the thirties of the Nineteenth century which required not only markets for surplus goods but fields for investment of surplus capital. The coming Railway age would soon solve this problem.

On 11 July 1853 Karl Marx summarised these results in the *New York Daily Tribune*. 'After the opening of the trade in 1813' wrote he, 'the commerce with India more than trebled in a very short time. But this was not all. The whole character of trade was changed. Till 1813 India had been chiefly an exporting country, while it now became an importing one, and in such a quick progression that already in 1823 the rate of exchange which had generally been 2s. 6d. per rupee sunk down to 2s. per rupee India, the great workshop of cotton manufacture for the world since immemorial times became now inundated with English twists and cotton stuffs. After its own produce had been excluded from England or only admitted on the most cruel terms, British manufactures were poured into it at a small or merely nominal duty to the ruin of the native cotton fabric once so celebrated. In 1780 the value of the British produce and manufactures amounted only to £ 386,152, the bullion exported during the same year to £ 15,041, the total value of exports during 1780 being £ 1,26,48,616. So that India trade amounted to only 1/32 of the entire foreign trade. In 1850 the total exports to India from Great Britain and Ireland were £ 80,24,000, of which the cotton goods alone amounted £ 52,20,000, so that it reached more than ¼th of the foreign cotton trade (and more than 60% of the total exports of India). But the cotton manufacture also employed now a ⅛th of the population of Britain and contributed 1/12th of the whole national revenue.' On 10 June 1853 in another article in the same paper he wrote, 'From 1818 to 1836 the export of twist from Great Britain to India rose in the proportion of 1 to 5,200. In 1824 the exports of British muslins to India hardly amounted to 6 million yards, while in 1837 it surpassed 64 million yards.'

The process of mass exploitation begun by the charter of 1813, culminated in the charter of 1833 which finally enthroned the ideal of laissez-faire. Western capitalism used this ideal as a weapon first to demolish the fabrics of mercantilist economy at home and then to destroy the village economy of India. Thereby it solved at the same stroke the problems of surplus good and surplus capital—for both it had found an inexhaustible market in India. It solved also the problems of cheap raw materials and cheap labour power—for with 'the arm of political injustice' (Wilson) it could seize the resources of an economically backward and agricuitural country abounding in both.

Notes

1. Rickard's evidence before the House of Commons Committee on E.I. Affairs, 1830.
2. Francis's letter to Lord North, challenged by Hamilton answered by Dutt and Sinha.
3. Rickard's 2 June 1813.
4. Munro in a letter dated 1 Feb. 1813, his evidence before the Parliamentary Committee, evidences of Hastings Teignmouth, etc.
5. Rickard's evidence before Lord's Committee, 1830.
6. Letter of court, 17 March 1769, 3 March 1775. Board of Trade letter 28 November 1778, re; silk winders—Blots and Verelst.
7. Parkuson, *Trade in Eastern Seas 1793–1813*.
8. The *East India Company 1784–1834*.
9. *Studies in the Development of Capitalism.*
10. Hamilton, *Trade Relations between England and India.*
11. The inequities of the system of advance to weavers was well-known in England through the writings of Bolts and Verelst and Ninth Report of Select Committee of 1783.
12. In 1797 the loss was to the tune of 4s. 3d. per small lb. First Report, Committee of Warehouses.
13. John Bainbridges'evidence, 1813.
14. *Report on Cotton Wool*, pp. 16–18.
15. *The Ninth Report, 1783.*
16. *Wellesley Despatches*, vol. V, p. 129.
17. Sullivan, 3 June 1813.
18. Lord's Select Committee, App. 1174.
19. Dobb, *Studies in the Development of Capitalism*, pp. 219–20.
20. Thomas Bracken's evidence—*Third Report, 1831.*

21. Braddock—before Lords' Committee, 1830.
22. Brecken, 1831.
23. Silk—Joshua Saunders, Indigo—J. Crawford.
24. Gisborne, Rickards, *Third Report*.
25. Shore's review of Sir Charles Trevelyan's Report.

22

Working of Coalbeds in Upper Assam in the Nineteenth Century

S.K. Barpujari

Hemmed in between the Eastern Himalayas, Southern Tibet, China, Burma and Bengal, the hills and valleys of the river Brahmaputra are said to contain valuable mineral wealth, the existence of which was little known till the last quarter of the eighteenth century.[1] Coal which was considered to be 'the mineral of first economic importance to Assam' was found in extensive beds in Upper Assam lying along the Lakhimpur (present Dibrugarh) and Sibsagar districts. The existence of this valuble 'hidden wealth' was recorded as early as 1826 by Captain R. Wilcox.[2] Mr. C.A. Burce, the early discoverer of tea in Assam also found traces of it on the banks of the river Saffry. Captain Jenkins, Commissioner of Assam and Agent to the Governor-General in the North East Frontier, reported as early as 1838, the presence of coal near Berhat and Jaipur.[3] Later discoveries and explorations reveal that coalbeds in Upper Assam extend along the northern front of the Naga-Patkai ranges facing the plains of the Sibsagar and Lakhimpur districts and further eastward upto the valley of the Noa-Dihing river to the frontiers of Burma.

Till the thirties of the last century, the authorities in Calcutta gave little or no encouragement to the exploitation of the coal resources in the North East Frontier. The meagre demand for this mineral, shortage of labour, transportation difficulties to and from Calcutta, and the insecure political condition of the frontier dissuaded private as well as state enterprise from undertaking coal operations. With the growth of the tea industry in Assam since the foundation of the Assam Tea Company in 1838, the demand for coal became considerable. To meet requirement of the tea industry in particular desultory attempts have been to work on the coalbeds on the feet of the Naga Hills which had extensive deposits of this valuable mineral. In 1837, Captain Hannay, Commandant of the Assam Light Infantry began work on dehalf of the government on the coal-fields between Jaipur and Berhat. The operations, however, suffered with the transfer of Hannay to Sadiya. Mr Sanders, Special Sub Assistant Cosimmissioner, took charge of the coal-operation. But as he possessed 'neither the energy nor the technical know-how' of coal-production, the project proved a failure.[4] Later he was placed in charge of the Dikhow field near Naginimora where also he proved no better. Attempts were nevertheless made by the Assam Tea Company to quarry the coal measures of Jaipur since 1840 to meet their growing demands.[5]

Captain Jenkins who was greatly interested in the economic development of Assam was not discouraged by Sanders' repeated failures. Rather this had convinced him the necessity of appointing an expert with sound knowledge of coal-mining to undertake the operation on a scientific basis. 'Until these several beds are examined by a competent authority' Jenkins wrote to the Governor-General in-Council, 'we may be losing time and spending money to great disadvantage.'[6] Anticipating that the government might at any time be induced to work any of the beds on its account, he made a survey of all the coalbeds 'discovered and supposed to exist' in Assam. Although his proposal received due consideration and his suggestion for appointing an expert was greatly appreciated by the Government of India, no attempt was made to implement the scheme.[7] However, the question of opening out the coal-fields engaged the attention of the Coal Committee which had met in Calcutta in 1840 and 1846.

With the introduction of Government Steamer Service in the Brahmaputra since 1847, the demand for coal increased. Situated as most of the coal-fields were near the upper terminal point of Steam Navigation at Dibrugarh on the Brahmaputra, it was recognised that successful working of coalbeds would usher in 'a revolution in the carrying trade by steamers on that river.'[8] In spite of this, the government of the day remained content by depending on private contractors who agreed to supply coal to the government steamers either at Gauhati or Dikhowmukh. It may be worthwhile to mention that no less a person then Maniram Dewan acted as a Government contractor for supplying coal to the Steamers plying in the Brahmaputra.[9] Jenkins on his own initiative continued to take interest in the matter. Under his direction, Mr. Thornton, Sub. Assistant Commissioner of Sibsagar accompanied by Mr. Mornay, Superintendent of the Assam Tea Company made a thorough inspection of the coalbeds on the banks of the river Dikhow which were discovered and partially worked at the expense of government by the late Mr. Sanders. The purpose of this inspection was to examine the possibility of supplying coal to the steamers from the coal-mines of Namsang in Naga Hills.[10]

The coalbed which Thornton and the party found then in operation by contractors was situated on the side of the Namsseso valley, down which flowed a rivulet called Namsseso. The thickness of the coal strata was about 10 feet, of which pure coalbed was from 3 to 4 feet. Mornay who had worked for sometime in the Bengal Collieries was of opinion that Namsang coal was of a very superior quality. Regarding the transport of coal by water Thornton said that the difficulty lies only near and under the hills where rapids are numerous.

He admitted that the difficulty of supplying coal from Namsang was 'great', but not 'insurmountable'. He foresaw no difficulty which could prevent the transport of coal by water to Gauhati.[11]

Although the Coal Committee discussed the question of opening out the coal-fields of Upper Assam, no systematic geological and economic investigation for coal was undertaken till the middle of the last century. However, frantic efforts were made in this regard on private initiative. To meet the requirement of its own tea factories, the Assam Tea Company had been working since 1840 the coal-mines near Jaipur. Another Company was floated about this to take up coal-production, that was the Coal and Timber Company or better known as M/s William Malcolm and Browne Wood. In 1850, this Company through its Attorney Mr. Browne Wood entered into agreement with the chiefs of Namsang and Kongan Duars for the liberty of cutting timber and working coal within their lands on payment of Rs. 60/- a year to each clan.[12] Captain Brodie, Principal Assistant, Sibsagar, did not interfere in the matter on the plea that the mines were situated some 10 or 15 miles within the Naga frontier which was beyond his fiscal jurisdiction. In 1854, the Assam Tea Company have acquired the rights over the mines through purchase from M/s William Malcolm and Browne Wood.[13]

In July 1854, Mr. G. Williamson, Superintendent of the Assam Tea Company preferred a claim in the court of the Principal Assistant of Sibsagar, the right of possession and working of the mines situated in the gorge of the river Dikhow . . . Holroyd, the immediate successor of Brodie who wanted to assert a claim to' the coalbeds in question on account of the government refused to recognise any such rights on the part of the Company to possession nor on that of the late coal and Timber Company 'to sell or will away what was not their own—as no tenure can be held vaild except that emanates from the Government of the country.'[14] Forwarding the case to the government, the Commissioner observed that, it was a question for the government to decide how far it would be wise to allow any persons European or native to make arrangement with the Naga tribes 'to hold or rent lands or to farm forests or to catch elephants or for other purposes' on their own accord. 'Any such general permission,' he added, 'might be attended with much mischief as likely to embroil the Government with the Nagas.' While urging the government to disallow any agreements made by foreigners, he desired that the government should assert its supremacy over all the Naga tribes bordering 'on Assam which would be conducive to the peace of the hills and the districts on the border'.[15]

In June 1856, the Lieutenant Governor of Bengal, without giving any definite decision on the particular question of the Assam Tea Company's claim declined to prohibit private persons from entering upon trading or agricultural speculation in the Naga Hills. He was convinced that 'if persons enter into agreements with the Naga tribes and mix with them in their own hills, conduct themselves discreetly and warily, and observe at all times a conciliatory and liberal course of conduct towards those whose labour they employ not very great risk is actually incurred.'[16] Consequently, the Assam Tea Company's rights over the mines remained on the same footing; and the rights were further extended and confirmed. The Company continued to quarry coal from these mines unmolested by the Nagas, and without any objection by the officers of the Government.

The first geological reference on coal resources of Upper Assam was made in 1865 by Mr. Medlicott of the Geological Survey of India. This was followed by systematic mapping of the coal bearing areas of Upper Assam.[17] A year later a notification was issued offering coal grants to the public. According to the terms of the notification the area of a single grant was not to exceed 640 acres and a surface rent of six annas per acre was fixed but no royalty was to be charged. However, the land was liable to resumption, if operations were not commenced within three years of the date on which the grants was made or work was suspended for five years or more. Seven grants in all were made under the new terms and conditions, but most of the grants had been subsequently resumed by the government as very little work was done.[18]

Consequent upon the Lieutenant Governor's order of June 1856, European and native speculators entered into the interior of the hills for the exploitation of the economic resources on a commercial basis. The entry of outsiders and their taking of lands, mines and forests either on sale, lease or rent led to disputes with the Nagas. Colonel Hopkinson, Commissioner of Assam, in his report to the Government was constrained to remark 'if our relations with the hill tribes have not proceeded from bad to worse, the improvement in them has not been sensible.'[19] In fact, the encroachment of tribal land for extension of plantation and exploitation of mines, of forests for elephants and Indian Rubber led to serious complications resulting from rent, tribute and boundary. To put an end to all such disputes, the Government of India promulgated in 1873, the Inner Line Regulations. Under these regulations, local authorities were empowered to prohibit British subjects generally, or those of specified classes from going beyond the line without a pass from the Deputy Commissioner. The Inner Line which was drawn up between the British territory and the independent Naga tribes made it difficult for outsiders to accept any grant beyond the line on under a tenure from any chief or tribe for exploitation of their forests and minerals.[20]

The Inner Line Regulations, it appears had little effect in the survey and operations of the coalbeds for the obvious reason that the official circles including Colonel Keating, the Chief Commissioner of Assam sought to attract private enterprise into the coal industry.[21] Keating perceived the necessity of the development of the Dikhow coal fields situated beyond the Inner Line. He submitted a proposal to the Governor-General in Council to aid the exploitation of the coal resources of this area. While submitting his proposal, he pointed out to certain claims preferred by the Assam Tea Company. The Governor-

General in-Council negatived his proposal as it would be in direct contravention to the Inner Line Regulations made two years ago.[22]

In 1874–75, Mr. Mallet of Geological Survey undertook a close and careful survey of all the coalbeds from the Tirap to the Disoi river extending over a distance of about 110 miles. Five coalfields have been named by him in his report; these being Makum, Jaipur, Nazira (Dikhow afid Saffay), Jhanzi and Desoi fields. Besides these, he also traced the existence of coal in the further extensions of the Naga Hills up the Dihing valley. Of the five fields named by Mallet, Makum field was considered to be of much importance by him.[23] In fact, it is even now considered the 'most important, attractive and well-developed coal field' in Assam. It covers an area 18 miles long and 3 miles wide tract in the south eastern corner of the Lakhimpur (present Dibrugarh) district near Margherita.

Inspite of the availability of the high grade Makum coal, speculators were wanting to take up operations in this field. In 1875, Colonel Keating framed rules of mining lease to attract private enterprise to the coal industry. Accordingly, the size of the grant was limited to 50 acres, and the holding of more than one site in the same grant was prohibited. But the real purpose of the rules was defeated as the terms were not sufficiently attractive.[24] Sir Stuart Bayley, Keatings successor, pleaded before the government for a revision of the rules as the existing ones 'would repel rather than attract capital.' His letter dated 22 March 1879 addressed to the Government of India in this regard states:

Unless indispensable preliminary of providing cheap and certain communication from the mines to the river is first undertaken by Government, it is certain that no lease will be so applied for. It can pay no one whose area is restricted to 50 acres to undergo the risks, with the certainty that competitors will profit by his failures; nor could it pay such individual speculators to attempt the improvement of communications. . . . Unless the Government are prepared themselves to provide these means of communications, he is convinced that the leases can only be profitably worked if sufficient inducement is given to a Company to provide their means of communication; and he is inclined to believe that in practice, the only sufficient inducement will be a virtual monopoly of one or the other of the coal-fields.[25]

These views of the Chief Commissioner received the approval of the Supreme Government as well as the Secretary of State for India and grants were made subsequently on the basis of the suggestions made by the local authorities.[26] In September 1979, the Manager of the Assam Tea Company on behalf of the Directors appealed to Sir Stuart Bayley for permission to work the Dikhow coal-field on an extended scale, 'a change which may induce the Nagas to claim an extended scale of compensation.' It was stated that the Company was agreeable to pay the government a royalty of four annas per tonne of coal extracted. Under ordinary circumstances, the Chief Commissioner would have certainly refused permission for making agreements with the Nagas without the knowledge of the district authorities; and would not have recognised any rights of the Nagas to minerals keeping in view that these actually belonged to the paramount power. Further in the case of the Assam Tea Company, he could totally ignore its claims as Section 7 of the Inner Line Regulations, V of 1873 expressly barred the acquisition or accrual of such rights.[27]

Stuart Bayley was, however, convinced that in view of the fact the Assam Tea Company purchased these rights whatever they were and have been working the mines smoothly for the last thirty years and that the interest of the state demanded that these mines should be developed, some kind of official recognition should be given to the aforesaid Company's claim. He recommended that the best form of recognition 'would be for the Deputy Commissioner in presence of both parties to have the conditions of lease reduced to writing and to have the boundaries within which mining is (sic) to be defined and marked off, and to make both parties agree that any dispute should be referred to him and that his decision should be accepted.'[28] In March 1880, the Governor-General in Council,, having regard to the peaceful conduct of operations for the last thirty years agreed to suspend the enforcement of the Inner Line Regulations against the Assam Tea Company and to allow it to continue working of the coal mines on certain conditions. These mines, situated a short distance within the Naga Hills were held on lease by the Assam Tea Company for a long time, but have net been worked till the end of century except for meeting their plantation requirements.[29]

Although in the last quarter of the nineteenth century there was great demand for coal by the tea factories, no steps were taken either by the planters or by the government to the exploitation of coal from the Makum field due to lack of transport. Coal required for the tea industry was mostly imported at a higher cost from Bengal. Consequently, need was felt for railway connections and with the formation of the Assam Railways and Trading Company in 1881 work on the Dibru Sadiya Railway was undertaken.[30] The construction of a metre gauge railway line connecting the coal measures on the Dihing with the Brahmaputra Dibrugarh in 1882 was an event of far reaching importance to the coal industry. In that year the Makum (Ledo) field was taken by the Assam Railway and Trading Company on lease. Since then work on this field was begun on right earnest by the above Company. The collieries are situtated in a line along the lower hills about four miles south of Margherita. Work on the Makum field was started by the Railway engineers and the name of Mr. George Turner, a mining engineer of South Staffordshire deserves particular mention in this connection. On his arrival in the Patkai Hills at the end of 1882, he saw nothing but 'jungles and outcrop' but on his departure a few years later he left 'working and prosperous collieries.'[31]

Work was begun at the Tikak, Upper Ledo and Ledo coal mines since 1882, and on the Namdang and Tirap mines in 1897 and 1898 respectively. The output of coal has risen steadily from 1,18,000 tons in 1889–90 to 2,42,000 tons in 1899–1900[32] and the capital invested in the collieries was about £ 3,60,000.[33] The working of the coalmines was of tremendous importance to the development of Eastern Assam. The tea industry in particular got a great fillip due to the availability of good quality coal at reasonable prices. At the same time, communication by rail, river and road improved, and which in its turn encouraged the establishment of markets and 'hauts' in different places in close proximity to the collieries. The lands strewn with coal were not suitable for rice; the greater part of it would have remained as impenetrable jungles had it not been cleared for coal-mining. With the concentration of labourers in the mining centres, the demand for rice increased considerably and the local cultivators earned profits by selling their surplus. Besides giving an impetus to agriculture, the collieries offered them an alternative source of employment in different kinds of work.

The changes brought about by foreign capital and enterprise in the coal-fields of Upper Assam has been graphically described by B.C. Allen in his Gazetteer for the district of Lakhimpur (1905) in the following lines:

A quarter of a century ago the hills near Margherita, and a belt of country at their feet 15 to 20 miles in width, were clothed with dense tree forest, the home of nothing more interesting and useful than wild beasts . . . . But on the bank of the Dihing an extraordinary change has taken place. The forest has been felled, the Makum garden has been put out with nearly 2000 acres of the finest tea, a flourishing bazar has been established . . . . Columns of smoke curl up into the air from the saw mills and the railway workshops, and the lower hills are dotted with fine bunglows, surrounded with trim lawns ad gardens.[34]

Notes

1. F. Hamilton, *An Account of Assam*, ed. S.K., Bhuyan, pp. 46–7. B.R. Pemberton, *Eastern Frontier of india*, pp. 85–6.
2. R. Wilcox, Memoir of a Survey of Assam, etc. (1825–28) vide Selection of Papers regarding the hill tracts between Assam and Burma, 1873, p. 5.
3. Cited in H.K. Barpujari, 'The Surveys and Operations at the Petroleum Springs and Coalbeds in Assam (1826–58)', vide *Proceedings Indian Hiistorcal Record Commission*, 1958, Trivandrum, vol. XXXIV, part II, pp. 69–7.
4. Ibid.
5. Ibid.
6. Ibid.
7. Ibid.
8. B.C. Allen, *District Gazetteer of Assam*, pp. 186–93.

9. T.E. Rogers, 'Coalbeds in Namsang Naga Hills', vide *JASB*, vol. XVII, 1848, pp. 489–91.

10. Ibid.

11. Ibid.

12. *Bengal Judicial Proceedings*, 26 July 1855, no. 56.

13. Ibid.

14. *Bengal Judicial Proceedings*, July 1854, no. 58.

15. Ibid., July 1855, no. 60.

16. Ibid.

17. *Account of the Province of Assam, Shillong*, 1903, p. 38. Cyril, S. Fox, *The Economic Mineral Resources of Assam*, p. 15.

18. B.C. Allen, *District Gazetteer of Assam*, pp. 186–93.

19. *Bengal Judicial Proceedings*, 1871, no. 30.

20. *Account of the Province of Assam*, p. 156, E. A. Gait, *History of Assam*, pp. 334–45.

21. *Foreign Political Proceedings*, March 1880 (B). nos. 316–7.

22. Ibid.

23. Cyril, S. Fox, *The Economic Mineral Resources of Assam*, p. 14, *Account of the Province of Assam*, p. 38.

24. B.C. Allen, *District Gazetteer of Assam*, pp. 187–93.

25. Ibid.

26. Ibid.

27. *Foreign Political Proceedings*, March 1880 (B), nos. 316–17.

28. Ibid.

29. Ibid.

30. P.C. Goswami, *Economic Development of Assam*, pp. 158–59, W.R.. Gawnthrop, *Story of Assam Railways and Trading Company*, pp. 26–32.

31. Ibid.

32. Substantial quantities of coal were sent to Calcutta and in 1893, the Company's stock of coal was sold to various Shipping Companies, but this was- discontinued due to unprofitability.

33. B.C. Allen, *District Gazetteer of Assam*, pp. 186–93.

34. Ibid.

23

Opportunism of Free Trade: Lancashire Cotton Famine and Indian Cotton Cultivation

Dwijendra Tripathi

SOME TIME ago, Professors J. Gallagher and R. Robinson propounded their famous thesis that economic aggression was the cornerstone of the British imperial policy during the nineteenth century, no matter what persons or parties were in office. The salient features of this policy, according to the authors, were overseas trade, investment, migration and culture. To support their hypothesis, the authors have cited, among many examples, the governmental promotion in India of products required by British industry.[1] The present article examines this thesis in terms of the British policy toward the cultivation of cotton in India during a period of virtual starvation of Lancashire mills caused by the interruption in the supplies of raw cotton from the United States.[2]

Several years before the American Civil War the British Cotton interests had realized the danger inherent in their too great a dependence on a single source of supply. They had pointed to the government the necessity of promoting cotton cultivation in India. During the past fifteen years the Manchester School of free Traders had taken up the cause and urged the government to adopt such measures as to enable India to be an alternative source of supply. Several enquiries conducted by experts had confirmed their faith in latent capacity of India which, if properly developed could, in their view, feed Lancashine.[3] After 1857, they has carried on their propaganda in a more systematic and vigorous way through the Cotton Supply Association formed that year. But since cheap cotton was available conveniently from a different source, the government, while sympathizing with the demand to promote cotton cultivation in India, remained inactive in practice. But the propaganda had its effect and when the War came, the press and the public looked to India with hopes and confidence.[4]

*29th Session at Patiala, 1967.

Manchester's demands relating to cotton cultivation in India were mainly two: (i) adoption of measures to increase the quantity of cotton cultivated in India and to improve its quality; (ii) enactment of a legislation to facilitate the purchase of waste land by Englishmen who by their superior skill might revolutionize the cultivation of the staple.[5]

As regards the first demand the government could do little in a legitimate way. Cotton was a subordinate crop in India grown mainly for internal consumption. Although the crisis in the British textile industry caused much excitement in the Indian cotton circles and during the first year of the War the Indians exported to Britain almost anything which resembled cotton wool, it was obvious that without increasing the acreage under cultivation, India could not feed Lancashire. There was no need for governmental action however. The free trader Sir Charles Wood, the Secretary of State, and Lord Canning, the Governor-General, believed that the market forces, the rising prices of the staple in the Liverpool market, would do the trick.[6]

A resolution of the Indian viceroy reflected this faith. Issued on 28 February 1861, the resolution urged the British merchants to send their agents to the cotton districts in the interior to procure whatever quantity was available and to adopt measures to reduce the number of intermediaries between producers and exporters. While promising to make available all possible statistical information, the Governor-General ruled out any step which might place the government 'in the position of the private capitalist cultivator or speculator' or in any way interfered with private enterprise. The Governor-General reiterated this 'first principle' of his policy in his instructions to the local governments of Bengal, Bombay and Madras to compile cotton statistics in each of the three presidencies. The handbooks which the local governments published within a year contained vital information regarding what had already been done in the field of cotton cultivation indicating the direction in which further efforts were necessary.[7]

To what extent these measures contributed to expanding the area of cotton cultivation could be anybody's guess. It was however necessary to improve the quality, for Indian short staple could be of little use to the British mills which had been designed for long staple varieties. In 1860 the government had abandoned the experiments which had been carried on since 1789 to grow exotic or foreign varieties, but the private efforts had continued. These were intensified in the face of British distress.[8] But there was little that the government could do without compromising its free trade attitude. As the pressure mounted, the Governor-General issued a resolution on 9 August 1861 announcing the offer of prizes in each Presidency to the grower of the largest quantity of cotton combined with the best quality during the current and the next cotton season. The ostensible purpose of this measure was 'to set the slow moving people of this country in motion', but Canning had an uneasy conscience about the propriety and equity of his action, for he suspected that it transgressed the 'Limits of Government's activity'. The Secretary of State, however, assured him of his support. 'I won't find fault with your prize', he wrote to Canning, 'It is quite right to do anything at present to show that the Government of India is alive to the crisis.' Wood, however, asked Canning not to repeat the offer of prizes.[9]

II

The cotton crisis had put the Government of Bombay in a difficult position. With jurisdiction over the largest cotton producing region, it had greater responsibility. Its action, therefore, had to be more drastic. In this context, two measures of this government assume special significance.

The act to check adulteration of cotton and fraud in cotton trade was a direct outcome of pressure from the Indian cotton interests. These evils had long hampered the growth of cotton trade. Indian traders would seldom ship their staple in a pure state; it was full of dirt and seeds and stones. There were a few regulations against such misdeeds, but they were not applicable to the whole of the Presidency. In any case their provisions were too inadequate. Convinced that adulteration and fraud had increased after the beginning of American hostilities, the Bombay Cotton circles became 'clamorous' for reform.

A private bill to check such practices was moved in September 1862 by a Bombay cotton merchant belonging to a famous Bombay firm—Michael Scott and Co. Justifying the measure, M.H. Scott, the mover, said that 'during the past twelve' months adulteration of Indian cotton had been greater than during the last ten years and that inferior cotton was shipped in the bags of superior variety. Pointing out that 'the subject of Indian cotton had attracted much attention' at the moment Scott pleaded for the adoption of his bill which provided for punishment of fraud or adulteration by fine not exceeding Rs. 1,000. After considerable debate the bill was passed in April 1863. Sir Bartle Frere, the Governor, though dissatisfied because the provisions 'did not go far enough', gave his assent, but he was not quite sure what the attitude of the Governor-General would be.[10]

Lord Elgin, who had succeeded Canning as Governor-General in March 1861, did not object and the act came into force on 1 February 1864. Under its provisions, the government appointed cotton inspectors to detect the cases of adulteration and fraud at the pressing sites, and also in the interior.

The legislation was more successful then the offer of prizes in achieving the objective but the problem of improving the quality continued to afflict the mind of the authorities. Wood, though convinced that there was little that the state could do in a 'legitimate way', anxiously enquired of Frere in May 1863 whether the government could adopt any measure if the conditions of the time failed to induce the cultivators to improve the quality of their produce. Frere was positive that the participation of the government in the processes of cultivation, cleaning, and packing was the only way to achieve the objective. He 'would not have suggested this two years ago' but since private skill and enterprise was not 'coming forward in time to be of use in the present crisis,' official interference, he emphasized, would be 'more than useful'.[11] Three months later he appointed G.F. Forbes, who had been associated with cotton experiments in Dharwar as Cotton Commissioner and gave him unlimited power to take any step conducive to increasing quantity and improving quality.[12] Frere had little doubt that Wood would acquiesce in his decision.

Forbes's activities, which had full backing and support of the Government of Bombay, threw overboard the 'first principle' of Canning's resolution of 28 February 1861. Forbes's first anxiety was to restore to its original purity the Dharwar acclimatized seed which had deteriorated as a result of the admixture of the exotic and native varieties. In order to achieve the objective Forbes decided to buy cultivated fields from the ryots in order to pick up separately cotton of different descriptions and thus to procure unmixed seeds for the next showing season. The government granted him a sum of Rs. 6,000, for this purpose. In the meantime, anti-cotton fraud legislation came into effect and Forbes's scheme became unnecessary and yet Forbes paid a sum of Rs. 800, to the contractors to cover minor expenses for keeping the seeds of different varieties separately. Later in order to ensure the success of the Dharwar acclimatized seed in Berar, Forbes reported to direct cultivation in 1864, although he had to pay exorbitant price for land while the cost of cultivation was 'extravagant in the extreme.' The experiment confirmed Forbes's opinion that Berar soil was suitable for growing better variety. On recommendation, the government of Central Provinces also decided early in 1865 to start experimental cultivation in Nagpore.[13]

III

The efforts to persuade the government to introduce sweeping land reforms in India, were only partially successful. As early as 1857, Lord Stanley, Wood's successor, had asked the Governor-General to consider the possibility of granting waste land to interested parties in fee simple and redeeming the land tax which was intimately connected with the problem of perpetual grant.[14] Nothing came out of these instructions for three years, and in his resolution of 28 February Canning maintained that the question was of no immediate concern to crisis.

British cotton interests, on the contrary, were of the opinion that a fee simple land tenure to which the Englishman were accustomed, would facilitate the settlement of India by Englishmen possessing superior skill to grow better cotton. They, therefore, represented to the House of Commons and the Governor-General. The latter, although resenting the tone and nonsensical arguments of these representations, issued an order on 17 October 1861, for under the impact of a 'real cotton famine' the nation and Parliament might follow the cotton interests.[15] Canning's order which authorized the sale of waste land at uniform rate irrespective of location and the redemption of land tax of a limited area gave 'general satisfaction' to England. *The Cotton Supply Reporter*, the official organ of the Cotton Supply Association, welcomed it, the *London Times* viewed it as the harbinger of a social revolution and the *Money Market Review* termed it as the 'Magna Carta' of India.[16] But Wood was unhappy. He ruled out the redemption of land tax, for this would result in the loss of revenue. He opposed uniform rates and ordered land survey in order to determine minimum price in each locality before effecting the sale.[17]

Obviously Wood's action was bound to delay the sale of waste land. He had taken almost a year to make up his mind and the issuance of his orders coincided with the controversy regarding a law of contract. The European settlers in India had agitated for years for an effective measure to compel the poor Indian cultivator to fulfil his promise to deliver a fixed portion of the produce in return for the money borrowed to finance his agriculture. The British cotton interests, after the onset of cotton crisis, set their heart on this demand pleading that a good contract law would augment India's capacity to supply Lancashire. They pleaded that breach of contract should be made a criminal offence.

The Indian authorities were sympathetic, but Wood was not. The demand for a contract law was too closely intermixed with the notorious indigo riots of 1860 and had gained momentum with the publication of the report of the Indigo Commission which had enquired into these ugly incidents. All efforts, pressure and persuasion failed to dissuade the Secretary of State from his deep-seated belief that a contract law would be interpreted as a 'special indigo measure.' Moreover, it would be unjust, he thought, to punish 'a breach of contract as a crime.' On his insistence the Government of India dropped in December 1862 a bill which had been initiated in March 1861.[18]

Manchester would not take it lying down. Convinced that it was Wood's obstinacy which barred the inflow of supplies from India, they decided to remove him from the scene. A former Finance Member of Viceroy's Council, Samuel Laing, who had crossed swords with the Secretary of State on the issue of Indian budget made common cause with them. Having failed to persuade Prime Minister Lord Palmerston to dismiss Wood, the cotton lobby in Parliament made an ignominious attempt to impeach the latter.[19] On the questions of waste land and contract law, the Manchester suffered an irreparable set-back.

The above account underlines the fact that the official policy toward cotton cultivation in India during the period of American Civil War was, at best, half-hearted. The Secretary of State withstood the Manchester pressure well and the Government of India allowed,, not without pangs of conscience, minimum deviations from what was considered the legitimate sphere of governmental activity in those days. True, the Supreme Government acquiesced in the activities of the Bombay authorities. But the relations between these two wings of Indian administration were never too happy during the entire period of crisis. Privately Sir Charles Trevelyan, the Finance Member of Viceroy's Council, expressed discomfort over the violations of the tenets of 'sound political economy' on the part of the Bombay Governor.[20]

The activities of the Indian authorities caused only minor dents on the official belief in the efficacy of free trade doctrine. But to attribute them wholly to the seeds of British industry is to reduce the problem of historical causation to utter simplicity. The needs of foreign policy also conditioned the British thinking and behaviour. The government had decided on a policy of 'honest, strict, and impartial neutrality' in the American question,[21] but a strong section of British public favoured the recognition of the Southern Confederacy. Lest the pro-confederate sentiments should gain momentum and force the government to abandon its neutrality, Lord John Russell, the Foreign Secretary, at the very beginning of the crisis had assured the Cotton Supply Association that his government would do its best to fill up the rupture in American supplies.[22] A strict adherence to the free trade policy would have run counter to this assurance, alientated not only the strong Manchester lobby but also the general public, and spelt doom to the government itself.

Thus the official attitude toward production of cotton in India during the American Civil War can be explained not so much by the theory of economic aggression, but by an element of opportunism in British politics. To this extent the Gallagher-Robinson thesis needs modification

Notes

1. Gallagher and R. Robinson, 'Imperialism of Free Trade,' *Economic History Review,* 2nd series, vol. VI, 1953, pp. 1–15. Also see Peter Hernetty, 'The Imperialism of Free Trade: Lancashire and the Indian Cotton Duties 1859–62', ibid., 2nd series, vol. XVIII, 1965, pp. 109–25; R.J. Moore, 'Imperialism and Free Trade Policy in India, 1853–64', ibid., 2nd series, vol. XVII, 1964, pp. 135–6; Peter Harnetty, 'India's Mississipi: The River Godavari Navigation Scheme, 1853–71.' *Journal of Indian History,* vol. XLIII, pt. III, December 1965, pp. 699–732. For the opposite view Oliver MacDonagh, 'The Anti- Imperialism of Free Trade', *Economic History Review,* 2nd series, vol. XIV, 1961–62, pp. 489–501.
2. For a good account of the crisis see W.O. Henderson, *The Lancashire Cotton Famine 1861–25;* also see Charles F. Adams, *Trans-Atlantic Historical Solidarity.*

3. These included Forbes Royle, *On the Culture and Commerce of Cotton in India and Elsewhere*, John Chapman, *The Cotton and Commerce of India Considered in Relation to the Interests of Great Britain, etc.*, Alexander Mackay, *Western India: Reports Addressed to the Chambers of Commerce of Manchester, Liverpool, Blackburn and Glasgow*, Henry Ashworth, *Cotton: Its Cultivation, Manufacture and Use*.

4. *Cotton, Supply Reporter*, 1 Sept. 1868; 1 December 1860, *London Times*, 12 April 1861; John Bourne, *The Cotton Crisis and How to Meet it: A Letter to Thomas Bazley Esqr.* Referring to the 'teeming opinions' in the English press on this question the *New York Times* wrote on 1 October 1861: 'There certainly never was a more melancholy display of ignorance, imbecility, and blind confidence. . . .'

5. *Cotton Supply Reporter*, 1 February 1861. They also urged a vigorous prosecution of public works to facilitate export of cotton from India. The present study however concentrates on the official attitude toward cultivation. The Government of India did spend a large sum to improve the internal transport. But since the free trade philosophy included public works among the legitimate governmental activities, these expendings, though injudicious in the face of a perennial deficit, can not be considered unjustified from a doctrinaire point of view. See Dwijendra Tripathi, 'An Echo beyond the Horizon: The Effect of the American Civil War on India' in Allan Nevins and Horold Hyman editors, *The Impact of the Civil War on Life and Liberalism Abroad*.

6. Wood to Canning, 18 February 1861, Halifax Collection (India Office Library, London), India Office Letter Book (cited hereinafter as IGLB), VI, 168; *Indian Empire*, Calcutta, 16 October 1861; *New York Times*, 4 October 1861; *Times of India*, 26 October 1861; D.E. Wacha, *Prernchand Roychand: His Early Life and Career*, pp. 28–29.

7. *Calcutta Gazette*, 2 March 1861; Government of India to Secretary of State, Letter no. 12 (Revenue), 25 July 1861, see the enclosure; also see *Cotton Supply Reporter*, 16 Sept. 1861.

8. *Reports of the Bombay Chamber of Commerce* for the year 1859–60, p, xxviii–xxxxiii; 1860–61 (Appendix A) and 1864–65 (Appendix K); The annual report of the Agri-Horticultural Society of India quoted in *Cotton Supply Reporter*, 15 March 1862; 15 October 1862.

9. Government of India to the Secretary of State, Letter no. 13 (Revenue), 13 August 1861; Canning to Wood, 2 September 1886, Indian papers of Lord Canning (Central Library, Leeds; these papers quoted with the permission of the Earl of Harewood), Letters to the Secretary of State; Wood to Canning 18 October 1861. Halifax Collection. IOLB.IX.28 and 186.

10. *Proceedings of the Legislative Council of Bombay Presidency* for the year 1862–63. pp. 106–10; Frere to Wood, 11 April 1863. Halifax Collection. Letters from the Governor of Bombay.

11. Wood to Frere, 4 May 1863. Halifax Collection. IOLB.XIII 34; Frere to Wood, 6 June 1863, ibid., letters from the Governor of Bombay.

12. Resolution of the Government of Bombay. 14 August 1863, quoted in *Cotton Supply Reporter* 1 October 1863.

13. Forbes to Chapman, 27 May 1865, quoted in *Report of the Bombay Chamber of Commerce* for the year 1864–65, pp. 198–207; Forbes to Chapman, 7 July 1865, quoted in ibid., pp. 209–38.

14. *Parliamentary Papers* (House of Commons), no. 327 (1862), 12.
15. *Cotton Supply Reporter,* 15 October 1858; Heywood to Mosley and Hurst, 15 May 1858, *Cotton Supply Reporter,* 16 September 1861; Grey to Mosley and Hurst, 2 July 1861, ibid., Canning to Wood, 22 July 1861, Indian Papers of Lord Canning, Letters to the Secretary of State.
16. For these and similar opinions see *Public Opinion,* London, 30 Nov. 1861; *Cotton Supply Reporter,* 2 December 1861.
17. Wood to Elgin, 10 February 1862, Halifax Collection, IOLBX.21; *Parliamentary Papers* (H. of C.) no. 431, I (1362), 1–14.
18. *Proceedings of the Legislative Council of India* for 1861, pp. 84–97, 178 241; ibid., for 1862, pp. 18, 215; Wood to Canning, 18 April 1861 and 10 July 1861, Halifax Collection, IOLB.VII.100, 184; Laing to Wood, ibid., Letters from Laing during his stay in England in 1861; Wood to Frere, 17 January 1862, ibid., IOLB.IX.206, 212; *Friend of India* (Serampore), 7 November 1862.
19. *Cotton Supply Reporter,* 1 Oct. 1862, ibid., 1 December 1862; *Friend of India,* 18 June, 1863, *India Bills and Acts,* 1863–64, Act XXIII of 1863.
20. Trevelyan to Wood, 21 November 1863, Halifax Collection, Letters from Trevelyan.
21. 3 *Hansard,* CLXY, 1209 (7 Mar. 1862).
22. British Foreign Office to President, Manchester Chamber of Commerce, 19 January 1861, *Cotton Supply Reporter,* 1 February 1861. For an excellent account of British policy in the American Civil War see Frank L. Owsley, *King Cotton Diplomacy,* also see E.D. Adams, *Great Britain and American Civil War.*

24

Economic Measures of Lord Ripon's Government, 1880–84

Sunil K. Sen

LORD RIPON is a famous name in Indian history. His government took important political and social measures in the direction of liberalising the Indian government. To the student of economic history the economic measures of his government are of much interest. We will review the economic measures which seems to indicate the beginnings of a shift in the industrial policy of the Indian government.

When the Indian government began to proceed with the construction of railways, roads, telegraphs, irrigation works, docks and public buildings, there was generated a growing demand for a wide range of goods, especially for iron and steel goods. There emerged what have been aptly called 'the three great consuming Departments'—the Railway, Military and Public Works Departments. The Civil Departments also purchased their requirements. The government became the single biggest purchaser of steel and engineering goods in the country and a big buyer of a variety of goods. The India Office through the Stores Department supplied these stores on receipt of indents from the Governor-General in Council. The Government of India issued from time to time, with the sanction of the Secretary of State, rules which governed the purchase of the stores. The question of the purchase of the stores became invariably linked with the wider question of the encouragement of Indian industries. Indian manufacturers eagerly expected to get a share of the rising government orders and receive encouragement, particularly in the initial years of development.

The policy of purchasing stores in the local market was first formulated in Lord Salisbury's Financial Despatch, dated 7 December 1876.[1] Lord Ripon's Government adopted an important resolution which was to guide the government in the matter of purchase of "*bona fide* Indian manufactures" (other than iron and steel work) in the years to come. A relevant section of this resolution, dated 10 January 1883, reads as follows: 'The Government of India

---

*24th Session at Delhi, 1961.

is desirous to give the utmost encouragement to every effort to substitute for articles now obtained from Europe, articles of *bona fide* local manufacture or of indigenous origin; and when articles of Europe and of Indian manufacture do not differ materially in price and quality, the Government would always be disposed to give preference to the latter; . . . There are many articles which may not be obtained in the local market but which can be made in the event of Government encouraging the manufacture.'[2]

What was new in this new policy declaration was the insistence on the importance of purchasing articles of '*bona fide* local manufacture' in the local market. Government officers could now freely obtain articles of Indian manufacture for the use of their departments. An important principle was laid down, and the Government of India did not depart from it. In the new Stores Rules issued in 1909, 1912 and in 1913, this principle was retained.[3] With regard to iron and steel work, however, this principle was not adhered to, and Indian manufacturers felt that there had been a retreat from the resolution.

Lord Ripon's Government adopted a number of resolutions between 1881–82, in which the substitution of Indian manufactures for European manufactures was recommended. It was stated that the government would enter into contracts with Indian manufacturers for the supply of the articles for 'five years in the first instance.' A list of articles of Indian manufacture was prepared, and mention was made of the local firms which could supply the articles.[4] The Annual Returns submitted by the Governor-General in Council to the Secretary of State show that the value of goods manufactured in India and substituted for stores hitherto imported through the Secretary of State rose from Rs. 39,42,421 in 1882–83 to Rs. 70,71,667 in 1883–84. It may be mentioned that the expenditure on stores produced in India rose appreciably in subsequent years.[5] The Returns reveal that Indian manufactures covered a wide range of goods. Indian industries supplied coal and coke, paper and pasteboard, cotton and linen and silk goods, woollen goods, leather and leather goods, oils, article made of wood, tools and plants. It seems that government spending stimulated the growth of some Indian industries, especially coal and coke, paper and pasteboard and woollen goods. The following figures have been taken from the Returns which will show the expenditure on coal and coke, paper and pasteboard and woollen goods manufactured an India.

I

Coal and Coke

Year (in Rs.)	Value
1882–83	3,54,824
1883–84	15,86,047

II
Paper and Pasteboard

| 1882–83 | 3,66,842 |
| 1883–84 | 3,79,060 |

III
Woollen Goods

| 1882–83 | 82,850 |
| 1883–84 | 1,01,854 |

It will be beyond the scope of this paper to examine the part played by government spending in India's industrial development. It is undeniable, however, that industrialisation was proceeding very slowly and in a lop-sided fashion. In a note prepared by Lord Ripon's Government an indication of the essential pre-requisite for India's industrialization is given in the following extract: 'Some gradual progress is being made in the direction of substituting Indian made articles for those of English manufacture; but it will not be possible to make any very sensible impression upon the total amount of stores imported from England until iron work and machinery ... can be manufactured in India.'[6] In this note the problem of India has been posed in an objective fashion. Industrial policy should be directed to promote the manufacture of 'iron work and machinery,' or real industrialization will remain a chimera. We will now briefly refer to the endeavours made by Ripon's government in the direction of developing Indian iron industry.

The Bengal Iron Works Company which had erected blast furnaces and foundry at Barakar suspended operations in 1879. It may be mentioned that attempts to manufacture pig iron at Porto Novo and at Kumaon had also ended in failure. The re-establishment of iron industry was a matter of supreme importance, and Lord Ripon's Government proposed to purchase the iron works. The home government was then pursuing a *laissez-faire* policy. Interference by the state in industry was considered to be fatal to efficient production. The state was to avoid participation in the productive process. A series of telegrams passed between the Government of India and the Secretary of State. At last the Secretary of State sanctioned the proposals 'in deference to your strongly-expressed opinions and urgent recommendation'. The Secretary of State thought it necessary to inform the Government of India that 'the objections entertained to your proposals were withdrawn with considerable reluctance.'[7] The Barakar Iron Works was purchased on 13 April 1882, for Rs. 4,30,761 and an additional amount of Rs. 16,442 was spent to purchase the stores belonging to the old company.[8]

It seems that *laissez-faire* was a dogma which conflicted with reality. The State was forced to participate in production, so that the iron industry could be re-established. The rapidly rising expenditure on railway stores was a fact which could not be ignored. Lord Ripon's government had taken important step in the direction of developing the iron resources of India. The Barakar Iron Works was run as a State enterprise between 1882 and 1889. It was put in charge of Ritter Von Schwarz, a German metallurgist; it successfully undertook the manufacture of pig iron and miscellaneous iron castings.[9]

Lord Ripon's government adopted an important resolution in the Finance and Commerce Deprtment on 4 August 1882, in which some tangible concessions were proposed to the iron industry. The government declared that they would part with the Barakar Iron Works to any Company which had 'sufficient capital, skill and resources' and proposed 'to take annually for ten years at fixed price not less than certain weight of the Company's manufactures'. The stress which Lord Ripon's government wanted to lay on the importance of establishing iron industry in India, is expressed in the first paragraph of this resolution. We reproduce this paragraph:

'The Government of India have, for some time past, had under special consideration the importance of developing the iron industry in India. The advantages which such development would afford both to state and public,—by cheapening the cost of railway construction and maintenance, and of works for improving the water-supply; by substituting metal for more perishable materials in buildings; by reducing the home charges and their concomitant loss by exchange; by creating for the population non-agricultural employment; and by increasing the means for profitable investment of capital,—are too well known to require lengthened exposition.'[10]

The resolution of Lord Ripon's government was not favourably received in England which was then passing through the period of the Great Depression. The 'Home Manufacturers' demurred. The *Economist* carried a campaign attacking the policy of Lord Ripon's government, which appeared to them to be 'a policy of protection to native industries'.[11] The Secretary of State, in his despatch, dated 16 November 1882, refused to sanction the proposals. It was pointed out that Indian manufacturers of iron 'must be supported by their own strength, and not relieved by artificial means from the natural competition of other countries'.[12] In a strongly worded despatch, dated 23 January 1883, the Governor-General in Council defended the policy of the government. They maintained that they 'rejected the idea of protecting Indian industries' and had totally abolished the import duties, despite the fact that the abolition of import duties 'has been regarded by a consiberable section of the Indian community as having been dictated in the interests of England'. The despatch concludes with these withering words: 'It is, we presume, certain that the establishment of the iron and steel industry would be viewed with disfavour by the persons interested in the manufacture of these articles in England. In this connection it is by no means improbable that even the most legitimate efforts to develop and encourage local industry will be represented by those interested in the matter as though such efforts involved the adoption of a protective policy on the part of the Government of India.'[13]

What was obvious to Lord Ripon's government was less obvious to the Secretary of State. In his despatch, dated 7 June 1883, the Secretary of State refused to the sanction the proposal to take a specified amount of the Company's manufactures at fixed price.[14] Thus the proposals of Lord Ripon's government were negatived. Nevertheless, a new policy of assisting Indian iron industry had been laid down, and the government had to modify their policy in subsequent years.

Lord Ripon left India in 1884. It is not fortuitous that Ripon is remembered as a friend of India whose journey from Simla to Bombay 'was a triumphal march such as India has never witnessed'.

Notes

1. Fin. despatch from, no. 477, 7 December 1876, B.
2. Fin. despatch to, no. 117, 28 April 1884, B.
3. See the Stores Rules of 1909,1912 and 1913 (CD—Stores, 1909, 1912, 1913 Pro. Vols.)
4. CD—Accounts and Finance, 1881, 1882, B.
   Woollen Cloth—The Cawnpore Woollen Mills; Egerton Mills; Bangalore Woollen Mills; Chemicals; Waldie and Co., Calcutta; Long cloth: Indian Cotton Mills; Padlocks: Roorkee Workshops; Linseel Oil: Gouripore Co., Calcutta, Handcuffs: Jessop and Co., Burn and Co., Richardson and Cruddas; Twine and rope: Ahmuty and Co; Paper: Bally Paper Mills; Ink: Sherafally Badruddin and Hormasji Rustamji, Bombay; Amrita Lai Ray of Calcutta.
5. The Annual Returns will be found in Fin. despatches from the Governor- General in Council to the Secretary to State.
6. Summary of Financial Results, Fin. despatch to, no. 76, 20 March 1883, B.
7. Despatch from, 25 August 1881 (CD—Accounts and Finance, April 1882, B).
8. Pin. despatch to, 4 August 1882, B.
9. See the Prospectus of the Bengal Iron and Steel Co. (CD—Coal and Iron. November 1889, B).
10. CD—Coal and Iron, September 1882, B.
11. CD—Coal and Iron, February. 1883, B.
12. Ibid.
13. CD—Coal and Iron, February 1883, B; Also see Fin. despatch to, no. 26, 23 January 1883, B.
14. CD—Coal and Iron, July 1883, B.

25

The Development of Modern Entrepreneurship in the Chettiar Community of Tamil Nadu, 1900–30

Raman Mahadevan

THE 'NATTUKOTTAI CHETTIARS', as distinguished from the other Chettys and Chittiars, are a Tamil-speaking business community hailing from a region which falls partly in the Ramnad district of Tamil Nadu and partly in the then independent principality of Pudukottai.[1] Though numerically insignificant—they numbered 10,000 in 1896 and 50,000 in 1930[2] the Chettiars were businesswise exceptionally enterprising. From about the early nineteenth century the Chettiars sought to invest a large part of their capital in the field of money-lending and trading in the various overseas countries such as Malaya, Ceylon, Burma, Indo-China, etc.[3] Much of the Chettiar capital that was to find its way into the various industries in south India from about the beginning of the twentieth century was largey accumulated in these overseas countries. From a mere 10 crores of rupees in 1896, their total assets had by 1930 shot up to Rs. 80 crores.[4] While conceding that a large part of their capital continued to remain locked as investment in money-lending and trading in the overseas countries, it should be noted that a part of their capital began to gradually find its way into the various industries in South India. Unfortunately, in the existing literature on this community, scanty as it is, the accent is essentially on their money-lending and trading activities.[5] To this day there has been practically no study on the history of their industrial activities.[6] This is partly the result of a heavy reliance by scholars on the Banking Enquiry Committee Reports of 1929–30 (which discusses, at great length, their banking, system only), and partly a failure to view growth and development of Chettiar capital in a historical perspective.

With the idea of undoing these misconceptions in a small way, I propose to examine the participation of Chettiar capital in the various industries in South India under conditions of colonial Rule. Those Chettiars who entered industry did so not by breaking away from their 'traditional activities', viz.

*34th Session at Chandigarh, 1973.

money-lending and trading, but combined the two. The transition from the stage of money-lending and trading to that of investment in industry was not entirely smooth; the old modes of business enterprise co-existed with the new.[7] This, in fact, was the distinctive feature of Chettiar enterprise in the period 1900–30. There were innumerable instances of Chettiars combining their money-lending and trade operation with the ownership of land and industrial enterprises. This peculiar phenomenon has, however, to be viewed in the light of: (*i*) the tremendous control of the Europeans over the various industries, the foreign trade and the money-market,[8] and consequent difficulty for Chettiars to invest, to any great exent, their surplus capital (generated through years of lucrative money-lending and trade in the overseas countries), in industry; and (*ii*) the positive discouragement, through the colonial state-policy, of inflow of Chettiar capital into India. Remittances into British-India were liable to be taxed as business-profit.[9] It is constraints such as these that would explain the smallness of Chettiar investments in the field of industry in the pre-1930 period. In fact, the entry of the Chettiars into modern industry in a big way in the post-1930 period was essentially due to: (*i*) the creation of a suitable environment for industrial investment which was the result of the weakening of the British hold over the Indian economy;[10] and (*ii*) changing economic and political conditions in the various South-East Asian countries, which made it less secure for the Chettiars to operate on their traditional lines.[11]

Let me elucidate very briefly the constraining condition under which sporadic efforts to stage an entry in industry were being made by the Chettiars in the period 1900–30. In practical terms, this meant facing up to stiff competition not only from the home industry in Britain (as in textiles,[12] but also from India-based industries under European control, such as those of Binny & Co., A. & F. Harvey & Co., Parry & Co., to name only a few. It also meant putting up with difficulties in procuring raw-materials, and in securing machinery and other accessories for industry.[13] More important, the Chettiars seeking to enter industry had to have a considerable amount of capital to be able to survive in a highly competitive market. These factors would serve to explain the relatively late entry of Chettiar capital industry in South India. The fact that there was a lesser degree of industrialization in Madras as compared to Bombay and Bengal should also be taken into consideration.[14]

Curiously, it was by way of textiles that the Chettiars, like the entrepreneurs of Bombay, entered industry; and what is more, until 1930, in the field of industry, their investment in textiles was by far the most.

The first bold Chettiar venture in the direction came with the setting up of the Malabar Spinning & Weaving Mill Co. Ltd. at Calicut, in 1888.[15] The capital for this company was principally subscribed by the ALAR Chettiar family, the zamindars of Devakottai, and the Desamangalam Namboodripad family of Travancore.[16] Till 1900, M/s. Kalianjee Soondeerjee & Co. and M/s. Vandarwandas Purshotamdas & Sons were the Managing Agents. In 1902,

ALAR (Somasundaram) Chettiar became the Managing Agent of the Company;[17] Rao Bahadur P. Somasundaram Chettiar was also, for some time, the Managing Agent.[18] The mill ran into considerable difficulties in the year 1899, but managed somehow to tide over it[19] and by 1920 was paying a dividend of 50% to its shareholders.[20] The Malabar Mill also had the distinction of being the first textile mill to be floated by a South Indian entrepreneur, but what is most remarkable is that it was established at a time when the European business houses like Binny & Co., A. & F. Harvey & Co., T. Stanes & Co., themselves had just entered or were entering the field of textiles.[21] The period 1900–14 is a striking contrast to the earlier period, in that there is a much greater degree of participation by the South Indian entrepreneurs in the textile industry.[22] In their earlier perod, viz. 1875–1900, most of the capital invested in the industry belonged either to the 'local English traders or Bombay capitalists.'[23]

Rao Bahadur P. Somasundaram Chettiar, the Managing Agent of the Malabar Spinning & Weaving Mill Co. Ltd., was among the successful South Indian entrepreneurs to enter during this period. In partnership with the ALAR Chettiar family he founded the Kaleeswara Mills at Coimbatore in 1910.[24] The paid-up capital for this mill, amounting to Rs. 6,50,000, 'was principally subscribed by Merchants, Bankers, and Vakils.'[25] In addition to Kaleeswara Mills, he also controlled the Calicut Tile Co., at Feroke in Malabar, a ginning factory and a bank at Ariyalur, in the Trichy district, a paddy-husking mill at Ami, in North Arcot district, and another ginning factory, at Pollachi, in the Coimbatore district.[26]

Besides promoting mills, the Chettiars were also acquiring defunct mills and starting them again. This was the manner in which the Koilpatti Mills was acquired by the Nattukottai Chettiar bankers, RMMST Vairawan Chettiar and MLM. Ramanathan Chettiar, in 1908.[27] The Koilpatti Mills was originally established at Koilpatti in Tinnevelly district, with a paid-up capital of Rs. 5,00,000 by 'some Muhammadans'[28] in 1892.[29] After a short while, the mill incurred financial losses, went bankrupt, and was ultimately closed down in 1908. Thereafter, 'the property came to court-sale, and was bought by two Nattukottai Chettis for nearly 7 lakhs of rupees.'[30] After remaining idle for nearly one and a half years, the mill was recommissioned and renamed as Kamakshi Mills. This, apparently, was only an 'ad hoc' and temporary arrangement, because by 1911 an altogether new mill was floated in place of the Kamakshi Mills. Named as the Chidambaram Vinayagar Mill, it was floated with a paid-up capital of Rs. 7,00,000. The original owners, RMMST Vairawan Chettiar and MLM Ramanathan Chettiar, held two-thirds of the shares.[31]

Between 1911 and 1920 no new textile mills were established in Madras Presidency. Though the 1914–18 War by cutting off imports and partially throwing open the domestic market to the Indian entrepreneurs, did afford an opportunity for the South Indian entrepreneurs to enter industry, they could not take advantage of these circumstances because the machinery and other accessories required for the mills had to be secured from Great Britain.[32] The entrepreneurs had, therefore, to wait for the war to end and, fortunately for them, the climate, both economic and political in the post-war period was extremely favourable for investment in industry. The lifting of the war time prohibitions and controls followed by the resumption of commercial intercourse with the overseas countries, resulted in a boom.[33] Moreover, the launching, in the 20s, of the non-cooperation movement, with its boycott and swadeshi programme, contributed towards strengthening the hand of the Indian entrepreneurs.

Karunuthu Theagaraja Chettiar, who was to emerge later as one of the leading figures in the field of textile industry, made his beginning in this period, when he established the Sir Meenakshi Mills in Madura.[34] It had a paid-up capital of Rs.14,07,700.[35] This was followed by the establishment of the Mahalakshmi Mills Co. in 1925 at Madurai, by S.S.N. Lakshmanan Chettiar.[36] As was the case with almost all the mills established by the Chettiars, the Managing Agents of these two mills were the founders themselves, their close relations, and members of their own community. The Managing Agents of these two mills were Theagaraja Chetty & Co., and S.S.N. Lakshmanan Chetty & Co.[37]

The famous AR AR SM family of Devakottai, also had a mill at Madras.[38] The exact date of its establishment is not known, but one can assume that it was set up sometime prior to 1925 for in that year the AR AR SM firm and its sudsidiaries, engaged in a wide variety of activity ranging from money-lending and trading to industry, was declared insolvent, and assignees were appointed by the High Court of Madras over all the estates belonging to the family.[39] Consequently, the AR AR SM Spinning Mills was acquired by Somasundaram Chettiar and was thereafter known as the Somasundaram Mills Ltd.[40] These were the only textile mills set up by the Chettiars until 1930.

The sugar industry was another field that attracted a certain amount of Chettiar capital. Once again, it was the established families of AL AR and AR AR SM Chettiar which acquired the two sick mills, viz., the Lakshmi Sugar Mills at Alwartirunagiri in Tinnevelly district,[41] and the Pettai Sugar Refining Co. at Tachanaloor, also in Tinnevelly district;[42] both these mills were engaged in producing sugar by refining jaggery.[43] The size of these enterprises was perhaps small, but the significant fact is that these mills were being acquired and operated at a time when the European business house, Parry & Co. had secured complete control over the production of sugar and spirit in the Madras Presidency.[44]

The Lakshmi Sugar Mills was established by a native of Allur. The mill, though small, could not, however, be worked successfully and changed hands several times before being acquired by the AL AR family.[45]

The Pettai Sugar Mill Co. was acquired by AR AR SM Somasundaram Chettiar in much the same way. It was found in 1895 by some Muhammadan businessman and worked until 1910, but thereafter incurred financial losses and passed into the hands of AR AR SM Somasundaram Chettiar, who had until then been assisting the mill financially.[46] The mill was then renamed as the AR AR SM Sugar Mill and had a paid-up capital of Rs. 3,00,000, subscribed by the proprietor himself.[47] That the mill was working successfully until 1925 is borne out by the fact that its paid-up capital for the manufacture of sugar was raised to Rs. 4,50,000 in addition to Rs. 2,50,000 raised for the establishment of a distillery.[48] Therein you have the classic case of a Chettiar entrepreneur not merely entering industry but also being prepared to introduce innovations and to venture out into new fields. However, with the failure of the entire network of the AR AR SM firms, the sugar mill passed into the hands of the official receiver, who was one AL VR ST Veerappa Chettiar of Devakottai.[49] The mill was subsequently named after him.

The spirit of enterprise and innovation shown by AR AR SM Somasundaram Chettiar in venturing into new fields is also exhibited in the attempt by the Chettiar to establish a paper mill at Punalur in Travancore State,[50] around the second decade of the twentieth century. The mill, however, suffered from the inevitable 'want of good machinery, chemicals and expert advice'[51] and was hence not a commercial success.

Another noteworthy Chettiar venture in the field of industry was the establishment of a modern cycle factory at Madras in 1925 by S.A.A. Annamalai Chettiar.[52] A member of the Burma Indian Chamber of Commerce, Annamalai Chettiar was also conducting, through his firms, considerable money-lending business in Burma.[53]

The Chettiars also established a large number of rice mills in the Tanjore district.[54] Of these, some of the prominent ones were those of the AR AR SM firm and the RM AR AR RM firm at Kuttalam, and that of MTTY firm in Kumbakonam.[55]

These, in short, were some of the industries in which Chettiar capital was sought to be invested. In the light of the evidence furnished in the preceding sections of this paper, one could quite justifiably conclude that Chettiar investments in industry as a whole were by no measure small, given the conditions of colonial rule, the state of industrialization in the Presidency, and the fact that an enormous amount of their capital was locked in the various overseas countries.

Besides these purely industrial enterprises, the Chettiars also promoted, and were associated with, a number of modern joint stock companies and banks. I shall now briefly consider some of these important companies which the Chettiars promoted. These were: (*i*) The South India Commercial Corporation, established in Madura, sometime in the pre-war period, with a paid-up capital of Rs. 1,00,000. The Corporation (of which SR MA R Ramaswamy Chettiar and RM Nagappa Chettiar were President and Secretary, respectively) apart from runuing a bus service between Madura and Karaikudi, was also engaged in importing motor cars and motor cycles from England;[56] *(ii)* The private firm of Ramaswamy & Co., established in Madras in 1907, by PLNK Meenatchi Sundaram Chettiar, ORMOM Subramanian Chettiar and ALAR Arunachellan Chettiar. The concern was principally engaged in importing various kinds of cloth from Manchester and Germany;[57] *(iii)* The firm of Muthoo & Co., which specialised in import–export business, founded by two leading Nattukottai Chettiar bankers-cum-merchants, PMA Muthiah Chettiar and SRMM CT Muthiah Chettiar;[58] and (iv) The three electric corporations set up in commercial towns of Devakottai, Kanadukathan and Karaikudi; also the result of Chettiar enterprise.[59] Lubin Bertran & Co., PSNC Palaniappa & Bros.[60] The Madras Railway Provincial Co.,[61] were some of the many such joint stock concerns floated by the Chettiars. The organisation of the their business (be it in the nature of industry or trade) on the basis of limited liability can be considered as constituting a new stage in Chettiar entrepreneurial activity, a stage heralding modern capitalist enterprise.

This trend was also carried over by the Chettiars into the field of banking. Thus, the Indian Bank Ltd., established as early as 1907, after the failure of Arbuthnot & Co., was backed by Chettiar finance to a large extent.[62] The bank, one of the first of its type in Madras, 'was intended by its founders to be purely indigenous in its aims and to . . . afford banking facilities to the Madras merchants and manufacturers.'[63] In the very year of the establishment of the bank, a capital of Rs. 17,75,000 was subscribed; of this, nearly two-thirds was subscribed by Chettiars.[64] The Chettiars closely associated with the bank since its inception were SRMMA Annamalai Chettiar, who later earned the title of 'Raja Sri,' PMA Muthian Chettiar, and SR M AR Ramaswamy Chettiar.[65] The diversion of capital by some of the wealthiest Chettiars, on howsoever small a scale, from money-lending to organised banking, was another significant step in the development of modern entrepreneurship amongst certain sections of this community; it was a definite advance over their traditional banking system in so far as the Chettiars now had access to greater resources (which in turn tremendously increased their financial power), and in that their risk was circumscribed to their share of the subscribed capital.

Those Chettiars who entered industry and other modern incorporated enterprises were essentially the influential Chettiars commanding enormous economic resources of their own. That there were differences of wealth within the community is often not brought out in the existing literature on the Chettiars; on the contrary, they are treated, though implicitly, as being some kind of monolithic community.

The period 1900–30 is significant in that one witnessed during this period the formation of business combines by the wealthy Nattukottai Chettiar families, such as those of the Raja Sir group (with its investment in the field of modern banking), and the Somasundaram and Karumathu groups (with their investment in textiles mainly).

The Japanese scholar, Shoji Ito's remarks on the supposed late entry of Chettiar capital into industry in Madras Presidency may be considered. Shoji Ito, in his article entitled, 'A Note on the Business Combine in India—with special reference to the Nattukottai Chettiars', published in the journal called *Developing Economies*,[66] has expressed the view that the adaptability of Chettiar traditional institutions to their traditional activities 'retarded their entry into the modern sector of the economy.'[67] He then goes on to argue that it was only with the bankruptcy of their traditional activities in Burma in the 30s that an occasion for entering industry presented itself to the Chettiars.[68]

That their entry into industry and other modern incorporated enterprises was not late, has been more than amply substantiated in the preceding sections of this paper; the very fact that the Chettiars were entering industry from the late nineteenth century onwards disproves the myth that the adaptability of their traditional institutions to their traditional activities retarded their entry into the modern sector of the economy.

As for the argument that the bankruptcy, in Burma, of the traditional activities of the Chettiars was the occasion for their investing in industry, it should be noted that the 1930 depression was basically a temporary crisis; there was no collapse of their financial structure.[69] It was a crisis; which made the system of money-lending temporarily less profitable and less secure than it has been in the pre-1930 period. Only those Chettiars belonging to the middle and lower strata of the community, and owning small amounts of capital, were hit by the depression; the wealthy families such as those of Raja Sir, in fact, stepped up their economic activities. This is borne out by the fact that between 1931–41 Raja Sir Annamalai Chettiar, one of the wealthiest members of the community, founded the Bank of Chettinad Ltd., the Chettinad Corporation Ltd., the Burma Commercial Corporation Ltd., and several other concerns which conducted extensive business in Burma, Malaya, Ceylon, Indo-China, etc.[70]

I am inclined to believe that Chettiar entry in a comparatively big way into industry and other modern incorporated enterprises, in the '30s was more because of the weakening of the hold of the Europeans over the Indian economy, and the consequent creation of a suitable environment for investment in industry.

Shoji Ito has overlooked what seems to me to be a peculiar feature or pattern in the evolution of Chettiar entrepreneurship under conditions of colonial rule. Thus, the Chettiars did not give up their traditional activities to enter into modern industry in the 1930s, but combined money-lending and trading operations with ownership of land and industrial enterprises. To cite an example, the AR AR SM firm, prior to its being declared insolvent in 1925, was on the one hand founding textile, sugar and rice mills, while on the other hand conducting money-lending business in Ceylon and trade in Madras.

Therefore, rather than examine the problem of the smallness, or the lack of, Chettiar investments in industry in terms of the hold of tradition over the

Chettiar community, and the role of social institutions in sustaining Chettiar activity in traditional grooves, it will be more meaningful to consider some of the more tangible material constraints that were at work against the entry of Chettiar capital into industries. These were, as indicated above, the monopolistic control of the Europeans over industry, foreign trade, the organised money-market, and the positive discouragement of any sort of repatriation of Chettiar capital from the overseas countries.

However, in spite of these hindrances, the Chettiars did manage to divert part of their capital from money-lending and trading into industry and other modern incorporated enterprises. To sum up one can say that the foundation of Chettiar capitalist enterprises was laid in this period 1900–30. Its consolidation took place in the post-1930 period.

Notes

1. A. Savirinatha Pielai, written evidence to the *Madras Banking Enquiry Committee Report*, vol. III, p. 1170; V.A. Seshadiri Sharma, *Nattukottai Nagarathar Varalaru* (Tamil) . . . (A history of the Nattukottai Chettiars), p. 69.

2. See A. Savirinatha Pielai, op. cit., p.1174 and *Dhanavanikan* an annual Chettiar journal published in 1930 from Kottaiyur. A.K. Chettiar, p. 369.

3. For an account of their activities in these countries see, *Malayavin Thotram* (Tamil) or *Happy Malaya* by P.N.M. Muthupalaniappa Chettiar. *The Nattukottai Chettiar Merchants and Bankers in Ceylon*—W.S. Weerasooria, 'The Chettiars in Burma—An Economic Survey of a Migrant Community—Allene Masters, *Population Review*, January 1957, vol. I, no. 1.

4. A. Savirinatha Pillai, op. cit., p.1174; Shoji Ito, 'A Note on the Business Combine in India, with Special Reference to the Nattukottai Chettiars', *The Developing Economies*, vol. II, Step. 1966, no. 3, p. 369.

5. P.J. Thomas, see 'Natthukotti Chettiars—Their Fanking System'; B.V. Narayanaswami Naidu, 'The Nattukottai Chettiars and their Banking System' in the *Paja Sir Annamalai Chettiar Commemoration Volume*, pp. 840–54 and pp. 457–72 respectively; V. Krishnan, *Indigenous Banking in South India*.

6. Perhaps the only exception is Shoji Ito's op. cit. But even Ito does not cover the ground adequately and concentrates more on their activities in the post-1940 period.

7. See P.J. Thomas, op. cit., p. 840.

8. A.K. Bagchi, *Private Investment in India 1900–39*, pp.188–91; S.T. Sadasivam, 'Three Hundred Years of Banking in Madras', *The Madras Ter Centenary Commemoration Volume*, 1939, pp. 257–60.

9. A. Savirinatha Pillai, op. cit., p. 1180.

10. A.K. Bagchi, op. cit., p. 206.

11. It was the coincidence of these two factors that would largely explain the Inflow of Chettiar capital into industry in the 30s in a much more vigorous manner than earlier.

12. P. Somasundaram Chettiar—Written evidence to the *Indian Industrial Commission,* 1916-17, vol. III, Madras and Bangalore; Question 110, p. 444.

13. P. Somasundaram Chettiar, op, cit., Q. 3, Q. 98, p. 444.

14. Written Evidence of Rao Bahadur P. Theagaraya Chetti to the *Indian Industrial Commission* 1916–17, vol. III, Madras and Bangalore, p. 51; see also A.K. Eagchi, op. cit., p. 189.

15. N.C. Bhogendranath, *The Developments of Textile Industry in Madras,* p. 11.

16. This oral testimony was given by ADAR Somanathan Chettiar when the writer interviewed him at Devakottai in June 1973.

17. N.C. Bhogendranath, op. cit., p. 12.

18. Rao Bahadur P. Somasundaram Chettiar's Evidence to the *Indian Industrial Commission,* 1906–17, vol. III, p. 443.

19. C.S. Chockalingam Pillai, *Biography of Devak ottai Rao Bahadur P. Somasundaram Chettiar* (in Tamil), pp. 3–4.

20. N.C. Bhogendranath, op. cit., p. 34.

21. Ibid., pp. 10–13.

22. Ibid., p. 15.

23. Ibid.

24. C.S. Chockalingam Pillai, op. cit., pp. 4–5.

25. Rao Bahadur P. Somasundaram Chettiar—Written Evidence to *Indian Industrial Commission,* vol. III, Q. 12, p. 443.

26. C.S. Chockalingam, op. cit., pp. 4–5.

27. H.R. Pate, *Madras District Gazetteer. . .Tinnevelly,* vol. I, Madras, 1917, p. 213.

28. Ibid., p. 213.

29. N.C. Bhogendranath, op. cit., p. 12.

30. H.R. Pate, op. cit., p. 213.

31. N.C. Bhogendranath, op. cit., pp. 12, 15; H.R. Pate, op. cit., p. 213. It was from the Thackers India Directory of 1915 that one secured the names of the two Chettiars who had acquired the old mill and floated the new. See *Thacker's India Directory 1915*—Section Commercial Industries—Sub-section Cotton Mills in Madras Presidency, p. 23.

32. N.C. Bhogendranath, op. cit., p. 25.

33. Ibid., p. 28.

34. Ibid., p. 28 and V.A. Seshadiri Sharma, op. cit., p. 133.

35. A.S. Pearse—*The Cotton Industry in India—Being the Report of the Journey of India.* See under List of Cottcn Mills in India in the Appendix, p. 242.

36. N.C. Bhogendranath, op. cit., p. 29 and V.A. Seshadiri Sharrra, op. cit., p. 151.

37. *Kothari's Investors Encyclopaedia,* 1949–50, pp. 282, 323. See A.S. Pearse, op. cit., p. 242.

38. A.S. Pearse, op. cit., p. 242.

39. W.S. Weerasooria, op. cit., p. 38.

40. A.S. Pearse, op. cit., p. 242.

41. This information was provided by ALAR Somanathan Chettiar when the writer interviewed him at Devakottai in June 1973.

42. See *Thacker's India Directory 1915*—Commercial Industries Section; Subsection Sugar Factories in Madras Presidency, p. 80; and H.R. Pate, op. cit., p. 226.

43. H.R. Pate, op. cit., p. 226.

44. A.K. Bagchi, op. cit., p. 190.

45. H.R. Pate, op. cit., p. 226.

46. Ibid., p. 226.

47. *Thacker's India Directory 1915*—Section Sugar Factories in Madras Presidency, p. 87.

48. *Thacker's India Directory 1923*—Section Sugar Factories in Madras Presidency, p. 87.

49. A. Savirinatha Pillai, op. cit., 1178 and *Thacker's India Directory 1929*—Section Sugar Industries, p. 70.

50. A. Savirinatha Pillai, op. cit., p. 1178.

51. Rao Bahadur SRM Annamalai Chettiar's remarks on the Punalur Paper Mill in the Legislative Council of Madras. See *Proceedings of the Council of the Governor of Fort St George*. July 1916–June 1917, p. 902.

52. See *Oolian* (the Tamil weekly published from Karaikudi; Editor: Rai Chockalingam), 10-11-25, p. 8.

53. The Burma Indian Chamber of Commerce—Report of the Committee and *Correspondence for 1925–26 and 1926–27* (Rangoon 1928). See under List of Members as on 31 March 1928, p. V.

54. A. Savirinatha Pillai, op. cit., p. 1178.

55. *Thacker's India Directory 1923*. See under Section Commercial Industries; Sub-section Rice Mills in the Madras Presidency, p. 77.

56. *The Vysiamitran* a Tamil weekly published by S.T. Ramanathan Chettiar at Devakottai. See the 12-1-1914 issue, p. 1.

57. Somerest Playne—Southern India—Its History, People, Commerce and Industrial Resources, 1914–15, pp. 692–96.

58. *Thacker's India Directory 1915*. See Section Madras; Sub-section Merchants Agents Trading firm etc., p. 65.

59. A. Savirinatha Pillai, op. cit., p. 1178.

60. *Thacker's India Directory 1915*; op. cit., pp. 62 and 5; see the 11-11-1921 issue.

61. *Dliana Vysia Oclian* (a Tamil weekly published from Karaikudi), p. 2.

62. M.S. Natarajan, 'A Study of the Capital Market of Madras Presidency, with special reference to its evolution and indigenous institutions,' Ph.D. Thesis submitted to the University of Madras, 1934, pp. 59–60; Shoji Ito, op. cit., p. 373.

63. M.S. Natarajan, op. cit., p. 60.

64. See Editorial of *Swadesmitran* (a nationalist Tamil daily) of 30 January 1908.

65. *Thacker's India Directory 1915*— See under Section Madras, p. 52.

66. The article was published in the September 1966, vol. IV, no. 3 issue of the journal.

67. Shoji Ito, op. cit., p. 374.

68. Ibid., p. 372.

69. This is confirmed by the following evidence:
"The Chettiars dominated foreign investments in Burma . . . even after the depression. It was estimated in 1941 that they were still the largest single foreign investors, holding 36 per cent of all foreign investments." See Allene Masters, op. cit., p. 23.

70. B.V. Narayanaswamy Naidu, op. cit., p. 472.

26

The Impact of the Great Depression on India in 1930s

Dietmar Rothermund

THE 1930s were a very important period of Indian history in which economic and political trends converged which influenced the course of subsequent events. The causes of these trends were not necessarily related to each other and their convergence was fortuitous. The emphasis on economic factors in this paper does not imply a belief in economic determinism. The analysis of economic trends is meant to provide a corrective to the preoccupation with political events which are in the limelight which the working of economic forces eludes the observer. Contemporary consciousness was also much more impressed with such striking events as Gandhi's Civil Disobedience Campaigns, the Round Table Conferences and Hindu–Muslim relations, whereas the impact of the Great Depression was felt but not easily understood by those who lived through it. But this impact greatly affected the political development during this period, patterns of cumulative causation as well as striking contrasts between economic conditions and political decisions can be observed with the benefit of hindsight.

In this paper only three trends will be studied which were originally independent of each other but then fell into a pattern which profoundly influenced the future course of Indian history: (1) The worldwide decline of agricultural prices, (2) British financial policy in India, (3) The Indian freedom movement and the development of the social base of the National Congress. The decline of agricultural prices, which was aggravated by British financial policy in India, made substantial sections of the peasantry rise in protest and this protest was articulated by members of the National Congress. After discussing at first the economic and financial trends the problem of peasant protest and its relation with the Congress will be taken up at the end of this chapter.

*41st Session at Bombay, 1980.

The Decline of Agricultural Prices

In the great wheat producing countries of the West the decline of agricultural prices set in even before the Great Depression. The stock market crash in New York in 1929 then caused a general crisis of confidence among all creditors and sent a shock wave of credit contraction around the world. Since the level of agricultural prices depended to a large extent on the availability of credit for stockpiling and forward trading the credit crisis removed the main, support of the agricultural price level, and the prices which had continued to be high ever since the First World War came suddenly down to the pre-war level.[1] Although India was no longer a major wheat importer or exporter and produced almost exclusively for a stable home market which was expanding with the growth of the population, the Indian wheat price immediately followed the world market price.

This was due to two mechanisms of transmission: (1) Australian wheat[2] competed with Indian wheat in the major port cities of India, (2) the credit network, about which more shall be said later on, discouraged buying above the world market rate. Considering the total amount of Indian wheat production and consumption the import of wheat was marginal, but as it concerned some of the major centres of urban consumption, its impact was of strategic importance. The British-Indian government which was always particularly eager to keep the Panjab happy, which was the main wheat-producing area in India, imposed in 1931 by special legislation a prohibitive import duty on wheat[3] and also saw to it that railway freight rates to the major ports were reduced, because the cheap supply of wheat by ship as against the more expensive rail-transport was one of the chief reasons of the supply of the port cities of India with Australian wheat. The duty did lead to a slight recovery of the Indian wheat price; it had to be re-imposed every year because the situation did not improve. Even when total world production of wheat was considerably reduced in 1933 there was over-production in the European countries which had so far imported wheat.[4] With the exporters sitting on their surpluses the world market price could not rise. Wheat prices remained low throughout the 1930s.

The fate of the rice price was determined by a very different set of circumstances; the areas of rice production and consumption were mainly in the East, and there was traditionally very little substitution wheat for rice. The rapid decline of the rice price which followed that of the wheat price with a time lag of about one year, was, therefore, not caused by the fall of the wheat price but was due to a similar pattern of overproduction in some countries which spoiled the price for all the others, too. In the late 1920s Siam (Thailand) and Indo-China stepped up their rice exports. India which still included Burma at that time was also a rice exporter, although its exports were marginal as compared to the large and stable home market. Japan played a crucial role, because the Japaanese government had stimulated rice imports after the rice-riots of 1919. The urban population had to be kept happy with cheap rice.[5] However, in 1928 there was a sudden change: the government placed an embargo on the import of rice, because of a surplus in the home market. This was originally imposed only as a temporary measure, but it was continued as indigenous overproduction increased.[6] In 1930 Japan produced about one Mill. t. rice more than during the corresponding period of previous year. In India the rice harvests had also been good and, as early as 1929, a serious congestion of rice stockd was noticed in Calcutta.[7] With the Japanese outlet blocked India tried to sell more Burmese rice to Europe. But there indigenous rice production had also increased.[8] Initially the marginal nature of Indian rice export meant that there was hardly any repercussion on the vast home market. But this situation changed when cheap rice was imported into India. In 1931 Japan, while still maintaining its embargo, began to export rice and after the devaluation of the yen in 1932 this rice was very cheap, indeed. Because India was still a rice exporter it was difficult to protect the internal price by an import duty as it had been done in the case of wheat. Nevertheless Indian representatives of the rice producing provinces clamoured for such an import duty, particularly whenever they were asked to endorse the re-imposition of the wheat import duty. The Government of India could point out that rice imports into India had proved to be insignificant: In 1930 they amounted to 7500 t., in 1931 to 18000 t., and in 1932 to 35,000 t.[9] But Ramaswami Mudaliar speaking in the Central Legislative Assembly in 1934 pointed out that by that time about 20,000 t. arrived in India every month and that Siam and Japan were practically dumping rice on India. He agreed that these imports were small as compared to total Indian production, but he emphasized the psychological effect of these marginal imports. The very news of a Japanese ship with rice on board landing in Madras immediately caused a sharp drop in the price of rice.[10]

The steepest drop in the rice price occurred in India even before these imports could make any impact. In 1930 the rice price was still at a high level and thus contrasted with the wheat price which had been declining for some time. In February 1931 when the new rice harvest reached the market the price was slashed by half.[11] After this dramatic fall it continued to decline until it reached its lowest point in February 1933. While the slow decline from 1931 to 1933 was undoubtedly due to the availability of cheap imports, the initial rapid fall was obviously due to the interpretation of the world market situation by the credit—and trading-network. It was perhaps one of the most striking examples of the dominant role which the world market played in India inspite of the fact that India was only marginally linked to the market atleast as far as foodgrains were concerned.

The grain prices remained depressed throughout the 1930s. Wheat was affected only for some time by protection, a further slump in the world market reduced the wheat price once more in 1934, whereas rice experienced a slight recovery at that time. After 1934 both prices stagnated at a fairly low level which more or less corresponded to the prewar situation.

British Financial Policy in India

The worldwide credit contraction which hastened the decline of agricultural prices was aggravated in India by a deflationary policy of the British-Indian government. The policy was aimed at maintaining the high exchange rate of the rupee which the British refused to devaluate inspite of constant Indian pressure. The basic decisions on that policy had been made before the depression began when the rupee was tied to the gold standard at a fixed exchange rate, 1 s 6 d. In order to defend the exchange rate against the challenge of the depression the Government of India resorted to a severe currency contraction. The circulating paper currency which amounted to about Rs. 185 crores in the years before 1929 was considerably reduced after October 1929 until it was down to Rs. 148 crores in September 1931.[12] The Government of India was obliged to maintain two reserves, the Paper Currency Reserve and the Gold Standard Reserve. The fate of these two reserves in the crucial years of the depression shows very clearly which external constraints determined British-Indian financial policy at that time. The Paper Currency Reserve consisted mainly of three elements: gold, silver and rupee securities. Sterling securities which were of some importance at an earlier time were negligible in this period. The gold in the Paper Currency Reserve amounted to about £ 22–24 Mill, until November 1930; then a steep downward trend set in: by May 1931 only £ 15 Mill, were left and by September 1934 this gold reserve had dwindled to £ 3 Mill. rupee securities followed the same trend. While in earlier years they had amounted to approximately Rs. 40 crores, they were down to Rs. 5 crores in June 1931. This was partly compensated by increasing the silver reserves which amounted to about Rs. 100 crores in earlier years and to about Rs. 130 crores in the second half of 1931. What happened to the gold which was drained out of the Paper Currency Reserve? A look at the changes in the Gold Standard Reserve will provide the answer.[13] In earlier years this reserve used to consist of £ 2 Mill, in gold and £ 38 Mill, in Sterling securities. From the beginning of 1931 this relationship changed. Sterling securities were reduced and more gold was put into this reserve. The highest amount of gold in this reserve was recorded in September 1931: £ 30 Mill. This was the time when Britain went off the gold standard. From this time onward the name of this reserve was really an anachronism, but the high amount of gold was kept in this reserve for some more time as a pawn in the hands of the creditor nation. The British government was deeply scared by the prospect of a British-Indian bankruptcy caused by a flight from the rupee; if this had occurred the British government would have had to pay India's debts and would have gone bankrupt, too. Therefore the British government insisted on a severely deflationary policy for British India. The bank rate reflected this situation; it remained at about 7 per cent until July 1932.[14] At a time when a national government would have tried to counteract the depression by a policy of devaluation and easy money, the British-Indian government was forced to pursue the very opposite course.

Britain's decision to go off the gold standard seemed to provide a new point of departure. The Government of India which had been informed only at the last minute of this important step issued an ordinance so as to prevent a run on its reserves. This ordinance practically implied that the rupee would be allowed to float.[15] When the Secretary of State came to know of this he immediately made the Government of India eat its words and used the platform of the Round Table Conference, then in session in London, to pledge British support for the exchange rate of 1 s 6 d. He then sent a homily to the Government of India warning them of the consequences of their policy. There would be a flight from the rupee, a steep rise of prices in India, hoarding of gold and silver would increase, the budget would be unbalanced and the government would encourage inflation, its reserves would not be conserved but dissipated because of the need to export gold to London to meet Indian obligations, India would be left on a silver basis and would default. Finally, he emphasized that there was no parallel between Britain and India as far as a drifting currency was concerned. Britain was still a great creditor but India was a debtor country with large obligations in Sterling.[16] The Government of India, particularly the Finance Member, Sir George Schuster were not convinced by these arguments, Schuster was willing to resign on this issue and the Viceroy, Lord Willingdon, backed him up and offered the resignation of his Government; for this he was severely reprimanded by the Secretary of State who compared this to the resignation of a general staff in the face of the enemy.[17] Willingdon, therefore, climbed down but Schuster reserved his right of individual resignation. But he did not need to take this courageous step, because the stream of distress gold which gushed out of rural India in the winter of 1931/32 made the whole controversy obsolete. Schuster gazed with amazement at the beautiful gold ornaments which were stacked in heaps in the currency offices of the government.[18] He regretted that they were there only to be melted down, but he did not understand the real problem of 'distress gold' on the contrary he congratulated the Indians on being able to sell their gold at a good price. As a liberal economist he could only welcome this dehoarding of gold.

The speed with which the gold was drained out of India was truly amazing. Keynes had once stated that gold in the pockets of people is rarely available to the government when it needs to tide over an emergency.[19] Under the special conditions which prevailed in India at that time this was not true and the Government of India was highly satisfied with the course of events. Of course, the people did not part with their gold voluntarily; they were pounced upon by the money-lenders who had practically stopped giving further credit and wanted to recover their capital from the peasantry.

The stream of gold increased liquidity and solved the problems of the British but it did not immediately lead to an easing of the credit situation in India. Credit contraction prevailed for some time; on top of this the Government of India appeared as a competitor on the Indian money market. It so happened that the Government of India announced a new issue of treasury bonds at 6½ per cent in September 1931 just before Britain went off the gold standard. Investors who had deposited their money elsewhere withdrew in order to buy these bonds. Some banks were severely hit by this run. The Provincial Co-operative Banks of Bihar and Bengal were so much affected by it that they had to appeal to the government for a guarantee.[20] Of course, in the long run government borrowing was also supposed to re-activate the money supply. Rupee securities in the Paper Currency Reserve which stood at Rs. 9 crores in September 1931 were increased to Rs. 59 crores by February 1932 and the note issue was also expanded, but it only reached the level of October 1929 once again in September 1934.[21] To begin with, the increase of Rupee securities in this reserve was simply meant to compensate for the gold which had been drained out of it. For all these reasons the stream of distress gold eased the credit situation only with a considerble time lag.

It was only by 1933 that the impact of the stream of gold could be felt. The bank rate was down to 3½ per cent, a rate lower than that prevailing even in slack seasons in pre-war times, and the Paper Currency Reserve was replenished with £ 30 Mill in gold.[22] This justified an adequate increase of the note issue. However, this easing of the credit situation generally benefited urban interests and the business community. The countryside remained depressed. The terms of trade which had been so sharply turned against agriculture with the decline in prices did not improve, and rural creditors were not willing to resume their earlier activities; they were still chasing their debtors in order to recover old debts.

The Development of the Social Base of the Indian Congress

Earlier campaigns of the Indian freedom movement had only touched the Indian peasantry marginally. In some local areas dedicated leaders had drawn the peasants into the movement in the 1920s. But the richer peasants remained outside the mainstream of Indian nationalism. The high prices which prevailed during and after the First World War benefited particularly those peasants who had free access to the market. In Northern India these strata had also derived considerable benefits from British-Indian tenancy legislation; they had therefore no reasons to be dissatisfied with the British Raj.[23] This was suddenly changed by the depression and the British found it hard to maintain their political credit with the peasantry. In the ryotwari areas they could do this to some extent by prompt remissions of revenue;[24] this was fairly successful with some regional exceptions—where specific conditions led to a confrontation between the peasants and the revenue authorities. In Northern India, particularly in the United Provinces and Bihar; this remedy did not work, because remissions to the zamindars did not automatically lead to rent reductions for the tenants. Most zamindars were indebted, the money-lender pounced upon them and they and the money-lenders pounced upon the tenants.[25] This explosive socio-economic conflict caught the Indian National Congress by surprise. Few leaders of the Congress had any idea about agrarian relations; leading a national movement against British rule they also did not want to take sides in class conflicts among Indians. Gandhi was particularly reluctant to get involved in such class conflicts which tended to erupt into sporadic violence. But, it so happend that the protest movements of the peasantry contributed new vigour to the Civil Disobedience Movement at a most crucial time. When Gandhi had started the movement in April 1930 the impact of the depression had not yet reached rural India. The Salt March and the subsequent demonstrations attracted a good deal of attention; but just when the momentum of this movement was lost the peasants in the wheat growing regions got restive because the decline of the wheat price hit them very hard after the harvest of 1930. By October 1930 'No Rent' Campaigns started in which some of the more radical Congress workers of Northern India eagerly participated.[26] The rice growing regions were still quiet because the rice price was not yet affected by the depression at that time, but the Western part of U.P. where wheat is grown became a mainstay of the movement. After some initial reluctance even Gandhi supported the cause of the peasantry. The Government of India was seriously concerned about the prospects of a large scale peasant rebellion and was, therefore, eager to come to terms with Gandhi.[27] Gandhi did not want to betray the cause of the peasantry but when the business community which financed the Congress campaign indicated that they would no longer be able to foot the bill, Gandhi had to arrive at a compromise and thus in March 1931 the Gandhi-Irwin Pact was concluded.[28] As had been pointed out earlier this was a period of severe financial stringency which placed the business community in very difficult position; it was therefore bound to sue for peace while the peasants remained in a militant mood. After the Pact was concluded the Congress could no longer openly support the 'No Rent' Campaign. The peasants were disappointed and when Civil Disobedience was resumed the peasantry of the wheat growing tracts showed by and large not much enthusiasm for it. But in the one year the rice price had declined even more dramatically than the wheat price. This affected the Eastern regions which now came into the forefront of the movement. Particularly Eastern U.P. and Bihar, here radical Kisan Sabhas sprang up, emerged as major areas of peasant unrest which was blended with the national movement.[29]

Congress involvement with the peasant movement in Northern India definitely helped to expand its social base. This was clearly shown by the elections of 1936 when the newly enfranchised upper strata of the peasantry voted for the Congress and not for parties favoured by the British. In extending the franchise the British had made it a point to get the occupancy tenants on to the electoral rolls.[30] Since these occupancy tenants had benefited from British-Indian tenancy legislation the British could have expected that under normal conditions they would have supported the government rather than the Congress which was still mainly town-based, but the impact of the depression upset all these political calculations.

The British made desperate bids to recover lost ground by introducing a spate of legislation for the relief of agricultural debtors, the scaling down of the debts, the restriction of interest rates, the curbing of the activities of money-lenders.[31] Earlier they had always refused to do anything about the limitation of interest rates because according to economic doctrine this would have been just as much as to try to suspend the law of gravity by legislation. Now they gave up all these reservations and even approved of the old Indian principle of damdupat, according to which the maximum amount of interest ought not to exceed the amount originally borrowed from the money-lender.[32] But in doing all this the British did not retain the allegiance of the peasantry and only alienated the business community which became more convinced than ever that only the Congress deserved, its support. After the easing of the credit situation due to the stream of distress gold the business community was again in a much better position to provide that support. The widening and strengthening of the social base of the Congress was, however, not an un-mixed blessing for its leadership. The Congress electorate of 1936 expected tangible benefits from Congress rule under provincial autonomy. It was not interested in the continuation of agitation but it expected Congress to take office and legislate in its favour. Because there were many elements in this electorate Congress had to be careful not to alienate one element while doing something for another. The only social group which the Congress did not need to worry about were the big landlords, because they were anyhow anti-Congress. The policy of the Congress ministries was therefore extremely cautious and to the more radical wing of the Congress it seemed to be almost reactionary. Nothing was done for the poorer peasants or those who had lost their occupancy rights when they fell into arrears of rent during the depression; a problem which was of particular importance in Bihar where the landlords had used this opportunity to extinguish occupancy rights on a large scale.[33] Peasants without occupany rights did not have the vote and politicians normally do not bend over backwards to do something for people who cannot vote for them. The extension of the social base of the Congress under the impact of the depression and its subsequent consolidation in a democratic process under the conditions of a restricted franchise greatly influenced its future development. The basic political alliances were made at that time; they were not greatly changed by the introduction of universal suffrage at a later stage.

Notes

1. Cf. M. Tracy, 'Agriculture in the Great Depression,' in H. vander Wee, *The Great Depression Revisited*, also Vladimir P. Timoshenho, *World Agriculture and the Great Depression*, Ann Arbor, 1933, vol. 5, no. 5.
2. Govt. of India. Legislative Dept., File 206/1933 C & G.
3. Govt. of India, Legislative Dept., File 242/1901 C & G (Wheat Import Duty Act), for the subsequent extension of this Act; see the following of the same department: 138 1932 C & G; 206 1933 C & G; 81/1934 C & G.
4. Govt. of India, Legisl. Dept., File 81/1931 C & G, note by D. Meek, DG Statistics.
5. R.H. Thomas Havens, *Farm and Nation in Modern Japan. Agrarian Nationalism 1870–1940*, p. 135f as quoted by Eernd Martin, 'Die Weltwirts-chaftskrise in Japan: Wirtschaftliche Konzentration and Sozziable Konflikte', unpublished paper 1980.
6. Govt. of India, Commerce Dept., File 110(1) T & E 1930 and File 1706—C 1932 = Commerce A, October 1932, Serial Nos. 1–32.
7. Commerce Dept., File 1706-C 1932, Note by Mr. Lindsay, 5 August 1929.
8. Commerce Dept., File 2019—C (6), Part B 1931 (Burma Rice Trade in Europe).
9. Government of India, Legis. Dept., File 81/1934 C & G (Statement made by G.S. Bajpai, Secretary, Education, Health and Lands).
10. Ibid.
11. Govt. of India, *Report on the Marketing of Rice in India*, pp. 544–45.
12. Govt. of India, Finance Dept., File 7(111) F 1935 (Statement showing composition of the Currency Reserve, December 1924 to March 1935 and of the Gold Standard Reserve, Statement changes of the bank rate, Presidence Banks and Imperial Bank, 1904–1935).
13. Ibid.
14. Ibid.
15. Government of India, Finance Dept., File 1 (10) F 1931; for the background to this decision, cf. Air George Schuster, Private Work and Public Causes. A Personal Record, 1881–1978, Cambridge 1979, p. 112ff.
16. Government of India, Finance Dept., File 1 (10) F 1931 (Secretary of State of Govt. of India, 23 September 1931).
    Impact of the Great Depression/Footnotes?
17. George Schuster, op. cit., p. 114.
18. Ibid., p. 175.
19. J.M. Keynes, Indian Currency and Finance.
20. Govt. of India, Dept. of Education, Health and Lands, File 3/1932 L & O (Proposal to guarantee cash credit of Rs. 30 lakh to the Bengal Provincial Co-

operative Bank from the Imperial Bank of India and financial position of Provincial Cooperative Banks in the several provinces).

21. Government of India, Finance Dept., File 7 (11) F 1935.

22. Ibid.

23. Dietmar Rothermund, *Government, Landlord and Peasant in India-Agrarian Relations under British Rule 1865–1935*.

24. Govt, of India, Dept. of Education, Health and Lands, File Lands (B).

25. Ibid.

26. Gyanendra Pandey, *The Ascendancy of the Congress in Uttar Pradesh 1936-1939, A Study in Imperfect Mobilization*.

27. S. Gopal, *Jawaharlal Nehru*, vol. I, p. 153.

28. Sumit Sarkar, 'The Logic of Gandhian Nationalism: Civil Disobedience and the Gandhi-Irwin Pact 1930–31' in *The Indian Historical Review*, vol. III, no, 1, July 1975, pp. 114–46.

29. G. McDonald, 'Unity on Trial: Congress in Bihar, 1929–39,' in D.A. Low, ed., *Congress and the Raj*, pp. 289–314.

30. Report of the Indian Franchise Committee, (Cmd. 4086), p. 35.

31. Cf. for instance the Bengal Moneylenders' Act of 1933 and similar legislation for provinces; for the United Provinces there was an Agriculturists Relief Act, an amendment of the Usurious Loans Act, a Reduction of Interest Act, and finally an Encumbered Estates Act (1934).

32. The principle of damdupat was included in the Bengal Moneylenders' Act and several other provincial act.

33. Rajendra Prasad et al., Report of the Bihar Kisan Enquiry Committee, 1937, unpublished paper, Rajendra Prasad Papers National Archives of India.

PART 5

Tensions and Struggles in the Coloinial Society

27

Nature of the Kol
Insurrection of 1831–32

J.C. Jha

T HE TRIBAL unrest of 1831–32, generally known as the Kol Insurrection, was a crude form of protest against all the recent changes and outside influences which had badly affected the tribal society. It was a gesture of despair. It was born out of frustration and anger–frustration with the new system of Government and laws, and anger at the people who either enforced them or took undue advantage of them.

The real tragedy of the tribal people of Chotanagpur was that their chiefs, alienated by their conversion to Hinduism and the English administrators, born and bred in the tradition of agricultural landlordism, had no sympathy with the tradition of tribal ownership of land or the idea of peasant-proprietorship. That was why the former brought in non-tribal settlers and the latter a complex administrative machinery run by unsympathetic people. Against these the tribal people found no remedy except unrest and violence.

In the course of their rising the tribal people were guilty of most heinous crimes, of banditry, murder and arson. But they knew no other method of effective social protest. According to Eric Hobsbawn, 'Social banditry, a universal and virtually unchanging: phenomenon, is little more than endemic peasant protest against oppression and poverty; a cry for vengeance on the rich and the oppressors, a vague dream of some curb upon them, a righting of individual wrongs. Its ambitions are modest: a traditional world in which men are justly dealt with.'[1] The tribal leaders were in their own society the equivalent of Robinhood or Rob Roy, rebels against landlords, bailiffs, merchants and usurers who were exploiting the tribal people. If their movements were 'blind and groping' that was because they were the movements of peasant protestants, extremely matriculate, not knowing how to express their legitimate grievances.

Thornton, Wilson and others voiced their belief that the events of 1831–32 were a mere spasmodic expression of tribal people's savagery and

*24th Session at Delhi, 1961.

propensity to plunder. A brief review of what the tribal people did when they broke out in violence and against whom their anger was directed will show that they were indeed savage in their attacks upon their enemies, savage perhaps from despair of securing justice by peaceful and orderly means. But it will also show that the outbreak was not an unconsidered, spasmodic affair, but one very closely connected with the oppression which they had suffered. The tribesmen had no hope of redress because the police were base and corrupt, the law court *amlas* were engaged in all sorts of illicit gains and the revenue officials tried to fleece them. In the face of this combined system of oppressive exactions, forcible dispossession of property, abuse and personal violence and a variety of similar tyrannies, the tribesmen found no other alternative than to make a desperate attempt to escape from this galling situation. Their retaliation, therefore, was as violent and unprecedented as the oppression had been on them.

Thornton described the rising as an orgy of mutual slaughter in which 'the hand of every man is against his neighbour.'[2] The Bengal Government noted of the rising that 'During the whole of its course and progress, though perhaps in a less degree in Palamau than within the Chotanagpur country, the worst excesses attended it. In the latter tract, from one part of it to the other, as the insurrection advanced, the people of the rude tribe of the Coles sacrificed numbers of those who fell into their hands, to their excited passions of revenge and hatred.'[3] There was a sort of madness and blindness and they could no longer see the light of reason. The Patna Commissioner, J. Master, reported the rising in lurid terms: 'Restless, wild and ferocious, they rushed into an insurrection scarcely paralleled for ferocity and eager for plunder, universally prone to violence and infuriated by real or imaginary wrongs, the whole population yielded to the unobstructed tide of rebellion—fire, rapine and murder marked their paths, nor was their vindictive spirit confined to those to whom their injuries were ascribed, but madly extended to unoffending females and helpless infants with the subtle determination of extirpating the whole area.'[4]

A number of cases brought to trial revealed the savage nature of the attacks to which many who failed or were unable to flee were exposed. The commonest feature was the hacking to death of victims who were killed even though they made no resistance. One Dahir Singh was dragged out of hiding, given two sword cuts across his back, two on the neck and finally his head was struck off by a *balwa*.[5] Shaikh Sagar, found hiding in the jungle was carried back to his village and then murdered by blows of a *balwa*.[6] In Thikochatti, a father and son were pulled from their hut, mercilessly beaten, and finally killed by having their heads hacked off with *balwas*.[7] At Tiku, six unhappy creatures, discovered sheltering in a hut were 'cruelly and wantonly butchered.'[8] In another case a Muslim family of eight, 'male and female, one advanced in years, several in the bloom of youth, and some in unconscious infancy', was completely annihilated.

The husband of a poor female had a rope of straw twisted round his neck by which he was forcibly dragged from his house and taken to the bed of a river at a short distance followed by his distracted wife. In his mutilated condition the victim was able to exclaim, 'You are resolved on my destruction. Kill my wife who stands there weeping'. On hearing this one of the assailants cut off the sufferer's head with a sword.[9] Women, children, the aged, none were spared. One woman's head was cut off to be presented to a God, and there were half a dozen cases of infants and babes in arms being killed.

Cases of treachery and brutality were in fact very common during the unrest. In one instance, a non-tribal family, which had returned from pargana Jashpur after supposed tranquillity, was offered pretended hospitality by a Kol and then the head of the family was murdered in cold blood.[10] In another instance the insidious information being conveyed to a secluded party in the hills, the family began its return journey. But no sooner had a member of the family approached the village than he was wounded severely and the assailants then seizing his arms and legs dragged him to a well into which they threw him and heaping upon him earth and stones thus terminated the wretched man's existence.[11] Hundreds of such heart-rending incidences were narrated before the trying magistrate and the sessions judge. It would be unnecessary to include them all in this paper, but it may be mentioned that these incidences show the pattern of behaviour of the tribal people. The terror of such actions can well be imagined, and from the earliest stage those who feared were possible victims could be found on the move, carrying off such valuables as they could. Their flight undoubtedly served to set off yet wider movements of non-tribal people, and so to spread the atmosphere of uncertainty and excitement. It also served to rouse the hopes of plunder among the tribal people through whose midst they had to pass and so in places gave to a movement begun as a rebellion against oppression the air of ordinary banditry.

Several methods were adopted by the tribal leaders to spread the rising: 'One was the beating of the *nagaras* or great drums; another the circulation of a '*dheori*' (a branch of a tree, usually mango)[12]; a third was to circulate arrows of war[13] like the fiery cross. The villages, which wished to join those by whom the arrows were sent, were required to return those arrows whole, and those who wanted to oppose them were to return them broken.

The arrows, later circulated, were accompanied by a notice to all foreigners to quit, and threatening messages to those who might remain or offer opposition.[14] The obvious motive of the tribal people was to so terrorize the non-tribal settlers as to make them abandon everything and flee from the whole tribal area.

The spread of the insurrection so quickly and so widely was only made possible, of course, by the absence of any effective check. The result was most shocking. As a newspaper correspondent put it, 'Finding so little opposition in their attack, and the soldier's life to be "a very merry kind of life, if taken smooth and rough", they proceeded from village to village burning and massacring every respectable person, and every foreigner, and forcing every Cole by the fear of instant death, to join their standards. Thus the fire of rebellion once lighted, the flames spread rapidly. The villagers, ever ready to fly to arms, and better themselves at the expense of their less numerous and more peaceable superiors, eagerly seized their bows and arrows, and pursued a course of the most cold blooded and heartless barbarity, in which they received no check until the arrival of the joint Commissioners.'[15]

It was a consciousness of the lack of any effective power in the field to check the rebels which caused the unusual alarm. Rumours were at one time afloat that Mirzapur near Banaras to the west of Palamau had been sacked by the Kols, and that the disturbances had occurred at Azimgarh. On 3 February 1833 it was reported in the *Meerut Observer* that for the last ten days the town of Mirzapur and the surrounding area was 'thrown into fearful consternation' by the intelligence of a body of about 5,000 men being assembled at a short distance, 'carrying plunder and rapine before them, and leaving desolation and misery in their rear.'[16] The *India Gazette* noted in its editorial column, 'from Chotanagpur to the frontiers of Oude there is a general commotion.'[17] (Even the people of Banaras were getting panicky lest they should be attacked by the Kols).[18] At one point it was rumoured that the Marathas were also joining the Kols from the south-west. Major Sutherland was probably right in saying that 'had the country between Chotanagpur and Calcutta on the one hand and Benares on the other, been inhabited by Danger Coles, the insurrection would have spread to those places'.[19]

The question naturally arises, with a rising so widespread and a rumour even wider, whether it was mainly an anti-British rising. Was there a concerted plan to throw off the British yoke? Master, the Patna Commissioner, argued that the Kols, who emigrated in vast numbers to Calcutta and other big cities in search of work, must have been familiar with the British enterprise, resources and power, and, therefore, they could never have thought of subverting such a power.[20] Metcalfe, perhaps voicing the opinions of Sutherland, his Private Secretary, who had personally visited the troubled area, believed, however, that the insurrection really had originated 'in the spirit of independence and (in) the belief that the opportunity of throwing off our yoke had arrived'.[21] W. Blunt, the third member of the Calcutta Council, however, disagreed with this view. 'Though the predatory habits of this people (habits which formerly prevailed more or less in all the Jungle Estates)', he remarked, 'may have rendered them ready auxiliaries to their discontented neighbours in Sonepur, but I cannot for a moment believe that either the Coles of Singhbhum or Nagpur could have entertained so wild a project (a project as far beyond their comprehension as their means) as that of subverting the British Empire.'[22] He, therefore, believed that they had no design 'beyond the immediate gratification of their revenge against those by whom they had suffered oppression.'[23] Indeed, it would seem clear that the ordinary mass of the tribal people were ignorant of the complex machinery of the British administration, scarcely knew a British official by sight, and were rising against much more immediate enemies, *thanadars* or salt *darogas*, money-lenders or *thikadars*. Those who would have gained most from the destruction of the Company's rule, the once-independent rajas and jagirdars, did not, in the event, ally themselves with the tribal rebels, and though they would not take a risk and actually support the British officials, they stood neutral. Some, indeed, got the best of both worlds; they used the tribal unrest to free themselves from the clutches of the money-lenders, and then carried merit with the authorities by turning on the rebels. The Rani of Patkum was particularly efficient in such double dealing.

So there was nothing so grandiose about the Kol insurrection as a national rising to secure independence from the British. The enemy which was attacked was a more local and particular one: the outsider (Hindu, Sikh or Muslim) who had clamped himself like a leech on the body of tribal society, and the petty and exacting government official. The Joint Commissioners put it succinctly when in February 1832 they wrote, 'The whole of the Moondas and Coles, who, we believe, compose about two-thirds of the population, have taken up arms against the respectable inhabitants of the country, burnt and plundered their houses and property, and expelled them.'[24] Once the expulsion of the foreigner was well under way, their property was of course thoroughly looted.

The unrest was then, in origin, a revolt of the dispossessed, of the helots against their masters. The statements of both prisoners and victims show that the Oraons, Mundas and others made the *Suds* their victims. Moneylenders, merchants and shopkeepers, land-grabbers and tax farmers, these were the people attacked; those foreigners who had been usefully integrated into the tribal economy, the *Chaukidars*, milkmen, and artisans were generally spared. Moreover, the non-tribal *amlas* (petty officials) of the Government who had fleeced the tribal people were also attacked. Thus, the Kol Insurrection was mainly a war of the tribal inhabitants of Chotanagpur against the non-tribal settlers and service- holders. The British came into the picture because they tried to oppose the tribal rebels to protect the non-tribal people and to re-establish law and order.

Notes

1. *Primitive Rebels*, 13.

2. Thornton, *History of British India*, vol. V, p. 203.

3. Bengal Government to Court of Directors, 25 September 1832, B.C. 1362/54223, I.O.L.

4. Master to Government, 17 January 1833, para 13, B.C. 1502/58893 I.O.L.

5. Master to Registrar, Nimamat Adalat, 22 October 1932, Trial no. 7, B.C. 1502/58893.

6. Ibid., no. 13.

7. Ibid., no. 18.

8. Ibid., no. 33.

9. Ibid., no. 104.

10. Ibid., no. 196.

11. Ibid., no. 115.

12. Master to Nizamat Adalat, 22 October 1832, case no. 22, B.C. 1502/58893.

13. Statement, Singrai, Enclosure, Russell to Government, 18 April 1832,. B.C. 1363/54226.

14. Sutherland to Government, n.d. para 8, B.C. 1363/54227.

15. 'P', Pitoria, n.d. Bengal Hurkaru, 15 February 1832.

16. Quoted in *India Gazette*, 8 March 1832.

17. Ibid., 9 February 1832.

18. Ibid., 10 February 1832.

19. Sutherland to Government, n.d. B.C. 1363/54227.

20. Master to Government, 17 January 1833, para 24, B.C. 1502/58893.

21. Metcalfe, *Minute*, 14 April 1832. B.C. 1363/54227. Sutherland thought that if the Kols had 'possessed either leaders or enterprise, they would undoubtedly have established themselves at our stations of Hazaribagh, Bankoorah and Sherghatty, perhaps at Gyah (Gaya) commanding the principal road between Calcutta and Benares and taking possession of some of the oldest territories, of the Company. Sutherland to Government n.d. B.C. 1363/54227.

22. Blunt, *Minute*, 4 Apr. 132, B.C. 1363/54227.

23. Ibid.

24. Joint Commissioners to Bowen, 9 February 1832, para 2, B.C. 1362/54224.

28

Agrarian Tensions and British Policy in Malabar

K.K.N. Kurup

Dᴜʀɪɴɢ ᴛʜᴇ last quarter of the nineteenth century, British rule and its landlord raj had to face new socio-economic problems in India. By that time the colonial relations had already dissolved an entire social fabric and integrated the economy and agriculture with the world capitalist system.[1] The forces released by the colonial government introduced considerable changes in the agrarian system and rural economy and subscribed ultimately to a parasitic-absentee land ownership. In brief, British rule was in a permanent alliance with landlordism. It stimulated sub-infeudation and encouraged the growth of intermediate tenure-holders. The agrarian system which came into existence under British rule was neither feudal nor entirely capitalistic. However, it provided for the emergence of an urban capitalist group. Prof. Eric Stokes writes:

Urban capitalists were more interested in rent-receiving or in controlling the disposal of peasant grown cash crops than in directly engaging in agriculture; so that the introduction of legal private property rights in land tended to lengthen the chain of intermediaries above the actual cultivator and left the peasant *petite culture* intact.[2]

Such a system, no doubt, accelerated agrarian discontent, tension and unrest in rural society.

The main purpose of this paper is to highlight tensions and new forces which appeared in Malabar rural society during the last quarter of the nineteenth century. The official policy of government with regard to the agrarian system in India clearly stated: 'It is most desirable that facilities should be given for the gradual growth of a middle class connected with the land without dispossessing the peasant proprietors and occupiers . . .'[3]

But in practice the peasants and occupiers were evicted out of their petty-holding everywhere. The structure of the agrarian system that originated under

*39th Session at Hyderabad, 1978.

Lord Cornwallis is 1973 remained unchanged. The ryots were left under the mercy of landlords and their interests were not properly safeguarded in the Anglicised legal system. A recent scholar, who has analysed agrarian tensions in Bengal, states that 'the great human surplus made the position of the peasants. precarious.'[4] Therefore, there was no proper improvement of land. Further no capital was available with the peasant as he was a victim of competitive rent. The landlord invested his capital in purchase of land rights, usury, etc., and not in the improvement of land. Such a practice ultimately led to economic backwardness and poverty in rural society. Malabar was not an exception to this general situation of colonial India.

The agrarian system introduced by the Company continued under the Crown also. However, new socio-economic forces which during this period compelled the government to look into the conditions of peasantry and eliminate tensions in rural society. The growth of cash economy, populations, cash crops, etc., were some of the new forces which pressurised the government to introduce social reforms and tenancy legislations. The liberal experiment in tenancy legislations, factory reforms, etc., of Lord Ripon during the Gladstonian era is a significant landmark in British policy in India.[5] It had an impact on Malabar also.

Since the establishment of colonial rule, the traditional society of Malabar had organised a series of revolts against the foreign authority. Though the revolts of Pazhassi and Kurichiyas represented a conservative character, they certainly involved elements of peasent-uprisings. The Company suppressed these revolts with the supports of local chieftains and big landholders. But tensions and disturbance again developed in Malabar Society, particularly in agrarian sections. The Moplah outbreaks of Malabar were violent expressions of rural tensions. As there was no systematic ideology behind these disturbances, they were influenced by religious sentiments also. However, their roots were agrarian discontent and rural poverty. It was in this situation that the government appointed William Logan, the district collector of Malabar, for specially enquiring into 'the general question of tenure of land and of tenant-rights in this region.'[6]

The Commission after considering various aspects of the agraian structure came to the conclusion that promulgation of tenancy legislations was an absolute requirement for ameliorating conditions in this region. The Commission also recommended legislative measures for introducing institutional changes. These recommendations were intended for bringing out social mobility to cope with the requirements of colonial government and its economy.

The Commission found that the extreme tenurial independence enjoyed by the landlords was responsible for rural tensions. 'The British Courts', stated Logan, 'backed up by police and magistrates and troops and big guns made the

Janmi's (landlord's) independence complete.'[7] Therefore, restriction, through statutory provision, was demanded by the Commission on this land owning upper class of rural society.[8] According to the Commission, the actual cultivators were hopelessly in debt and hopelessly in arrears with their, in many ways outrageous rents.[9] He recommended to the government to encourage the formation of small gardens by small holders who should be securely left to gather the fruits of the trees they planted.[10] Ultimately, the commission desired a direct settlement of revenue with this class of small holders. In principle, the proposed revenue system was based on ryotwari. It was intended to support the lower strata of the agrarian section against the highhanded and arbitrary dealings of the upper class of landowners or *Jammis*. The Commission recognised the significance of a policy of pacification of the lower sections in the agrarian structure. It criticised the revenue policy of Munro which practically supported the upper section and completely neglected the lower class of peasants in the rural society. The Commission stated:

It was thought, no doubt, that the ryotwari system provided for all contingencies; whereas if any, even the smallest inquiry had been made into the condition of the actual cultivators of the soil of Malabar, as apart from ideal ryots, it would have been at once apparent that the ryotwari system altogether failed to provide for such a state of thing as existed in Malabar then, and as exists now. When the ryot of our revenue account is, as so often happens, the holder of a fat appointment in some public or private office, who has perhaps never seen the piece of land, of which he holds the title deeds and Patta, it is clear that Sir Thomas Munro's ideal ryot has fallen away from his traditions, and has become something very different from the ryot sketched in Sir Thomas Munro's papers. The result was natural enough; the pity is that it was not foreseen and guarded against, for in Malabar the actual cultivators are rapidly degenerating into insolvent cottiers.[11]

The revenue system introduced by Munro and his supporters was a substantial landlord settlement. The 'peasants' with whom the government settled land revenue were of the elite landholding castes. They sub-infeudated their land to the inferior landless castes.[12] Therefore, agrarian tensions in Malabar involved the elements of caste-antagonism also. The Commission recommended an immediate revenue settlement with the occupying tenants. Such a settlement would make them loyal to the British authority. Simultaneously, the system would increase production as well as the revenue.

During the last quarter of the nineteenth century, like many other districts in India, Malabar also began to produce on a significant scale for the world market. Growth of plantations and extensive cultivation of cash crops were on immediate effect of this development. But this was effected without the mode of peasant agricultural production undergoing any fundamental change. An agrarian revolution was expected by the early British administrators like

Cornwallis with the introduction of freely alienable proprietory rights in land. However, this innovation did not bring any structural changes in the productive system of rural society.'British hopes of the emergence of capitalist agriculture,' states Eric Stokes,'whether at the peasant or superior level, were disappointed, and the class stratification of rural society by legal revolution into landlord and tenant was never properly consummated.'[13]

In this circumstance, full utilization of the agrarian section for colonial needs largely depended on institutional changes. The Commission realised the significance of institutional changes in Malabar, especially among the land community in Malabar belonging to the Nayar caste. Their major problem was the matrilineal joint family or Tarawad system. By the end of the century, this historical institution had disintegrated owing to western impact and several economic factors.[14] According to this system a man's own acquisitions during his life-time descended at his death to the common stock of his Tarawad and not to his own children. Legally the children had no claim on their fathers' self acquired property.[15] Therefore, there was no motive or stimulus for the members of the joint families to exert or participate in wealth producing activities. This situation was fatal to individual of self acquired property by will during one's own life time and to save the Nairs from the false position in which they were placed by tradition.[16]

It was, therefore, recommended not only for tenancy legislation for eliminating agrarian tensions but also for social reforms for enforcing institutional changes in traditional society. It criticised the matrilineal inheritance and corporate land control by joint families. Although many of the findings of the Commission were not immediately considered by the government, much socioeconomic legislations for Malabar in the later years was largely moulded by its findings.[17] The western educated professional group in Malabar gradually compelled the government to promulgate legislation in favour of individual inheritance to one's father's property and abolition of corporate land ownership. This group supported the growth of individualism in rural society. The government also cooperated with them in breaking up traditional society by enforcing legislative enactments. The ultimate purpose was the integration of a rural agrarian structure based on subsistence economy with that of the capitalist system of colonial rule. It initiated the beginning of a long process of social mobility.

Notes

1. Bipan Chandra, 'Presidential Address'(Modern India) in *Indian History Congress: Proceedings of the Thirty-second Session, Jabalpur,* 1970, vol. II, p. 22.
2. Eric Stokes,'The First Century of British Colonial Rule in India: Social Revolution or Social Stagnation' in *Past and Present,* no. 58, February 1973, p. 150.

3. Secretary of State, Despatch no. 14, 9 July 1892 in *Report of the Land Revenue Commission, Bengal*, vol. I, pp. 338–39.

4. Chittabrata Palit, *Tensions in Bengal Rural Society*, p. 203.

5. S. Gopal, *British Policy in India: 1858–1905*, pp. 129–79.

6. G.O. (Madras) Judicial Department, no. 281, 5 February 1881.

7. *Malabar Special Commission: 1881–82, Malabar Land Tenures*, vol. I, para 122.

8. A statement showing the number of *Janmis* in Malabar is given by the Commission as follows (ibid., para 234).

Taluks	Minor Janmis Number	Principal Janmis Number	Total
Chirakkal	4,650	42	4,692
Kottayam	349	32	381
Kurumbranad	3,109	66	3,175
Wynad	343	26	369
Calicut	4,852	56	4,908
Ernad	1,387	113	1,500
Walluvanad	2,152	179	2,331
Palghat	3,319	96	3,415
Ponnami	3,424	219	3,643
Cochin	50	—	50
TOTAL	23,635	829	24,464

9. Ibid.

10. Ibid., para 139.

11. Ibid., para 87.

12. An analysis of this relationship is given in Dharma Kumar, *Land and Caste in South India*, p. 72ff.

13. Eric Stokes, op. cit., n. 2, p. 150.

14. Robin Jeffrey, *The Decline of Nayar Dominance: Society and Politics in Trevancore: 1847–1908*, p. 181 ff.

15. *Malabar Special Commission*, n. 7, paras 481–4.

16. Ibid., paras 485–87.

17. Malabar Marriage Act IV of 1896 and Madras Marumakkathayam Act of 1932 belong to such category.

29

Emigration of Biharis to Mauritius in 1859–70

Satyanarain Prasad

THE ABOLITION of the slave trade from the British Empire in 1838 gave birth to the problem of labour in the British colonies. The dearth of labour adveresly hit the plantation industry of Mauritius, Grenada, Jamaica, Trinidad, etc. Mauritius, a sugar producing colony, needed labourers well-adept in the art of sugar production to tone up its languishing industry. Bihar, a sugar producing province, with its unemployed inhabitants caught the attention of the Mauritius Government.

The labourers were recruited according to Indenture system. This system required them to enter into contracts with the employers. The contracts enjoined them to serve the employers for five years. During this period they could neither change masters nor demand higher wages in spite of the rise in prices. The employers, on the other hand, provided them with free quarters and medical facilities.[1]

Like other colonies Mauritius too maintained its office-depot for the recruitment of labourers. It also employed recruiters to procure workers. They were called *Arkatees.* They recruited labourers from distant places. It was a profitable profession and was carried on by all sections of population. The people of Bihar, going to Calcutta, in search of employment, came in touch with the recruiting agents. They offered them food and clothes and thus lured them to their depots in Calcutta. From there the labourers, without their knowledge, were shipped to different colonies. Though no complaint of force or fraud was made, the moment the workers accepted the help of the agents they fell into their clutches from which there was no escape.[2] Thus, the likes and dislikes of the emigrants were ignored. They were treated like dumb cattle and were driven to colonies of which they knew nothing. The cheap labour available in India led to unhealthy competition among the various colonies, which resulted in a fall in the number of emigrants going to Mauritius. In 1858, 810 old emigrants (sometimes persons employed in Mauritius also recruited

*31st Session at Varanasi, 1969.

labourers when they visited their homes for short periods) despatched 14,722 persons, in 1859, 873 imported 10,393 souls. In 1860, the number of old emigrants got reduced to 135, who could send only 1,811 persons to Mauritius.[3] The total number of persons going to Mauritius was 6,091 in 1860–61 against 17,606 in 1859–60. Among them 3,756 or nearly half belonged to Bihar. The unscrupulous behaviour of the recruiting agents was mainly responsible for the fall in the number of emigrants to Mauritius.[4]

This alarmed the Mauritius Government. In its minute of January 1861, it requested the Government of India to put boards at the entrance and in the public room of every depot depicting the name of the colony to which it belonged, both in English and Indian languages, so that the emigrants might not be misled by the agents.[5]

The Lieutenant-Governor accepted this suggestion and asked the Protector of Emigrants to put the names of the colonies at the gate of the Emigration Depot to check misrepresentation and fraud. He was also asked to see that the emigrant should not be deceived and should go to the colony he intended to go.[6]

The government had no power to interfere with the work of the agents engaged in recruiting labourers so long as they did not violate the law of the land. Act XXIV of 1852, however, empowered the magistrate to prosecute a person who 'seduces away coolies on false representation'. With the increase in the number of Emigration Depots the chances of corruption and malpractices also increased. So the government asked the Protector of Emigrants to examine the intending emigrants carefully and to acquaint them with their destination.[7]

The Special Commissioner, H.N.D. Beyts, appointed by the Mauritius Government, arrived in Calcutta in March 1861 to watch the working of the Emigration Depots and to submit report.[8] The report described the method of recruiting labourers 'radically defective'. It requested the Government of India to take some concrete steps to check the evils otherwise they would hamper the proper working of the Depots and would even lead to the prohibition of the emigration of labourers. The want of any rule to regulate the activities of the agents gave them license to indulge in all sorts of nefarious activities.[9]

To give the system of recruitment a clear and sound footing, the Special Commissioner suggested the registration of recruiters with full particulars at the office of the Protector of Emigrants. A recruiter should be permitted to recruit for only one Depot at a time and that also with the permission of the District Magistrate. Every licensed recruiter should be asked to wear the badge of his Depot in three languages. It should be made incumbent on the part of the recruiters to accompany the recruits to the office of the Protector and to bear the responsibility for their care and comfort in the way. Provision should be made for the examination of the recruits individually and not in batches. To control the activities of the recruiters recommendation was made for the payment of their remuneration through the Protector's Office 'once every six months, at an average rate to be fixed by the Protector.'[10]

The Government of Bengal regarded these suggestions very 'desirable, necessary and proper' likely to check the unscrupulous and fraudulent means adopted by the recruiters. But as to the last suggestion regarding the payment of the recruiters the government agreed with the first part of the proposal that they should be paid through Protector's office, but it was not in favour of fixing the amount to be paid to them.[11]

To remove the grievances of the Mauritius Government and to control the activities of the recruiters the government passed an Act in 1864. Act XIII of 1864 insisted upon the interrogation of the labourer by a Magistrate regarding his choice for the colony, the nature of work he would have to perform there, before his embarkation. Provision was also made for the medical examination of the labourer and for the issue of licenses to the recruiters. Only the Protector of Emigrants could grant licenses. The Magistrate could also refuse to register any person, if he failed to answer his queries, or if he, in his opinion, was seduced by the recruiters. The Act, thus, tried to curb the activities of unscrupulous recruiters.[12]

To enforce these rules strictly the Protector of Emigrants at Calcutta, Captain Burbank, was asked to get a number of tickets printed, showing the number of labourers, the registration number, the district of registry, the name of the depot for which he was recruited. The Registering Officers had to distribute these" tickets after filling them among the labourers.[13]

In the Patna Division under Act III of 1863, 4,993 persons were registered, while the number of persons registered under Act XIII of 1864 was 1,010. The district of Shahabad alone registered 2,450 persons, Patna had 1,638 persons to its credit, while 1,915 persons were registered in Bihar. In North Bihar, Champaran registered only nine persons under Act XIII of 1864, while 92 persons were enrolled in Tirhut under Act III of 1863. The return of Saran, on the other hand, was blank.[14] Bhagalpur Division registered 5,311 persons under Act III of 1863.[15] Thus the provision of the Act regarding the registration of the labourers worked satisfactorily in Bihar.

In 1865–66, 19,963 persons went to different colonies. The number of persons despatched to Mauritius was 15,115—the highest. Among them more than half belonged to Bihar. This was due to the famine of 1866 which threw many people out of employment.[16] The district of Arrah supplied the largest number of emigrants, Sahebagnj came next, the third place was occupied by Chapra or Saran while Tirhut was at the tail of the list.[17]

The rapid pace of emigration to Mauritius came to a halt due to the restriction imposed on the stay of the labourers in the colony over a certain period. The work they had to do during this period was also decided. Their remuneration was fixed on 'an average of' Rs. 12-4-0 per month. This ebbed the rising tide of emigration to a considerable extent. From January 1866 to March 1866 only four ships left Calcutta for Mauritius.[18]

In 1866–67, 10,175 persons embarked for different colonies. Of them only 478 persons proceeded to Mauritius on two ships while the number of people going to British Guiana, Trinidad, Jamaica and St. Vincent was 4,509, 2,993, 1,705 and 490, respectively. In 1867–68, emigration to Mauritius was further reduced to 313. British Guiana and Trinidad received 3,001 and 1,840 new comers during this period, respectively. The sharp fall in the number of emigrants to Mauritius was due to the failure of crops in the colony on account of severe drought resulting in the want of labourers and rise in prices.[19] Besides this, the reduction in the rate of wages to Rs. 4 per month rising up to Rs. 6 in the fifth or last year of service must have affected the choice of the emigrant in choosing that colony. The Protector of Emigrants did not think that the reduction in the wages of labourers had retarded their emigration to Mauritius because of 'its comparatively close proximity to India.'[20] To some extent this may be true, but the emigrants were going to earn money. So, they might have chosen the colony which paid them higher wages.

The slow rate of emigration to Mauritius was soon reversed. From 1868–69, the number of emigrants began increasing. During this period 1,237 souls sailed for the colony, while in 1869–70, their number increased to 1,499, an increase of 262 persons from the previous year.[21] This year, as usual, Arrah topped the list in sending labourers to Mauritius from Bihar. It sent 389 workers, Sahebganj or Gaya sent 175 souls while the number of labourers hailing from Chapra was 89.[22] The close proximity of the colony to this country, the improved state of agriculture might have again lured the labourers to this colony.

In 1870 the Protector of Emigrants requested the Government of Bengal to fix a limit on the number of emigrants going to different colonies. But the government did not comply with the request as it would be tantamount to putting arbitrary restraint on emigration and thus interfering with the labour market. It could only prevent unfit persons from embarking on board a ship.[23] The period was the heyday of capitalism. The theory of laissez-faire had been accepted by the government. So, it did not want to put a check on the number of emigrants going to different colonies.

Thus, the government tried to curb fraud and malpractices practised in the recruitment by making rules. It was also not blind to the other side of the medal, such as moral, hygenic and sanitary aspects of emigration.

In 1860, the government instructed the Emigration Agents at Calcutta and Madras to see that the ships carrying emigrants to different colonies should contain at least one-fourth females to the total number of males. This was done to check corruption among the emigrants. The despatch of a large number of females was to benefit not only the emigrants but the colonial governments as well because it would make them permanent residents there. This would solve the problem of labour in the colonies.[24]

The Mauritius Government welcomed the gesture of the government. The Special Commissioner from Mauritius requested the Governor-General to permit female emigrants to enter into contracts for working there. This would lessen the burden on their male relatives and would enhance their income. Moreover, there was no logic in debarring females who worked in India to earn their livelihood. He assured the government that women contracting for service would be engaged in light work such as 'weeding, planting or manuring sugarcanes and drying or bagging sugar.' The Special Commissioner also proposed to recommend that even after signing the contract, if a woman was found physically unfit to work by the Medical Officer of the Estate where she had to work or by the Government Medical Officer of the district, she would be freed from the terms of the contract without paying any indemnity. Again, if any woman would be hindered from working due to justifiable reasons, she would be free to abstain hereself from the work without 'incurring any punishment of forfeiture.'[25] The government had no objection in permitting the female emigrants to enter into contracts if the assurances from the Special Commissioner were adhered to.[26]

In the year 1861–62, the percentage of women going to Mauritius was 24.3,[27] while it was 29.59 in 1863–64.[28] In 1866–67, the proportion of females to males reached 35.1 per cent.[29] Thus, the percentage of females was increasing. Not satisfied with this, the Government of India made a rule which fixed the proportion of females to males 50 on board a ship. This created a lot of difficulties. It was found to be extremely difficult to procure such a large number of women. It led to the recruitment of undesirable persons and prostitutes to fill the quorum. The presence of such women was objectionable both on 'physical and moral grounds.' So, the Government of Bengal urged the Secretary to the government of India to relax the proportion of females to males to 25 per cent.[30]

The Government of India complied with its request and allowed it the discretion of sending 25 per cent females as emigrants.[31] The proportion of females to males on ships going to Mauritius was always satisfactory. During 1867–68, it was 45.10 per cent—the highest, in comparison to the percentage of females going to other colonies. During this period, the percentage of females sailing for British Guiana and Trinidad was 29.97 and 43.71, respectively.[32] The Emigration Report for the year 1869–70 expressed satisfaction on the compliance of rules regarding the percentage of females to males by different colonies. In 1869–70, the percentage of females to males emigrating to Mauritius was 40.53.[33] Thus, Mauritius maintained its popularity with Indian women.

The government also tried to provide civic amenities to the emigrants. This is why it made provision for the inspection of depots, formulated rules regarding the space allotted to an emigrant in the ship. In 1864, the government took strong action against the officers of a ship, Earl of Clare, for supplying bad food to the emigrants returning from Mauritius and for assaulting a female emigrant.[34] It disqualified the ship from carrying any emigrant so long as it remained under the charge of the Commander and Medical Officer who had totally neglected the emigrants.[35]

The depots where the emigrants were kept before embarkation were incharge of the agents of contractors. They supervised the work of licensed recruiters and arranged for the boarding and lodging of the emigrants. These depots were not properly looked after. They often housed more persons than their capacity.[36] This led the Governor-General-in-Council to issue a supplementary rule which required the presence of the Surgeon-Superintendent at the time of store inspection along with the Protector and Medical Inspector of Emigrants. The new rule made it incumbent on the part of the Surgeon-Superintendent to submit his report in writing.[37]

As a result of this measure, the sanitary condition of the depots improved. The rate of mortality was moderate. Only in the Mauritius depots the deaths were 'more numerous' in comparison to other depots. Here out of 1077 persons 29 died in 1866–67, whereas in the Demerara and Jamaica depots, out of 7,220 persons 75 died. In the Trinidad and St. Vincent depots 4,116 persons were admitted of whom 26 died. The cause of the excessive death in the Mauritius depot was the admission of famine stricken persons who swarmed Calcutta. The Emigration Agents helped the Surgeon in improving the sanitary condition of the depots.[38]

The government also took care for the comfort and health of the emigrants on voyage of a ship. In 1867, it turned down the request of the Emigration Agent of Mauritius to ship the emigrants without medical men.[39] In July 1867, the government made certain amendments in Act XIII of 1864. A ship was not allowed to carry more than 350 passengers. The married couple were to be provided with a separate compartment.[40] The 12''per state adult' was the space allotted to an adult.[41] In 1870, the Governor-General-in-Council passed a rule under Section 63 of Act XIII of 1864, which asked the Masters and Surgeons of the ships to report any occurrence likely to affect "the health and safety" of the emigrant.[42] This ensured the safety of life and health of the emigrants. The rate of mortality decreased considerably. In 1869–70 out of 1,691 persons going to Mauritius only three persons died.[43]

The emigrants had gone to Mauritius to earn money. So, the Government of Mauritius framed rules for the remittance of money to their relatives in India. Immigrants, who wanted to send money to India had to deposit in the Immigration Office, which issued them a receipt. The Immigration Office was instructed to send the money to the Treasury at the end of every week. The Protector of Immigrants was to be informed every month about the amount received in the office and other details. He had to send reports every month regarding the money received and the names of persons to whom it was to be paid in India to the Emigration Agent in India. They had to distribute the money in the three Presidency towns of India. In the interior, Mauritius sub-agents or collectors or sub-collectors were empowered to disburse the money. The Agents had to submit quarterly reports about the disbursement of money both to the Protector of Immigrants and to the Auditor-General.[44]

The Government of India appreciated the soundness of the principle of payment.[45] But it recommended the extension of time for payment first to two months and then to six months due to distance and ignorance of the people. After twelve months, according to the rules of the Indian Post-Office, the money was to be forfeited.[46]

The rule regarding the transmission of money was enforced in April 1866. From that time till 1870, about 142,190 rupees came to India. The value of the jewellery and gold brought by the Indians could not be ascertained.[47]

The Ordinance of 1845, had required the emigrants to return to India after fulfilling their contracts.[48] This ordinance ensured their safe return to India. But it also put a check on their liberty. They were not free to go to the place of their choice. So, on the suggestion of the Protector of Immigrants, the Secretary of State for India decided to make an amendment in the ordinance allowing the emigrants to go anywhere from Mauritius after completing the terms of the contract. The Protector of Immigrants, was, however, required to transmit to the British Consul of the place where the emigrant was going, the details about him besides registering his name.[49] This measure was taken for the safety and protection of the emigrants leaving the colony.

In the second quarter of the nineteenth century, emigration from India to different colonies was very brisk. Mauritius was one of the most popular colonies among the Biharis. Both Mauritius and Bihar produced sugar. So, a large number of labourers went there from Bihar. Moreover, the climate of the colony was similar to that of India. Arrah, Chapra, Gaya and Patna supplied the largest number of emigrants. The various laws framed by the Government regarding recruitment and for safeguarding the life, liberty and health of the emigants worked satisfactorily.

Notes

1. C. Kondapi, *Indians Overseas 1838–1949*, p. 8.
2. From J.H. Young, Commissioner of Burdwan, to the Secretary to the Govt. of Bengal, no. 28, dated the 6 February 1861.
3. Minute, no. 5 of January 1861 by His Excellency the Governor of Mauritius.

4. From Capt. C. Eales, Protector of Emigrants at the Port of Calcutta, to J.D. Gordon, Jr. Secy. to the Govt. of Bengal, no. 250, dated the 28 May 1861. (The number of persons going to Mauritius from several districts of Bihar was as follows—Arrah-985, Birbhum-7, Bhagalpur-10, Chapra or Saran-239, Hazaribagh-385, Muzaffarpur-78, Patna, Azimabad, Jullesore or Monghyr-552, Purulia-492, Purnia-4, Ranchi-439, Sahebganj or Gaya-166. Total 3,756).

5. Minute, no. 5 of Jan. 1861 by His Excellency the Governor of Mauritius.

6. From J.D. Gordon, Jr. Secy. to the Govt. of Bengal, to the Protector of Emigrants at Calcutta, no. 52, dated the 4 April 1861.

7. Ibid.

8. From Capt. C. Eales, Protector of Emigrants at the Port of Calcutta, to J.D. Gordon, Jr. Secy. to the Govt. of Bengal, no. 250, dated the 28 May 1861.

9. From H.N.D. Beyts; Sp. Commissioner from Mauritius to W.S. Seton-Karr, Secy. to the Govt. of Bengal, no. 11, dated the 13 April 1861.

10. Ibid.

11. From J.D. Gordon, Jr. Secy. to the Govt. of Bengal, to the Secy. to the Govt. of India, Home Deptt., no. 101, dated the 9 August 1861.

12. C. Kondapi, op. cit., p. 13.

13. From A. Eden, Secy. to the Govt. of Bengal, to the Commrs. of Chittagong, Cuttack, Chota Nagpore, Assam, Patna, Bhagalpore, Dacca, Nudea and Burdwan, no. 199, dated the 12 January 1865.

14. From G.F. Cockburn, Commr. of the Patna Divn. to the Secy. to the Govt. of Bengal, no. 77 dated the 28 Mar. 1865. (The number of persons registered in each office was as follows—Gaya-433, Sherghatty-1, 482, Patna-908, Danapur-70'), Barh-24, Arrah-1, 817, Buxar-493, Sasseram 140.)

15. From A. Money, Commr. of the Bhagalpore Division and Sonthal pergunnahs, to the Secretary to the Govt. of Bengal, no. 476, dated the 31 May 1865. (The following is the number of labourers recruited from various places till 1864. Bhagalpur-1, 176, Monghyr-2, 852, Turnia-41, Darjeeling-41, Rajmahal-1, 081, Pakur-5, Dumka-5, Deoghur-25, Godda-25.)

16. *Bihar and Orissa District Gazetteers*, Saran, p. 6, Champaran, p. 61, Gaya 120; *Bengal District Gazetteers*, Darbhanga, p. 70, Purnea, p. 100, Muzaffarpur, p. 71.

17. From Capt. C. Burbank, Protector of Emigrants Calcutta, to J. Geoghegan, Offg. Jr. Secy. to the Govt. of Bengal, no. 186, dated the 15 May 1865. (number of persons despatched to different colonies. Mauritius-15, 115, British Guiana-2, 842, Trinidad-1, 498. Number of persons sailed for Mauritius from the diferent districts of Bihar is noted below—Bihar-19, Bhagalpur-8, Chapra or Saran 629, Arrah or Shahabad-5, 647, Hazaribagh-54, Purnia-1, Ranchi-7, Sahebganj or Gaya-383, Tirhut-1.)

18. From Capt. Burbank, Protector of Emigrants, Calcutta, to J. Geoghegan, offg. Jr. Secy. to the Govt. of Bengal, no. 178, dated the 8 May 1866.

19. From C. Burbank, Protector of Emigrants at Calcutta, to S.C. Bayley, Esq. Offg. Sec. to the Govt. of Bengal, no. 127, dated the 5 April 1867; From S.B. Patridge, Surgeon, Government Medical Inspector of Emigrants to Capt. A. Baker, Offg. Protector of Emigrants, Calcutta, 13 May 1867.

20. From Capt. C. Burbank, Protector of Emigrants, Calcutta, to S.C. Bayley, Offg. Addl. Secretary, to the Govt. of Bengal no. 143, dated Fort William, the 17 April 1868. (The number of persons going to Mauritius from different districts of Bihar, in 1867–68, is listed below—Arrah or Shahabad-106, Chapra or Saran-23, Danapur-1, Hazaribagh-13, Monghyr-3, Muzaffarpur-8, Patna or Azimabad-21, Purulia-5, Purnia-2, Ranchi, Sabibganj or Gaya-29, Tirhut-1.)

21. From J.G. Grant, Offg. Protector of Emigrants at Calcutta, to A. Mackenzie, Offg. Jr. Secy. to the Govt. of Bengal, no. 179, dated Fort William, the 31 May 1870.

22. Report of the Government Medical Inspector of Emigrants for the official year 1869–70. (The following were the number of persons going to Mauritius from different districts of Bihar. Arrah-389, Bihar-3, Bhagalpur-8, Chapra/Saran-89, Hazaribagh-16, Monghyr-8, Purnia-1, Muzaffarpur-35, Patna or Azimabad-94, Purulia-1, Ranchi-15, Sahibganj or Gaya-175, Tirhut-1.)

23. From A. Eden., Secy. to the Govt. of Bengal, to the Protector of Emigrants, no. 3628,, dated Fort William, the 29 October 1870.

24. Circular from His Majesty's Principal Secretary of State to Colonial Govts., dated the 24 September 1860.

25. From H.N.D. Beyts, Special Commissioner from Mauritius, to C. Eales, Protector of Emigrants, Calcutta, dated the 30 April 1861.

26. From J.D. Gordon, Jr. Secy, to the Govt, of Bengal, to the Protector of Emigrants, no. 83, dated the 8 July 1861.

27. Conclusion drawn from the table exhibiting the number and description of the East Indian Emigrants who have left for Calcutta for British and French Colonies from the year 1861 to 1870 and the numbers returned therefrom. Progs, no. 29 May 1870.

28. From Capt. C. Burbank, Offg. Protector of Emigrants at the Port of Calcutta, to S.C. Bayley, Jr. Secy. to the Govt, of Bengal, no. 101, dated the 4 May 1864.

29. Conclusion drawn from the table exhibiting the number and description of the East Indian Emigrants . . . and the numbers returned therefrom.

30. From S.C. Bayley, Offg. Addl. Secy. to the Govt, of Bengal, to the Secy. to the Government of India, Home Deptt., no. 982, dated Fort William, the 24 February 1868.

31. From E.C. Bayley, Secy, to the Govt. of India, Home Deptt., to the Offg. Addl. Secy. to the Govt. of Bengal, no. 1245, dated Fort William, the 10 Mar. 1868.

32. From Capt. C. Burbank, Protector of Emigrants, Calcutta, to S.C. Bayley, Offg. Addl. Secy. to the Govt, of Bengal, no. 143, dated Fort William, the 17 Apr. 1868.

33. From J.C. Grant, Offg. Protector of Emigrants at Calcutta, to A. Mackenzie, Offg. Jr. Secy. to the Govt. of Bengal, no. 179, dated Fort William, the 31 May 1870.

34. From Capt. C. 3urbank, Offg., Protector of Emigrants at the Port of Calcutta, to S.C. Bayley, Jr. Secy, to the Govt. of Bengal, no. 118, dated the 23 May 1864.

35. From A. Eden, Secy. to the Govt. of Bengal to the Colonial Secy, to the Govt. of Mauritius, no. 1244T, dated Darjeeling, the 2 July 1864.

36. From E.T. Dalton, Commr. of Chota Nagpore, to A. Eden, Secy. to the Govt. of Bengal, no. 465, dated the 15 March 1866.

37. Notification, no. 2847, 17 July 1866.

38. From S.B. Patridge, Surgeon-Supdt., Govt. Medical Inspector of Emigrants, to Capt. A. Baker, Offg. Protector of Emigrants. Calcutta, dated the 13 May 1867.

39. From H.L. Harrison, Jr. Secy. to the Govt. of Bengal, to the Offg. Protector of Emigrants, Calcutta, no. 2437, dated the 29 May 1867.

40. From Capt. C. Burbank, Protector of Emigrants, Calcutta, to H.L. Harrison, Jr. Secy. to the Govt. of Bengal, no. 189, dated the 13 July 1867.

41. From S.C. Bayley, Offg. Addl. Secy. to the Govt. of Bengal, to the Protector of Emigrants, Cal., no. 981, dated Fort William, the 24 February 1868.

42. Notification no. 321, Home Department, Fort William, the 18 January 1870.

43. Report of the Govt. Medical Inspector of Emigrants for the Official year 1869–70.

44. Rules for the transmission of money from Mauritius to India on behalf of Immigrants, Progs, no. 19, May 1866; Regulations for the remittance to India of the savings of coolies in the West Indies and other colonies. Progs, no. 7, February 1867.

45. From S.C. Bayley, Jr. Secy. to the Govt. of Bengal, to the Offg. Under Secy, to the Govt, of India, Home Deptt., no. 709, dated the 8 February 1867.

46. Ibid., From the Duke of Buckingham and Chandos to Governor H. Barkley, dated Downing Street, the 6 July 1867.

47. From C. Eales, Emigration Agent for Mauritius, to the Offg. Protector of Emigrants, Calcutta, no. 47, dated the 8 April 1870.

48. Extract from Report no. 61 of 1860 from the Protector of Immigrants.

49. From J. Cosmo Melville, to the Under Secy, for the Colonies, dated India Office, the 24 August 1860.

30

Condition of Labour in the Coalfields of Bengal and Bihar, 1890–1920

Pabitra Bhaskar Sinha

Although the coal mining industry was more than one hundred years old in 1890,[1] and had assumed an important place in the economy of India, no serious attempt to know and ameliorate the condition of the miners seems to have been made during those hundred years.[2] It was only in 1890 when Lord Cross, then Secretary of State for India, forwarded to the Government of India a copy of the proceedings of the Berlin Conference of 1890, and asked the government to consider the advisability of undertaking legislation for the inspection of mines, and for the regulation of employment therein of women, young persons and children, that public interest was aroused on the condition of labour in the coalfields.[3] It was reports of this intention of the government which led to the formation of a mines sub-committee by the Bengal Chamber of Commerce and Industry in February 1891 to watch the course of legislation and focus commercial opinion upon the problems which were to emerge, and early in 1892 this mines sub-committee became the Indian Mining Association.[4] In 1893 Mr. James Grundy, one of the Inspectors of Mines in England, was appointed to inspect the Indian mines and to report on regulations he would recommend for the protection of the miners.[5] From this time the details about the actual working and living conditions of labour in the coalfields of Bengal and Bihar came to the knowledge of government and the public, but it took a long time to sufficiently improve the condition of the miner.

The earliest of the miners were the Bauris (a low-caste tribe of mixed Hindu origin) of Burdwan, Bankura and Manbhum. They were physically weak and degenerate, but possessed greater skill and mental ability than the hardier types of aboriginals by whom they have been largely replaced. The latter are the Santhals, the Kols, the Koras and the Gonds who inhabit the hilly and forest-clad country stretching from western Bengal to the Madhya Pradesh.[6] But, as the area of mining operations extended and more and more new coal mines were opened, the number of these hill tribes fell far short of the

*30th Session at Bhagalpur, 1968.

demand of labour in the collieries of Bengal and Bihar. Gradually the Bhuinyas, the Rajwars, the Gops, the Lodhs, the Pasis, the Kurmis, the Nunias, and the Beldars came to settle as miners in the collieries. They came from southern Bengal and western districts of Bihar. Besides, the numerous tribes who are collectively known as the Bilaspuri miners were also recruited. In addition there was a small number of Muslims locally known as Meas or Jolhas.[7] In 1894 James Grundy, the Inspector of Mines in India, recorded the names of as many as forty-nine castes and sub-castes working in the Giridih coalfield.[8] Numerically the Kurmis held the first place, then came the Koiris, the Goalas, the Khaviwars, the Telis, the Dhanuks, the Ganjus, the Bedias, and the Santhals.[9]

The usual method of recruitment of mines labour was to send a European officer to the country-side accompanied by a clerk and Sardars who by means of advances prevailed upon a large batch of villagers to come down with them. The results were not always satisfactory. Sometimes, the labourers being new to the work and surroundings, finding that they lacked the requisite skill to earn much, that considerable physical exertion was required, and that picks hurt their hands, were dissatisfied and ran away on the first opportunity.[10] Some coal mining companies who had cultivable lands used to offer plots of land to the miners either free of charge or on nominal rents. The miners hold these lands on the condition of working in the mines.[11] There were also the recruiting contractors who supplied labour. However, as the number of mines increased, the mining population almost doubled in thirty years time, i.e., from about 75,000 in 1890 to about 1,40,000 in 1920.[12]

This vast human material assembled together in the coalfields of Bengal and Bihar to meet the demands of industrialization, was of the rawest character, and with a few exceptions they were illiterate. They were drawn from scattered villages and hamlets in different parts of the country, and they had little knowledge in the art of living in large and fixed communities. They were generally cultivators and agricultural labourers in their village homes or semi-nomadic hill-tribes. It took them a long time to settle down to a routine life of long hours of work underground or in machine rooms, weekly payment of wages, and the cheerless smoke-filled atmosphere of the collieries. At the beginning it was hoped that within a few decades there would emerge a generation of regular miners who would be inextricably bound up with the interests of the coal mining industry. But the expectations were belied by the fact that the miners never felt at home in the colliery and the management had done nothing to train up the children of the miners to become skilled and interested workers in the colliery. Therefore, whenever, colliery life became irksome, they returned to their villages where some kind of work had been always available for them, and in most cases they were secured against want by the joint family system.[13]

The story behind the village cultivators and labourers taking to the dreary life of a miner had been always similar. Heavy pressure of population on land was the chief cause of migration of labourers to the coalfields. The small cultivators having incurred a debt were attracted to the mines by the comparatively high and constant wages, and found there the means to satisfy their landlord and money-lender.[14] Many among them used to leave their families behind in the village, regularly remit a portion of their wages to their families, and returned there periodically to look after their affairs. Particularly during the sowing and the harvesting seasons there was exodus of labour from the coalfields to the villages. There was yet practically no mining population such as existed in European countries, consisting of a large number of operatives trained from their youth to one particular class of work and dependent upon employment at that work for their livelihood.[15]

Even in the last decade of the nineteenth century the method of mining in India was primitive. Small Beam engines did the combined work of pumping and winding. Ship's windlasses were a common form of engine for winding. Nearly all the large concerns had pits worked by gins the wheels of which were turned by women labourers. For lighting purposes underground, tin lamps were used. The oil burnt in them was thin mineral oil from Burma or Kerosene that smoked badly.[16] Electricity came into use much later. No daily reports were kept of the condition of the workings, the Manager relying on the report of the underground Sardars. Very few collieriers kept up plans up-to-date or otherwise.[17] In most of the mines there was no attempt made at ventilation. The bad efforts of such a system, greatly increased by the smoke from the oil burnt in the lamps used by the miners in all parts of the mine working, caused irreparable damage to the health of the miners and sapped out their energgies. The smoke filled the galleries to such an extent that it was impossible to see, and the want of sufficient air was so great that sometimes light would not burn, and a person felt that he could not long live in such a place. It was calculated in 1894 that even in the best managed colliery the average life of a miner was not more than 21½ years.[18]

Death-rates by accidents in the coal mines of Bengal and Bihar were also high. In 1894 Mr. James Grundy, the first Inspector of Mines in India, reported that the accidents had been more due to ignorance and negligence than due to natural causes or mechanical failures. Of 62 mines visited by him only 36 mines had plans, only 9 had erected air-stoppings, and coalfires for cooking or warmth were frequently to be found burning in underground galleries. Fortunately, the Indian coal mines are free from inflammable and obnoxious gases.[19] The following table illustrates the number of deaths by accident in one particular year.

TABLE 30.1[20]: Deaths Caused by Accidents in the
Coal Mines of Benigal and Bihar during 1894

No.	District	Above Ground		Below Ground		Total
		Males	Females	Males	Females	
1	Burdwan	1	1	26	6	34
2	Hazaribagh	1	1	9	—	11
3	Manbhum	—	—	2	1	3
	TOTAL					48

The numbesr of serious accidents causing loss of a limb or the miner mained for life, was also high. In 1894 in the coalfields of Bengal and Bihar 10 persons including a woman were severely injured and maimed for life. As the mines became deeper and more machineries came into use the number of accidents in coal mines increased by leaps and bounds. In the Manbhum district alone, in 1913, 142 accidents occurred killing 131 persons and seriously injuring 63. Next year, i.e., in 1914, 139 accidents occurred killing 86 persons and seriously injuring 75.[21] The serious accident in the Chourashi colliery in the Manbhum district in the evening of 22nd October 1913, by fire and explosion, will be long remembered. Not less than 30 persons lost their lives on the spot and many were severely wounded.[22] The Bhowra colliery disaster (Manbhum district) at 2.30 a.m. on 4 February 1916, occurred when the roof of the mine collapsed. 45 persons who were working or resting undergrond were killed, and 5 men, 11 women and 8 children who were asleep in the quarters on the surface were killed being suffocated by the debris of the fallen building.[23] It was estimated in 1920 that the accidents and subsequent fatality in the coal mines of Bengal and Bihar were due to the following reasons.[24]

Misadventure	49.73%
Fault of deceased	30.78%
Fault of fellow-workmen	6.07%
Fault of subordinate official	3.94%
Fault of Management	9.48%
TOTAL	100.00

Although the direct share of responsibility of the accidents in the coal mines of Bengal and Bihar on the part of the management and the mine official was small, indirectly they should share the full responsibility for the accidents. There was absolutely no arrangement to train the miners in safety precautions and first aid, and supervision was slack. In spite of the fact that the Mines Act of 1901 had laid down rules for safety measures and daily inspection and supervision by the certified managers and assistant managers, they never exercised adequate control on the subordinate officials and miners under their charge.[25] Sand-stowing of abandoned and dangerous underground galleries was not a practice, and the use of electricity was a new phenomenon. As a consequence, falling of mine roofs and fire and explosion due to electrical short circuit were common. The accidents always took a heavy toll of life due to the presence of women and child labour.[26]

Women and children comprised about half of the total labour force in the coalfields of Bengal and Bihar. First the Santhals had brought their womenfolk to work along with them in the collieries. Thereafter, all castes trained their women to go underground. The absence of carriers for the men, unwillingness of women of other castes to carry coal for men of another caste, and envy at better wages earned by the miner who had been assisted by his wife and family, to a great extent brought this about.[27] In 1914 out of a total coal mine labour of 83,527 in the Manbhum district 22,297 women and 343 children above twelve were employed underground, and 9,752 women and 1,438 children worked above ground.[28] When in 1894 it had been proposed to prohibit women and children from working underground, there was a strong opposition from the miners themselves. They sent a petition to the Lieut. Governor of Bengal requesting him not to accept the proposal, for they thought that the proposal had been brought to rob them of a part of their fair earnings and to make their wives and daughters idle at home and unchaste.[29] With regard to woman and child labour the Government of India felt that they form an 'integral part of the family-gang system of labour' and their work was valuable. A Government Report said: 'It would seem that the employment underground of growing children must tend to produce stunted bodies and impaired health . . . . But the actual employment of children is not the only question to be considered. It must also be decided whether they are to be prevented from going below ground, even if not employed. This question is closely connected with that of the employment of women; as it is possible that to forbid the mothers to take their young children below with them might, in some cases at least, practically amount to preventing them from going down themselves.'[30] Coal mining industry was expanding rapidly at this time, and it required a large number of labourers. The Mines Act of 1901, therefore, prohibited the employment of children below twelve underground. But the practice of taking small children below working age to underground workings by their parents continued, as they had no one above ground to look after them.[31]

In the 1880s the wages were as low as a pice a maund of coal for the miners working underground, and he earned about 2½ annas a day. The wages of surface labour were 2 annas per day.[32] The women received 5 pice and the children 3 pice per day. Even at a time when rice sold at 25 to 30 seers per rupee, it required the earnings of all the members in a family to meet the both ends. With the rapid march of industrialization the prices of commodities of daily necessity increased, and by 1902 the wages were raised from 8 to 12 annas for an underground worker. The unskilled surface labourers earned from one annas to 4 annas per day. Women and children were paid in the same rate and received 1½ annas for surface and 2 annas for underground work.[33] There was no fixed hours of work and the underground miners worked for more hours to earn more. The miners did not suffer much hardship due to rise of prices during the World War I since there had been a very brisk demand for their services and liberal wages were paid everywhere.[34]

On some old and nearly all the newer fields the miners lived in their villages and hamlets near the collieries. The Santhals particularly preferred to live in their own houses erected by themselves, thatch for the roof and wood for the pillars being supplied by the company. The houses were of the type usually seen in Chota Nagpur villages: rooms grouped round a courtyard, mud walls and mud floors plastered with a mixture of cowdung and earth.[35] The bulk of the labour, however, was housed in what are known as 'lines' or 'dhowras'. A 'line' or a 'dhowra' was a long building divided into compartments by cross walls. Each compartment measured about 10'X 10'x 7', with an opening on one side for entrance and exit. Many of these 'lines' faced directly to a more or less public open space. In some cases there was a low wall in front which served a screen for the 'line'. The door provided was not repaired once it was erected, and could not be closed against an intruder either during the day or during the night. No limit was placed on the number of individuals who might occupy one of the compartments into which a 'line' was divided, and no question was asked as to the relationship which existed between the male and female occupants. Besides being unseemly and indecorous to a degree, this promiscuous housing of the sexes had a pernicious influence on the people as a whole, and the temptation to laxity of morals which it entailed was telling injuriously on the social life of the people of the locality and even of those who had remotely come into contract with the life as it was lived in the 'cooly lines'.[36] In the case of the smaller Indian-owned collieries the accommodation for the labourers was most insanitary and unsuitable. Some of the huts were such that a miner could only creep in through the door, and could not stand upright when inside.[37]

There was no toilet accommodation provided for the residents in the 'cooly lines'. The Committee set up for the Regulation and Sanitation of Mines in India in 1896, were strongly opposed to recommending any general rule for the erection of toilets by the colliery owners. They said that toilets were not required as there had been plenty of open country about where the miners could relieve nature. For toilets underground they were of the opinion that it would be sheer waste of money to construct one, for the miners would never use such toilets.[38] The lack of toilet accommodation was an outrage on the inherent modesty and self-respect of the female members of the community. The density of population in the coalfields of Bengal and Bihar increased so rapidly that within a very short period there was hardly any open country or jungles near the 'cooly lines' where the women-folk could relieve nature safely without being intruded upon by the gaze of passerby.

In the absence of toilets and arrangements for the disposal of night soil and refuse, the colliery areas quickly became a veritable breeding ground of all sorts of diseases and source of epidemics. Jharia town became a menace to the coalfield as several outbreaks of plague had their starting point 'in that most unsavoury spot'.[39] The provision of drinking water was never adequate, and the miners used water accumulated in coal pits for drinking as well as washing purposes. As a consequence every year cholera and smallpox took a heavy toll of life. In one year in the Manbhum district 397 persons died of cholera and 10 persons of msall-pox.[40] This was the case in normal year when the diseases had not spread as in epidemics. The only colliery where better sanitary arrangements and adequate supply of drinking water were available was the East Indian Railway Company's colliery at Giridih. This colliery also could boast of a well-maintained hospital and first-aid facilities, and qualified doctors. It also ran a family benefit scheme contributed by the Company as well as the miners for the benefit of the family of a sick or dead miner.[41] Other collieries had very little hospital facilities and they depended much upon the physicians and sanitary officers of Asansol and Jharia Mines Boards of Health,[42] set up by the government in 1912 for improving the condition of health and sanitation in the coalfields. Of course, the collieries whose owners had been members of the Indian Mining Association were looked after by the doctors of the Association.

There was no school for the young children of the miners except one in the East Indian Railway Company's colliery at Giridih. Drinking was a common vice. In the gloomy atmosphere of the collieries the miner and the members of his family had no place or provision for recreation. Without any moral training in early life, the miner spent a sizeable portion of his income on liquors to snatch a few hours of forgetfulness of his miserable condition.[43] As he started earning more wages, he spent more on his drinks, and in 1917 there was an increase of 50% over the figure of 1916 in the sale of country spirit in the coalfields of Chota Nagpur division.[44]

During the World War I the importance of the labour in the coalfields was recognized when the collieries of Bengal and Bihar had to increase the output for the war purposes and simultaneously face scarcity of labour owing to the indenture of Indian labour to Mesopotamia and France. By the end of the War there was a general increase of wages of the miner, and this coincided with a betterment of housing and living conditions. The proceedings of the International Labour Conference, held at Washington in October 1919, furnished the impetus which led to several Acts for the improvement of the condition of labour in the coalfields by the Indian Legislative Assembly. Ultimately, the Indian Mines Act of 1923 and the Mines Regulation of 1929 removed many of the ills present in the living and working conditions of the labour in the coalfields of Bengal and Bihar.

Notes

1. The first coal mines were opened by Messrs Sumner and Heatly during 1774–75 in Birbhum and Pachet. cf., *Journal of the Asiatic Society of Bengal*, vol. XI, pt. II, 1842, pp. 8151-5.

2. One is obliged to come to this conclusion because of the dearth of any detailed information either in the Government Records or newspapers and journals. The present writer, however, has come across a pamphlet 'The Indian Coal Mines: Is Legislation Necessary to Regulate their Working?' by T.H. Ward. Asst. Manager, E.I.R. Collieries, published in Calcutta in 1885 to review a paper by one Mr. Joseph Chater. Mr. Ward in his pamphlet has supported legislation for regulating the mines, but has not supplied any useful information about the condition of labour in Indian mines.

3. Papers regarding Legislation for the Regulation and Sanitation of Mines in India, Govt. of India, Deptt. of Rev. and Agri., 1896, p. 1.

4. cf., *Indian Mining Association, Report of the Committee for 1892–93*.

5. *Report of the Inspection of Mines in India for the Year Ending 30 June 1894*, p. 1.

6. R.R. Simpson, 'Social Conditions of Mines in India', *Transactions of the Mining and Gelogical Institute of India*, vol. XXVII, 1932, p. 89.

7. Ibid.

8. *Report of the Inspection of Mines in India for the Year Ending 30 June 1894*, pp. 50–51.

9. *Memoirs of the Geological Survey of India*, vol. VIII, 1871, p. 292.

10. B. Foley, Report of Labour in Bengal, p. 35.

11. Ibid.

12. The figures have been compiled from *Census of India*, vol. V of 1891 and 1921.

13. *Report of the Indian Factory Labour Commission, 1908*, pp. 18–19.

14. *Bengal District Gazetteers*, Manbhum, Calcutta, 1911, p. 180.

15. *Census of India*, 1911, vol. V, p. 529.

16. *Trans. Min. and Geol. Inst. of India*, vol. IX, 1914, Presidential Address by F.J. Agabeg, pp. 21–22.

17. *Report of the Inspection of Mines in India for the Year Ending 30 June 1894*, pp. 11–18.

18. Ibid., p. 58.

19. Ibid., p. 14.

20. Papers regarding Legislation for the Regulation and Sanitation of Mines, in India, op. cit., Addenda to the Report, p. iv.

21. Govt. of Bihar and Orissa, Municipal Deptt., Commercial Branch, Prog, no. 30 of June 1915. All the Proceedings cited here are of the same Deptt. of the Govt. of Bihar and Orissa.

22. Prog. no. 32 of April 1915.

23. Prog. no. 45 of Dec. 1916.

24. *Trans. Min. and Geol. Inst. of India*, vol. XVI, 1921, 'Accidents in Indian Mines', by R.R. Simpson, p. 36.

25. Prog. no. 32 of Mar. 1917.

26. *Trans. Min. and Geol. Inst. of India*, vol. XVI, 1921, loc. cit., pp. 32–35.

27. *Trans. Min. and Geol. Inst. of India*, vol. VIII, 1913, 'Labour in Bengal Coal Mines' by E.C. Agabeg, p. 27.
28. Prog. no. 30 June 1915.
29. Report of the Inspection of Mines in India for the Year Ending 30 June 1894, pp. 88–89.
30. Papers regarding Legislation for the Regulation and Sanitation of Mines in India, 1896, op. cit., p. 3.
31. Prog. no. 30 June 1915.
32. *Trans. Min. and Goel. Inst. of India*, vol. IX, 1914, loc. cit., p. 22.
33. *Report of the Chief Inspector of Mines in India for the Year Ending 31 December 1902,* p. 3.
34. Prog. no. 16 July 1918.
35. Prog. no. 32–41 of Feb. 1981. See also Report of the Chief Inspector of Mines for the Year Ending 31 December 1902, p. 3.
36. Prog. no. 35 December 1916.
37. Prog. no. 27 December 1916.
38. Papers regarding Legislation for the Regulation and Sanitation of Mines in India, op. cit., p. 22.
39. Prog. no. 13 February 1913. See also *Tran. Min. and Geol. Inst. of India*, vol. V, 1910. Presidential Address by S. Heslop. p. 22.
40. Prog. of May 1917. Report from Deputy Commissioner, Manbhum.
41. *Report of the Inspection of Mines in India for the Year Ending 31 December 1897*, pp. 2–4. Also see the Report of the Deputy Commissioner, Hazaribagh in Prog. of July 1913.
42. Prog. no. 13–20 of Feb. 1913.
43. *Trans. Min. and Geol. Inst. of India*, vol. XV, 1920, pt. I, Presidential Address, p. 18.
44. Prog. no. 16 July 1918.

31

A Pioneer of Workingmen's Uplift and Welfare Work in Bengal: Sasipada Banerjee

K.L. Chatterji

THE NINETEENTH century saw the beginning of new stirrings in the minds of the Indian people. Raja Ram Mohan Roy was the pioneer of social reform and religious movements in the nineteenth century. A true humanist and a reformer he wanted to raise the Hindu society. With this object he founded the Brahmo Samaj. The work begun by him was carried forward by Devendra Nath Tagore and Kesav Chandra Sen. A very powerful preacher, Kesav Chandra's fervent devotion, wonderful eloquence and missionary zeal carried the influence of the Brahmo Samaj far outside the limits of Bengal. Everywhere the Samaj had played a notable part as a reforming and uplifting agency. Its services in the cause of elevating the position of the common people deserve unstinted praise. The condition of the common people attracted, the attention of one of our countrymen. He was Sri Sasi Pada Banerjee who lived in Baranagore, a suburb of Calcutta. Before Sasi Pada the condition of the workingmen attracted the attention of Brahmananda Kesav Chandra who took up missionary activities for the spread of Brahmoism in India. Within his missionary activity he included the upliftment of poor and uneducated people. J.B. Pheare wrote in an article with the caption 'The problem of civilisation in India' in *Calcutta Review*: 'Throughout the middle and the lower middle classes of the country an existing system of instruction is spreading an amount of elementary information which cannot fail ultimately to produce important consequences in regard to the mental condition of those classes, however, seem to be still unaffected by an educational effort from either without or within, and they constitute a dead weight of obstructive ignorance, prejudice and superstition, which is perfectly appalling in its magnitude. It is a hopeful system of the healthiness of social progress in Bengal that the task of attacking this enormous evil is fearlessly approached by some earnest-minded

*32nd Session at Sabalpur, 1970.

native gentlemen unaided by the state. Obviously instruction and enlightenment must be brought to this portion of the population in a special mode. Their extreme poverty deprives them both of the means and of the time for availing themselves of the ordinary schools. Evening schools, such as those at Baranagore maintained by the very zealous and praiseworthy exertions of Baboo Sasi Pada Banerjee and those lately set on foot by the association over which Baboo Kesav Chandra Sen presides, appear to afford almost the only avenue by which the lower labouring classes can be invaded in the absence of government organisation for the purpose.'[1]

As early as 1866, Sasi Pada at the age of 26, turned his attention to the labouring classes in the local jute mills. He was an inspired disciple of Baboo Kesav Chandra Sen. On 1 November 1866 he called a meeting of all workingmen of that locality to discuss their condition and explained to them how due to ignorance they were being exploited by the employers. He perfectly understood that without education much could not be done for their betterment. So he wanted to start a night school for the workers. After listening carefully all the workers present in the meeting accepted the night school.

As it would be convenient Sasi Pada took the help of Magic Lantern and by it showed the pictures to the workers. By this aid the workers got initiative. This feature was completely new and unique in the development of education.

On the next day, Sasi Pada founded the first ever established night school for the workers in India. At that time, most of the workers resided in Kamarpara, Ariyadaha and Kutighata near Baranagore. Borneo Company had a jute mill at that locality. Sasi Pada went to its Calcutta office and requested the owner of the mill, Mr. Alexander, to give a site for the night school. On 1 June 1869, the General Manager of the Company, Mr. Maire, permitted Sasi Pada to establish a night school within the mill area and allotted a small room for it. That was a thatched hut. All of a sudden, fire broke out after 13 days and the room was completely gutted. But soon the Company constructed a room and again the night school started from 5 July 1870. Sasi Pada and his brother, Kedarnath, were the teachers who, free of cost, taught the workers. This noble initiative was very much applauded by the editorial article of Harish Chandra Mukherjee's *Hindu Patriot*.[2]

A step forward in organisation was taken by the establishment in August 1870, of the Workingmen's Club, which continued for a long time to be the central body and rallying place for all who came under the influence of the movement. The club held its meetings at the houses of the members, and great was the enthusiasm displayed not only by the men but also their mothers, wives and sisters on these occasions. The meetings were frequently attended and addressed by the sympathising visitors from Calcutta such as Baboos Dwarakanath Ganguly, K.K. Mitra, and Kali Sankar Sukul.[3] Lectures on different subjects chiefly of a moral and practical character were delivered in these meetings, and the effects of these, issuing, as they did, from hearts that deeply and actively sympathised with all the trials and difficulties of the members, began soon to be visible in their thrifty and temperate habits and their improved morals.

The next attempt of Sasi Pada was to curb the habit of drinking of the poor workers. He assembled the workers on 27 August, 1870, and delivered lectures by which the workers were convinced about the harm of drinking and gambling. He established a Temperance Association. Most of the workers became members of the association. For temperance work, he would go personally among the drunken labouring people and once had been placed inside the 'hajat' through the intrigues of the opposition parties. He also placed a ban on palm trees. His speech was published in the *Burmingham News:* "The rule of the British Government in India had been conducive of great good in many respects to the latter country, but there was one great blot on their management of the sale of intoxicating liquors . . . a once noble temperate people were rapidly being turned into an intemperate and vicious race. Even the best-educated and promising young men were seduced by the temptation offered and fell victims to the effect of temperance, for men addicted to drunkenness soon met their death in a climate like that of India. In order to stay the further progress of intemperance the speaker and a number of influential native gentlemen formed a Temperance Society in 1866, and the pledge that was to be taken was that of total abstention from all intoxicating liquors . . . . As soon as the society was started the promoters did all in their power to reclaim their fallen brothers with great success followed in nearly every instance. The wine shops, too, were visited, as those addicted to drinking would not attend the lectures given . . . . Drinking places had been converted into places for instruction and reading classes now assembled where the drunkards used to congrerate."[4]

To increase the habit of thrift among the working classes, Sasi Pada started an 'Anna Bank' like the 'Penny Banks' of England, in 1870 before the government Saving Bank were established. In fact, his experiment was an eye-opener to the Government to whom was supplied a scheme by Sasi Pada himself. Government sanctioned a private scheme for the appointment of a local board, and appointed five to eight locally respectable residents to work with such banks. The first Local Board Bank of the kind was opened in Baranagorh on 4 February 1871. The *Indian Mirror* gave the following account of the opening ceremony, 'As an earnest of the work meant to be done in connection with this movement, we learn that a sum of rupees 390 was deposited, on the occasion, the number of depositors being no less than sixteen . . . . It is also proposed to confer the full benefit of the measure to the working men and women of the place."[5]

Another step which specially showed Sasi Pada's interest in the welfare of the working people and drew them closely to him, was the strenuous efforts he made to bring to justice a certain police sub-Inspector who had committed a brutal outrage on a poor working women and brought a false charge of rioting against a number of workingmen in order to screen himself from the consequences of his own crime. The innocent men were acquitted. Their feeling is written in a farewell address to Sasi Pada on the eve of his departure for England in 1871: 'We are very poor, there is no one in Baranagore to help us in any way, but it is only you who have been labouring heartily for our good. It is impossible to state here how much benefit we have derived from the 'Workingmen's Clubs' which have been established by you with a view to improve our character . . . . The lectures have changed our character in many respects so that some have given up the habit of drinking and other vicious habits, and are now leading an honourable and peaceful life . . . . You love us so much that whenever any one of us is sick, you visit him at his sickbed and freely give medicines to those who cannot afford to buy them. What more shall we say, we honour you as our father.'[6]

It may be pointed out that the workers irrespective of caste and creed were welcomed and equally treated by Sasi Pada. His efforts were not confined to improving the condition of the Hindus; he had before his eyes also the miserable condition of the Muhammadan working classes. On 20 October 1872, he addressed a meeting of Muhammadans and on the 10 December of the same year he established a school for boys belonging to that community.

To supplement the work connected with the elevation of the workingmen Sasi Pada started an illustrated monthly in May 1874, which was wholly devoted to the service of these people. This was the first illustrated labour monthly, the *Bharat Sramajibi* (The Indian Labourer, with a circulation of 15,000—almost unique in those days. It is in this labour journal that there appeared the first workingmen's poem in the Bengali language, by the young firebrand Sivnath Sastri, *'Utho Jago, Sramajibi Bhai'* (Rise, awake, labourer, my brother). The aims and objects of the paper were published in the *Indian Daily News*.

'Under the above title (*Bharat Sramajibi*) is now published at Baranagore in the neighbourhood of Calcutta, a monthly Bengali journal of 8 pages octavo, with woodcut illustrations, price one pice per number. It is purely an educational paper and its object is to supply a means of supplying the moral and intellectual condition of the working classes by short and simple articles on descriptions of natural phenomena on objects of general interest, accounts of native arts and manufactures and the application of science to the improvement of such arts and other useful purposes exemplified in more advanced countries, biographical sketches of individuals whose characters and careers may be likely to exercise beneficial influences on the readers, and advise any suggestion on subjects bearing on their own welfare on their duties to their fellow-men, whether of their own class, or of their employers, or of the community in general such as may tend to make or keep them worthy and respectable members of society.'[7]

For the recreation of the workers Sasi Pada arranged holiday trips. In the annual meeting he addressed the workers who assembled at his place. He wrote some songs specially designed for the occasion. The Workingmen's Association of London, upon hearing, of the occasion through their President Mr. Hardson Spratt sent a letter of congratulations on 12 August 1874.[8]

However, Sasi Pada, like a large number of other Indian reformers, suffered from a limitation. He failed to realise that essentially it was the colonial social order, imposed on India, by the alien British, which was responsible for the misery, backwardness and degradation of the toiling masses of our country. Rather, he held that the indifference of our educated upper classes and the soulless attitude of the local English bureaucracy were responsible for the misery of the working people of India. This extremely partial and one-sided awareness of the reality, led Sasi Pada to have much illusory faith in British liberalism and he believed that he could obtain 'paternal' help from them, provided the case of the Indian workers was properly represented. In consequence, Sasi Pada, despite his passionate attachment to the cause of the working people of India, spread among them, not an embryonic nationalistic or anti-imperialistic consciousness, but rather tried to inject the 'Paternalist' idea about British rule.

There were various other activities of Sasi Pada Banerjee which will not be possible for us to mention in this brief paper. He was not a great orator, nor was he a popular writer, but he was a tireless worker with an unerring instinct for those classes of the society, which were vital for national development.

Notes

1. *Calcutta Review,* 1871, vol. LII, no. 103, pp. 65–6. It would not be out of place to mention some of the most valuable sources from which we can form a correct estimate about the life and work of Sri Sasi Pada Banerjee. Some of the books or pamphlets were written in English, but some of them were in Bengali also: S. Tattwabhusan, *Social Reforms in Bengal;* K.C. Kanjilal, *Karmajogi Sasi Pala; Albion Banerjee, An Indian Pathfinder—Memoirs of Sebabrata Sasi Pada Banerjee;* Sitanath Tattwabhushan, *Romance of a Great Indian Social Servant;* Sitanath Tattwabhusan, *Elevation of the Masses and the Depressed Classes:* Motiwaja, *Biography of Sasi Pada Banerjee;* S.N. Roy Chowdhury, 'Life-story of Seba Brata Sasi Pada in Nutshell', *Calcutta Review; The Bengalee; Brahmo Samaje Sasi Pada O Maner Bal*—One Brahmo; Dwarkanath Ganguly, *Mababarshiki; Som Prakash; Sanjibani: Tattvabodhini Patrika.*
2. Personal interview with Sri Probhat Chandra Ganguly, son of celebrated Dwarkanath Ganguly.

3. Sita Nath Tattwabhusan, *Social Reforms in Bengal*, p. 8

4. *Birmingham Daily News*, 10 August 1871, quoted by Albion Banerjee in his book *An Indian Pathfinder*, p. 33.

5. *Indian Mirror*, February 1871.

6. Sitanath Tattwabhusan, *Social Reforms in Bengal*, p. 9.

7. *Indian Daily News*, 11 December 1873.

8. *Journal of Natinoal Indian Association*, February 1874.

32

The Agrarian Problems in the Punjab and the Unionist Party, 1923–45

S.D. Gajrani

T HE PRINCIPAL purpose of this paper is not to make an exhaustive study of the Unionist party, but to focus the attention on those aspects which contained seeds of tension and conflicts. With this perspective in view, significant factors have been highlighted.

The year 1923 is considered a landmark in the modern history of the Punjab. During this year, the agriculturist's movement after a long struggle of 20 years through the forums of various political groups,[1] attained atleast in the Punjab, a concrete shape as a political organization by the victorious emergence of the Unionist group in the Punjab Legislative Council[2] under the joint leadership of Sir Fazl-i-Hussain and Chhotu Ram. The following factors brought the two leaders closer.

It was alleged by Sir Fazli that the government circulars promising more employment to the agriculturists had remained unimplemented. Thus, he appealed to the Sikh and rural members seeking support against the no-confidence motion that had been moved against him in March 1923. At this time, Chhotu Ram had also limitations of his own. The *Arya Samaj* had by its remarkable role, set the agriculturist community on the path of awakening and education in different areas of the Punjab. As the *Samaj* was split up into two factions, one of the agriculturists, and the second comprised the non-agriculturists, urban and educated classes, Chhotu Ram led the former group himself. He had realised that the complete salvation of the agriculturists was possible only through their organization because the majority in the *Arya Samaj* was not prepared to concede to them a preferential treatment in its educational and economic programmes.[3] Hence, both the leaders were in dire need of each other's help to achieve their ends, stated above.

Second, his constant efforts for organizing the *Jats* of all the communities under the banner of *zamindara* Association set up m 1917[4] and *Jat Sabha* had annoyed most non-*Jat* Sikhs who were opposing his movement. They criticised

*43rd Session at Kurukshetra, 1982.

him on the ground that he was dividing the Sikh community. In fact, it was alleged by all the sections of Hindus and Sikhs that the *zamindara* movement was *anti-Mahajan*, anti-*Brahmin*, anti-Sikh anti-*Arya Samaj*.

Thus, both the leaders were forced by the prevailing circumstances to join hands and they ultimately founded the Unionist party at the close of 1923 to stem the tide of communalisn.[5] Within a brief period of two years, it became a considerable force,[6] as the backward and indebted agriculturists of the Muslim Community joined the *zamindara* movement. It is noteworthy that many Sikh agriculturists also started joining the *zamindara* Association under the joint leadership of Kharak Singh Dhillon and Kirpal Singh Mann.[7] But it evoked little interest and response from the upper strata of Muslim Community.

It will be appropriate to cite here creed aims, and programmes of the Unionist Party:

First, it was to take up economic reconstruction and reorganisation of agricultural and industrial life of the province so as to cope with the problem of unemployment, to study and promote the commercial interests of the province. It was to promote industries with special emphasis upon cottage industries in rural population, to improve methods of marketing, including the reforms of objectionable market usages and practices.[8] However, it is to be remembered that it was to promote the interests of masses without undue encroachment on the interests of capitalists, big landlords and moneyed people. This vividly exhibits its character.

Second, it was to effect rural uplift by infusing the real and enlightened spirit in village communities and making every village a unit of true social and national life and to ensure religious and cultural integrity of each community as the best basis of lasting national unity, denying the claims of any community to dictate to other communities and in the case of conflicts, settling the disputes and differences on the principle of toleration. It was also to provide equal facilities and opportunities for all, with special solicitude for the backward classes and areas whether rural or urban.[9]

Third, the Unionists were to attain dominion status by all constitutional means at as early date as possible. The securing of an honourable status for Indians overseas; the establishment in the province of provincial autonomy defacto; the acceptance of the community of economic interests as the true basis of political parties, irrespective of caste, creed or religion were other important objectives of this party. It was to develop national respect to press for economy at the centre, i.e., the Government of India. It was also to encourage independence of thought and freedom of speech and to discourage sacrifice of public interest to personal ends; and to secure purity of administration to distribute fairly and equitably the burden of taxation; to eliminate all excess in the cost of administration, so as to promote funds for beneficient activities.[10]

It will not be out of place to state that the party, above all, considered the Reforms Act of 1935, to be most unsatisfactory, but since it was the law of the land, made after prolonged inquiries and struggle, the party was determined to get the best possible result out of it. Whether or not the constitution would permit national efforts to obtain good results, the party was under no illusion, but was determined to make strenuous efforts to secure the objects mentioned above. Success was contingent upon the measure of national ability, integrity, industry and cohesion that might be forthcoming. Thus, its formation, popularly known among the masses as rural or *zamindara* party, brought the agriculturists from all the communities under one banner[11] and banished the Muslim League from the province for atleast two decades and lessened the political dominance of the urbanites, both Hindu and non-Hindu.

With these aims, and ways, the Unionists formed the Government in 1923.[12] After the formation of its ministry the Unionist party assured of freedom from the pressure of the Muslim League, which had been progressively growing weaker during 1924–26,[13] on the Muslim members of the Punjab Legislature, who also formed a majority in the party, should have easily implemented its aims and programmes, yet the latter had to face heavy odds right from the beginning. First, the Hindu Sabha faction led by Raja Narindra Nath, backed by some other legislators who had been a political challenge to the Urban vested interests in the formation of their ministry, had mobilised all their energies to overthrow the Unionist ministry.[14] Second, the leadership[15] of the Unionist party clashed with the Governor Malcalm Hailey who desired and partly manoeuvred with the help of the above group for the continuation of cases against the outgoing President of the Provincial Legislature.

When the governor did not succeed in his attempt, he tried to veer Sir Fazli and Chhotu Ram round to his viewpoint. The two leaders, though moderate and constitutional in their methods, strongly held that the government was wrongly manoeuvring in the legislature to undermine the Unionist position. Now Abdul Qadir and Sardar Mohinder Singh were elected President[16] and Vice-President[17] respectively by the Unionists, true to the principle of communal harmony. Let it be clear, the two leaders persistently advised the agricultural folk to follow constitutional methods so that they could advance financially, socially as well educationally and receive training in the art of self-government.[18]

To achieve its objectives, the Unionists now tried to secure the support of the Sikh landed aristocracy, since under the Reforms Act of 1919 the system of minority representation had been given to them. In fact, it was the common economic programme which united all the Unionists and this programme was to keep intact the Punjab Alienation Act as a measure of protection to small landholders and backward classes.[19] The Unionist Party always claimed that it was founded to protect small as well as the big landlords against the Urban (largely Hindu) money lending and commercial groups.[20] This party could give to its ideology a living form, when it set up a few institutions[21] which alongwith a Urdu weekly *Jat Gazette* not only repulsed the nationalist attack on this ideology, but mobilised opinion to gather enough pressure in order to secure economic concession and reservation of services for agriculturist class.[22] Besides the needs for the *Jats* to unite into one community of *zamindars* was also advocated.[23] In many of his articles published in the *Jat Gazette*, Chhotu Ram had depicted the exploitation of *zamindars* by the black *banias* and corrupt officials. The Unionists, therefore, had been pleading that no land revenue should be charged from those who possessed two acres of irrigated land, or five unirrigated acres of land or who were assessed for land revenue up to Rs. 5.[24] They also supported the demand of the agriculturists that the land revenue should be charged on income tax basis.[25]

However, it is interesting to note that once they captured power in 1937, they refused to implement either of the two demands even when pressed by Congress leaders. We can realise easily the importance of these two demands when we take into account the fact that 17.5 lakh cultivators fell under the category of those paying rupees five or less as land revenue.[26]

Thus, the result was that the Punjab Kisan Committee had a number of conferences during the year 1937, at different places such as Anandpur, Gobindpur, Chhajewal, Dhaudhar, Bhakna and many more places.[27] During the course of these conferences, the Punjab Kisan Committee focused the peasant movement mainly on the general demands of the peasantry, i.e. reduction in land revenue and *abiana*. Now, the Congress activities almost coalesced with the Punjab Kisan Committee activities, in the rural areas. The Congress activities continued unabated throughout the provinces though the Unionists made the best efforts to obstruct the spread of Congress influences in the rural areas. The Congress workers also cooperated with the socialists and the communists. Their propaganda was making headway in the district of Lahore, Amritsar, Jullundur and Hoshiarpur, but the Congress was too weak to successfully counter the Unionist party. It was due to the majority the Unionists commanded in the new legislative Assembly and also the support of the National Progressive Party and the Khalsa National Party.[28]

Another significant point worth noting is that the Congress and its allies wanted to win over a large section of the agriculturists against the British authorities. To achieve this they had decided to launch an anti-recruitment and agrarian agitation. But before they could do so, the Unionist Party introduced several bills[29] of agrarian legislation. The Unionists expected that such laws would be opposed by the Congress and that this was the best means of weaning the agriculturists away from the Congress.[30]

Indeed, by launching agrarian legislation the Unionists focused their attack on the money-lenders and carried on practical legislation against them. By doing so they tried to influence over a large section of peasantry. It has been said that the gulf between the town and the country created by the Act of 1900,[31] became the hub of the programme of this party—a party of the landlords. It also offered consistent opposition to the Indian National Congress as well as the support to the government during the war period. In fact, the Unionist party contained a large number of government pensioners, retired Indian Army officers, and higher grade members of the police force.[32] In its formation, the British bureaucracy succeeded in creating an institution which became a bulwark against the Congress or left influence.[33] Let it be admitted, that when the Congress defended the money-lending class from the attack of the Unionists it indirectly helped the Unionist party to project itself as a pro-peasant government, atleast for some time.

To consolidate its position in the countryside, the Unionists organised *Zamindara* Conferences in different districts to convince the agriculturists that it was a *Zamindara* Government working for their welfare and best interests. Party spokesman pointed to agrarian legislation designed to bring practical benefits to them.[34] During the course of these meetings they criticised the Congress party and boasted that in agrarian legislation they had stolen a march on the Congress,[35] in the province. In fact, after coming into power in 1923, for a long spell, the Unionist Party had fed the countryside an identity of the Congress with the money-lender and had created a generalised mistrust of the Congress amidst the peasantry.[36]

It is essential to take stock of the Muslims' activities resulting from the government attitude especially when they were a majority community in the province but had not been given representation in the Punjab Legislature proportionate to their community, because of the Lucknow Pact. The Unionist party took up their cause. Its leaders, whether Muslim or Hindu, in their campaign for Communal harmony, advocated due representation for the Punjab Muslims in and outside the Punjab Legislative Council.[37] To substantiate, one instance is cited here. Though in the elections to the Punjab Legislative Assembly in 1936–37, the Unionist captured 101 seats out of the total of 175.[38] By virtue of this majority, they could have all the ministers out of their own ranks, yet, true to their widely proclaimed principles of communal harmony and due representation, in the Unionists of six, there were three Muslims, two Hindus and one Sikh.

Let us not enter into the details relating to Muslim politics in the Punjab due to lack of space. Still some facts are cited here to have a clear picture of the relationship between the Unionists and the Muslim League. The former under Sikandar Hyat's leadership decided to join Muslim League some time in October 1937, but on their own conditions, i.e. the Unionist Ministry and the Unionist party were to continue as before in the Punjab Legislative Assembly. Sir Sikandar defined this duality by saying that, 'in provincial matters he was a Unionist, but in all India affairs a Muslim Leaguer.'[39] However, the League as an organisation was practically non-existent in the Punjab.[40] Moreover, Sri Chhotu Ram became the real leader of the Unionists after Sikandar's death and the former openly declared that he would have nothing to do with the league.

The Communist Party explained the Unionist-League conflict of March 1944 as a conflict between pro-imperialist landlords,[41] anti-imperialist patriotic organisation of the Muslims.[42] The Communists considered the League alliance with the Unionists (Sikandar–Jinnah pact which lasted for 7 years) as a short sighted policy on the part of the League as the league had become a mass organisation in the Punjab by itself. Now the Communists desired to form a coalition in such a way that the Unionists' ministry could be replaced by the people's ministry backed by the Muslim League, the Congress, the Akalis and the Communists.[43]

Now the Muslim League held meetings in the rural areas; but the number of audience was very small. In these meetings, the League leadership criticised the Unionist party and the *Zamindara* League.[44] With this, effective counter-meetings were held by the Unionist Party. The Premier also dismissed Shaukat Hyat from the post of ministership. At this movement, the league ministries in other provinces faced defeats and the Unionists could display the strength and Unity of their party in the budget session. All these factors finally lowered the prestige and influence of the Muslim League in the Punjab.[45]

In brief it would be appropriate to observe here that the Sikandar–Jinnah pact, in spite of the fact that it did not result in making Muslim League strong in Punjab, did circumscribe the activities of the Muslim Unionist party by itself even it so wanted; it could not spread out in other provinces, because legislators in those provinces were also the leaders of a considerable section of the Muslims.

Thus Unionist party, undoubtedly faced stiff opposition from different quarters, such as the non-agriculturists Hindus party,[46] the Muslim League, the Akalis (till 1942)[47] and a number of times from the Congress and the British bureaucracy. But despite all these heavy odds, the party had some achievements to its credit. Let us see to what extent this party succeeded in redressing the grievances of the rural masses coming to the efforts made by it, to achieve the above objectives, first of all, it aimed at educating the people of the province, especially the agriculturists.[48] Keeping in view all the defects in the then existing system of education, the Unionists brought forth some important proposals in 1923, with a view to improving the existing state of education in the Punjab.[49]

The over all result of all the efforts in this respect is partly reflected in increased investment in education. For instance, expenditure on education in the state rose from Rs. 6.76 lakhs in 1920–21 to Rs. 11.5 lakhs in 1925–26 and Rs. 154.19 lakhs in 1936–37. In 1944–45, Rs. 231.69 lakhs were provided for the development of education.[50] This excludes additional expenditure on the education of Europeans and Anglo-Indians and an Industrial education.

The Unionists took another radical step for the social upliftment of the rural masses (particularly peasantry), by providing sanitation, drinking water, medical and other facilities. In 1924, the government spent 10.3% of the funds allocated for the purpose for rural development,[51] and the rest was spent in Urban areas. However, due to their efforts, the share of the rural areas was raised to 15.7% in 1925–26, 26.4% in 1926–27 and 53.2% in 1927–28.[52] It is notable that such high allocation was for rural development and the rest was spent in urban areas.

The 'Creed' of Unionist Party made a provision of equal facilities and opportunities for the backward classes, whether rural or urban.[53] The party was committed to getting backward castes government lands on easy terms of payment. To cite a few instances, after the Great War, the government conferred about twenty thousand *bighas* on the *Kamins* and other backward classes.[54] Similarly, during 1940–44, it got distributed among them nearly three thousand *acres* of crown land in the Punjab and another one thousand acres among the members of the criminal tribes of whom 75% of beneficiaries were again the scheduled castes.[55]

The most remarkable measure improving the working conditions of the workers and labourers enacted by the members of the Unionist Party was the Trade Employee Act.[56] Another important step taken by the Unionist members was during the first ministry (1924–26) enactment of the opium (Punjab Amendment) and the Punjab Excise (Amendment) Act;[57] This was part of programme and of reducing consumption of liquor as a special evil. Again its members were prominent supporting the Punjab Suppression of Immoral Traffic Bill of 1935 presented by a non-Unionist member.[58] In 1939, it also supported the prevention of Extravagant Dowries Bill, introduced by a Congressite.[59]

The Unionist Party paid due attention to the problems of land revenue which concerned the party's main supporters, the landholders. The Unionists' efforts in the field of land reforms began in 1926 when their party got the Punjab Revenue (Amendment) Bill, passed by the Punjab Legislative Council.[60] The Bill asked the Government to fix the land revenue at not more than ⅓rd of the net assets instead of the then existing rate of ½ net assets.[61] Though the bill was vetoed by the Governor, because he had political difference with the Unionists.[62] The Unionists without being discharged, intensified their efforts and further raised their demand by asking that the maximum land revenue should be assessed at the ¼th of the net assets with the proviso that in no subsequent resettlement should be enhanced by more then 23% of the preceding assessment.[63] The government ultimately gave way by legislating, the Punjab Land Revenue Act, 1928, conceding the preceding demands.[64] Apart from the slashing of land revenue, they impressed upon the government, especially during the economic depression, to give very liberal remission in land revenue. Another reform which this party stressed upon was the abolition of *Acrage Rates* which was charged by the government to recover in 7 years Rs. 60 lakhs, the amount the government had incurred on digging watercourses, construction of culverts and preliminary surveys and demarcations. This effort resulted in an assurance by the Government that *Acrage Rates* would either be remitted or abolished.[65] In 1927, the *Chahi* rate was rationalised[66] and reduction was given in the irrigation duty during 1933–42.[67] Peasant welfare fund aiming at the special efforts for the progress of agriculture and the rural, folk was institued.[68]

Due to the efforts made by this party in the field of irrigation agriculturists became self dependent to a large extent. Practical shape was given to the *Kharif* canal extention scheme in 1940.[69] Thai Project, Haveli Project on canal in Pind Dadan Khan were completed in 1942 and 1944[70] respectively. New schemes of tubewell irrigation from western Jamuna canal were taken in hand,[71] and many more works were completed. Thus the efforts made in the field of irrigation were comprehensive as is borne out by the figures: e.g. canal irrigated areas had increased from about 8.8 million acres in 1923–24[72] to 16.5 millions acres in 1939–40.[73] At the same time the area under the cotton cultivation rose from about 1.35 million acres in 1920–21[74] to about 3.13 million acres in 1937–38.[75]

Attesting the same point planning committee and Mr. Darling observed that the irrigational improvements during the period resulted in a great stimulus to the trade and industry in the province.[76]

Before we discuss the efforts made by this party in the field of industry let us remember that its leadership also criticised the excessive *Malikana* rate that was realised as a part of rent from the grantees in the colonies.[77] Consequently, the government suspended the realization of *Malikana* for three harvests and further assured to reconsider the issue at a proper time.[78] At the same time one section in the party opposed the government's policy of selling Crown land through auction, thereby only capitalists could purchase that.[79] They demanded its distribution among the agriculturists of famine-striken areas.[80]

On the other hand, efforts were made to introduce many modern techniques for increasing the agricultural yields.[81] For this purpose, the number of co-operative societies was increased from 133 in 1924 to 237 in 1926 and their number stood at 1477 in 1939.[82] The Unionist Party also got enacted the Punjab Consolidation of Holdings Act 1936 (further amended in 1948) introducing compulsion in this regard, if it was objected by any owner of land. Area consolidated in the Punjab increased steadily, improving the prospect of large-scale farmers. From 5376 *acres* consolidation in 1923, it rose to 21,258 *acres* in 1926, over 100,000 *acres* in 1938 and 157,211 *acres* in 19 3 9,[83] and thus, by the close of 1939 more than million *acres* had been consolidated.[84]

It was again this party which ended a long standing injustice to the small landlords, when it passed for the reclamation of waste lands while under the old policy, big landholders managed to get much above the quota of additional canal water allowed for the purpose, under the new policy introduced by the Unionist Party's government, reclamation work commenced from the head of a tributary with the lands affected greatest by barrenness, whether these belonged to small agriculturists or big landlords and gradually reached the tail.[85] However, it is to be remembered here that the Unionists granted these concessions to small farmers just to avoid agrarian unrest and ultimately agrarian agitation in the province.

Thus, it may be concluded that the contribution of the Unionists' government to farms and fields covered almost all their aspects. The policy that the Unionists had adopted to accomplish its aims in this field was rather significant, while using the Unionist government's authority to bring about the changes, its leaders laid distinct emphasis on using the media of the social and democratic institutions like arbitration and conciliation Boards, Marketing Committees and Co-operative societies of various kinds which endeavoured to give a training to the agriculturists for self-improvement by involving them in their activities which led to non the less satisfactory reslts.

Notes

1. *Jat Sabha*, All India *Jat Mahascibha* and *Zaminclara Sabha* were some of the important political groups.
2. *The Tribune* (Lahore), 12 January 1933, p. 4; R.S. Shastri, *Chaudhary Chhotu Ram: Jivan Charitra*, (Hindi), p. 80; *Pioneer*, (Allahabad), 12 January 1945, p. 5. Mitra's *Indian Annual Register*, vol. I, 1944, p. 218; *PLCD*, vol. XXII, March 10, 1944 (This party was set up with its headquarter at Rohtak by the efforts of All India *Jat Mahasabha* and it remained in power for atleast 20 years. However, the Sikh and the Muslim *Jat* agriculturists were allowed to be its members. Soon its activities spread to the entire province), vide A. Hussain, *Fazli-Hussain: A Political Biography*, p. 156; R.S. Sharma, *Haryana Ka Itihas*, p. 84.
3. Y. Shastri, *Khastri-Jation Ka Uthonopattan*, (Hindi), pp. 626, 629; R.S. Sharma, *Haryana Ka Itihas*, pp. 86–8.
4. Its Headquarter was at Lahore, vide *Jat Gazette*, (Rohtak), 12 January 1918, pp. 10–12.
5. *18 Months of Provincial Autonomy in the Punjab*, (Lahore), 4 April 1930, p. 3; Y.P. Bajaj, *Sir Chhotu Ram and His Work* (unpublished Ph.D. thesis), Kurukshetra University, 1972, p. 85).
6. Gopal Madan, *Sir Chhotu Ram: A Political Biography*, p. 19; *Jat Gazette*, (Rohtak), December 1924; A. Hussain, op. cit., pp. 150–60.
7. *Jat Gazette*, (Rohtak), 2 Apr. 1923, 9 July 1923, 23 March 1927, 26 June 1927; R.S. Shastri, op. cit., pp. 93–96.

8. Its creed, aims and objects are quoted from the 'Punjab Unionist Party Rules and Regulation' published by the Punjab Unionist Party headquarters Secretariat, Lahore. Given in All India *Hindu Mahasabha* Papers, (Private paper sections, NMML, New Delhi), A. Hussain, op. cit., *Jat Gazette* (Rohtak), December 1924, A. Hussain, op. cit., pp. 150–60.

9. *PLAD*, vol. I, 1937, p. 320; A. Hussain, op. cit., pp. 154–55, Y.P. Bajaj, 'Land Revenue Reforms of the Unionist Party', *The Punjab Past and Present*. Y.P. Bajaj, op. cit., Appendix-XX; 'Chaudhary Chhotu Ram: The Weak and Raising The Fallen', *The Punjab Past and Present*, vol. V, part I, April 1971, p. 165; *18 Months of Provincial Autonomy in the Punjab*, 1 April 1938, p. 1; Mitra's *Indian Quarterly Register*, vol. II, 1938, pp. 122–23.

10. File no. 19, Institution-III, NMML (Private Papers Section) New Delhi; *Jat Gazette*, 1 July, 1931, p. 2.
Jat Gazette, 15 June 1927, p. 4; 1 June 1931, p. 1; 5 December 1941, p. 5; 8 January 1941, p. 5; 29 January 1941, p. 6; *The Tribune*, (Lahore), 17 September 1933.

11. Ibid.

12. H.G. Rowlinson and H.L.O. Garrett, eds., *Great Men of India*, p. 359;. Khushwant Singh, *History of the Sikhs*, vol. II, p. 224.

13. G. Adhikari, Pakistan and National Unity: The Communist Solution,. p. 22.

14. R.S. Shastri, op. cit., pp. 123–28.

15. Particularly Sir Chhotu Ram and Sir Fazl-i Hussain.

16. A. Hussain, op. cit., p. 160; R.S. Shastri, op. cit., p. 129.

17. Ibid.

18. *The Tribune*, (Lahore), 11 January 1945, p. 3; R.S. Shastri, op. cit., p. 129.

19. This point is made clear in the aims and objects of the party. See A. Hussain, op. cit., pp. 154–5.

20. Ibid., p. 318, Kanson, J. Henery, ed., *Contemporary Problems of Pakistan*,. p. 7.

21. *Jat Mahasabha Samiti*, All India *Jat* Conference, and *Jat* Heroes Memorial School were the main institutions, vide Madan Gopal, op. cit., p. 161; *Jat Gazette* (Rohtak), 12 February 1918, p. 11; A. Hussain, op. cit., p. 155, R.S. Sharma, op. cit., p. 84.

22. Madan Gopal, op. cit., p. 161.

23. *The Tribune* (Lahore), 30 Apil. 1938.

24. Y.P. Bajaj, op. cit., p. 345.

25. Ibid., p. 351. (The Income tax up to Rs. 2000 was exempted from income tax but no such exemption was allowed in the assessment of land revenue.) This is based on the views expressed by various members in the Punjab Legislative Council Debates of the period under review.

26. Ibid. Chaudhary Prem, 'Social Basis of Sir Chhotu Ram's Politics',. *The Punjab Past and Present*, p. 345.

27. These places were situated in the districts—Hoshiarpur, Gurdaspur,, Ludhiana, Ferozepore and Bhatinda, respectively.

28. The National Progressive Party—a semi-Communal party, represented the interests of a section of the Urban Hindu Commercial group and Raja Narendra Nath led this group. The Khalsa National Party represented the aristocracy and the intellectuals, vide All India *Hindu Mahasabha* Papers. (Private Papers Section) NMML, New Delhi.

29. Ibid.

30. *The Tribune* (Lahore), 17 January 1937.

31. Bhagwan Singh Josh, *Communist Movement in India*, pp. 116–17 (but it does not appeal to the reason as has been stated by Bhagwan Josh that the Unionist were able to rally behind the whole of the Punjab countryside).

32. Ibid., p. 116; *National Front*, 3 July 1938.

33. The British Policy, conceived with enough foresight in 1900, of driving, wedge between the countryside and the city to stem the tide of nationalism in the countryside was thus crowned with success in the formation of the Unionist Party, vide Madan Gopal, op. cit., p. 111.

34. Home Department, File no. 18/9/1938, Political, NAI, New Delhi.

35. Madan Gopal, op. cit., p. 116.

36. Bhagwan Josh, op. cit., p. 148.

37. R.S. Shastri, op. cit., p. 204, *PLCD*, vol. XIV, 20 Mar. 1929, pp. 243–44; Y.P. Bajaj, op. cit., Appendix XX (Out of 71 seats filled in by the election, 35 had been allocated to the Muslims). For more details see *Jat Gazette*, 1 January 1931, p. 1; *Indian Annual Register*, vol. I, 1927, p. 431; A. Hussain, op. cit., p. 358.

38. *18 Months of Provincial Autonomy in the Punjab*, pp. 8–9; *Civil and Military Gazette*, (Lahore), 21 Oct. 1937.

39. Sajjad Zaheer, *Light on League-Unionist Conflict*, pp. 24–8.

40. Ibid., p. 19.

41. The Unionist Ministry which was not only anti-national but also anti-Kisan Ministry of the big *Zamindars* vide Bhagwan Josh, op. cit., p. 147.

42. For details of the conflict between the two factions, see Sajjad Zaheer, op. cit., pp. 26–27.

43. Ibid., p. 15 (For details see Report of the Political situation in the Punjab for the second half of November 1945, Home Department Political, NAI, New Delhi.

44. Home Deptt. File no. 18/2/1945 Political, NAI, New Delhi.

45. Bhagwan Josh, op. cit., p. 175, for details also see *People's War*, vol. III, no. 23, 31 Dec. 1944, no. 32; February 1945, no. 37, 11 March 1945.

46. Some agriculturists and rural Hindus like Baldev Singh and Pt. Nanak Chand had also joined this group, vide Gurcharan Singh, *Ankhi Surma*, (Punjabi), p. 130.

47. In this regard K.C. Gulati, notes that Akali opposition to the Unionist Party ended in 1942, when Sikander-Baldev Pact was concluded on 15 June 1942, vide K.C. Gulati, op. cit., p. 113; *The Tribune*, (Lahore), 16 June 1942, Mohinder Singh, *Sardari-Azam*, (Punjabi), pp. 103, 104; *Akali Patrika*, 16 June 1942.

48. *PLCD*, vol. X, 24 Oct. 1939, p. 62; *Punjab Government Report of the Compulsory Education Committee*, 1930, p. 4, Punjab Government, *Land of Five Rivers*, pp. 2–6; Proceedings of the Department of Education of India, File no. 1–2A, Oct. 1917.

49. For details, see *PLCD*, vol. X, 7 March 1925, p. 141, vol. XV, 7 March 1930, pp. 330–31; A. Hussain, op. cit., 134.

50. The Punjab budgets with detailed estimate for 1920–21, to 1944–45. Regarding the increase in the number of schools to all kinds, see *Annual Report*, XXIII, 27 July 1933, pp. 1070–72; *Punjab Administration Reports*, 1923–24 to 1938–39.

51. *PLCD*, vol. VI, 13 March 1924, p. 565.

52. Ibid., *PLAD*, vol. X, 15 March 1927, p. 165. *PLCD*, vol. VI, 1924, p. 565; XXVI, 25 February 1935, p. 97; *Jat Gazette*, 15 Jan. 1927, p. 4. For details about public welfare works in the rural areas in various fields, also see *PLAD*, vol. 1, 13 July 1939, p. 440. Punjab budgets detailed estimate for 1936–37 to 1944–45, *Punjab Govt. Gazette* (Extraordinary), 2 May 1940, p. 257; Mitra's *Annual Register*, 1941, p. 266; R.S. Shastri, op. cit., p. 628; *PLCD*, vol. VIII, 7 February 1925, p. 1088; vol. XXIII, 13 March 1933, pp. 359, 1016–97.

53. *PLAD*, vol. XV, 4 January 1941, p. 270.

54. R.S. Shastri, op. cit., pp. 301, 302; *Jat Gazette*, 9 January 1946, p. 3.

55. *PLAD*, vol. XXII, 10 March 1944, pp. 488–89; vol. XXIV, 19 Feb. 1945, p. 2.

56. Mitra's *Indian Annual Register*, 1941, p. 266, *Indian Year Book*, 1940–41, pp. 527–30; *PLCD*, vol. XIII, 30 Apr. 1930, p. 1237.

57. *Punjab Govt. Gazette*, part II, 1926; *PLCD*, vol. VIII, 5 March 1925, pp. 311–13, 316–17; vol. VII, 12 Nov. 1924, p. 355. (For details see *Excise Administration Report*, 1938–39.)

58. *Punjab Govt. Gazette*, (Extraordinary) ending 31 December 1935, pp. 77–80, *PLCD*, vol. XXVI, 21 February 1935, pp. 44 and 80.

59. Ibid., part V, 3 Nov. 1930, pp. 85–90, 92, 95; *PLCD*, vol. X, 20 Oct. 1939, p. 146.

60. A. Hussain, op. cit., p. 10.

61. Deptt. of Education, Health and Lands Year 1926, File no. Land Feb.3-B.

62. A. Hussain, op. cit., p. l00.

63. *PLCD*, vol. XI, 8 May 1928, pp. 1009. 17, 47, *PLAD*, vol. XIII, 4 March 1940, p. 49; vol. XV, 27 January 1941, p. 313.

64. Punjab Land Revenue Act, 1928, Section 48-B; A. Hussain, op. cit., p. 149. *The Tribune* (Lahore), 6 February 1933, p. 7; *PLCD*, vol. XXVI, 6. Feb. 1935, (for figures) see *The Tribune* (Lahore), 27 April 1930, pp. 3–4.

65. *PLCD*, vol. XXVIII, 10 Mar. 1936, pp. 47, 320, 515, 521; A. Hussain, op. cit., pp. 149 and 160.

66. *PLCD*, vol. XXIII, 28 Feb. 1933, p. 55; Mitra's *Indian Quarterly Register*, vol. I, 1927, p. 369; *PLCD*, vol. XXIV, 5 March 1934, p. 515; vol. XXIII, 21 March 1933, p. 605.

67. *PLAD*, vol. XIX, 10 March 1942, p. 184; vol. XXI, 16 March 1943, p. 357.

68. *Jat Gazette*, (Rohtak), 8 Sept. 1943, p. 8; *PLCD*, vol. XXIV, 51 Mar. 934, p. 95; vol. XXIII, 21 Mar. 9133, pp. 643, 655, 652–63; Report on the *Abiana* Committee (by the Punjab Government, 1933, p. 47; T. Ram, op. cit., p. 12, *PLCD*, 10 March 1942, p. 184; Dept. Health, Education and Lands, Year 1926, File no. Lands May 20-21-B; File no. 17(27) F.D. 1944; also year 1938, File no. 22(27) ED-1984; 52(79) E.D.-1948; 22(80) FD-1948 NAI, New Delhi.

69. *PLCD*, vol. II, 5 March 1940, p. 32.

70. Mitra's *Indian Annual Register*, vol. II, 1940, p. 187 (For detailed information also see Y.P. Bajaj, op. cit.)

71. *PLCD*, vol. XII, 7 March 1925. p. 140, 13 March 1925, p. 506; vol. XXVIII, 1936, pp. 59 and 993; *PLAD*, vol. I, 22 June 1927, p. 501; 2 July 1937, p. 947; vol. VIII, 29 March 1939, pp. 860–61.

72. Board of Economic Enquiry Commission Publication no. 52, p. 47.

73. Ibid., Supplementary 3 to Publication no. 52, p. 1.

74. *Statistical Abstracts of British India 1911–12 to 1920–21*, pp. 316–510.

75. *Report on the Operations of the Agricultural Deptt.*, Ending 30 June 1939, p. 72.

76. Ibid.

77. *PLCD*, vol. XXVIII, 10 Mar. 1936, p. 314; vol. XXIII, 5 March 1934, p. 515.

78. *PLCD*, vol. XXIV, 1934, pp. 31, 322.

79. *Jat Gazette* (Rohtak), 22 November 1930. p. 3.

80. Ibid.

81. M.L., Darling, *Punjab Peasant in Prosperity and Debt*, pp. 29–30, 84, 133–34, 264.

82. The Annual Report on the working of cooperative societies in the Punjab for the year ending 31 July, 1923 to 31 July, 1927; also year ending 31st July, 1940; *Jat Gazette*, (Rohtak), 15 June 1927, p. 41.

83. Achievement of these societies is further brightened when it is studied that their work was steadily opposed by the Patwaris, because practice of legal gratification were generally slashed, vide ibid., A. Ullah, *Co-operative Movement in the Punjab*, pp. 257–28; *PLAD*, vol. VIII, 16 March 1939, p. 210, vol. III, 8 March 1938, p. 570.

84. *PLAD*, vol. VIII, 16 Mar. 1939, p. 210; B.S. Saini, *Socio-Economic Condition of the Punjab 1930 39*, p 204, *Punjab Govern ment Gazette*, (Extraordinary), 6 November 1936, pp. 167–70; also of 8 March 1945, (Extraordinary), p. 33.

85. *PLAD*, vol. XXII, 16 March 1943, p. 355.

33

Parties and Politics in Indian Trade Union Movement: Early Phase 1917–24

Sanat Bose

The purpose of the present article is to trace

(a) the forces which accelerated the growth of organised labour movement in India (through trade unions);
(b) the counterforces tending to retard this growth; and
(c) to analyse the problems which emerged in the field of trade unionism, out of this action and reaction.

The fact that some books and articles dealing with this subject already exist, does not minimise the need to study them afresh because, first some of these problems persist even today and second, they raise certain fundamental questions relating to trade unionism itself which should be raised and analysed again and again. Split in the trade unions leading to the formation of a number of central trade union bodies (AITUC, CITU, INTUC, etc), is neither accidental nor the results of whimsical actions on the part of leading trade unionists. It has a history of its own and is directly or indirectly involved with the following basic question: what are the roles and goals of trade union movement? Obviously, the answer to this question cannot be singular; because the issue is also intimately connected with the socio-political attitude and outlook of the answerer. Functions of trade unions cannot be entirely divorced from the general current of socio-political movements. It is 'politics' that gave birth to Indian trade unions and it is 'politics' again that accelerated or retard their growth at different points of time.

It will be interesting to get some idea about the founder leaders of Indian trade union movement, in terms of their ideology and role. For this purpose, we may group them in the following manner:

*39th Session at Hyderabad, 1978.

(a) Social workers (Baptista, Jhavala, Ginwala, Andrews, etc.): This group was motivated by the ideal of social upliftment of the downtrodden. For them, the working class was only one section of the society—the most oppressed and exploited section. It was therefore an object of pity. The worker's poverty, ignorance and helplessness called for sympathy and consideration from the more favourably placed. They considered it a social obligation to focus their problems and hoped, by pleading for social justice, they would be able to convince their employers to take steps with a view to ameliorating their plight to some extent.

Their contribution to the growth of trade unions cannot be minimised. B.P. Wadia, who was mainly responsible for building up the Madras Labour Union, may be considered as belonging to this group.

If in a subsequent period this group's hold over the working class slackened, that was inevitable because of the changed circumstances which called for a different type of ideology to guide labour movement. Philanthropy, even in its purest form, can act as a catalytic force in accelerating social movements up to a point. Beyond, it either becomes a brake or dies away slowly.

Along with such people, another group should also be mentioned. They were motivated primarily by personal considerations (gain in social status or profession), though they also claimed to be social workers. Quite a number of such leaders were lawyers by profession and some were employees themselves who wanted to exploit the situation for their personal promotion, etc.

(b) Moderate politicians (N.M. Joshi, etc.): They belonged ideologically to the well known Liberal Party of the day. Their 'moderate' political thinking—and hence their socio-economic outlook reflected in their attitude to trade unionism, its role and goal. By and large, they wanted to build up trade unions on the model of the British Trade Union-Congress. They had a poor understanding of the significance of anti-imperialist movement vis-a-vis the growth of trade unions. In other words, they wanted trade unions to remain aloof from the general current of anti-imperialist politics of the Congress. They also believed in 'politics' but politics of a different nature. Hence, it was no accident that some of them also thought of forming a separate political party again on the model of the British Labour Party. As they did not realise that circumstances which gave birth to the British Labour Party did not obtain in a colonial country like India, they failed to achieve their objective. But they genuinely believed that conditions of the Indian worker could be definitely improved through constitutional means—appropriate labour legislation at home and putting pressure on the government through the efforts of the newly set up ILD.

Naturally, the line of demarcation between these two groups was very thin, because though known as social workers or philanthropists, most of the leaders belonging to the first group also did hold some political views which were very close to the line of political thinking of the Moderates. Thus, sharing as he did,

Mrs. Annie Besant's 'Home Rule' politics, Mr. Wadia was also the Assistant Editor of her newspaper, *New India*. So he cannot be called a strictly non-political social worker. Similarly, though not actually connected with 'politics', 'Andreas' close association and collaboration with Gandhi, particularly in trade union activities, makes it difficult to identify him only as a Christian philanthropist.

Being basically constitutionalists in their outlook, these leaders tried to conduct their union activities accordingly. Both these groups therefore discouraged militant working class actions, including strikes. If, on some occasions, they had to lead a strike, that was because events forced them to do so. They wanted to settle matters through negotiation with employers whenever possible.

(c) A section of the Congress leaders (Jawaharlal Nehru, C.R. Das, Lala Lajpat Rai, Subhas Bose, etc.): They belonged to 'left' of the anti-imperialist movement, and lent their support to the workers' movements with a view to drawing the latter into the fold of their political movement. (Some extremists like Nani Gopal Mukherjee of Jamshedpur Labour Association also actively participated in organising workers). It is to be remembered that these leaders did not participate in trade union activities in their individual capacities only. The Congress itself was also keen to organise labour for the same purpose. Thus at its 31st session (Amritsar 1919), the following resolution was passed: 'This Congress urges its Provincial Committees and other affiliated associations to promote labour unions throughout the country with the view of improving social, economic and political conditions of the labouring classes and for securing them a fair standard of living and a proper place in the body politic of India.'[1]

It is well known that these Congress leaders did not share any common social or political ideology. Their common point of focus was concentrated on anti-British struggles. Hence their approach to trade union activities varied from individual to individual and from one situation to another.

The role of Gandhi as a trade union organiser also comes under the above group because he was the most influential Congress leader. But his principles of trade unionism and trade union activities were not equally practised by other Congress leaders. In the early period at least, Gandhian principles of trade unionism as propounded by him in course of his activities in Ahmedabad (1918); did not serve as the main guideline for other trade unionists including those belonging to the Congress. Probably one of the reasons for this divergence of views and activities between Gandhi and other Congress leaders was their relative stature in the field of Indian politics. By virtue of his unique position which enabled him to claim both labour and employer as his friends, he could get certain things done in certain ways which others could not. His role could not be 'immitated'. If we compare the relationship that was established between

Gandhi and the Sarabhais of Ahmedabad (during and after the famous Ahmedabad labour strike of 1918) on the one hand and between C.R. Das and the Tatas (during and after the famous Jamshedpur labour strike of 1920) on the other, we shall see that these two leaders were not equally acceptable to the capitalists: Gandhi was much more acceptable than even C.R. Das (or Subhas Bose at a later period).

(d) The different Communist groups which had not yet coalesced into the Communist Party of India: These scattered groups were actively working in Bombay, Calcutta, Cawnpore and Lahore. Strictly speaking, their activities in the field of trade unions do not fall in the period under discussion, though they had started their political activities from 1920 onwards. In spite of their initial handicap because of late entry into this field, and of the tremendous difficulties under which they had to operate, they rapidly made up the time lag and from 1925, became a decisive force in Indian trade union movement. It was on these communists trade unionists that the Russian Revolution of 1917, cast a positively lasting influence. Inspired by the Socialist Revolution and guided by the Third Communist International they for the first time brought in the concept of class and class struggle in the field of Indian labour.

Thus stood, broadly, the different groups of trade union leaders in the early phase of trade union activities in India.

Let us now take up the main features of labour movements in the period under discussion. They may be summarised in the following manner:

(a) Though white collar (including Anglo-Indian employees) unions or associations came into existence earlier (Amalgamated Society of Railway Servants of India and Burma, 1897, Printers Union, Calcutta, 1905, Postal Union Bombay, 1907, etc.), working class unions, once they started (in the immediate post-World War I period), spread out and grew up at a more rapid pace.

(b) With the rapid growth of labour unions, the influence of social and philanthropic workers on the labour organisations began to decay. During this period objective conditions gave rise to widespread and intense labour unrest, which could not be controlled or forestalled by this group of leaders. It was not possible for organisations like the Social Service League (1910), with their limited outlook and objectives, to grasp the significance of this new trend that was developing in the working class. Through the formation of trade unions, the latter was gradually emerging as a distinct class, groping for a class identity and looking out for its class enemies.

(c) Labour unrest was primarily centred around demands for wage increase, bonus, shorter hours of work and stopping misbehaviour of employers. On certain occasion and in certain centres, current anti-

British political movement also made its impact on the working class. The strike of Assam Tea Garden workers (Chargola Exodus, 1921) is a case in point. But its participation in the current political movement should not be exaggerated.

(d) Strikes were frequent but usually lasted for short periods. Closure of factories for longer period was due more to 'lockouts' than to strikes. Since the mill owners were not under any social or legal obligations, they could declare lock out at any time, and it was practised with a view to crushing organised labour movements. It was difficult for workers to hold out for a long period and for the sake of survival they would leave for their village home whenever mills remained closed for a long period. This usually brought about a lull in trade union activities in the post-strike period, accompanied by a fall in union membership.

(e) In general, the government apparently followed a policy of 'non-intervention' unless 'law and order' problems were apprehended. It was taken for granted that for all 'law and order' problems the workers alone were responsible, and suitable steps would accordingly be taken to tackle this problem. Thus whenever it did intervene, it was for the purpose of unholding the employers' cause, either in the name of preserving 'law and order' (Jamshedpur Labour Strike of 1920) or acting as arbitrator.[2]

(f) Up to 1926, there were no pro-labour legislations excepting the amended Factories Act (1922), while a good many anti-labour legislations were still in force (Masters and Servants Act, Workmen's Breach of Contract Act, some Sections of the Indian Penal Code, etc.).

Circumstances responsible for the birth of trade unions and trade union activities in the immediate post-World War I period were summarised in the following report submitted by the Viceroy to the Secretary of State for India:

(a) 'The pressure of high prices, wages having risen very considerably (?) in the last 12 months, but not uniformly and not having kept pace with prices.

(b) 'The general belief that profiteering is freely practised by middle men and retail dealers.

(c) 'The knowledge that very large profits are being made by capitalists, mill owners in particular.

(d) 'The general shortage of industrial labour which has recently been accentuated by the increased demand of rapidly expending industrial establishments and aggravated by the ravages of influenza, the results of which have been most obvious in crowded towns and have in consequence kept away country labours. (This aspect was also reiterated by the Viceroy in 1917, while announcing abolition, of Indenture system of labour recruitment for British Sugar Plantation Colonies like Br. Giana, West Indies, etc.)

(e) 'The reluctance of employers to grant increase of pay till discontent with existing conditions has manifested itself in the shape of a strike.'[3]

All the above factors combined to produce widespread labour unrest throughout the entire country. Starting with the Bombay textile workers' strike (August 1917), labour unrest spread out and engulfed all the industrial centres of the country.

A rapid resume of strike-struggles may be made in this connection. In 1919, 16 strikes took place in Madras. There were a number of strikes in Bengal jute mills, Bihar, and Assam tea gardens. A general strike was organised in Bombay.

In 1920, about 200 strikes took place all over the country, and in Madras alone 62 strikes were declared.

In 1921, about 400 labour disputes have been noted. In 174 cases the strikers demanded higher wages, and in 75 cases, it was bonus. 'Personnel' problems caused 63 disputes, and in 10 cases, the issues involved were leave and other matters. In Bombay, 162 strikes were declared, the figure for Bengal being 135. Cotton and woollen mills accounted for 164 strikes, while the corresponding figures for engineering, jute and railways were 31, 28, and 28.

Out of these strikes, 88 were successful and 82 were partially successful.[4]

Workers had as yet neither emerged as a mature proletariat class with its own class consciousness, nor become active participants in the political movements of the day. Since the anti-imperialist movement launched by the Congress was not based on a clear formulation of its objectives, hesitancy and reluctance in organising and extending trade unions and union activities developed. For example, it did not clearly formulate its views on the role of working class *vis-a-vis* the dichotomy existing between foreign and Indian capital. This also led to half-hearted attempts by Congress leaders to bring the working class into the fold of nationalist movement.

The Congress leaders therefore failed to see or establish appropriate link between trade union movement and the anti-imperialist movement that was being led by them. The greatest stumbling bloc to this coordinated movement was Gandhi himself. His views and utterances on labour and labour problems made this confusion worse confounded. For instance, on the issue of political strikes, Gandhi's view was expressed thus: 'In my opinion, it will be the most serious mistake to make use of labour strikes for political purpose. It does not require much effort of the intellect to perceive that it is most dangerous to make political use of labour until labourers understand the political conditions of the country and are prepared to work for the common good. The greatest political contribution, therefore, that the labourers can make at present is to improve their own condition, to earn better income, to insist on the right to demand proper treatment by their employers. The proper evolution, therefore would be for the labourers to raise themselves to the status of part proprietor. Strikes, therefore for the present, should only take place for the direct settlement of the labourers' lot and, when they have acquired the spirit of patriotism, for the regulation of prices of their manufacturers."[5]

According to Gandhi the condition of a successful strike therefore, would be:

(a) The cause of the strike must be just.
(b) There should be practical unanimity among the strikers.
(c) There should be no violence used against non-strikers.
(d) Strikers should be able to maintain themselves during the strike period without falling back upon Union Funds and should therefore occupy themselves in some useful and productive temporary occupation.[6]

Gandhi's attitude to the growth of trade unionism was also reflected in his opposition to the AITUC. Probably he intuitively felt such a step would have far reaching consequences and would draw the working class away from the path chalked out by him. (That is why he advised the Ahmedabad Labour Association not to affiliate with the AITUC). He also did not share the views of the founder leaders of the Trade Union Congress. He was, however, absolutely confident that his views will ultimately triumph. His statement in this connection, is worth noting: 'A time will come, when it will be possible for the Trade Union Congress to accept the Ahmedabad method. But I am in no hurry. It will come in its own time.'[7]

Gandhi's views were however not apparently shared by other Congress leaders; otherwise they could not have participated in the work of founding the Trade Union Congress. In the face of Gandhi's sharp views, it is difficult to explain how could other Congress leaders agree to participate in the activities of the newly formed AITUC.

Having noted Gandhi's views, let us try to present the views of the older type of labour leaders the right liberals, who were still very active and whose contribution towards the formation of the AITUC cannot be historically minimised. Two such leaders were F.J. Ginwala (a solicitor) and S.H. Jhabvala. Either as president or as secretary, they were actively associated with a number of unions, and naturally these unions had more or less the same type of objectives. These objectives were:

(a) 'to promote friendly feelings and to foster a spirit of brotherhood and cooperation among workmen in Bombay;
(b) 'to consider the question of their various disabilities with regard to their work and wages and to try to bring about their removal by all lawful and constitution (sic) means;

(c) 'to promote friendly and harmonious relations between the workmen and their superior authorities;

(d) 'to maintain funds for the relief of members when sick or in distress, and for the relief of dependents of the deceased members;

(e) 'to improve the conditions of workmen by initiating schemes of benefit insurance, provident funds, cooperative credit-society, medical relief and such other kindred benefits; and

(f) 'generally to ameliorate the social, educational and economic condition of the workmen and their dependents.'[8]

The above objectives reflect the views of this section of trade union leaders. They had no quarrel with the prevailing socioeconomic order and hence did not wish to take any step which would strike at the roots of that system. For them, anti-imperialist politics was taboo, and revolutionary politics still more. Yet these leaders were also in favour of forming a central labour union: Baptista himself was the Chairman of the Reception Committee of the First Session of the AITUC, which was presided over by Lala Lajpat Rai, a confirmed left nationalist of the day.

In the context of all that has been noted above, how do we account for the formation of the AITUC in 1920? To our mind, it was brought about by the following factors.

(a) a spate of intense labour unrest (as mentioned earlier) recurring frequently and simultaneously at all the industrial centres of India, creating an objective basis for starting trade unions seriously;

(b) through such trade unions, fulfilling the urge of a section of labour leaders (mainly belonging to the moderate group), to represent Indian labour in the different official bodies, particularly the newly formed ILO;

(c) through such international bodies like the ILO, to bring pressure on the government to pass pro-labour legislations with a view to defending the interests of labour;

(d) to lead working class struggles through constitutional means;

(e) the role of the ILO, which insisted on having unofficial labour representatives on its body. This condition could not be fulfilled unless some sort of a centralised labour union was formed which would act as the mouthpiece of Indian labour and elect its own representatives for the ILO.

Leading trade unionists did not fail to avail themselves of this opportunity. In the absence of further data, coupled with the state of working class consciousness that existed at that time, it is difficult to conclude that the Indian working class itself was seriously feeling the need to form a central labour union like the AITUC. This doubt is further strengthened when one looks at the composition of leaders who participated in the first Session of the AITUC.

As a matter of fact, the leading personalities responsible for founding the AITUC consisted of philanthropists, moderates, and left nationalists. They could participate jointly because their views regarding the role of trade unions and trade union movements *vis-a-vis* capital, were basically identical, though their political views particularly with respect to freedom movement were different.

This contradiction prevailing among the founder leaders of the AITUC, was to persist throughout the subsequent history of this, body and bring about disastrous consequences later on.

Notes

1. V.B. Karnik, *Indian Trade Unions*.
2. Madras Labour Advisory Board, a few Courts of Enquiry.
3. Quoted by Sukomal Sen in his book *Working Class of India*, 1977, p. 138.
4. J.S. Mathur, *Indian Working Class Movement*, pp. 21–2.
5. Quoted by V.B. Karnik in *Indian Trade Unions*, p. 37.
6. Ibid., pp. 85–6.
7. Quoted by Sukomal Sen in *Working Class of India*, p. 154.
8. A.R. Burnett-Hurst, *Labour and Housing in Bombay*, 1925, p. 102.

34

The Unsettled Adivasi World of Malda in the First Three Decades of the Present Century

Sivaji Koyal and *Ramkrishna Chatterjee*

CHOTANAGPUR AND Santal Parganas were in the throes of an acute agrarian crisis during the second half of the nineteenth century. The loss of land which was their only source of income forced the Santals, Mundas and Oraons to move out in different directions. Malda was one district which was to be largely settled by these adviasis, especially the santals. In course of this paper an attempt will be made to study the settlement of the adivasis in Malda during the first decade of the present century, their deteriorating relations with the landlords and the resulting tension culminating in their eviction from their lands. This study will be meaningful for it will help us to demonstrate the unsettled nature of the adivasi world under the British rule.

Movement Towards Malda

Round about 1880 the adivasis of Chotanagpur and Santal Parganas began to move out from their home land towards Malda. In 1901 the Santal population in Malda was returned as 52,000 and the decade following saw a further increase of over 14,000.[1] So far as Oraons are concerned some 3,000 of them were settled in Malda at the time of the settlement operations.[2] There were Mundas also but their figure has not been recorded. The census figures (census of 1931) indicate that in Malda the Santal population stood at 72,145 and the Oraons at 4,961.[3] It was discontent at home which prompted migration. Chotanagpur in the nineteenth century was a scene of exploitation, the zamindars being the exploiters and the adivasi peasants the exploited. The spirit of antagonism between the two stemmed from such causes as heavy incidence of rent, the system of collecting heavy predial dues (rakumat) and the system of levying predial services (bethbegari). The rapacity of the money-lender was another form of exploitation. All these fell heavily on the adivasi peasant and the process of land alienation was accelerated. Often he had no other option but to move out. Much the same was the case with Santal Parganas. The Santals whose labour was required to cultivate the new estates were enticed by false promises of high wages or rent-free farm to leave their jungle homes and become tenants of the new landlords or agricultural labourers. Soon after their acceptance of service, the Santals were enslaved as agricultural serfs, or mercilessly exploited as tenants."[4] Naturally the Santals too like their breathren in Chotanagpur were often forced to migrate and settle in different districts of Bengal like Malda. It was the zamindars of Malda who had induced the Santals to migrate to this district to clear the jungles, and terrace the slopes in the Barind region.[5] However, here as in other parts of Bengal things were not much different from what they were in Chotanagpur and Santal Parganas. But registering protest against the existing order of things was not an easy task. In these regions of Bengal the non-adivasi milieu was too formidable for a rebellion of the type Chotanagpur and Santal Parganas had witnessed.[6] Be that as it may, Barind was to witness an uprising which was the result of unbearable oppression of the adivasis.

Landlord–Tenant Relations Strained

Much the same exploitation which the Santals and Oraons had experienced earlier in their homelands awaited them in the territory newly settled by them. The zamindars in Malda showed no interest in the economic welfare of their tenants or in agricultural improvements.[7] What led to ill feeling between the zamindar and the ryots were the illegal enhancements of rents, exaction of various *abwabs*, the non-grantal of rent receipts, the levy of interest at high rates by the mahajan, the low price of agricultural produce which was again due to the economic depression of the third decade of the present century. With these may be added the rapacity and oppression of the agents, *gomastas* and *peadas* of the zamindar. These various types of malpractices flourished in the Barind where the adivasis lived and they caused much ill feeling between the zamindar and the tenant.

Origin of Troubles

Trouble started round about 1910 when the zamindars of Tauzis Numbers 586 and 587 Habibpur Police Station tried to enforce an enhancement of rent. At that time the Santals were holding the cleared lands at very low rates, or rent free. Soon after this incident, the Santals made a representation to the Governor. Mr. Vas, the Collector who was asked to arbitrate caused the lands to be measured and the rent was settled at six annas per bigha, also provision was made for the payment of arrear rent. Since this time the Santals have stood by this Settlement, but the government could not compel the zamindars to abide by it. The Bulbuli Estate, for example, tried its hand at rent enhancement. Such attempts have caused friction, for the ryot have always resisted, such attempts on the part of the zamindars.

Illegalities in the Grant of Rent Receipts

One more factor which led to ill feeling between the adivasi ryots and the zamindars can be traced to the non-grantal of rent receipts and also to irregularities and illegalities practised by the zamindar's *naibs* and *gomosias* in matters of grant of rent receipts. The following illegalities were usually practised:

(a) The whole or part of the rent was realised without the grant of a receipt and without crediting the amount to the estate accounts.

(b) In cases of part payment the tenant was told that a rent receipt will be granted when he had paid up the demand in full.

(c) When a payment was made on account of rent the amount was credited to arrears, and no mention was made of the year for which the payment was made. The *lahuri* or *hisabana* was also deducted by the landlord's agent at the time when rent receipts were granted.

High Scale of Abwabs

The Bengal Tenancy Act of 1885 clearly prohibits the exaction of *abwabs* and various extra legal cesses from the ryots. But in Malda it was realised by almost every zamindar and their scale was higher in the Barind a elsewhere. This was so because the adivasi was ignorant of his legal rent. The scale of *abwabs* varies considerably from estate to estate. The following examples will help us to form some idea."[8]

Thana	Estates	Abwabs
1. Habibpur	Bulbuli Singabad	On the average as four in the rupee. The tenants have to pay between Re. 1 and Rs. 2 to see the landlord.
2. Old Malda	Girija Kanto Das and others	The *abwabs* vary from as. 4 to as. 8 per rupee. Also the cost of rent receipts and subscription to various festivities were realised. On the average one-third of the legal rent were laid as *abwabs*.

Suppression of Civil Court Notices

Taking opportunity of the ignorance, improvidence and illiteracy of the adivasi, his more educated neighbours always thought of cheating him out of his land. The method which was commonly practised and which was easy also was to use the Civil Court, and by suppressing its processes to get an exparte decree. In this manner dispossession of tenants through the Civil Court had been a common practice in the Barind. Mahajans, tahsildars, touts—all resorted to this practice. Pleaders living in English Bazar were also known to have purchased Santal's holding in rent sale after suppressing notices. We have figures for the years 1928–33 obtained from the Civil Court which show the number of cases heard exparte, and the percentage of such cases to the total number of cases. The figures were as follows:[9]

1. *Rent Suits:*
   (a) Cases heard exparte   881
   (b) Percentage   88
2. *Mortgage Suits:*
   (a) Cases heard exparte   172
   (b) Percentage   82

Economic Depression of 1920s

Another contributory factor in the deteriorating tenant–landlord relationship was the low price of agricultural produce brought about by the economic depression which occurred roundabout 1928. In the context of this depression the tenants found it difficult to make rent payment and the zamindars unreasonably thought that the tenants were deliberately withholding rent and making the depression issue a pretext.

Defects in Legislation and Alienation of Land

The net result of all these high-handed activities of the zamindars and their agents was land alienation. The Santals lost occupancy rights on not less than one-half of the area held by Santals to money-lenders and other non-agriculturists and in the majority of cases they became *adhiars* without any rights.[10] This was so because of the defects in the tenancy legislation and in its execution. Chapter VII A of the Bengal Tenancy Act was extended to Santals of Malda in 1923 and to the Oraons there in 1927. Under its provision no adivasi can transfer land by a sale or mortgage without the Collector's permission in writing. Unfortunately this provision was nullified in practice because the

Collector was not given any statutory power to compel the money-lender to accept his terms to which he arrived at after calculating how much land should be sold or what should be the terms of the mortgage and what was the amount owing to the money-lender. It appears that law was meant to be preserved in the stature and not to be put into practice or enforced. In fact the Bengal Tenancy Act, 1885 failed so far as the adivasis of Malda are concerned in the determination of a fair rent protection against eviction and prevention of alienation of land to non-agriculturists, the cherished objectives of the said legislation. All these go to show that the law and the method of its application and enforcement did not always play a remedial role and did not serve the interests of those rights and interests it sought to safeguard.

Discontent Takes a Rebellious Form

This unbearable oppression on the adivasis did not go without protest all the time. After all protest, in the form reprising, was in their tradition. The Santals of Malda similarly 'Started a rather serious movement.'[11] The leader of the movement was Jitu Santal. Jitu 'began to collect money from the Santals and persuaded them to believe that the British Raj had come to an end and that he would thenceforth act as the leader of the Santals.'[12] The dictum of Jitu was that the 'payment of rent to landlords had been prohibited and the only payment required was a basketful of paddy to himself.'[13] Such activities of Jitu reminds us of the pattern of movement initiated by Sidhu, Kanu in the Great Santal Uprising of 1855. 'The activities of Jitu culminated in an incident during which the police had to open fire on the Santals. This happened in 1932. It appears that on 3 December a large number of Santals had taken possession of the Adina Mosque, one of the protected monuments in Pandua, and converted it into a place of Hindu worship. They refused to allow any Muhammadans to go there'[14] and proclaimed their independence and refused to leave it when ordered by the District Magistrate. The police had to open fire, several Santals were killed or wounded and one constable died from the effects of a wound by a poisoned arrow.[15] Resistance against oppression was thus stamped out.

The movement initially had a religious bias. One Kasheswar Chakrabarti founded a sect, named Satyam Sibam in the year 1905. May Santals joined the sect.[16] The reasons why the Santals could have been converted to this sect and why the Santals occupied the Adina mosque as well as how this movement 'tended to get mixed up with politics' are very pertinent to understand the social base of Jitu's uprising. We are keeping this very important aspect of the movement out of the scope of the present paper for this requires investigation of source materials.

Conclusion

The story of exploitation in Malda is much the same as Santal Parganas in 1855 and Chotanagpur in 1895–1900. Adivasis became victims at the hands of zamindars and mahajans. Starting from 1855 right till the fourth decade of the present century, the adivasis have struggled against their opponents. While the trickeries of the zamindars and their agents were the same old ones and legislation failed again and again to protect the adivasis, there was a continuity in the adivasis' mode of protest, they demanded the end of the British Raj and the establishment of their own Raj, they fought with their traditional weapons and a messianic leader was there to lead them. Thus adivasi world is said to be in a state of turmoil and unrest.

Notes

1. *Final Report of the Survey and Settlement Operation in the District of Malda, 1928–35* (hereafter referred as *FRSSO*).
2. Ibid.
3. Ibid.
4. S. Fuchs, *Rebellious Prophets*, p. 46.
5. Barind is situated east of the River Mahananda and comprises of thanas Bamangola, Gajole, Habibpur, Old Malda, Gomastapur Nachole and Nawabganj.
6. S. Sungupta, *Santal Rural Economy*, p. 7.
7. *FRSSO*, Malda, 1928–35.
8. Ibid.
9. Ibid.
10. Ibid.
11. J.C. Sengupta, *West Bengal District Gazetteer, Malda* 1969, Calcutta, p. 62.
12. Ibid.
13. *FRSSO*, Malda, 1928–35.
14. J.C. Sengupta, *West Bangal, District Gazetter, Malda* 1969, Calcutta, p. 62.
15. *FRSSO*, Malda, 1928–35.
16. J.C. Sengupta, *West Bengal District Gazetter, Malda* 1969, Calcutta, p. 62.

Index